"Many Christians avoid Old Testament books like Kings because they don't see what stories about ancient kings have to do with their lives today. Tony Merida does a masterful job explaining these books and showing their incredible importance for our lives. Like ancient Israel, we need a king who not only follows God's Word Himself, but a king who can lead us to follow God's Word. The bad news for ancient Israel was that all of their kings failed. Tony proclaims the good news for us: what they longed for, we have—the King of kings, Jesus Christ!"

Jonathan Akin, pastor, Fairview Church, Lebanon, Tennessee

"In this outstanding commentary set, my friend Tony does what he does best—bringing the realms of deep theology and actual practice together. The content, layout, and thought flow of this commentary are extremely helpful. For a pastor-teacher, this is precisely what is needed: timely, thoughtful, and Jesus-centered."

Alex Early, author of *The Reckless Love of God*

"The authors of this commentary are aware of the needs of the pastor. It is readable, provides insight for application, and is helpful in discerning the Christ markers of the biblical text. This clearly written commentary will not only help pastors as they prepare to preach but the people who listen to their sermons!"

Scott M. Gibson, Haddon W. Robinson Professor of Preaching and Ministry, Gordon-Conwell Theological Seminary

"Tony Merida has written a commentary on 1 and 2 Kings that hits all the right notes. It is exegetically helpful, pastorally insightful, culturally relevant, devotionally beneficial, and most importantly it is all those things in a Christ-centered and Christ-exalting way. Both the pastor and the church member will find Tony's work to be profitable for increasing their understanding of God's dealing with His people in this particular time and place and of the need that all God's people have for a greater king—Jesus Christ."

Zach Weihrauch, pastor of Preaching and Vision, Gateway Heights Church, Cleveland, Ohio

AUTHOR **Tony Merida**

SERIES EDITORS **David Platt, Daniel L. Akin, and Tony Merida**

CHRIST-CENTERED
Exposition

EXALTING JESUS IN
1 & 2 KINGS

HOLMAN
REFERENCE
NASHVILLE, TENNESSEE

SERIES DEDICATION

Dedicated to Adrian Rogers and John Piper. They have taught us to love the gospel of Jesus Christ, to preach the Bible as the inerrant Word of God, to pastor the church for which our Savior died, and to have a passion to see all nations gladly worship the Lamb.

—David Platt, Tony Merida, and Danny Akin
March 2013

TABLE OF CONTENTS

ACKNOWLEDGMENTS

I must say thank you to some people who made this commentary possible. First of all, thanks to Imago Dei Church. I'm so thankful to God for your love for the Word. I will never forget the time we spent studying 1 and 2 Kings on Sunday mornings. God was so gracious to us during those weeks.

Thanks to the elders of Imago Dei Church. What a joy it was to preach through Kings! I love laboring in the mission with you all.

I'm indebted to our Aspire interns, who helped with this manuscript. I'm especially grateful to Seth Brown for the final edits and for helping with the discussion questions.

I also want to express my gratitude to God for the work of five commentators in particular: Dale Ralph Davis, Philip Graham Ryken, John W. Olley, Paul R. House, and Iain W. Provan. I hope I have cited each of these men sufficiently. I couldn't have finished this commentary without their hard work and scholarship. I'm not an Old Testament scholar. I'm a pastor who tried to preach through these very challenging books! I learned a ton as a result of this study, and much of that was due to their lives and labors.

I must always thank my dear companion, Kimberly, and my five kids: James, Joshua, Angela, Jana, and Victoria. I'm a happy and blessed husband and father. I had such a sweet time discussing Kings as a family before and after Sunday mornings.

Finally, to the King of kings, Jesus: thank You. I want my life to be spent for Your kingdom. May You, risen Savior, receive this work as an offering of worship. May You use it to build up Your church, which You purchased with Your own blood, and advance Your cause on the earth.

Tony Merida

SERIES INTRODUCTION

Augustine said, "Where Scripture speaks, God speaks." The editors of the Christ-Centered Exposition Commentary series believe that where God speaks, the pastor must speak. God speaks through His written Word. We must speak from that Word. We believe the Bible is God breathed, authoritative, inerrant, sufficient, understandable, necessary, and timeless. We also affirm that the Bible is a Christ-centered book; that is, it contains a unified story of redemptive history of which Jesus is the hero. Because of this Christ-centered trajectory that runs from Genesis 1 through Revelation 22, we believe the Bible has a corresponding global-missions thrust. From beginning to end, we see God's mission as one of making worshipers of Christ from every tribe and tongue worked out through this redemptive drama in Scripture. To that end we must preach the Word.

In addition to these distinct convictions, the Christ-Centered Exposition Commentary series has some distinguishing characteristics. First, this series seeks to display exegetical accuracy. What the Bible says is what we want to say. While not every volume in the series will be a verse-by-verse commentary, we nevertheless desire to handle the text carefully and explain it rightly. Those who teach and preach bear the heavy responsibility of saying what God has said in His Word and declaring what God has done in Christ. We desire to handle God's Word faithfully, knowing that we must give an account for how we have fulfilled this holy calling (Jas 3:1).

Second, the Christ-Centered Exposition Commentary series has pastors in view. While we hope others will read this series, such as parents, teachers, small-group leaders, and student ministers, we desire to provide a commentary busy pastors will use for weekly preparation of biblically faithful and gospel-saturated sermons. This series is not academic in nature. Our aim is to present a readable and pastoral style of commentaries. We believe this aim will serve the church of the Lord Jesus Christ.

Third, we want the Christ-Centered Exposition Commentary series to be known for the inclusion of helpful illustrations and theologically driven applications. Many commentaries offer no help in illustrations, and few offer any kind of help in application. Often those that do offer illustrative material and application unfortunately give little serious attention to the text. While giving ourselves primarily to explanation, we also hope to serve readers by providing inspiring and illuminating illustrations coupled with timely and timeless application.

Finally, as the name suggests, the editors seek to exalt Jesus from every book of the Bible. In saying this, we are not commending wild allegory or fanciful typology. We certainly believe we must be constrained to the meaning intended by the divine Author Himself, the Holy Spirit of God. However, we also believe the Bible has a messianic focus, and our hope is that the individual authors will exalt Christ from particular texts. Luke 24:25-27,44-47 and John 5:39,46 inform both our hermeneutics and our homiletics. Not every author will do this the same way or have the same degree of Christ-centered emphasis. That is fine with us. We believe faithful exposition that is Christ centered is not monolithic. We do believe, however, that we must read the whole Bible as Christian Scripture. Therefore, our aim is both to honor the historical particularity of each biblical passage and to highlight its intrinsic connection to the Redeemer.

The editors are indebted to the contributors of each volume. The reader will detect a unique style from each writer, and we celebrate these unique gifts and traits. While distinctive in their approaches, the authors share a common characteristic in that they are pastoral theologians. They love the church, and they regularly preach and teach God's Word to God's people. Further, many of these contributors are younger voices. We think these new, fresh voices can serve the church well, especially among a rising generation that has the task of proclaiming the Word of Christ and the Christ of the Word to the lost world.

We hope and pray this series will serve the body of Christ well in these ways until our Savior returns in glory. If it does, we will have succeeded in our assignment.

David Platt
Daniel L. Akin
Tony Merida
Series Editors
February 2013

1 Kings

Kingship

Main Idea: The writer recounts how Solomon succeeded David in coming to the throne and also provides David's final instructions to his son.

I. **Introduction**
   A. 1 Kings 1–2
II. **Who Is the King (1:1-53)?**
   A. A suffering king (1:1-4)
   B. A self-appointed king (1:5-10)
   C. Servants of the king (1:11-27)
   D. A sovereignly appointed king (1:24-53)
III. **What Should the King Do (2:1-46)?**
   A. Keep the covenant (2:1-4).
   B. Reign (2:5-46).
IV. **Who Is Your King?**

Introduction

What possible relevance does this antiquated book have for our lives? I mean, other than helping you win at Bible trivia or giving you some potential names for your kids, what benefit is there in examining the book of Kings?

As we shall see, Kings is relevant for our lives. Paul said, "For whatever was written in the past [in the Old Testament] was written for our instruction, so that we may have hope through endurance and through the encouragement from the Scriptures" (Rom 15:4). In Kings, as in other Old Testament books, we find instruction, encouragement, and hope. We need these blessings in order to endure faithfully.

Kings belongs to the history section of the Old Testament, a section referred to as the Former Prophets. It includes Joshua, Judges, Samuel, and Kings. In Joshua God's people conquer the promised land as promised in the story of the patriarchs and the exodus. In Judges a number of interesting figures like Gideon, Deborah, and Samson lead the nation for a period of about 400 years. Judges, as a whole, shows the nation of Israel in a downward spiral, in need of a godly king. In 1 Samuel we find the account of the prophet Samuel and the beginning of the monarchy. The story of Saul, the first monarch, is found in 1 Samuel. David looms in the background of 1 Samuel as the king to come. Second Samuel is the story of David's reign.

The books of 1 and 2 Kings (originally one book) cover about 370 years of history starting from the end of David's reign. His successor is Solomon, the third larger-than-life king, about whom we read in the first eleven chapters of 1 Kings. After Solomon, there are a number of other kings. The final scene shows the kings in exile.

The message of 1 Kings is *decline* and 2 Kings is *fall* (Dever, *The Message of the Old Testament*). Seeds of decline appear in the beginning of 1 Kings and take on different appearances throughout (ibid.). The book opens like many books close (e.g., Genesis, Joshua), with the leading figure dying. This is fitting since Kings is about the decline of the kingdom—a decline that ends in a judgment.

We will make a number of applications in our study, but let me introduce three broad applications that appear throughout this story of decline. Kings is about *worship*, the *word*, and *weakness*. First, God's people were called to **worship** God alone, but Kings tells the sad story of idolatry among God's people. Though Solomon builds the great temple for worship, he falls prey to idolatry as well. Then the kingdom is divided because of idolatry (1 Kgs 11:33-35). We regularly read about what each king did with the "high places" or idols. Did he tear them down or not? The kings are judged based on this all-important matter. Since a more important question doesn't exist than "Whom will you worship?" we see that Kings is most relevant for our lives.

Second, regarding the **word**, God previously told the people how to live. Much of the content in the first five books of the Bible (esp. Deuteronomy) is referred to in Kings. The people were supposed to live by God's word, but the kings and their people failed to do so. In Kings God raises up prophets, most famously Elijah and Elisha, who perform great wonders and speak God's word to the people. Later in the book Josiah recovers the word and leads a reformation. Since we too are a people of the book, we need to consider and apply this message of Kings.

Regarding **weakness**, the story of Kings shows us that every human leader has limitations. After the monarchy divides, all of Israel's kings fail. Judah's kingdom, however, is somewhat mixed. After Solomon (who appears to be continuing the power and the glory of Israel through his unparalleled wisdom, only to drift into folly and shame), two kings are exemplary: Hezekiah and Josiah. Six kings of Judah are praised, but with the caveat, "The high places were not taken away." These are Asa, Jehoshaphat, Joash, Amaziah, Azariah, and Jotham. The other kings are condemned. It's obvious that another King is needed.

So Kings is a story that involves the sinfulness of kings and the people they represent, their persistent idolatry, and associated injustice. It's a story of a sad decline and the need for another King, the ultimate Son of David. In Genesis a promise was made to Abraham: "I will make . . . kings come from you" (Gen 17:6; cf. 35:11). God kept His promise and in the fullness of time sent forth the King to end all kings, Jesus.

In addition we find various topics in Kings like political maneuvering, material prosperity, power plays between nations, alliances, violence, injustice, war, international trade, compromised worship, dying children, and many more familiar experiences (Olley, *Message of Kings*, 20). Through it all we meet God. Judging? Yes, but also dispensing mercy and providentially controlling human history. We meet the God of promise and salvation, who orchestrates a royal line that will ultimately culminate in David's greater Son.

Kings speaks to everyone, every church, and every nation that might be going through turmoil. In the midst of turmoil, chaos, and confusion Jesus said the people were "weary and worn out, like sheep without a shepherd" (Matt 9:36). He came to save a rebellious people. And eventually the God over history will "bring everything together in the Messiah, both things in heaven and things on earth" (Eph 1:10).

1 Kings 1–2

Due to space restrictions and the nature of this commentary, we're going to cover a lot of ground in each chapter. I will look at the text historically, theologically, and practically, making appropriate Christ-centered, gospel-saturated connections. My plan is to give an overview of many sections. I call what I am going to do "sectional exposition" rather than verse-by-verse exposition, since we will not always treat every single verse, but we will cover every section. We will hit the major units of thought and try to cover the main theological emphases in each chapter. You will do well to read for yourself and discuss more of the pieces with others.

The dominant idea in chapter 1 is *kingship*. Olley says, "The seventy instances of the noun *king* or related verb is the most in any chapter of the Bible" (*The Message of Kings*, 39). Immediately King David is mentioned, then the big question is, "Who will replace David?" Will David act as king? Will Adonijah's conspiracy to become king work? What will happen to Solomon? So consider two questions related to kingship: Who is the king? What is the king to do?

Who Is the King?

1 KINGS 1:1-53

As we examine this first chapter, notice *a suffering king, a self-appointed king, servants to the king*, and *a sovereignly appointed king.*

A Suffering King (1:1-4)

The story begins with Israel's famous king, David. But all isn't well with him. He is *old* and *cold.* They cannot manage to get him warm, so they opt for another solution. They do a "Miss Israel Beauty Pageant" and select the stunning Abishag to care for him and increase his vitality. Later, Adonijah will attempt to take her for himself (for his own devious reasons).

Is Abishag's beauty intended to excite David sexually? The passage does have several sensual overtones like "lie by your side" (cf. "in your arms" in Gen 16:5; 2 Sam 12:8; Mic 7:5) and "was not intimate with her" (cf. Gen 4:1). Olley reminds us, "This is to be read in the context of a court where the king has a number of wives and concubines (2 Sam 5:13; 15:16)" (Olley, *Message of Kings*, 41). Whatever their intentions, David doesn't respond to her beauty.

Chapters 1–2 paint a picture of a suffering king who no longer has his previous physical or political power. David slew giants, killed lions with his hands, conquered kingdoms, and nurtured sheep. Now he is dying, feeble, and powerless. His declining life illustrates the declining nation itself. A few applications emerge.

We must face our frailty. At some point all of us will begin feeling the effects of aging and physical decline. Our bodies will not function properly, and many of us will find ourselves on a deathbed. We will die, like David, not accomplishing all that we set out to accomplish. What should you remember in those days? You should remember that your identity isn't bound up in what you can do. Your identity is in who God has made you to be in Christ. You aren't your gifts. Don't let your abilities lead you to pride, and don't let your inabilities lead you to despair. You aren't your accomplishments.

David Martyn Lloyd-Jones is one of my heroes. He preached in London for several years, God used him in his generation mightily, and his work continues to impact people. When Lloyd-Jones was dying of cancer, he was unable to do all that he used to do. However, Lloyd-Jones knew that his joy and identity were not bound up in how he could perform. He reflected on the words of Jesus as he talked to his biographer, saying, "Don't rejoice that the spirits submit to you, but rejoice that your names are written in heaven" (Luke 10:20). He then said, "Our greatest danger is to live upon our activity. The ultimate test of a preacher is what he feels like when he cannot preach. Our relationship to God is to be the supreme cause of joy" (quoted in Iain H. Murray, *David Martyn Lloyd-Jones: The Fight of Faith 1939–1981*, 738). What should give us great joy in our living, and in our dying, is our relationship to God through Christ (2 Cor 4:16-18). Don't rejoice ultimately in what you look like, in what you have, or in what you can do, but in the fact that your name is written in heaven.

There is a need for transitional plans. I realize this may seem unnecessary and even unspiritual. But is it? We don't see from David the type of training Jesus did with His disciples or Paul did with Timothy (2 Tim 2:2). In the next paragraph David doesn't reprimand Adonijah. He never disciplined him, as a father must do. What about Solomon? Did David spend sufficient time with him? We don't know all the details, but we do know that David is dying and things are shaky. Similarly, churches and organizations often fall apart because no one has trained future leaders. Let this text remind us of the importance of preparing the next generation of leaders, fathers, mothers, and missionaries. We must train and deploy faithful kingdom servants.

A Self-Appointed King (1:5-10)

Whenever succession is needed, emotions tend to rise. Sometimes war and violence occur, and many times manipulative conspiracies are at work. Here, in his pride, and in view of David's weakness, Adonijah tries to make himself king. Of course, he was next in David's line. He was the fourth-born son. Absalom (the third son) was put to death (2 Sam 18:9-17) after killing Amnon, the oldest son. No one knows what happened to the second son, Chileab (2 Sam 3:2). Perhaps he died young. On the other hand, David himself was the youngest son of his family. The oldest has not always had priority. At any rate, Adonijah should have been with his dying father; instead he was up to no good.

Adonijah had several problems, even though on the surface he looked like a king.

First, Adonijah exalted himself (v. 5). He has a lust for power and praise. He does the opposite of what the Scriptures teach, namely, to "humble yourself" (1 Pet 5:5-6) and put others ahead of yourself (Phil 2:3-4). God exalts the humble but opposes the proud (Prov 6:16-17). God will sometimes exalt the humble to positions in this life (Ps 75:6-7). Ultimately, in the next life, God will exalt those who have humbly served Him (Luke 14:11). Adonijah personifies Psalm 49:12 (ESV): "Man in his pomp will not remain" (cf. 49:20).

Adonijah had a "yearbook theology." Do you remember getting a yearbook in high school? If you were like me, one of the first things you did was immediately look for *your* picture. That was not because you hadn't already seen it. You probably picked it out! It was already framed and hanging in the family's house. Still, I went straight to that picture. I made sure they spelled my name correctly. What's next? Sports pictures. I flipped there, and then to the clubs, looking for my pictures. A yearbook theology is self-centered. It is an "it's all about me" spirit. This view of life is lived out in the decisions we make, the way we spend our money, and even the way we read the Bible. We often go to the Bible for personal reasons, without any intent of seeing the nature and glory of God. We need a Yahweh-centered theology instead of a yearbook theology; we must desire to exalt God instead of self.

We see this spirit everywhere in pop culture. It's a self-absorbed, self-addicted world. In reality TV, for example, many are famous for no good reason. They are stuck on themselves. The production team follows these individuals around and teenagers want to be like them, perpetuating a self-exalting culture. Find a better model: Jesus. He actually had something to boast in, yet made Himself nothing and served others. Then the Father exalted Him. He now gives us the power to live out an others-focused life. Adonijah should have been concerned about his dying father, but he was doing what he always did, thinking about himself.

Second, Adonijah sought his own pleasure. He had always gotten what he wanted; added to his spoiled nature was his handsome appearance (v. 6). Here is a spoiled, attractive, self-centered man—a recipe for disaster. Apparently, David never disciplined him because he was busy doing other things, or perhaps because he favored him to the point of not rebuking him. He never used the "purpose-driven paddle," as one of my friends calls it. Let this serve as a warning to fathers: Children must be disciplined. We discipline them because we love them, just as the Father disciplines us (Prov 3:11-12; Heb 12:7).

Third, Adonijah sought the wrong counsel. Verses 7-10 describe how he confers with Joab and Abiathar instead of Zadok the priest, Benaiah, or Nathan the prophet. This reminds me of the proverb, "The one who walks with the wise will become wise, but a companion of fools will suffer harm" (Prov 13:20). Adonijah accumulated supporters who wouldn't contradict him. He turned away from the prophet because he wanted to do things his way. We commit this error when we fail to seek counsel from God's Word. When people are considering marrying an unbeliever or pondering how to spend money without first studying God's Word, they aren't living under the authority of Scripture.

Fourth, Adonijah opposed God's king. He acts as the serpent in this story. He represents the evil one. He tried to become king by the "Serpent's Stone." The word *Zoheleth* (v. 9) means "slithering" (Leithart, *1 and 2 Kings*, 37). Because of his serpentine character, Solomon will put him to death. Solomon later said, "A king favors a wise servant, but his anger falls on a disgraceful one" (Prov 14:35). The enemy always opposes God's plan. Adonijah is about to reap the harvest of shamefully opposing God's king.

We can learn from Adonijah. He teaches us of our need to submit to God's will and God's Word instead of pursuing our own self-interest or listening to those who only tell us what we want to hear. Our purpose in life, as the Westminster Confession says, is to glorify God and enjoy Him forever. Adonijah has his own confession: "To glorify self, and pursue my own enjoyment." Even though his name means "Yahweh is my Lord," he doesn't live like it.

We should be aware of Adonijah types in the church as we remember what true Christian leadership is. In the New Testament we read of a guy named Diotrephes who "loves to have first place among them, [and] does not receive us" (3 John 9). Here Adonijah puts himself first, doesn't respect the leaders God has put in place, and doesn't seek godly counsel.

Biblical leaders have a calling and are known for godly character. On the surface Adonijah is everything one might want. He's gifted and attractive. But leadership isn't about giftedness as much as it's about *Christlikeness.* Let's be careful in appointing people to leadership. We should put more stock in their true character than in their ability and external appearance (1 Tim 3:1-7).

Servants of the King (1:11-27)

In response to Adonijah's power play, the first of many prophets in Kings appears: Nathan. He isn't on the Adonijah bandwagon. In the following verses Nathan speaks to Bathsheba (vv. 11-14), Bathsheba speaks to David (vv. 15-21), and then Nathan speaks to David (vv. 22-27).

Nathan is very important in this story. He stirs David to action. He stands in the gap. His first appeal is to Bathsheba. He has spoken to David face-to-face, but now he takes an indirect approach. Some argue that he has bad motives here, and we certainly want to read Kings without rose-colored glasses, but it seems to me that he wants what's best for the kingdom.

Bathsheba honors the king (v. 16) and reports the situation. We are reminded of what brought her to the court in the first place. David may have been Israel's greatest king, but he was not perfect. Yet God used him despite his failures, just as he continues to use individuals today.

Bathsheba is concerned for the kingdom, and she understands that if David doesn't appoint Solomon, then she and her son will be rivals to the throne. According to Chronicles, God promised that Solomon would sit on the throne (1 Chr 22:9-10; cf. 2 Sam 7:12-13). David himself had appointed him (1 Chr 23:1; 29:22) and charged him to build the temple (1 Chr 22:6). Thus Adonijah is attempting to overthrow Solomon, not fill a power vacuum (Leithart, *1 and Kings,* 31).

Since Bathsheba is concerned for the kingdom, she ends by saying, "The eyes of all of Israel are on you" (v. 20). They were looking for an answer. It's David's responsibility to appoint a king.

While she speaks to David, Nathan directly addresses the king respectfully (vv. 22-27). Previously, Nathan had told David a parable to get a response, but now he asks a question.

Small acts have big consequences. Don't ever underestimate one thing that you do for the kingdom of God. It might be simple conversations with a student or coworker about the gospel, spending time with a person going through a trial, inviting someone to a worship service or small group, caring for a single mom, opening up your home for others, forgiving a brother or sister, or supporting missionaries. Nothing is insignificant when it's done for the glory of King Jesus. Whatever influence you have, you should use it for the advancement of the kingdom.

A Sovereignly Appointed King (1:28-53)

Following this conversation with Bathsheba and Nathan, David responds by making Solomon king (vv. 28-37). Though Adonijah may have looked more like a king than Solomon, Solomon comes to the throne by promise. He comes to the throne the way we come into the kingdom: by grace, not by performance or merit.

Olley says regarding Bathsheba, "She who initially had become the object of David's lust, and whose husband had been a pawn to sacrifice, is now the recipient of the words that guaranteed her safety and the safety of her son" (*Message of Kings*, 45). We see grace here also. David is leading in his weakness. David acknowledges that while he is the Lord's anointed, he himself isn't the Lord. He invokes the name of the Lord, showing that he is submissive to the Lord. He also acknowledges that the Lord delivers from "difficulty" (v. 29), implying that God has intervened in this crisis.

Next we see the crowning of Solomon (vv. 32-40). David tells the trio, Zadok, Nathan, and Benaiah, to put Solomon on the king's mule and bring him to Gihon. This was a symbol of kingship that marked Solomon as the favored son (cf. Zech 9:9, Matt 21:1-11). He also tells them to anoint Solomon as king and blow the trumpet. In verses 38-40 they fulfill the king's commands, and a boisterous party results. The writer says, "The earth split open from the sound" (v. 40).

Once Solomon is declared king, Adonijah gets the news (vv. 41-45). Jonathan the priest quickly pledges allegiance to David, calling him "our lord." He reports, "Solomon has even taken his seat on the royal throne" (vv. 46-48). As a result of the news, "all of Adonijah's guests got up trembling and went their separate ways" (v. 49). Adonijah goes to the altar, as a holy place, believing it will protect him from Solomon (invoking Exod 21:12-14?). Solomon says that if he will show himself worthy, then he will not put him to death. Verse 53 says that Adonijah submits to Solomon, though one wonders if this is just outer expression. Is he truly paying homage to the king?

This account makes us think of David's greater Son, Jesus. It calls to our attention Palm Sunday. Jesus would ride into the city on a donkey. The people would shout "Hosanna." He was the rightful king who dispensed mercy, not to those who are worthy but to every unworthy person who bows the knee to His lordship. One day, Paul says, "every knee will bow—of those who are in heaven and on earth and under the earth—and every tongue will confess that Jesus Christ is Lord, to the glory of God the Father" (Phil 2:10-11). What a merciful King we have in Jesus! His throne is greater than the throne of David or Solomon. His name is more famous than that of David or Solomon. "Something greater than Solomon is here" (Matt 12:42; Luke 11:31).

Submit to Christ's kingship with gladness. His kingdom is an everlasting kingdom (1 Tim 1:17). Submit to His kingship sincerely. Don't just mouth pious words. Jesus said that on the last day, "Not everyone who says to Me, 'Lord, Lord,' will enter the kingdom of heaven, but only the one who does the will of My Father in heaven" (Matt 7:21). He will say to them, "I never knew you" (Matt 7:23). Don't just make a decision because others are doing it, and don't trust in some ritual that is empty of meaning. Repent and turn to the King in surrender.

We have answered the question, "Who is the King?" and now we will answer the second question.

What Should the King Do?
1 KINGS 2:1-46

Final words are important. In David's final words he gives Solomon a "spiritual charge," urging him to obey God's word (2:1-4). These final words remind us of Moses' instruction for Israel's king (Deut 17:14-20) and remind us of his charge to Joshua (Josh 1:6-9). They are also reminiscent of the blessed man of Psalm 1. Solomon is to walk in the law of the Lord, mediate on it, and experience blessing.

David also gives Solomon a "political charge." He tells Solomon what he should do with the threats to the kingdom (vv. 5-9). Solomon carries out this advice in verses 13-46. I will focus most of my attention on verses 1-4.

We might break down the spiritual charge and political charge by simply saying that the king is to *keep the covenant* and *reign*. With both of these, we see that Solomon is to be vigilant, not passive.

Keep the Covenant (2:1-4)

As David is dying, he issues his command to Solomon. Notice the writer's choice of words: "As the time approached for David to die" (v. 1). It reminds us of the psalmist's words, "My times are in your hands"

(Ps 31:15 ESV). Dying David tells his son to "be strong and be courageous like a man" (v. 2; cf. 2 Tim 2:1; Eph 6:10; 1 Cor 16:13). We might expect a father to say something like David says. When I go out of town, sometimes I say to my oldest son, "Be the man of the house."

But what makes a man "a man"? Physical strength? Career success? Sexual conquest? Political power? Belonging to the Million Miler club? Athletic dominance? No. If these are the only things we live for, then we are wasting our lives as men. David gives us a simple understanding of godly manhood: obedience to God's Word. The Word makes the man.

David tells his son/king to walk in God's ways, which are found in the statutes, commandments, judgments, and testimonies written in the law of Moses (2:3). These words emphasize the totality of God's Word.

Nothing is wrong with having vocational ambition, but God's Word puts these pursuits in proper perspective. It helps us understand them.

Solomon's kingship was supposed to be founded on God's Word. He was to rule differently from others. He was not supposed to lead as a law unto himself. He was to keep God's law.

The benefit of following God's Word is clear at the end of verse 3: "So that you will have success in everything you do and wherever you turn." While God would continue to be faithful to David's line because of His promise (2 Sam 7:14-16), Solomon wouldn't enjoy the blessing if he didn't follow God's Word.

The same is true for us. We are blessed when we walk in God's Word (Ps 1). This doesn't mean we will never suffer. It means we will experience blessing in a variety of ways. Jesus said, "Everyone who hears these words of Mine and acts on them will be like a sensible man who built his house on the rock" (Matt 7:24). Jesus says those who know Him will bear fruit. Those individuals are wise. They enjoy the blessing of having a firm foundation, even when the floods come.

In verse 4 David mentions a double blessing for obeying God's word. He says not only will Solomon have personal blessing but he will also have a *perpetual dynasty*. Solomon was David's son, and God promised David an everlasting kingdom. The continuity of the dynasty depended on obedience to God's word. On the one hand, this was clearly a conditional promise (cf. Ps 132:11-12).

However, God made other promises that were unconditional (2 Sam 7:16). So which kind of promise was this? Was it conditional or unconditional? This is a tension raised in the Old Testament that Jesus Christ resolves.

Solomon, like his father and the other kings, would fail. They couldn't keep the law perfectly. Yet God would keep His promise of preserving the kingdom, and eventually one would keep the law perfectly: Jesus. Christ came down, keeping the law perfectly. God kept His promise; Christ the King kept the covenant.

God's promises to David were both conditional and unconditional. Conditional in that the king had to live out the demands, but unconditional in that God stated that wrongdoing on the part of David's successors would not lead to the end of the dynasty. The kingdom came on the king's obedience and by God's own promise. God's promise never failed, and God's ultimate King never failed. This is why we bow down to Jesus and why we call him "King of kings."

Build your life on the Word of God and worship the hero of the Word: Jesus. What a King we have! Sin is our attempt to make ourselves king; salvation is in Christ, the King substituting Himself for His servants. He lived the life we could not live and died the death we should have died. Now He is the risen and reigning exalted Lord. Glorify and enjoy Him.

Reign (2:5-46)

After telling Solomon to keep the covenant, David gives him instructions about two enemies of the kingdom and one friend. Apparently, David thinks Joab is too dangerous to be allowed to live once David is gone, so he recommends for him to be eliminated. Joab had long served as the commander of David's army, but he occasionally tried to pursue his own agenda, and he had blood on his hands from his actions against Abner (2 Sam 2:18-23; 3:1-39) and Amasa (2 Sam 20:1-10; 20:23). Joab was dangerous. One can only wonder why David never brought him to justice earlier (see 1 Chr 2:13-16).

David also gives orders regarding Shimei, the pro-Saul Benjaminite who cursed David and threw stones at him previously (2 Sam 16:5-14). Later Shimei regretted what he had done and asked for mercy, which the king granted, promising not to put him to death "today" (2 Sam 19:18-23). David admits that he swore he would not kill him on that day, yet he encourages Solomon to "bring his gray head down to Sheol with blood" (v. 9). Perhaps he was saying that Solomon was not bound to this promise of sparing Shimei, as David had been.Some wonder about David's counsel. Was this brutal? Was David acting like "the Godfather" in the old movie, killing off all of the rivals to secure his own power? Is this an example of David's failure? Shouldn't he have already dealt with these guys? There are many questions here. We have to remember that these were kings; it was their job to render justice. Further, they were divinely anointed kings, and any assault against his royal person was an attack against the kingdom of God (e.g., 1 Sam 24:6). Opposition was no small thing. We must realize the importance of securing the kingdom. All of these things must be considered as you make your judgments. David instructs Solomon to use wisdom in dealing with these individuals.

Twice David mentions Solomon's "wisdom" (vv. 6,9). He will receive more wisdom in the following story (3:5-14), which is essential for leading people in a godly way.

In between these two calls for the death penalty is a story of kindness. David instructs Solomon to reward old friends. Barzillai had provided bread and supplies when David ran from Absalom (2 Sam 17:27-29). He was loyal to the king and made personal sacrifice for the kingdom.

Verses 10-12 report David's death. His 40-year reign was the greatest of Israel's history. He was buried in the city he built. Later, other kings will be judged in comparison to David. Verse 12 notes the succession: Solomon's "kingship was firmly established." It's noted again at the end of the chapter: "So the kingdom was established in Solomon's hand" (v. 46). God is keeping His promises.

On earth we have human rulers. But ultimately, the psalmist said, "The LORD has established His throne in heaven, and His kingdom rules over all" (Ps 103:19). God is the Ruler of all, and He allows us the happy and holy privilege of embracing His rule.

David's death points to the need for another king. Peter would preach at Pentecost that David was "buried, and his tomb is with us to this day," but Jesus, the Holy One, would not see corruption (Acts 2:22-36). Jesus would rise from the dead as the ultimate King.

Let me summarize verses 13-46. Here Solomon acts according to David's instructions. He deals with the enemies his father mentioned and with other threats. In verses 13-25 **Adonijah** is executed after he makes another play on the kingdom. Because he was with the king's concubine, Abishag, it amounted to a claim on the throne (though she may not have technically been a concubine, she did attend to the king; 2 Sam 16:20-22). Solomon interprets it as a wicked conspiracy. After we read about Adonijah's execution, we read about his associates. **Abiathar** is banished from office (vv. 26-27). **Joab** is executed because he is still conspiring with Adonijah and because David wanted him executed (vv. 31-34). In verse 35 Solomon then replaces Abiathar and Joab with Zadok and Benaiah. As for **Shimei**, he is confined to Jerusalem and threatened if he ever leaves (vv. 36-38). He didn't abide by this warning and was put to death (v. 46).

In his depiction of the events, the writer simply tells this story without saying whether these actions were necessary or condoned. He doesn't comment on motives either. He does say that Solomon is the king and these rivals have been eliminated. I think Solomon is acting justly, though I understand the concern over these actions. As mentioned, these threats were serious. Adonijah was told that he would not die if he didn't act wickedly (1:52), but he did act wickedly. Joab should have been dealt with earlier. Shimei acted foolishly by not obeying orders.

One thing is certain: God knows. The writer of Proverbs said, "All a man's ways seem right to him, but the LORD evaluates the motives" (Prov 16:2). The King of all the earth will judge perfectly. Throughout the Psalms we read of God's justice: "For Yahweh, the Most High, is awe-inspiring, a great King over all the earth" (Ps 47:2). "Your throne, God, is forever and ever; the scepter of Your kingdom is a scepter of justice" (Ps 45:6). "Righteousness and justice are the foundation of Your throne" (Ps 89:14).

Perhaps this is a story of mixed motives, much like the story of our lives. This doesn't justify injustice, but it does highlight human weakness in leadership and the need for a perfectly just King and a better kingdom. Thankfully, God, by His grace, made good on His promise and gave us the Ruler we need in Christ.

Now, on this side of things, we understand that zeal for the kingdom today doesn't mean taking lives but rather giving up our lives for the good of others and the glory of God. And we know that one day we will give an account to the King of kings.

Who Is Your King?

While we know the rest of Kings tells the story of decline, another King would eventually reign: Jesus. Is He your King? We have already noted the superiority of the kingship of Jesus. He is the perfectly righteous, infinitely wise King. He is majestic, merciful, and eternal. Paul exalted Christ, saying that He is "the blessed and only Sovereign, the King of kings, and the Lord of lords, the only One who has immortality . . . to

Him be honor and eternal might" (1 Tim 6:15-16). Bow to this One who has invited you to His table. Submit to Him. Love Him. Trust Him. For He has come, as Isaiah and others promised:

> For a child will be born for us, a son will be given to us, and the government will be on His shoulders. He will be named Wonderful Counselor, Mighty God, Eternal Father, Prince of Peace. The dominion will be vast, and its prosperity will never end. He will reign on the throne of David and over his kingdom, to establish and sustain it with justice and righteousness from now on and forever. The zeal of the LORD of Hosts will accomplish this. (Isa 9:6-7)

Reflect and Discuss

1. How can the prospect of death influence the way a person lives?
2. What are some ways believers can spiritually invest in others so that, when they die, their influence lives on?
3. What is the biblical picture of leadership?
4. What does self-exaltation say about one's beliefs?
5. How might believers today attempt to exalt themselves?
6. Describe how Jesus led others during His time on earth.
7. Solomon was born of David and Bathsheba's relationship, which began in sinfulness, yet Solomon was divinely appointed as king. What does this teach about God and His providence?
8. Why did Adonijah ask for Abishag as his wife?
9. Is Solomon merciful or harsh to his enemies? Why?
10. How might believers today honor or undermine godly leaders?

Solomon's Wisdom

1 KINGS 3:1–5:18

Main Idea: The new king, Solomon, attained and used God-given wisdom.

I. **Understanding Wisdom**
II. **The Wisdom of Solomon**
   A. Early warning signs (3:1-4)
   B. Seek wisdom (3:5-15).
   C. Use wisdom (3:16–4:20).
   D. Spread wisdom (4:21–5:18).
III. **Someone Greater than Solomon Is Here.**

In the opening chapters of Kings, Solomon's reign is established. The right king was appointed to the throne, even though some questionable actions were taken. In chapter 3 we see more of Solomon's leadership, witness positive and negative acts, and we are told the reason for Solomon's greatness: God gave him wisdom.

Understanding Wisdom

To help us think about the importance of wisdom, let us consider a few questions. What type of person is worth admiring? How do you evaluate someone's significance? According to the world, for many young ladies (and some older ladies), outer appearance is the determining factor of value and worth. It's evidenced in films, magazines, songs, and many other contexts. Problems like eating disorders and addictions to plastic surgery arise with this quest for a perfect appearance. I read this week of a young model who was "leaving her career for God," citing that she didn't want to use her body to promote sex any longer. She described the sad scene of her modeling world: teenage girls getting into black SUVs late at night, getting home early in the morning, and standing in front of the mirror sobbing because they thought they were "fat." One girl was so bulimic that she involuntarily threw up everything she ate. For these young ladies everything sadly revolves around one's figure. I also heard of a pop star who said that her greatest fear when she turns

70 is that she would no longer be "hot." Being "hot" is the central desire not only for her but also for the many girls who seek to emulate her.

The book of Proverbs, however, gives a different vision of what ladies should desire: "Charm is deceptive and beauty is fleeting, but a woman who fears the LORD will be praised" (Prov 31:30). That lady is worth emulating. A woman should be concerned with fearing the Lord, not being "hot." Fearing the Lord is the wise life. Proverbs also shows us that "the fear of the LORD is the beginning of wisdom" (Prov 9:10). The lady worth admiring and emulating pursues wisdom, which means she submits to God, reveres God, and worships God. Proverbs says, "A beautiful woman who rejects good sense is like a gold ring in a pig's snout" (Prov 11:22). The attractiveness of a beautiful ring is likened to the attractiveness of a lady, but that beauty is nullified if it's in an undesirable situation—in this case, in obstinate stupidity. Ladies, pursue wisdom.

What about men? The same applies. Adonijah and Absalom illustrate how men may be suitable for magazine covers but aren't worth following because they lack godly wisdom. Don't determine your significance and worth by external appearance but by internal submission to God.

Let me ask an additional question: How should a Christian measure spiritual growth? Don't be deceived by certain Christian subcultures. Being able to name a bunch of preachers doesn't equal spiritual maturity. Reading numerous articles at *The Gospel Coalition* (or any other Christian website) doesn't equal spiritual growth either. Spiritual growth is also more than being emotionally moved in a worship gathering, more than attending lectures, and more than hearing sermons. One can do all of these things and still live in total rebellion. You can have a head full of theology but have a train wreck of a life or marriage. One can cry during a set of songs but be addicted to porn.

One of the concerns for the apostle Paul was for Christ's church to grow in *wisdom* (Eph 1:17; Col 1:9). If a person isn't growing in wisdom, he isn't growing in maturity.

What then is wisdom? The topic is complex. An entire chapter could be written on it. Let me try to mention six interrelated dimensions of biblical wisdom (though I'm sure more could be listed). First, wisdom has a **worship** dimension. As mentioned, the fear of the Lord is the starting place for wisdom. If you don't worship the real God, then you aren't wise according to Scripture. You can be intelligent, win at Trivial

Pursuit, and have more degrees than Fahrenheit, but if you aren't a worshiper of God, then you aren't wise.

Second, wisdom has an **insight** dimension. Wise people have insight into spiritual truth (Prov 4:6-7). They possess an ever-increasing thirst for wisdom (Prov 9:8-9), unlike the fool, the mocker, or the simple one who rejects it and is wise "in his own eyes" (Prov 13:1; 26:16). In the New Testament we read that the Holy Spirit opens up our eyes to give us wisdom and insight so that we may know God better (Eph 1:17-21; 1 Cor 2:14-16).

Third, wisdom has a **discernment** dimension. The wise person can read a situation and make the right decision, as we will see Solomon do in 1 Kings 3:16-28. Proverbs echoes, "Anyone with a wise heart is called discerning" (Prov 16:21; cf. 17:24). Paul prays that the Philippians would grow in knowledge and all discernment (Phil 1:9).

Fourth, wisdom has a **moral** dimension (Prov 14:16). Throughout Proverbs, wisdom and purity go together. A wise person has discretion. Proverbs addresses youth because they need discretion ("young man" in 1:4; also "My son")—for example, they should avoid prostitutes (Prov 5–7). The wise prefer good over evil (1 Kgs 3:9; Prov 3:7-8). In James wisdom involves virtues such as "pure" and "peace-loving" (3:17-18). The wise person is open to correction as well.

Fifth, wisdom has a **justice** dimension. Proverbs opens by speaking of this: "For receiving wise instruction in righteousness, justice, and integrity" (1:3). After speaking of the God who gives wisdom, Solomon says, "Then you will understand righteousness, justice, and integrity—every good path" (Prov 2:9). Leaders are particularly praised for using wisdom to do justice. In Proverbs 8 wisdom is personified as a lady, and she says, "It is by me that kings reign and rulers enact just law; by me, princes lead, as do nobles and all righteous judges" (Prov 8:15-16; cf. 29:4). At the end of Proverbs, the king's mother taught him this: "Speak up, judge righteously, and defend the cause of the oppressed and needy" (Prov 31:9). We will see an example of this in Solomon's life in chapter 3.

Finally, wisdom has a **skill** dimension. The book of Proverbs describes the wise person as the one who is skillful in building. God in wisdom "founded the earth" (Prov 3:19). Lady Wisdom was "a skilled craftsman" (Prov 8:30). Leithart says,

> In Scripture, wisdom is more closely associated with the skill of
> the woodcutter than the ecstasies of the mystic. The Hebrew

word for wisdom means "artistic skill" (Ex 28:3; 31:3; 35:31; 1 Kgs 7:14). . . . Proverbs is a book of instruction concerning skillful living, teaching how to construct a life that is attractive, fitting, and beautiful. (Leithart, *1 and 2 Kings*, 43)

Solomon's skill was displayed in a variety of ways, such as in his political actions and in the building of the temple.

How does one acquire wisdom? The "humble" find wisdom (Prov 11:2) by practicing humble acts. As this passage teaches (and others teach, e.g., Jas 1:5), we should earnestly ask our gracious God for wisdom. We should also study Scripture to grow in wisdom (Prov 7:1-5). Paul says the Scriptures are "able to give you wisdom for salvation through faith in Christ Jesus" (2 Tim 3:15). People go everywhere looking for wisdom—John Tesh, Oprah, Dear Abby, and Dr. Phil to name a few popular sources. Go to Scripture, for God makes "the inexperienced wise" (Ps 19:7). We should also seek biblical community to grow in wisdom. We read in Proverbs, "The one who walks with the wise will become wise, but a companion of fools will suffer harm" (13:20).

We must also point out that wisdom is found ultimately in and through Christ. Wisdom isn't just a set of ideas. Wisdom is in a person. In Christ are "all the treasures of wisdom and knowledge" (Col 2:3). How can you experience the six dimensions of wisdom just listed? In Christ. In Christ we come into a relationship with God enabling us to worship God with a healthy fear. In Christ we can have insight and discernment as we put on "the mind of Christ" (1 Cor 2:16). In Christ we see what a wise, godly life looks like; and in Christ we have power to live it out. In Christ we can judge righteously. In Christ we see what a skilled craftsman looks like, as He created the world we live in and is now building the kingdom of God. To walk away from Christ is to walk away from wisdom.

The Wisdom of Solomon

Early Warning Signs (3:1-4)

Solomon's life contains both positive and negative examples. Some people paint Solomon in a positive light until chapter 11; however, the early chapters of Kings also reveal some negatives. These four early warning signs become greater and greater sins for Solomon later. While he "loved the LORD" in 1 Kings 3:3, Solomon was a man with a divided heart. What were these early warning signs?

Solomon chose the wrong woman. This was not wise! He "made an alliance with Pharaoh king of Egypt by marrying Pharaoh's daughter" and he "brought her to live in the city of David" (v. 1). This verse emphasizes marital relationship (Olley, *Message of Kings*, 59). She probably wasn't a believer. Therefore, Solomon was unequally yoked with an unbeliever.

The Bible supports the marriage between couples of different races but not of different faiths (2 Cor 6:14). God explicitly forbade the marrying of a foreigner in Deuteronomy 7:3-4 because of the danger of apostasy. Thus, Solomon is already breaking David's charge in 1 Kings 2:1-4 to keep the law of Moses. His love for foreign women eventually led him down an awful path of idolatry (1 Kgs 11:1-2). Let him stand as a warning to those who are in a relationship with someone who isn't a Christ follower. Solomon lacked wisdom because he didn't have a proper reverence for God and His word.

Solomon formed an alliance with Egypt—of all places! Egypt has negative connotations throughout the Old Testament (though a future hope for the Egyptians' salvation was promised in Isa 19:19-25 and Ezek 29:13-16). He probably intended to secure peace between the nations with this royal marriage. In those days this type of union was common. The problem is that God wanted His people to trust in Him alone, and the Egyptians had been enemies of God. In Deuteronomy God predicted that Israel would have a king, and He gave them specific instructions, like following His law, not taking too many wives, and not returning to Egypt to form close relations with them (Deut 17:14-20).

Here's an important application: don't conform to the patterns of the world, even though some actions make sense to the world. Solomon was living out the values of his culture, but he was violating God's word. A prevalent example of this today is cohabitation. When people talk about cohabitation, they have many reasons couples should live together. They say things like, "You should test drive the car before you buy it." "It's economical." "You need to see if you're compatible." The problem is it's not God's plan for marriage. Repeatedly we come back to this fundamental issue: Under whose authority are you living? What are you allowing to shape you? Culture? Feelings? Or Scripture? The writer of Proverbs says, "The one who trusts in himself is a fool, but one who walks in wisdom will be safe" (Prov 28:26). Don't trust in your own mind or the minds of others, but look to God's Word for wisdom, and you will experience freedom and fulfillment.

Solomon worshiped at the high places. High places have a negative connotation, as the rest of Kings demonstrates. They were elevated places where people worshiped false gods. Why is Solomon worshiping there? At least three views exist. One view claims that since the temple had not been built, it was acceptable to worship at the high places (2 Chr 1:3 doesn't mention "high places" and says that "the Tent of Meeting was at Gibeon," viewing this in a positive light). Perhaps Solomon was just expressing that David's God was his God. Another option is that Solomon was being disobedient in worshiping there (Deut 12:2-4). If so, that God appeared to him is a result of divine grace not Solomon's obedience (Ryken, *1 Kings*, 75). The third view is that Solomon was delayed in building the temple because his heart was distracted with other things, such as his foreign wife (Provan, *1 and 2 Kings*, 45). Verse 15 says after Solomon meets with God at the high places, then he goes to Jerusalem to worship. This was either because he was wrong to go to Gibeon and in wisdom changed places or because it was previously permissible to be at Gibeon, but now he will be building the temple in Jerusalem. Regardless of your position, Provan says the "potential for disaster is clear enough, and 11:33 will tell us of a people who eventually follow Solomon into sin" (ibid., 45).

Solomon's love was fragile. We must admit that he was a lot like us. He loved the Lord, but he also had false loves. We face the same struggle. In the words of Luther, Christians are at the same time righteous and sinners (*simul iustus et peccator*).

Solomon's conflicted heart highlights God's grace in his life and in our lives. It also highlights the need for us to kill sin before it kills us. Paul said, "Do not let sin reign in your mortal body, so that you obey its desires" (Rom 6:12). Don't allow these false loves to remain, but put them to death so that your devotion to Yahweh may be wholehearted.

Turning to some positive examples, let us apply three principles related to wisdom: seek wisdom, use wisdom, and spread wisdom.

Seek Wisdom (3:5-15)

Despite Solomon's foolish decisions, the following verses show a positive example. In 1 Kings 3:5-15 five times the word "ask" is used, and five times the word "give" is used. God invites us to ask for wisdom, and God loves to give it. First Kings 2 mentioned Solomon's wisdom (2:6,9). Some argue that he was behaving like every other ancient Near Eastern king; he needed God's gift of wisdom to lead differently.

Solomon's request (vv. 5-9). In his request for wisdom, we can learn at least three important lessons. To start, Solomon **roots his request in the gospel**. He says,

> You have shown great and faithful love to your servant, my father David. . . . You have continued this great and faithful love for him by giving him a son to sit on his throne, as it is today. (v. 6)

At first glance you may just think that Solomon is talking about his dad—and he is. But this mention of David is rooted in God's covenant promise to have a son of David sit on the throne. While Kings shows us the nation in decline, it also shows us the faithfulness of God.

If Solomon can marvel at God's faithfulness to appoint him as king, how much more should we marvel at God's faithfulness to set forth Christ as King? The New Testament mentions Jesus' identity as the Son of David mentioned several times. The opening of Matthew reads, "The historical record of Jesus Christ, the Son of David, the son of Abraham" (Matt 1:1). When Mary is told about the upcoming birth of Christ, Gabriel said to her,

> He will be great and will be called the Son of the Most High, and the Lord God will give Him the throne of His father David. He will reign over the house of Jacob forever, and His kingdom will have no end. (Luke 1:32-33)

When Paul writes to the Romans, he says that Jesus was "a descendant of David according to the flesh" (Rom 1:3). "The lion from the tribe of Judah, the Root of David, has been victorious," the elder in Revelation 5:5 says.

One reason for a lack of prayer is a feeling of unworthiness. But our prayers, like Solomon's, are founded on the gospel. We can approach God because God is kind and merciful, and He keeps His promises. He is the God who saves sinners through Jesus Christ, our King. If you think, "I can't pray and ask for anything. I'm not good enough." You are right! But Christ is! Meditate on the grace and faithfulness of God as you pray.

Next, Solomon **demonstrates humble dependence**. He says, "I am just a youth with no experience in leadership" (v. 7). This doesn't refer to his age (for he was old enough to father a child) or to complete ignorance (he acted competently in the previous chapter), but to his child-like dependence. Here, Solomon shows us what childlike, dependent prayer looks like. He confesses that the job is over his head because he is king over "a people too numerous to be numbered or counted" (v. 8). I can imagine my eight-year-old child's response if I said, "Go play in the NFL." He would feel a bit inadequate! Solomon is admitting the same kind of inadequacy.

Here we find another reason for prayerlessness. We arrogantly believe in our own self-sufficiency. A self-righteous person doesn't ask God for help. The desperate child goes to God and asks. Perhaps you say, "Yeah, if God came to me and said, 'Ask Me,' then I would." He has said this to you! Jesus said, "Keep asking and it will be given" (Matt 7:7). He illustrated this by saying that if a son asked his father for bread, he would not give him a stone (Matt 7:9). He continued, "If you then, who are evil, know how to give good gifts to your children, how much more will your Father in heaven give good things to those who ask Him!" (Matt 7:11). My son just last week asked me to go eat pizza. I didn't say, "Hey let's just eat some candles and a Nerf football." I care for my children, and I want to feed them. How much more with our perfect Father! Go to God with a humble, childlike dependence.

James says that you do not have because you do not ask, and when you do ask, you desire to feed your flesh (Jas 4:2-3). Solomon, however, **asks for the right gift: wisdom**. He prays, "So give Your servant an obedient heart to judge Your people and to discern between good and evil. For who is able to judge this great people of Yours?" (3:9). His understanding of wisdom includes a fear of the Lord (he acknowledges who God is and what He has done), just governance, discernment of good and evil, and by implication the skill to lead well.

You might think, "Yeah, that's Solomon. He needs wisdom. He's a king. But not me." You are right in that he needed wisdom, but you are wrong in thinking you don't need it. Whatever you do in this life in the name of Jesus is important. Greater responsibility and honor will come for those in the next life who have been faithful with the small things in this life (Luke 16:10). The janitor who uses God's gifts of skill and wisdom to scrub toilets orderly, on time, and to the glory of Christ may find himself honored by Christ with a greater and more glorious realm of responsibility than the famous megachurch pastor who did his work for the praise of people (Russell Moore, "Personal and Cosmic Eschatology," 915). Don't underestimate small things. Jesus said those who welcome the marginalized will be rewarded at the resurrection of the just (Luke 14:14). Hosting others requires skill and wisdom.

Seek wisdom. It is more valuable than jewels (Prov 8:11). God grants it because He is abundantly generous and gracious.

God's response (vv. 10-15). The writer says, "Now it pleased the Lord that Solomon had requested this" (v. 10). God wasn't bothered by Solomon's request. God delights in the prayers of His people, especially prayers that aren't self-centered but instead are about serving God's people. Don't expect God to answer prayers like, "Please help me break into this house" or "Please help me escape from the police" or "Please help me get into this strip club." God is pleased to answer prayers that serve His mission.

We also see God's prerogative to give Solomon more than he requested. God promises also to give him riches and honor that surpass other kings, and if Solomon is faithful, He promises to lengthen his days. We shouldn't read this like a trick—"If I ask for wisdom, will God give me a new Escalade?" We should read it as a simple example of Matthew 6:33—"Seek first the kingdom of God and His righteousness, and all these things will be provided for you" (an interesting feature of this passage is the mention in 6:28-32 of Solomon's attire and how God clothes the flowers more magnificently). The best gift Solomon received was wisdom.

Solomon awakes from the dream. He goes to worship in Jerusalem, the future place of the temple. He offers sacrifices. Why? He has learned the right place to worship, but there is more. It seems that with this gift of wisdom comes an understanding of the need for mercy.

This sacrifice foreshadowed the ultimate sacrifice offered by Jesus. The easiest way to turn away from wisdom is to turn away from seeing your need for Christ. When you arrogantly fail to recognize your sinfulness and need for forgiveness, then you are turning away from wisdom. The person who goes through the day not realizing the need for the Savior isn't wise.

Use Wisdom (3:16–4:20)

After teaching us to seek wisdom, Solomon demonstrates two ways we should use wisdom. He uses wisdom to bless the powerless, and he uses wisdom to lead faithfully and skillfully.

Use wisdom for the powerless (vv. 16-28). Many became prostitutes in those days out of economic desperation or by voluntary slavery. They could have been desperate widows who were trying to stay alive, or they could have chosen this lifestyle over other alternatives (though this option seems unlikely). We don't know.

The story is pretty straightforward, but we're left without a lot of details. Did they intend to get pregnant? What was their plan for the babies? Did they plan to help each other with the children while the other was "working"? We don't know. In our day would they have preferred an abortion? We can only speculate. One thing is for certain: they weren't the most respected members of their society. Yet the king uses his wisdom and cares for them, even though some probably would not give them the time of day.

In the first half of the story, the king listens; in the second part the king speaks. What he says is shocking, and it's genius.

One woman presents her case (vv. 17-21); then the other simply denies the claim (v. 22; cf. Prov 18:17). There are no independent witnesses so this is a difficult case—she said, she said. Solomon responds by calling for the "sword" (v. 24). He will use it to administer justice. His unexpected words are these: "Cut the living boy in two and give half to one and half to the other" (v. 25). Since there is no proof, one might reject the plaintiff's case. But Solomon understands the relationship between a mother and a child, so he appeals to that motherly instinct to find the truth. He uses discernment to administer justice. The rightful mother says, "Give her the living baby, but please don't have him killed." The lying woman says viciously, "Cut him in two" (v. 26). Solomon relies on God's wisdom to give the baby to the right mother, the one who helped to save her child by her compassion. As a result, Israel was "in awe of the king because they saw that God's wisdom was in him to carry out justice" (v. 28). The king is living out the values of his God who is "executing justice for the exploited" (Ps 146:7). The psalmist said, "The mighty King loves justice. You have established fairness; You have administered justice and righteousness in Jacob" (Ps 99:4).

We have much to learn here about caring for the powerless. Solomon sees beyond her being a prostitute to her being a mother (Olley, *Message of Kings*, 28). He values her as we should value everyone created in God's image. Don't dismiss individuals who are in dark situations, for we were in a dark situation as well. Perhaps you are caring for individuals who are marginalized. That is wonderful! Value those who aren't valued, giving evidence that you are a kingdom citizen.

We also should remember that we need wisdom to care for the various groups of the powerless. We need discernment to care for rescued victims of trafficking on an organizational level, governmental level, church level, and personal level. We need wisdom on how to do transitional assistance for those who come out of foster care and orphanages. Couples adopting need wisdom to pursue the fatherless carefully and justly, as a lot of recent concern has developed related to the integrity of international adoptions. We need benevolent wisdom on how to bless the single mom and the lonely widow, the homeless and the prostitute.

Further, we need to pray for leaders who work on behalf of those in need. Paul tells us to pray for "kings and all those who are in authority" (1 Tim 2:2). Currently, many political leaders defend the need to protect kids in schools, tightening up security, but allow for the unborn (the most powerless in society) to go unprotected. We are called to be a voice for the voiceless and to pray for God to change leaders' hearts (Prov 21:1).

After Solomon dies, many kings fail to administer justice and defend the needy. However, the Old Testament has a sustained word of hope that the Messiah will ultimately come. Jeremiah spoke God's word: "I will raise up a Righteous Branch of David. He will reign wisely as king and administer justice and righteousness in the land" (Jer 23:5). Jesus Christ is the ultimate wise King that was promised. His wisdom was displayed in His ability to discern a person's heart (like the woman at the well). His mercy, justice, and wisdom were put on full display at the cross (1 Cor 1:24). He will eventually return to this broken world and establish His everlasting rule, in which there will be no more evil. We stand in awe of that King today, and we long for His appearing.

One way to see the connection of Solomon's reign and Jesus' superior reign is by considering Solomon's prayer in Psalm 72:1-17:

> God, give Your justice to the king
>   and Your righteousness to the king's son.
> He will judge Your people with righteousness
>   and Your afflicted ones with justice.
> May the mountains bring prosperity to the people
>   and the hills, righteousness.
> May he vindicate the afflicted among the people,
>   help the poor, and crush the oppressor.
> May he continue while the sun endures
>   and as long as the moon, throughout all generations.
> May he be like rain that falls on the cut grass,
>   like spring showers that water the earth.
> May the righteous flourish in his days
>   and prosperity abound until the moon is no more.

May he rule from sea to sea
 and from the Euphrates to the ends of the earth.
May desert tribes kneel before him
 and his enemies lick the dust.
May the kings of Tarshish
 and the coasts and islands bring tribute,
 the kings of Sheba and Seba offer gifts.
Let all kings bow down to him,
 all nations serve him.
For he will rescue the poor who cry out
 and the afflicted who have no helper.
He will have pity on the poor and helpless
 and save the lives of the poor.
He will redeem them from oppression and violence,
 for their lives are precious in his sight.
May he live long!
May gold from Sheba be given to him.
May prayer be offered for him continually,
 and may he be blessed all day long.
May there be plenty of grain in the land;
 may it wave on the tops of the mountains.
May its crops be like Lebanon.
May people flourish in the cities
 like the grass of the field.
May his name endure forever;
 as long as the sun shines, may his fame increase.
May all nations be blessed by him
 and call him blessed.

Here, Solomon is praying for himself, as the royal son in need of wisdom. He prayed for help to rule justly and defend those in need (vv. 1-4), as demonstrated in the case of this compassionate mother. (Mercy and justice go together—mercy for the victim and justice for the perpetrator.) The prayer also involves a cry for justice in the future kingdom (vv. 5ff) and the messianic rule. Jesus came announcing his arrival, saying that part of His purpose was to "set free the oppressed" (Luke 4:18). In His ministry Jesus demonstrated mercy and justice by ministering to those in need. At the cross Jesus' mercy and justice were put on full display. There, Jesus died for those who had broken God's law—satisfying the justice of God by taking their penalty and demonstrating the love of God by saving sinners. We are part of His kingdom. We await with anticipation the "not yet" part of the kingdom. Then we will know everlasting peace.

Use wisdom to lead others faithfully and skillfully (4:1-20). The writer says that Solomon "was king over all Israel" (v. 1 ESV). At the end of the unit, he says, "Judah and Israel were as numerous as the sand by the sea; they were eating, drinking, and rejoicing" (v. 20). Moses longed for this land, Joshua conquered enemies for it, David subdued it, and now Solomon and the people are enjoying it. God kept His promises. You too should enjoy the promises of God in celebration and thankfulness.

In between verses 1 and 20, we see evidence of Solomon's structure, organization, and diplomacy that led to such happiness. Religious, political, and economic leaders are mentioned here. The first four are possibly the inner cabinet (vv. 1-3; Olley, *Message of Kings*, 69). Next we read of a second level of leaders (vv. 4-6). The term "forced labor" in verse 6 doesn't refer to men with whips barking threats to slaves. It probably refers to putting one's self into the service of another family due to economic pressures. Then we read that Israel was divided into 12 administrative districts for taxation purposes (vv. 7-19; Olley, *Message of Kings*, 70). In verse 20 we read of the great growth of Israel (cf. Gen 22:17). The growth demanded wisdom in organization (for more, see Provan, *1 and 2 Kings*, 54–56).

Business leaders need wisdom to organize a growing business to go from "good to great, to built to last," in the words of Jim Collins (*Good to Great*, 188). Families need wisdom to organize their lives for effecting childhood development. Children need wisdom to prioritize their lives and complete their tasks. College students and graduate students need wisdom to give proper attention to family, work, studies, and the church.

Church leaders need wisdom as the church grows. In Acts 6 a need arises to care for widows. At that point the church had grown tremendously, and the apostles could not manage this legitimate need. So they appoint some leaders and allocate responsibilities for effective shepherding.

The goal of organization in a church is for disciple making, community building, and mission. Organization alone will not change anyone's life. The purpose is to facilitate growth in the best possible way. It's possible to spend all of one's time in structure and forget that ministry is about people (this point is made well in Marshall and Payne's excellent book *The Trellis and the Vine*). This need for sufficient structure to provide effective contexts for personal and discipling relationships demands wisdom. Thankfully, we aren't left on our own, for God gives wisdom to those who ask, and God gives the spiritual gift of administration to some in the church (1 Cor 12:28).

The happiness in the kingdom at this point in the Kings narrative points ahead to another kingdom. We await the King's arrival when we will sit down with our Messiah-King at the end-times banquet.

Spread Wisdom (4:21–5:18)

Next we read of the wisdom and glory of the king spreading among the nations. Solomon's rule extended "over all the kingdoms from the Euphrates River to the land of the Philistines and as far as the border of Egypt" (4:21). This large area, which is further explained in verse 24, corresponds to the promise to Abraham in Genesis 15:18. Verse 21 also says these nations "offered tribute and served Solomon all the days of his life." As a result of the massive amount of food and resources coming into Israel, all of Israel was blessed ("in safety . . . under his own vine and his own fig tree," 4:25). Solomon's reign initially brought prosperity and peace. This scene reminds us of Micah's description of the kingdom in the "last days" (Mic 4:1-5), in which the nations come into Zion and everyone sits without fear under their own vines and fig trees. It also sends our minds forward to a messianic feast described by Jesus (Matt 8:11). The nations are invited into the kingdom of God. It's our job as ambassadors of the kingdom to extend that invitation.

In verses 26-28 we detect some problems, however. Solomon is violating another command. In Deuteronomy 17:16 the king is forbidden to go to Egypt or to make the people return to Egypt to "acquire many horses." In 1 Kings 10:26-29 we see him breaking this command again, right before we read of his apostasy in 11:1. Provan says, "It is a bomb that will tick away quietly, along with all the others in 1 Kings 1–11, until the combined explosion occurs in 11–12" (*1 and 2 Kings*, 59).

Despite this negative note Solomon's wisdom continues to attract attention. He surpasses everyone in wisdom, even those known for wisdom (vv. 29-32; cf. Matt 2:1-12). He was famous in all the surrounding nations (4:31). Solomon's gift of wisdom was displayed by his speaking of proverbs and his singing of songs (v. 32; e.g., Song 1:1).

In 1 Kings 5 Solomon takes advantage of his friendly relationship with the next-door king, Hiram of Tyre, to obtain help in building the temple. This is made possible by a time of peace (God put all David's enemies "under his feet"; v. 3; cf. Ps 110:1; 1 Chr 22:7-10; 28:2-3). Hiram was previously involved in David's building project by supplying wood, carpenters, and stonemasons (2 Sam 5:11; Hiram also built impressive worship centers; House, *1, 2 Kings*, 122). The Sidonians were experts in building techniques (v. 6).

Solomon asks Hiram for skilled men and materials, especially the cedars, and promises to pay Hiram's servants. Hiram negotiates, saying that his men should deal with cutting and transporting the wood (in contrast to Solomon's desire for cooperation; v. 6). Then Hiram tells him that he should pay his royal household. Solomon receives trees; Hiram receives food. Goods are leaving Israel for another king. This seems like a peaceful arrangement.

In verses 13-18, however, it seems that Solomon ignores Hiram's counterproposal in verse 9. Instead of Hiram's men cutting and transporting the wood, Solomon sends a task force of 30,000 men to Lebanon to serve for three-month periods, making an annual total of 120,000 men! The rotation includes working one month in Lebanon and two months in Jerusalem. Another massive group (150,000 men) works in the hills cutting the stone for the foundation. Some rightly question Solomon's use of "forced labor" here. Many details are omitted (for a more positive take on "forced labor," see Provan, *1 and 2 Kings*, 65, and Davis, *1 Kings*, 56–57). The men of Gebal (north of Tyre) also assisted them.

Solomon negotiates with Hiram but also ignores him. Solomon's rule over the nations mentioned in 4:21 applies here, for Solomon is dominant over the king of Tyre. While his integrity is questioned at various points, Solomon's wisdom to build such a place is truly impressive.

Solomon's wisdom and glory are spreading in numerous ways. His proverbs, songs, building project, diplomacy, economic success, organizational skills, and leading national prosperity all attract worldwide attention.

Someone Greater than Solomon Is Here

We have the sacred calling to make the wisdom and glory of our King known among the nations. Our King and His kingdom deserve all that we can give.

In Matthew 12 Jesus, referring to Himself, says that "something greater than the temple is here" (12:6); "something greater than [the prophet] Jonah is here" (12:41); and, regarding the wisdom of Solomon, "something greater than Solomon is here" (12:42). Jesus elevated Himself above the three greatest institutions of Israel—prophet, priest, and king.

Jesus is superior to Solomon. He never drifted into idolatry or made foolish decisions that led Him into sin. He was the sinless King. He always did that which pleased the Father, being the ultimate example of the proverb, "A wise son brings joy to his father" (Prov 10:1).

Jesus also had superior wisdom. In Isaiah the Messiah has the "spirit of wisdom" resting on Him. In Nazareth they marveled at Jesus' wisdom (Mark 6:2). The same word for "parables" is the word for "proverbs." Jesus spoke with infinite wisdom in these parables. Not only did He astonish people with His teaching, but His work on the cross has also "become our wisdom"; it is "folly to some," but to us who believe, it is "the power of God" (1 Cor 1:18-25,30).

Jesus' temple is greater than Solomon's since He is our temple! He is the place we go to for worship (Mark 14:58).

Jesus' kingdom is more glorious. It's better organized, as the Spirit of God works to create order, not chaos (demonstrated at Pentecost, a reversal of Babel). He creates in us the fruit of the Spirit that leads to harmonious relationships. Jesus' kingdom is bigger than Solomon's kingdom, with people from all nations coming into it all the time. This was the promise given to Abraham. It was partially seen in Solomon's reign, but in Christ it is coming entirely true. Jesus' kingdom consists of greater happiness and peace, for we know His kingdom cannot be shaken (Heb 12:28).

As the King's people, we spread the wisdom and glory of our King by proclaiming the gospel and doing deeds of mercy and justice. We are called to spread His glory among the nations (Ps 96:3).

The biblical vision of Christ's kingdom is awe inspiring. It will extend from shore to shore until it finally covers the earth with the glory of God as the waters cover the sea (Hab 2:14). We want to see the nations swept up in this glory. Phil Ryken says it well: "Our desire is for the Lord Jesus Christ to receive as much honor as possible, from as many people as possible, in as many places as possible, for he alone deserves all the glory" (*1 Kings*, 107).

The wisest act one can do is repent of sin and put faith in King Jesus. Pay true homage to Him. Say, "You are my King. I am Your servant. I will submit to Your will. I will listen to Your wisdom in Your Word."

If you have received Christ as your Savior-King, then seek our gracious God for wisdom. Seek wisdom to help you lead your family, make wise decisions in your vocation, serve others in the church, and spread the King's wisdom and glory among the nations.

Reflect and Discuss

1. Why might Solomon have made a marriage alliance with Egypt?
2. What are some ways believers today compromise their faith with worldliness?
3. Is it significant that God continues to bless Solomon even though he is an imperfect king? Why?
4. Why is wisdom so valuable?
5. Describe how you have personally seen the benefits of godly wisdom.
6. People of all nations came to Solomon for wisdom. How might believers today be a beacon of wisdom to the world?
7. Why did Israel enjoy such prosperity during this time?
8. For what purposes does God bless His people?
9. How can we see wisdom in the life of Jesus?
10. Was Solomon ever foolish? How so?

Solomon's Temple

1 KINGS 6:1–9:9

Main Idea: The construction of the temple and the prayer of dedication show us the uniqueness, faithfulness, holiness, grace, and mission of God.

I.   **Treasure the Promises of God (6:1,37-38).**
II. **Marvel at the Holiness of God (6:2-10,14-36).**
  A. The size of the temple (6:2)
  B. The structure of the temple (6:3-10,14-36)
III. **Submit to the Word of God (6:11-13; 7:1-12).**
  A. Solomon's heart (6:11-13)
  B. Solomon's house (7:1-12)
IV. **Use Your Skills to the Glory of God (7:13-51).**
V.   **Pour Out Your Heart to God (8:1-66).**
  A. Celebration and sacrifice (8:1-13,62-66)
  B. Blessing (8:14-21,54-61)
  C. Sevenfold petition (8:22-53)
    1. A prayer for justice (vv. 31-32)
    2. A prayer for rescue (vv. 33-34)
    3. A prayer for provision (vv. 35-36)
    4. A prayer for deliverance (vv. 37-40)
    5. A prayer for outsiders (vv. 41-43)
    6. A prayer for victory (vv. 44-45)
    7. A prayer for restoration (vv. 46-53)
VI. **Listen to the Warning from God (9:1-9).**

Prepare for an all-you-can-eat meal. I don't mean a cheap buffet but a five-star Brazilian steakhouse! In these chapters the uniqueness of God, the faithfulness of God, the holiness of God, the grace of God, the mission of God, the warnings of God, a marvelous prayer, and many more soul-strengthening truths about God's greatness are set before us.

Solomon had many construction projects (cf. 1 Kgs 9:10ff; 2 Chr 8). Here, we read of his personal palace and the most important project: the temple. Solomon's temple stood for four centuries, and it was the only building the people rebuilt after the exile. After we read of the construction of the temple, we read of Solomon's prayer of dedication.

From the previous chapter we know that Solomon, the incredibly wise yet sometimes foolish king, is reigning over Israel in a time of great prosperity. It was a season of peace, great wealth, remarkable literature, and worldwide fame. In chapters 5–8 we read of another reason for Solomon's fame. God promised that Solomon would build the temple to the glory of God (8:5-21; 2 Sam 7:12-16). Here we see that promise being fulfilled.

Some of the technical language we meet here leaves us with questions. I'm not going to try to answer all of these questions because that's not the purpose of this commentary. Further, we should probably assume that the original readers had background knowledge and could fill in some of the blanks. Some details are better covered in 2 Chronicles 2–8; you should read it along with Kings. Also, some details are omitted because of the nature of the book itself. Kings isn't a construction manual. The information here isn't meant for you to go build a temple! It's here for you to behold God's glory.

Our hearts should be moved to worship with the psalmist who proclaimed, "Splendor and majesty are before Him; strength and beauty are in His sanctuary" (Ps 96:6). David dreamed of seeing the splendor. He said, "I have asked one thing from the LORD . . . to dwell in the house of the LORD all the days of my life, gazing on the beauty of the LORD and seeking Him in His temple" (Ps 27:4). Indeed, many psalms come to mind like this one: "Worship Yahweh in the splendor of His holiness" (Ps 29:2). As we reflect on the beauty of God's holiness, may we also reflect on these words: "Be holy, because I am holy" (Lev 11:45; 1 Pet 1:16). The temple should cause us to elevate our concept of God and, in seeing Him, cause us to worship and serve Him with more passion.

I want to make five applications from these chapters. The first four come from the construction of the temple (chs. 6–7), and the last one, which has several components, comes from chapter 8. A warning follows these.

Treasure the Promises of God
1 KINGS 6:1,37-38

We noticed in chapter 5 that the king used his wisdom to acquire the necessary materials for the temple. Thousands of workers were needed.

Now, in the 480th year after the people came out of Egypt, in the fourth year of Solomon's reign, they begin building (6:1). This date is about theology as well as chronology. The writer shows us the continuation of the story of redemption. We're reading about a new era in redemptive history. The exodus was that great event in the history of Israel in which God brought out His people from bondage (after 430 years of slavery; Exod 12:40). God had promised to deliver them from Egypt (Exod 6:6), and God later promised that Israel would settle in the land and build a house for Him (Exod 15:17; Deut 12:10-11; 16:2; 2 Sam 7:12-13). Throughout these chapters, a repeated refrain is that *God keeps His promises*.

We might think God takes a long time, but remember, God doesn't play by a shot clock! He keeps His promises, but it's on His own timetable. Our job is to trust Him, to wait on Him. God also promised that Messiah would come, and in the fullness of time He did (Gal 4:4). In Scripture we read of the great redemption provided by Jesus. In Him we find ultimate freedom and rest. We now await the fulfillment of the last act in the redemptive drama. And that day will come. Luther said, "There are two days on my calendar, today and 'that day.'" We can be certain that "that day" will come.

Paul prayed that the Ephesians would "know what is the hope of His calling" (Eph 1:18). Biblical hope isn't a wish. It's a settled reality. You can take God at His word. You can trust that God cares for His people. You can trust that all things are working for the good of those who love Him and are called according to His purpose (Rom 8:28); that His glory will one day be revealed (Rom 8:18); and that this light, momentary affliction will give way to eternal glory (2 Cor 4:17). Treasure His promises.

At the end of the chapter, the writer says the temple was completed in seven years (6:38), or more precisely seven years and six months (Provan, *1 and 2 Kings*, 67). God keeps His promises so we should treasure them.

Marvel at the Holiness of God
1 KINGS 6:2-10,14-36

The Size of the Temple (6:2)

In the wilderness wandering God's people built a tabernacle, which was a portable structure used for worship. The temple, however, was a permanent residence. The temple was similar to the tabernacle in structure, but it was bigger and more glorious in every way. The temple was measured in cubits. A cubit was about 18 inches. The temple was about 90 feet long (the distance from home plate to first base), 30 feet wide (a first down in football), and 45 feet high (a four-story building). It had the same proportions as the tabernacle, only quadruple the size. Ryken notes, "Roughly speaking, it was about the size of a church sanctuary that would seat 250 people, but proportionately it was narrow and tall—the height of a four-story building" (*1 Kings*, 138).

Therefore, the temple was *not* on the scale of the Seven Wonders of the World. It wasn't huge. Of course, it was placed up high on the mountain for people to see, and it was designed with amazing skill and expensive items, but what made it most impressive was its purpose. It was the place where God's name dwelled (1 Kgs 8:19).

Since a picture is worth a thousand words, an image is provided below. We will describe some of these elements.

The Structure of the Temple (6:3-10,14-36)

We could highlight the temple construction in three parts: the exterior (vv. 3-10,14), the interior (vv. 15-28), and the furnishings (vv. 29-36).

Verse 7 records an interesting aspect of the **exterior** construction project: "The temple's construction used finished stones cut at the quarry so that no hammer, chisel, or any iron tool was heard in the temple while it was being built." In chapter 5 Solomon deployed thousands of men to the hills to acquire stone for the temple, which they brought back to the city. These skilled workmen cut the material perfectly and then *without a sound* put each stone where it belonged. Remarkable skill! (I think I may institute this rule at my house!)

The off-site cutting and dressing of stones could stem from an earlier prohibition about the use of iron tools in constructing sacred buildings or altars (Deut 27:5; Josh 8:31). I think it has more to do with the idea of reverence. The prophet said, "But the LORD is in His holy temple; let everyone on earth be silent in His presence" (Hab 2:20). These men were doing holy work in quiet reverence.

Regarding the important **interior**, the writer describes the elaborate adornments and boards. Then he describes the holy of holies or the most holy place (vv. 16ff). A three-part plan included the court, the holy place, and the "most holy place." The most holy place was at the rear of the house, occupying some 30 feet, a third of the temple. Most of the

SOLOMON'S TEMPLE, Exterior View (LOOKING WEST)

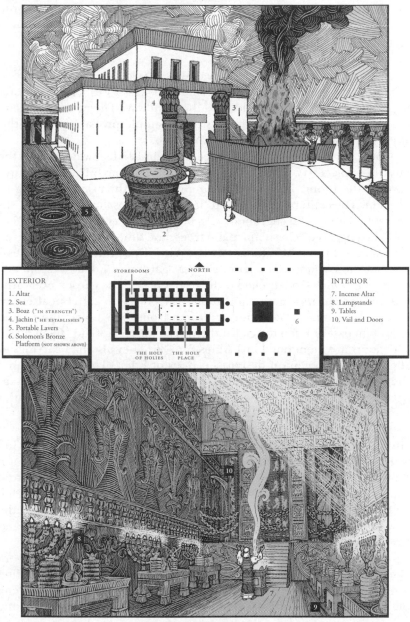

EXTERIOR

1. Altar
2. Sea
3. Boaz ("IN STRENGTH")
4. Jachin ("HE ESTABLISHES")
5. Portable Lavers
6. Solomon's Bronze Platform (NOT SHOWN ABOVE)

STOREROOMS

NORTH

THE HOLY OF HOLIES THE HOLY PLACE

INTERIOR

7. Incense Altar
8. Lampstands
9. Tables
10. Vail and Doors

SOLOMON'S TEMPLE, Interior View (LOOKING WEST)

Israelites would never see the things in it since it was an area reserved for the priests. The most holy place housed the ark of the covenant, where atonement was made and which served as God's footstool! Hebrews mentions that it was also an earthly copy of God's heavenly throne room (Heb 9:23-24).

Among the **furnishings** described, we see Solomon's temple was covered in "pure gold" (6:20-22,28,30). This was extraordinary! It denotes the glory of God. Was this gold used the right way? The writer makes no judgments. No negative word exists, so we should probably just see this as an act done to honor the glory of Yahweh.

Two cherubim, each about 15 feet high and 15 feet wide, graced the most holy place (vv. 23-28). The wings of these magnificent creatures covered the room! They were like guardians of the ark, reminding us of Eden. They also magnified God' majesty. The psalmist says God "sits enthroned above the cherubim" (Pss 99:1; 80:1; Isa 6:1-3)

The engraved "cherubim, palm trees, and flower blossoms" covered the walls and the inner doors (v. 29). Why? To signify God's holiness? Yes. But there's more. The temple was a "garden of Eden" like the tabernacle, in which God dwelled with His people. In the garden every tree was "pleasing in appearance and good for food" (Gen 2:9). But after our first parents sinned, God banished them from their home and placed cherubim east of Eden to "guard the way to the tree of life" (Gen 3:24). The doors are mentioned in 1 Kings 6:33-36. They also had carvings of cherubim and botanical designs—echoes of Eden. The doors allowed the priests into the presence of God but also kept others out of God's presence. As for the most holy place, only the high priests could enter once a year on the Day of Atonement.

The temple pointed back to Genesis and to the tabernacle, but it also pointed ahead to the person and work of Christ. Jesus was "God with us" (Matt 1:23), who became flesh and "dwelt among us" (John 1:14). He became the new temple, allowing us, who were cut off from God, to have access to God through His once-and-for-all sacrifice (Heb 10:19-22; Eph 2:18). These parts of the temple also point ahead to the new heavens and the new earth in which paradise will be regained and God will forever dwell with His people (Rev 21:3).

The work done in the temple of God also reminds us of the work God is doing in our own lives. We are "living stones" that God is building into a "spiritual house" (1 Pet 2:5). God isn't finished with us—His temple! How is God shaping us? God is chipping away what doesn't belong and is fitting us together. He uses pain, suffering, trials, and temptation. He uses Bible reading and prayer to shape us as well. God is shaping us personally and communally. Paul says of God's church that we are a "holy temple in the Lord," and we are "built together into a dwelling place for God by the Spirit" (Eph 2:21-22 ESV). God is sanctifying His church, His new temple (2 Cor 6:16; Col 3:16-17). There were great temples in places like Athens, and a great temple in Jerusalem, but now a greater temple is being built, namely God's people.

Submit to the Word of God
1 KINGS 6:11-13; 7:1-12

Solomon's Heart (6:11-13)

Tucked in the middle of the details of the temple is God speaking to Solomon. God often interrupts us! He uses various circumstances to get our attention and fix our eyes on His Word.

This interruption highlights what Solomon was to remember in the midst of his work; that is, apart from God's word, this was just another building project. If Israel doesn't follow God's word, then they won't enjoy all the benefits the temple signifies. God says that Solomon will experience God's blessing if he obeys the commands. These blessings include an everlasting dynasty and the presence of God.

Despite the importance of the temple, what God desires from His people isn't a building but obedience. God was after Solomon's *heart*. While God doesn't tell him to stop building, He reminds Solomon what is most important: obedience to God's word. External work is secondary to one's interior life. The Israelites often failed to remember this fact (e.g., Jer 7:1-34). God was after their obedience, yet they often trusted in "the temple of the LORD" to keep them from judgment (Jer 7:4).

What God says here is basically what David previously said to Solomon (1 Kgs 2:4). Solomon knew this, but walking in the commands was another matter.

I was counseling someone close to me this week, and she was telling me of her husband who knows the Bible. He even text messages verses to others, but the life he is living consistently contradicts what he knows and says. His sin is leading the children to become jaded toward him because of such hypocrisy. He has knowledge but does not implement the truth. God wants us to be "doers of the word and not hearers only" (Jas 1:22).

Is there any hope? Yes. But as we have said, Solomon could not keep the "if statements" of the covenant. But a real Promise Keeper came—Jesus Christ. Ryken says, "[Jesus] kept all the 'if' commands of the law that open up all the 'then' promises of the gospel for everyone who believes in him" (*1 Kings*, 145). God promises that He will dwell in our hearts through faith (Eph 3:15) and that He will never leave us or forsake us (Heb 13:5), even to the end of the age (Matt 28:20). Because of Jesus, these promises are ours. Because of Jesus we can be forgiven for our law breaking, and because of Jesus we have power to obey Him faithfully.

Solomon's House (7:1-12)

Solomon's palace takes about twice as long to finish (13 years) as the temple. It consisted of five parts, the "House of the Forest of Lebanon," the "hall of pillars," the "Hall of Judgment," and a palace for him and one for Pharaoh's daughter. Verses 9-12 describe the expensive materials used.

The writer doesn't tell us how we interpret this section. Do we take it positively? Was this an example of God's blessing and a sign of God's splendor like the temple? Or was this an example of Solomon's self-indulgence and divided heart? Were Solomon's priorities out of line? Positively, it seems like a good thing that he lived near the temple. He was close to God's presence, and he used the palace to render justice (cf. Ps 72). Negatively, one could call this extravagant. The language of 6:38 and 7:1 highlights an emphatic contrast, perhaps suggesting that his priorities were out of order (Provan, *1 and 2 Kings*, 69). We are probably safe in saying he was a man with mixed motives at best.

However you resolve the issue, we should remember that we must submit to God's Word concerning wealth, home, and worship buildings. In the New Testament we read about an indulgence that is sinful (Luke 12:17-21) but an extravagance that at times is acceptable (Mark 14:3-9; Davis, *1 Kings*, 64). As believers, we need to seek God's Word for counsel regarding wealth and seek to use it wisely. I don't think it's wrong to spend money on a nice house or a place for worship, but we need to remember a few things. Regarding the temple, we should never compare a church building to Solomon's temple. We are in a new era. We don't need to spend millions upon millions of dollars on a place for corporate worship because we have our temple already in Jesus. Even if the need for a large place exists, it seems best to build simple structures.

We aren't called to compete with the new Dallas Cowboys stadium. We need to put the glory of God on display with our lives.

Regarding our homes, Christians should think about building, buying, or renting their homes with ministry in mind. Certainly, one can enjoy the fruit of work and be thankful for a nice place to raise a family, but think about how to host people when you think about your home. And even if Solomon isn't demonstrating misplaced priorities in this text, it's possible that you and I could do this. Our stuff isn't more important than the kingdom. Christians should take care of their houses but shouldn't idolize them. Be careful that culture doesn't influence you in these matters. Once again, the call is to order our lives after God's Word.

Remember also Matthew 6, where Jesus teaches that we shouldn't worry about our most basic needs but rather trust our heavenly Father. He says, "Learn how the wildflowers of the field grow," and "not even Solomon in all his splendor was adorned like one of these" (Matt 6:28,29). Then He says, "If that's how God clothes the grass of the field, which is here today and thrown into the furnace tomorrow, won't He do much more for you—you of little faith?" (Matt 6:30). You can trust God. You don't need to have a massive home or great wealth, and you need not worry about your basic needs; instead you should simply "seek first the kingdom of God" (Matt 6:33) and rest in the promise that God will take care of you.

Use Your Skills to the Glory of God
1 KINGS 7:13-51

In these verses we read of the fixtures of the temple. A skilled craftsman, Hiram of Tyre, from the tribe of Naphtali (not the Hiram from chapter 5), fashions the gold and bronze items. Hiram's work is reminiscent of Bezalel and Oholiab, who were skilled and gifted to construct the tabernacle. God gifts people in the arts and for craftsmanship.

Hiram makes four basic items and their accessories in 7:15-47. First, he makes a pair of massive **pillars** (vv. 15,21-22). One pillar was called "Jachin" ("He will establish") and the other "Boaz" ("in Him is strength"). These names signified a message, much like a basketball point guard might call a play saying, "Five" (Davis, *1 Kings*, 73). These single words conveyed much meaning. These pillars conveyed the firmness of God's promise to *establish* David's throne (cf. 2 Sam 7:12-16) and

God's mighty *strength* to accomplish it. David's royal Psalm 21 begins and ends with this word "Boaz" (*strength* in English): "LORD, the king finds joy in Your strength. . . . Be exalted, LORD, in Your strength (Ps 21:1,13). It's possible, maybe even probable, that this pillar was to remind people of this psalm. Therefore, standing in front of the temple proper were these two pillars, "He will establish" and "In Him is strength"—the promise of God and the power of God exalted.

What a great reminder to us today that our strength is in the Lord (Eph 6:10; 2 Tim 2:1) and that God's kingdom through Christ, the greater Solomon, is established forever (Luke 1:32-33). The temple would fall, but as Luther wrote, "His kingdom is forever" ("A Mighty Fortress Is Our God"). We don't need these pillars today, but what we do need is this message written on our hearts, as we seek to do God's will in this life.

On top of each pillar stands an ornate capital (vv. 16-21). The capitals were decorated with rows of fruit and chains of flowers—more echoes of the garden. The pomegranates remind us of the priests who had pomegranates on the fringes of their garments. We also read of lily work, symbols of life and love. These also remind us of Eden.

Second, Hiram made a large holding tank called a "molten sea" or "**cast metal reservoir**" (7:23-26). It was designed to hold lots of water (about 11,000 gallons). He decorated it with gourds and made its lip in the shape of a lily. The stand consisted of 12 bronze oxen (perhaps a sign of the 12 tribes of Israel). It was for washing and maybe even conveys the idea of God ruling over the chaotic waters and all creation.

Third, Hiram made 10 **water carts** to hold smaller basins for other temple rituals (7:27-39). Each basin contained about 200 gallons of water. The stands had four wheels and were decorated with cherubim, lions, and palm trees (7:27-37).

"What is up with all this water?" you might ask. These basins demonstrate God's concern for cleansing. The priests had to keep themselves ceremonially pure to do their work (2 Chr 4:6). They washed themselves and the animals.

Of course, God is still concerned with cleansing, but there are some differences. First, all believers are God's priests now (1 Pet 2:5). We no longer need to offer sacrifices; instead we offer our praise, our prayers, and our proclamation of the good news to the world (Heb 13:15). Second, we have a better cleansing. Through Jesus we can be truly cleansed. There is an initial cleansing when we come to Christ

(Titus 3:5), then a renewed cleansing that we need daily (1 John 1:7; 2 Cor 7:1). Positionally, we are holy as God's people because of Jesus, but practically we need to experience fresh cleansing daily.

Fourth and finally, he made smaller "**basins, the shovels, and the sprinkling basins**" (vv. 40-47). Such elements were used for temple ceremonies. In verses 48-51 we read that Solomon completes the furnishings by having the equipment made. We read of "the gold altar" that was likely used for the burning of incense (cf. Exod 30:1-4), symbolizing the prayers of the people; "the gold table that the bread of Presence was placed on," which represented God's presence and provision; 10 lampstands (cf. Exod 25:31-40), which gave light, signified glory, and conveyed the idea of life through both the tree of life and the light (House, *1, 2 Kings*, 135); and bowls, wick trimmers, sprinkling basins, ladles, fire pans, and more that are covered in pure gold. "So all the work King Solomon did in the LORD's temple was completed" (v. 51). Then Solomon brings the items David had dedicated into the temple (2 Sam 8:11; 1 Chr 22:14).

Ralph Davis points out that 2 Chronicles (chs. 3–4) spends much less time on these details than the writer of Kings. You might wonder, "Why all this information? Who cares about pomegranates and basins and fire pans and pillars?" While many have little patience for this section, the author seems to relish it. He loves describing the liturgical elements (Davis, *1 Kings*, 75–76). Why? Perhaps because he thinks one should use their technical mind and artistic skills to the glory of God. Hiram, with his artistic skill, like the men who made the worship elements for the tabernacle, made beautiful things for God's temple.

What about you? Are you using your God-given gifts to create things for the glory of your Creator? That is what you were made to do. Whether you are an artist, a musician, a writer, a cook, a plumber, a teacher, an athlete, a tech guru, a doctor, or something else, use your gifts for God's glory and the good of others.

The Presbyterian missionary Elizabeth Freeman and her husband John were pioneer missionaries to India. After only seven years they were seized in a Muslim uprising and shot in cold blood. Earlier Elizabeth had written these words to one of her nieces:

> I hope you will be a missionary wherever your lot is cast,
> and as long as God spares your life; for it makes but little
> difference after all where we spend these few fleeting years, if

they are only spent for the glory of God. Be assured there isn't anything else worth living for. (Ryken, *1 Kings*, 198)

Indeed. Be assured! Nothing is worth living for except the glory of God. And on top of this grand purpose, we are given the presence of God to carry out the mission of God.

Pour Out Your Heart to God
1 KINGS 8:1-66

In chapter 8, after the ark is brought into the temple, Solomon offers up a magnificent prayer to God. The structure of chapter 8 seems to have a great emphasis on verses 22-53. Following Porten and Davis, consider this scheme:

    Celebration and Sacrifice (vv. 1-13)
        Blessing (vv. 14-21)
            Prayer of Dedication (vv. 22-53)
        Blessing (vv. 54-61)
    Celebration and Sacrifice (vv. 62-66)

Following this chiastic structure, one can see that what comes in the middle of the sandwich is of great importance (Davis, *1 Kings*, 80; see also Leithart, *1 and 2 Kings*, for a possible structure of 1:1–12:24 that places the section we are considering, 1 Kings 6:1–9:9, at the center of the narrative of Solomon). We can divide this prayer, then, into three parts: celebration and sacrifice (vv. 1-13,62-66); blessing (vv. 12-21,54-61); and prayer of dedication—a sevenfold petition (vv. 22-53). The first and last parts highlight God's mystery and clarity. The second part exults in God's faithfulness, and the second blessing includes a benedictory prayer. The third part highlights God's forgiveness. With these attributes of God in mind, let us consider the need to pray to this God.

Celebration and Sacrifice (8:1-13,62-66)

This chapter begins with Solomon bringing the ark, this great symbol of God's presence, into the temple (vv. 1-3). Everyone involved in the process offers sacrifices in view of personal and national sin and in praise to the God who forgives and provides (vv. 4-6). We see here the holiness of God and the necessity of blood in order to enter into His presence.

    In verses 6-9 the ark reaches its destination: the most holy place. We are given a description of the massive poles and of the contents of the ark: nothing "except the two stone tablets that Moses had put there at Horeb" (v. 9). God's Word and God's presence are thus linked together.

Then we see the amazing results. A cloud fills the house and the priests "were not able to continue ministering" because of the cloud (v. 11). Why? The cloud represented God's glory. The writer says, "The glory of the LORD filled the temple" (v. 11). This same wonder happened in the tabernacle in Exodus 40:34-35. The disciples also experienced an awesome glory cloud at the transfiguration of Jesus (Mark 9:2-3). One day we will see glory for ourselves, as Jesus prayed in John 17:24.

As we see throughout chapter 8, God's attributes are mysteriously and majestically joined together (Davis, *1 Kings*, 79–93). Here, we see mystery and clarity joined together. God is on the one hand hidden and on the other hand revealed. The cloud reveals His glory and conceals His glory (cf. Pss 18:11; 97:2). His clarity is revealed by what is in the ark: His Word. His Word is clear. He has clearly taught us His ways. The cloud points to His obscurity—we can't know everything about Him (though we have sufficient knowledge to know Him). Davis says, "He satisfies your need for clarity but not your passion for curiosity" (Davis, *1 Kings*, 82).

You can know God today. He has made Himself known in His Word and in His Son. But when you come to know Jesus, you realize that God is inexhaustible. The psalmist said, "His greatness is unsearchable" (Ps 145:3). You were created to know this God and to know Him more and more.

Of course, these sacrifices point to how we are reconciled to this God. The animal sacrifices provided temporary atonement but ultimately couldn't completely satisfy God's wrath against sin. We needed a perfect sacrifice, and we have it in the Lamb of God. Because of Jesus' sacrifice, we can celebrate. Because of His sacrifice, the only thing left to offer is our lives (Rom 12:1-2).

In verses 12-13 Solomon responds in awe and underscores the mystery of God's transcendence and immanence. God dwells in thick darkness (transcendence, hiddenness) but is also immanent (dwelling among His people in the "exalted house"). May we too stand in awe of His glory.

At the end of the chapter, more sacrifices are made (vv. 62-64); then a great feast is held for seven days. The people were full of joy and gladness (vv. 65-66). In this we see another "joining together," except this time it isn't a joining together of God's attributes but rather our response to His attributes: fear and festivity. God is to be feared; sacrifice is required. God is also to be enjoyed; celebration should exist among God's delivered people.

Blessing (8:14-21,54-61)

After the initial celebration and sacrifice, Solomon turns his attention to speak to the people. He is speaking about God in a worshipful manner. He is exulting in God's faithfulness. He ties together God's covenant to David and the exodus, both of which highlight God's faithfulness (vv. 15-16). Next he reflects on God's words to David, that David's son would build a house (vv. 17-19). This also highlights the faithfulness of God. Finally, Solomon exults in God's choice of him to build the temple (vv. 20-21).

What about you? Do you exult, rejoice, and delight in God's faithfulness? If not, then I would recommend you do what Solomon is doing here: consider the word of God. Consider how God has kept His promises.

Look at the second blessing in verses 54-61. Solomon again stretches out his hands toward heaven (v. 54; cf. v. 22). Only this time he isn't standing but kneeling. Perhaps he began standing but poured out his heart with such passion that he ended up on the ground.

Again he says, "May the LORD be praised!" (v. 56; cf. v. 15). He praises God for His faithfulness. He says, "Not one of all the good promises He made through His servant Moses has failed" (v. 56; cf. 6:1; 8:16). What a statement! Not one word of God has ever failed, and not one word of God ever will fail! You can trust in His word forever!

Then the praise turns into a three-part benedictory prayer. First, **he encourages the people to recognize their need for God's presence**. He says, "May the LORD our God be with us as He was with our ancestors" (v. 57). Solomon recognizes that just as God was with Moses, Gideon, Jeremiah, and others, he and his subjects also needed His presence.

Second, **he prays that God would "incline our hearts to him"** (v. 58 ESV). Solomon pleads with God that the people may love God's word and do His will. We should pray this! "Incline our hearts to him." What does this mean? One theologian said, "Love is inclination" (Shedd, *Dogmatic Theology*, 208). That is, whatever we are inclined to do is what we love the most. This is a prayer for God to work in our wills so that we don't love anything more than Him, so that we are totally devoted to Him. The psalmist prayed, "Incline my heart to your testimonies, and not to selfish gain" (Ps 119:36 ESV).

This may be a good place to think about true conversion. Conversion is the change of affections. Paul writes, "Therefore, if anyone is in Christ, he is a new creation" (2 Cor 5:17). In conversion our wills are inclined to something new. When some people hear the gospel, they think, "Oh, I've tried that, and it didn't work." Often they've only performed a religious ritual but have never had their affections changed. Others say they're believers, but they live a double life because they have never been changed. Christianity is about internal transformation. A Christian is one who loves Christ, and to love Him our hearts must be inclined to Him. Now, as Christians, every day we are praying that God would incline our hearts to Him so that we may do His will.

Third, **he pleads with God to uphold Israel's cause** (vv. 59-61). Notice the reason: "That all the peoples of the earth may know that Yahweh is God. There is no other!" (v. 60). Solomon desires for the nations to know the true and living God. God isn't a tribal deity exclusive to Israel but the only living God who deserves the worship of all nations (vv. 41-43).

Solomon concludes with a charge to Israel to be faithful (cf. Josh 24:14). Every generation has this charge to be faithful to the God who is always faithful to His people.

Sevenfold Petition (8:22-53)

The prayer Solomon offers is important to understanding Kings. It's basically a summary of every prayer that would be prayed in the temple in the future (Spurgeon, "Solomon's Plea"), organized with seven petitions, perhaps to signify perfection. These petitions begin in verse 31.

Leading up to these petitions, Solomon praises God for His uniqueness. God is the only God. God is the faithful, redeeming, covenant-keeping God (vv. 23-26). Verses 27-30 transition into the seven petitions. Solomon reminds us that God isn't confined to a building (Acts 17:24-25). Indeed, the highest of heavens cannot contain Him. Yet God has chosen to make His "name" dwell in the temple (vv. 18,19,20). God is high and lofty, but He hears the prayers of the meek and lowly (Isa 66:1-2).

The listening nature of God is noted in the next verse and then appears throughout the following petitions. Notice the phrase "hear in heaven" (vv. 32,34,36,39,43,45,49). Solomon understands that the temple was to be a place to petition God, and He would hear there, but He was not confined there. God's "hearing" is done in heaven.

On this side of the cross, we have no temple; we have something better, namely, Jesus. Through Him we can pray anytime, anywhere, as Jesus told the woman at the well (John 4:21-24). And we know God hears the prayers of His people. "Call to Me and I will answer you" (Jer 33:3; cf. Ps 91:15; Jer 29:12). What is more, we have a better Mediator than Solomon. Jesus Christ our King is our eternal Intercessor (Rom 8:34; Heb 7:25), and the Holy Spirit dwells within us, allowing us to commune with God (Eph 2:18). Pour out your heart to this transcendent and immanent God.

Since God hears the prayers of His people, what should they pray? The following seven petitions highlight both the *severity* and the *mercy* of God (vv. 31-53). Five of these petitions—the first four and the last one (vv. 31,33-34,35-36,38-39,46ff) address sin situations. Consequently, a prayer for forgiveness is offered throughout (vv. 30,34,36,39,50). One of the main purposes of the temple is forgiveness. The other two petitions will be noted below. Let's ponder these seven petitions. (I'm indebted to Ryken, *1 Kings*, 224–36, for the following headings.)

Petition 1: A prayer for justice (vv. 31-32). The first petition concerns a legal case where insufficient evidence makes it difficult to render a verdict. God is called on to condemn the guilty and clear the innocent. Even though Solomon was wise, he couldn't possibly rightly judge all things (cf. Exod 22:9). Solomon acknowledges God's righteousness and justice. God is the one who "judges impartially" (1 Pet 1:17). We should also pray for justice to be done and for God to grant us wisdom when we are called on to execute justice.

Petition 2: A prayer for rescue (vv. 33-34). The second petition concerns a defeat in battle because of Israel's sin and their need for rescue and return. Israel often lost battles because of their previous sin (Josh 7:1-5; 1 Sam 4:1-11). Solomon understood Israel's human nature and thus prayed for God to forgive them and bring them back to the land.

Petition 3: A prayer for provision (vv. 35-36). Sometimes the sin of God's people would bring about problems with the land (Deut 11:13-17). This actually happens later in 1 Kings in the days of King Ahab. The people turn away, and there is no rain for three years (1 Kgs 17:1; Jas 5:17). After Elijah overcomes the prophets of Baal and prays for rain, God provides for His people (1 Kgs 18:41-45; Jas 5:17-18).

Petition 4: A prayer for deliverance (vv. 37-40). This prayer sounds similar to the third. Solomon lists a host of disasters that might befall the people because of their sin (v. 37). Later we will read of Hezekiah stretching out his hands in prayer for deliverance when the nation of Assyria, led by Sennacherib, besieges Jerusalem (2 Kgs 18–19). Hezekiah prays for deliverance from this threat (2 Kgs 19:14-19), and God hears his plea and answers him (2 Kgs 19:20,32-36).

We shouldn't always make a one-to-one correlation between disasters and God's judgment. Our nation isn't in a covenant the way the nation of Israel was. However, we need to remember that God calls us to obedience, and when we fail, there are consequences (and those consequences could be in the form of disasters, if God so chooses). When we fail, we need to repent.

We also need to remember the simple truth that God hears us when we pray. Elijah and Hezekiah illustrate this truth. James encouraged his people to pray, reminding them that "Elijah was a man with a nature like ours" and he prayed fervently and God acted (Jas 5:17-18).

Petition 5: A prayer for outsiders (vv. 41-43). Solomon expresses a desire for the nations to know and worship the God of Israel. He mentions the "mighty hand" and "outstretched arm" of God, signifying God's salvation (Deut 4:34; 5:15). Here we are reminded that God chose Israel that they might be a blessing to the nations (Gen 12:1-3). The temple was designed to be a "house of prayer for all peoples" (Isa 2:3; 56:7; Mark 11:17). In the Gospels we read about the temple being used as a place for nationalistic pride, warfare, and economic gain (John 2:13-17). It was never intended for that purpose.

Many examples of outsiders being drawn to Israel's God appear in the Old Testament. One of them is Ruth. Others appear right here in the book of Kings, like the queen of Sheba and the widow of Zarephath. We also read of Naaman, who comes to Israel to be healed of leprosy after an Israelite slave girl testifies of God's power. Naaman confesses, "I know there's no God in the whole world except in Israel" (2 Kgs 5:15). In the New Testament many outsiders are brought to faith, such as the centurion and Cornelius (Matt 8:5-13; Acts 10–11).

Many people don't understand that God desires the salvation of all nations. Some wrongly categorize Christianity as a "Western religion." In some bookstores it's placed under such a heading. The fact is, many Eastern countries are seeing more explosive growth in the church than the West. The gospel is for the nations. The promise to Abraham was about the nations. Here, at the steps of the temple, we find a prayer for the nations. In Revelation we see the culmination of this passion. So if people ask you, "Where did you get your passion for the nations?" you should simply say, "I read the Bible." For if you take the nations out of the Bible, you leave only the table of contents and the maps!

Are you praying for outsiders to come to know Jesus? Are you joining God in this mission to see outsiders come to faith in Jesus? A difference to note is that in the Old Testament the nations mainly came *into* Jerusalem, but in the New Testament the Christians were together in Jerusalem at Pentecost, but then the mission went *out from* Jerusalem. We are to go into the world to show and to tell the gospel.

Petition 6: A prayer for victory (vv. 44-45). Like the previous petition this petition is about war. However, this prayer is about victory in God's cause. In 2 Chronicles 20 the Moabites and Ammonites come against King Jehoshaphat and Judah. Jehoshaphat gathers everyone and they seek the Lord's intervention. He alludes to 1 Kings 8, and they pray, "For we are powerless" and "we do not know what to do, but we look to You" (2 Chr 20:12). Miraculously, God intervened and delivered His people. Of course we are in a different kind of battle now, but we need to pray for God's help to gain victory against our enemies (Eph 6:10-20).

Petition 7: A prayer for restoration (vv. 46-53). Here we find the fifth request for forgiveness. This is a "worst case scenario" (Davis, *1 Kings, 89*). The people of God are going into exile because of their sin. This is exactly where the book of Kings is headed. A second exodus will be needed because of their sin. Solomon's prayer is based in reality. He says in verse 46, "There is no one who does not sin." Yet he understands that restoration and grace are possible if the people plead for it. We find prayers like this during Israel's exile. Daniel was exiled in Babylon and prayed for the restoration of Israel (Dan 6:10; cf. 9:3-19). Daniel's prayer brought an answer to Solomon's prayer. God did forgive the people and bring them back to the land.

We too need to be reminded that our greatest problem is a sin problem. But we have great hope in Christ. He is the sin-bearing Savior, the sin-forgiving Savior. Due to the nature of sin, we need constantly to be repenting of sin and seeking cleansing from our merciful God. Our culture doesn't want to believe anything is a sin, and in their denial they are blinded to their need for the One who came to save His people from their sins.

Looking back over this section on the temple construction and temple dedication, we're reminded of some important truths:

- *Treasure the promises of God.* He redeems. He saves.
- *Marvel at the holiness of God.* Worship in the splendor of His holiness.

- *Submit to the Word of God.* God is after the heart, not just what you build.
- *Use your skills to the glory of God.* All of your talents should be used for the good of the kingdom.
- *Pour out your heart to God.* Praise God. Bless God. Celebrate the goodness of God. Pray for justice, rescue, provision, deliverance, outsiders, victory, and restoration.

Listen to the Warning from God
1 KINGS 9:1-9

We aren't done! The temple narrative isn't finished! After this, the writer says, the Lord appeared to Solomon a second time. He first appeared at Gibeon, where He blessed Solomon with wisdom. Such wisdom was used for the building of the temple. God now assures Solomon that His name will dwell there and that He will hear prayer.

However, this appearance comes with a warning (vv. 4-9). There is a condition for continued blessing: obedience. The particular issue mentioned is idolatry. God says if they worship false gods, then Israel will become a byword and a proverb and the temple will become a pile of ruins. Provan notes, "The 'if' of verse 6 cannot in reality be anything other than a 'when' (8:46)" (*1 and 2 Kings*, 83). The people will chase other gods, and Israel will be carried away. He adds, "The temple is no sooner built than we hear of its inevitable end" (ibid.).

Thus, we are left with a focus on Solomon's heart. That is a good place for us to end. The warning to the Hebrews comes to mind: "Watch out, brothers, so that there won't be in any of you an evil, unbelieving heart that departs from the living God" (Heb 3:12).

Everyone will worship something or someone. What or whom do you worship? Let us remember that someone greater than Solomon is here. Jesus has come to show us the glory of God. He never sinned or fell short of the glory of God. He lived a perfectly righteous life and died a substitutionary death. He conquered the grave, and now we need to submit our lives to this King. Don't give your heart to another lover. Instead, see in Christ all that you need. In Him there is freedom, rest, joy, power for holiness, and access to God in prayer. Let His peace rule in your heart (Col 3:15). Look to the Savior-King-Temple who outshines all the beauties of this world. Behold "the light of the knowledge of God's glory in the face of Jesus Christ" (2 Cor 4:6) with the eyes of faith and be changed by the Spirit of God.

Reflect and Discuss

1. Why is the temple significant in the life of the Israelites?
2. What does the temple communicate about God's character?
3. Are the intricate details of the temple structure important? Why or why not?
4. Why is it important that God's people walk in holiness?
5. Are holiness and God's presence related in any way?
6. Hiram, along with Solomon, also had wisdom. Was it different from Solomon's wisdom? How so?
7. How does God continue to give His people wisdom today?
8. How might God's people use wisdom to glorify the Lord?
9. Name some of the characteristics of God found in Solomon's prayer (8:22-53).
10. How does God respond to Solomon's prayer?

The Wise Fool

1 KINGS 9:10–11:43

Main Idea: The collapse of Solomon's reign underscores our need for a King greater than Solomon.

I. **Solomon's Tainted Glory (9:10–10:29)**
   A. Solomon's position (9:10)
   B. Solomon's protection and provision (9:11-22,24)
   C. Solomon's righteousness (9:25)
   D. Solomon's wisdom (10:1-13)
   E. Solomon's wealth (10:14-29)
II. **Solomon's Tragic Collapse (11:1-43)**
   A. His downfall was predictable (11:1-2).
   B. His downfall involved deliberate disobedience (11:1-3).
   C. His downfall stemmed from a heart problem (11:1-9).
   D. His downfall involved persistent sin (11:2-9).
   E. His downfall was a gateway to apostasy (11:5-8).
   F. His downfall caused devastating results (11:9-43).
III. **What Should We Say at Solomon's Funeral?**

Chapters 9 and 10 are like taking a field trip to observe the grandeur of a building or a city. We read of the cities Solomon built and the massive amount of gold he accumulated. We also read of a fascinating meeting with the queen of Sheba. However, the story moves from the golden age to a cold grave. In chapter 11 we read the sad commentary on Solomon's sins, their devastating consequences, and a brief statement of his death. We read of massive gold and incomparable wisdom, and then we finish at a graveside.

Solomon is a paradox. He was the wisest man ever, yet he made some foolish and destructive choices (like having 700 wives!). He was an incredibly blessed man, but he didn't always steward God's blessings faithfully. He knew God's law, but he didn't keep it. He led the nation to a golden age (peace, prosperity, profitable trade, and a magnificent temple), yet he also led it into decline and set it up for collapse.

Solomon serves as both example and warning. Like Solomon we need to learn how to steward God's gifts responsibly. We have a sinful tendency to take good things and use them wrongly. Sex, money, food, and influence are wonderful blessings when used accordingly for God's glory, but they can be abused and can destroy lives.

Therefore, we need to learn from this story—the story of Solomon's tainted glory and his tragic downfall. His rise to greatness is something to behold, but it's short-lived and impure at times. Solomon's glory is "under a cloud, destined to fade away" (Provan, *1 and 2 Kings*, 84). In studying his life we must learn to avoid his sins and to marvel at the One greater than Solomon.

Solomon's Tainted Glory
1 KINGS 9:10–10:29

Solomon's life and reign reveal glimpses of Jesus' glory. By examining some Messianic categories provided in chapters 9–10, we can navigate through the narrative and set our minds on the ultimate Son of David who fulfilled the categories. Let me point out five aspects of Solomon's kingly glory that were present but not perfect.

Solomon's Position (9:10)

The section opens up with some chronology: "At the end of 20 years" of construction activity. At this time 24 years of Solomon's reign were complete (6:1,38; 7:1). He had the privilege of being the king, but he also served as a *mediator*. In the previous chapters Solomon built "the LORD's temple," which was a place for sacrifice and prayer. Immediately following this, we find Solomon praying for his people (8:12-66). He offers a sevenfold petition to God on their behalf, and God responds by saying, "I have heard your prayer" (9:3). Solomon is communing with God, interceding on behalf of the people in a priestly way. What a unique privilege he had!

Second Chronicles 7 records a portion of this story not revealed in Kings. After the prayer and the dedication of the temple, we read a promise that has become popular. God says, "If My people who are called by My name humble themselves, pray and seek My face, and turn from their evil ways, then I will hear from heaven, forgive their sin, and heal their land" (2 Chr 7:14). In the previous sevenfold petition, Solomon asked God to hear the people when they pray (1 Kgs 8:22-53). Here in

2 Chronicles 7 God says that the people do indeed have access to Him and that He will "hear from heaven." Now the people have a place of prayer in the temple (the new garden of Eden) and the promise that God will hear their prayer. Solomon serves as a mediator for them.

A *greater Mediator.* Of course, Solomon doesn't fulfill this role perfectly. Only Jesus would become the ultimate Mediator. Paul tells us that Jesus Christ is the only mediator between God and humanity (1 Tim 2:5). Through Christ we now have access to the Father (Eph 2:18). He is the way back into the garden, our new temple, giving us access to God. Because of Jesus, God can and does hear our prayer. We have One who has gone before us, a perfect, sinless Mediator, Jesus, who "lives to intercede" for us (Heb 7:25; cf. Rom 8:34).

Solomon's Protection and Provision (9:11-22,24)

We first read of Hiram, king of Tyre, in chapter 5. He gave supplies for the temple. (A different Hiram built the furnishings for the temple; 7:13ff.) What chapter 5 hints at, chapter 9 shows us. Hiram was very much a "junior partner" in his relationship with Solomon (Provan, *1 and 2 Kings*, 84). Hiram gives Solomon gold "for his every wish," and in return Solomon provides him with 20 cities (1 Kgs 9:11-12). For some reason Hiram is dissatisfied with this trade, so he names the cities "Land of Cabul" (unknown meaning, perhaps "Like Nothing" or "Worthless"). This probably had to do with the amount of gold he gave to Solomon (Konkel, *1 and 2 Kings*, 198). Despite the apparent displeasure with the trade, Hiram continues to send men to the sea to bring more gold to Solomon (vv. 26-28; 10:11-12,22).

While Solomon's trading practices probably continued to bless the people, it seems that we have another example of Solomon watching out for his own interests more than the interests of others. This problem seems to have escalated in his later years. We read less about the people and more of Solomon's wealth in chapters 9–11. Previously we read that all of Israel lived "under his own vine and his own fig tree" (4:25). Has Solomon's power and wealth led him to love gold more than people? Is he using his wisdom to do justice and lead the nation faithfully, or is he using it to acquire more wealth?

Next the writer tells of Solomon's magnificent construction projects and the massive amount of workers needed (vv. 15-19). Many of these workers appear to have been enlisted unjustly (5:13,21; 11:28; 12:14). This is another example of glory under a cloud.

Impressively, we read of the following construction projects: "the supporting terraces," "the wall of Jerusalem," "storage cities," "the chariot cities," and "the cavalry cities." Then the writer says, "And whatever Solomon desired to build in Jerusalem, Lebanon, or anywhere else in the land of his dominion" (v. 19). Thus, Solomon strengthened the defenses. Six cities formed a line of defense from north to south: Hazor, Meggido, Gezer, Lower Beth-horon, Baalath, and Tamar. These were fortified towns that protected the people and the trade routes. He had to rebuild Gezer because Pharaoh destroyed it. All of these were strategic passes that Solomon controlled for the benefit of the nation. Hazor was strategically located in the north. Megiddo was an intimidating fortress that controlled one of the major passes along the coast of the Jezreel Valley. Gezer was on the road from Joppa to Jerusalem. Upper and Lower Beth-horon were areas that controlled access to the highlands of Judea from the coastal plain through the Aijalon Valley. Baalath refers to several cities in Canaan.

What about his wife? She receives a new separate home (v. 24). In chapter 11 we will read more of Solomon's woman troubles and their disastrous implications.

In verses 20-22 we read of the subjugation of Solomon's enemies. In 2 Chronicles 8:3 the Chronicler says, "Solomon went to Hamath-zobah and seized it." Solomon wins a military victory.

The writer tells us of 550 men in particular who worked under Solomon (1 Kgs 9:23). As already mentioned, Solomon's administrative skills demonstrated his God-given wisdom. And we know that in the kingdom of Christ a much greater administration exists thanks to the outpouring of the Holy Spirit, who gives gifts to His people (including administration) so that God's people can work harmoniously and effectively.

In 1 Kings 9:26-28 we see that Solomon also built a navy. Sailors are sent to serve Solomon. These ships are probably for both protection and trade (10:22). Ophir was a place known for an abundance of gold (10:11).

A greater Protector and Provider. King Solomon serves as a provider and protector to the people, but because of his failures, he pales in comparison to the true Son of David. Christ is our protector and has all power in heaven and earth (Matt 28:18). He is a victorious warrior who not only protects but also provides all good things to those who seek His kingdom (Matt 6:33). He supplies our needs according to His riches in glory

(Phil 4:19). Unlike Solomon, who acquired much gold for himself, we have a King who shares His spiritual riches with us (2 Cor 8:9).

Solomon's Righteousness (9:25)

The writer of Kings describes Solomon's sacrificial offerings. The Chronicler goes into more detail in 2 Chronicles 8:12-16. (As a whole Chronicles provides a more idealistic vision of the monarchy than Kings does. Many of Solomon's problems aren't mentioned in Chronicles.) Chronicles shows Solomon obediently keeping the feasts and making the sacrifices. He set an example, a pattern of righteousness. However, his pattern of righteousness was not perfect because Solomon was disobedient to the covenant.

Greater righteousness. Christ, however, fulfilled all righteousness. Peter says Christ gave us an example that we might walk in His steps (1 Pet 2:21). Christ alone committed no sin (1 Pet 2:22). Not only that, but He also died on behalf of those who sinned: "He Himself bore our sins in His body on the tree, so that, having died to sins, we might live for righteousness" (1 Pet 2:24). We can only be righteous through Christ, our perfect example and ultimate sacrifice.

Solomon's Wisdom (10:1-13)

Here we read of the queen of Sheba (present-day Yemen). This area was famous for perfumes, incense, gold, and gems. She is attracted to Solomon because she heard of his fame "connected with the name of Yahweh" (v. 1). The nations are being drawn to the God of Israel (cf. 8:41-43,60; Josh 9:9). Once again we see that God isn't a mere village god or even a national god but a global God.

When she comes, she tests him with hard questions and gives him "gold in great abundance" (v. 2). Solomon then answers all her questions. She marvels at Solomon's wisdom, his house, his servants, and his splendor.

Verses 6-9 continue describing how her breath was taken away by the king's wisdom and prosperity, the happiness of his servants, and his execution of justice. Again we read of more gold, spices, and precious stones being given to Solomon in unparalleled quantities.

Greater wisdom. Even more than Solomon, Christ astounded everyone by His wisdom (Mark 6:1-2). His fame spread because of His authoritative teaching (Mark 1:27-28). He answered all of their questions and left them silenced (Mark 12:34).

There is another obvious and powerful connection to Christ here. For Christ refers to the queen of Sheba in Matt 12:42 and Luke 11:31. In these passages Jesus tells us that we have not seen the last of her. He uses her as an example of the effort others should take to hear His word. The queen of Sheba traveled hundreds of miles to hear Solomon. Like the Ninevites she had a small portion of God's truth and responded positively to it. In these passages Jesus is comparing the queen to the Gentiles who were not "in the loop" like the religious leaders; yet they responded to Christ's word positively. Jesus said that those who reject Him will stand condemned, and the queen of the South will be "pointing her finger at you" (Davis, *1 Kings*, 109).

The application is clear: you know far more than the queen of Sheba, the Ninevites, or even the religious leaders of Jesus' day because you have the whole Bible. Don't be resistant or indifferent! You must listen and believe or face the consequences. Seek Jesus. Study His Word—even if you have to travel far, make sacrifices, relocate, get up early, or stay up late. Hear Wisdom and the good news of His kingdom. You have no excuse. Paul says, "All the treasures of wisdom and knowledge are hidden in Him" (Col 2:3). So come to Him and pay homage to Him, for there is no one else like Him.

Are you taking every effort to study the Scriptures personally? What about attending corporate worship? If you aren't a Christian, are you earnestly seeking the truth?

I was in Boston a few years ago speaking to a large group of college students from universities around New England. A group of international girls was on the second row taking avid notes. During the break I asked them, "When did you become Christians?" One said, "We're not Christians. We're still searching." That sounds very much like the queen of Sheba—diligently seeking truth. I was happy that they were spending their weekend to study God's Word. Don't put Christ on the shelf. Consider His claims and His Word, or you will face the consequences of indifference and unbelief.

As we think about Solomon's glory spreading to the Gentile nations, we're reminded that this too pales in comparison to the global glory of Christ. Psalm 72 reminds us that though some of Solomon's prayer came to pass, not all of these petitions could be accomplished through him. They would be fulfilled through the King of kings:

> *Let all kings bow down to him,*
> *   all nations serve him. . . .*

May his name endure forever;
  as long as the sun shines,
  may his fame increase.
May all nations be blessed by him
  and call him blessed. (Ps 72:11,17)

We also know that one day "the kingdom of the world [will] become the kingdom of our Lord and of His Messiah" (Rev 11:15). Concerning the greater Solomon's kingdom, we can say indeed, "The half has not been told" of what is about to be displayed to His people.

Solomon's Wealth (10:14-29)

The word "gold" appears 10 times in 10:14-22. In chapter 9 we read of 9,000 pounds of gold (v. 14), then 16 tons of gold (v. 28), and here in chapter 10, 25 tons of gold (v. 14). Solomon made stuff with this gold, such as decorations for his palace (v. 16), overlaid his throne with it (vv. 18-20), and made household items with it (v. 21). He accumulated silver (v. 21), chariots, and horses (v. 26). We read a summary statement of his wisdom and wealth in verses 23-25, including how rulers brought tribute to Solomon. Solomon was a rich man.

Problems abound here. Deuteronomy 17 is an important text on how the king should live and rule, and Solomon doesn't obey these commands. Instead of following the law, he acquired many horses for himself, sent the people back to Egypt, acquired many wives, and acquired large amounts of silver and gold (cf. Deut 17:16-17). Further, we read that God wanted the king not to have his heart "exalted above his countrymen" (Deut 17:20).

While God promised to bless Solomon with wealth, Solomon has become "the rich fool" who is laying up treasure for himself instead of "being rich toward God" (Luke 12:13-21; notice how Jesus mentions Solomon in v. 27). Jesus said, "Watch out and be on guard against all greed because one's life isn't in the abundance of his possessions" (Luke 12:15). Solomon's wealth started out as a blessing, but he was not responsible with it and lusted for more of it. At the end of his life, he wrote, "The one who loves money is never satisfied with money, and whoever loves wealth is never satisfied with income. This too is futile" (Eccl 5:10). Indeed, Solomon had the pleasures of this life (Eccl 1–2) but ended up saying that what matters most is to "fear God and keep His commands" (Eccl 12:13).

Paul provides some important teaching on wealth:

> But godliness with contentment is a great gain.
> For we brought nothing into the world,
> and we can take nothing out.
> But if we have food and clothing,
> we will be content with these.
> But those who want to be rich fall into temptation, a trap, and
> many foolish and harmful desires, which plunge people into ruin and
> destruction. For the love of money is a root of all kinds of evil, and
> by craving it, some have wandered away from the faith and pierced
> themselves with many pains. . . .
> Instruct those who are rich in the present age not to be arrogant or
> to set their hope on the uncertainty of wealth, but on God, who richly
> provides us with all things to enjoy. Instruct them to do what is good,
> to be rich in good works, to be generous, willing to share, storing up
> for themselves a good reserve for the age to come, so that they may take
> hold of life that is real. (1 Tim 6:6-10,17-19)

The wealthy aren't charged to become poor but rather to learn how to
use their wealth, treasure God above all, and serve others faithfully.

Greater glory. Despite Solomon's personal, inordinate desire for
gold, the wealth of the kingdom does remind us of the future messianic
kingdom. Isaiah says,

> . . . the wealth of the nations will come to you. Caravans of camels
> will cover your land—young camels of Midian and Ephah—all of
> them will come from Sheba. They will carry gold and frankincense and
> proclaim the praises of the LORD. (Isa 60:5-6)

Isaiah uses images of an Arabic caravan bringing in massive amounts of
gold. Resting camels cover the ground like flies. Of course, the gold and
frankincense are symbols of wealth of the East, used by the wise men
who brought gifts to the infant Jesus to fulfill this picture partially. What
is the goal of this ultimate fulfillment? It isn't to repay anyone. It isn't to
say the Jews are a superior race. It's for the "praises of the LORD." That's
it. Jesus deserves our praise and our grateful offerings (Oswalt, *Isaiah*,
541). In Revelation we read, "The kings of the earth will bring their
glory into [new Jerusalem]. . . . But only those written in the Lamb's
book of life" will enter there (Rev 21:24,27).

Solomon's glory is magnificent in many ways, but his glory was incomplete, short-lived, and tainted. He and others may have thought he was at the pinnacle of his reign, but he didn't care for his soul appropriately. His lack of attention to his spiritual life leads to his fall in chapter 11.

Solomon's Tragic Collapse
1 KINGS 11:1-43

In chapter 11 Solomon's sins are on full display. The first 10 verses show the tragic fall, while the following verses reveal its devastating consequences. What led to Solomon's downfall? Let me point out six characteristics of Solomon's downfall. It's important that we understand the nature of this collapse so that we may avoid one of our own.

His Downfall Was Predictable (11:1-2)

The opening verses shouldn't shock us in light of 1 Kings 3:1, where he wrongly married Pharaoh's daughter (cf. Deut 7:17). Solomon started down the wrong path and never corrected himself. Ryken rightly says, "We start falling into sin long before we ever fall into disgrace" (*1 Kings*, 295).

Solomon is a case study on the subtlety of sin. Along with marrying Pharaoh's daughter, there are other warning signs, like his questionable political actions in chapter 2, worshiping at the high places, taking horses from Egypt, debatable actions in building his own palace, the questionable integrity of his trading practices with Hiram, misuse of wealth, and the use of forced labor. Now these "small sins" lead to this big disaster.

You cannot let sin go unchecked and think everything will be fine. You must deal with it head on, immediately, and aggressively. What sins should you seek to kill? All sins! How many spiders do you need to eat to damage your body? One! The Puritans used to compare small sins to baby snakes. They're small but deadly, and if you let them live, they will grow into huge serpents (Ryken, *1 Kings*, 297).

His Downfall Involved Deliberate Disobedience (11:1-3)

Solomon couldn't plead ignorance or accident. He knew God's clear word revealed in the Scriptures. He was not to take a foreign wife, nor was he to take many wives (Deut 7:3-4; 17:17). He was to be different from pagan kings. Further, the Ten Commandments forbid coveting and adultery as well (Exod 20:14,17). Ultimately he broke the first commandment (Exod 20:3), which will cause you to break the others. Solomon knew this but intentionally and defiantly chose to disobey God for political and selfish reasons.

As mentioned earlier, he deliberately disobeyed Deuteronomy 17 in multiple ways. God had good reasons for these commands—His commands are always for our good. Kings were forbidden to take a foreign wife because of the threat of idolatry. The prohibition against taking many horses was so the people would not trust in horses and chariots but rather trust in God (Ps 20:7; Deut 20:1). They were not to return to Egypt because God rescued them from Egypt and threw Egypt's horses into the sea (Exod 15:1).

What makes matters even worse is that Solomon wrote about these issues. Concerning forbidden women, he wrote three chapters in Proverbs about staying away from them, yet we read that he had 700 wives who were princesses and 300 concubines (1 Kgs 11:3). I doubt he even knew their names! Concerning wealth, he wrote, "Anyone trusting in riches will fall, but the righteous will flourish like foliage" (Prov 11:28). Yet he lived more for wealth than for righteousness.

Once again, it's one thing to know the Word of God, and it's another thing to live by it. God doesn't simply want you to know information about the Bible; He wants you to obey it. Solomon deliberately chose to disobey the Word of God, and it led to his downfall.

His Downfall Stemmed from a Heart Problem (11:1-9)

Six times in the first nine verses, we read of Solomon's heart being led astray: "*heart* after their gods" (v. 2 ESV); his wives "turned his *heart* away" (v. 3 ESV); "turned away his *heart* after other gods" (v. 4 ESV); "his *heart* was not wholly true to the LORD his God, as was the *heart* of David his father" (v. 4 ESV); and "the LORD was angry with Solomon, because his *heart* had turned away from Yahweh" (v. 9).

Solomon's story began with the statement, "Solomon loved the LORD" (1 Kgs 3:3); now it ends in a tragedy, "Solomon loved many foreign women" (11:1). Notice also the phrase "deeply attached" (v. 2). Usually, the Hebrew word behind this phrase describes someone being faithful to God (Deut 13:4), but here Solomon is clinging to foreign women who led his heart astray.

All sin is an inside job. We live out of the overflow of the heart. To say it another way, sin problems are worship problems. Because Solomon's heart was given to other lovers, he fell hard. James says, "Then after desire has conceived, it gives birth to sin, and when sin is fully grown, it gives birth to death" (Jas 1:15). Do you see that? It begins with desire; it leads to death. The problem isn't "out there" but "in here"—in the heart.

Solomon offered orthodox prayers, spoke good proverbs, and wrote wonderful poetry, yet his heart was not wholly true to God. He abandoned the love he had at first (cf. Rev 2:4). What about you? Do you find your heart flirting with different sins? Are you headed for a tragedy?

We will worship something or someone. Whom will you worship? If you don't worship the God of the Bible through His Son Jesus Christ, then you will experience what the psalmist said in Psalm 16:4: "The sorrows of those who take another god for themselves will multiply." My friend, you are multiplying your sorrows when you give your heart to idols (sports, peer approval, success, sex, power, money). You're turning from the only source of everlasting joy. The psalm goes on to say, "In Your presence is abundant joy; in Your right hand are eternal pleasures" (Ps 16:11). Solomon's heart went after other gods, and it eventually led to his downfall.

His Downfall Involved Persistent Sin (11:2-9)

The writer says Solomon's heart was turned "when he was old" (v. 4). He didn't have a brief lapse into sin. The progression of sin seems to have gone on gradually until he eventually collapsed when he was old. Repeated words reveal the persistent nature of his turn from following Yahweh: *turn* (vv. 2,4,9), *follow* (vv. 5,6,10), and *heart* (vv. 3,9; Olley, *Message of Kings*, 116). Even though the Lord "appeared to him twice" (v. 9), Solomon continued down the wrong path.

His heart wasn't "wholly true to the LORD his God, as was the heart of his father David" (v. 4 ESV; cf. v. 6). The writer uses David as an example here and in other places (see 11:38; 14:8; 15:5). We know David sinned with Bathsheba and in other situations, but David's fall was followed by a broken and contrite heart and repentance. From David we have Psalm 51, a prayer of repentance and renewal. Consequently, the biblical writers can speak positively of David (e.g., Acts 13:36).

How will you finish your life? Simon Peter had a grave lapse in sin, but Jesus restored him and Peter died heroically, serving Jesus faithfully.

You cannot change the past, but by God's grace, you can be restored and finish well.

If you have fallen into sin, follow the model of David, not Solomon. Solomon saw the problem but didn't repent. This story provides a warning. David's story gives us hope. What should you do if you sin? You should repent like David, but that's not what we naturally want to do. We want to deny sin, rename sin, redefine sin, ignore sin, manage sin, or shift the blame for sin. What should we do? We should hate sin and constantly repent of it. Believers admit their sin, accept God's mercy, find help among God's people, and change the way they live.

Because your inner person is hidden, you might appear to be doing fine but actually be withering away spiritually. If your soul is withering away, don't persist in sin. You can be a supermodel but be spiritually empty. You might have just received a raise but find no joy in it because your soul isn't at peace. You could be on the fast track to success as a young businessperson but not be in sweet communion with God. You can be an "A+" student but be in constant darkness spiritually. On the flip side you could have cancer and no physical strength but on the inside be soaring in praise to God! You might be unemployed, but you can still dance when you hear of God's faithfulness and grace.

Daniel Doriani told how Henri Nouwen assessed his own soul. Nouwen was a tenured professor at Notre Dame, Yale, and Harvard. He was internationally known for his writing and instruction. He then shocked everyone when in his mid-fifties he decided to leave Harvard to work with people in Toronto with mental handicaps. He wasn't going to be training the best and brightest but those who couldn't dress themselves. Some were mute. Even though he was the "spiritual advisor" of the place, he also changed diapers and cared for others physically. Why would you leave Harvard to go work with mentally disabled individuals? Nouwen said it was motivated by love for God, who loved him when he was poor and weak and commands us to do the same. Nouwen also stated that as he grew older he began asking the question, "Am I getting closer to Jesus?" As he reflected, he saw that he was praying poorly. He was isolated from others. He sensed that his soul was withering away even though he was teaching spiritual disciplines to the best and the brightest. He prayed and believed that God wanted him to leave the world of fame and to care for these precious individuals (Doriani, "The Wise Fool").

Solomon's story is the other side to Nouwen's story. Nouwen's friends told him he was doing great, like Solomon, but Nouwen paid more attention to God speaking in his heart. Solomon was doing some things well, but he listened to his friends and disregarded vital spiritual warning signs. As a result, he eventually collapsed. Solomon's persistent sin eventually led to his downfall.

His Downfall Was a Gateway to Apostasy (11:5-8)

Solomon lapsed into evil worship practices. Once his heart was drawn away from the living God, widespread idolatry occurred. Strangely, Solomon worships the gods whose nations he conquered and controlled (House, *1, 2 Kings*, 167). Yahweh had demonstrated that the so-called gods of those nations were impotent and nonexistent (cf. Ps 96:5). Yet Solomon abandoned the living God in favor of those counterfeits. This makes no sense, but then idolatry never makes sense (Jer 2:11-13).

Solomon worships the fertility goddess Ashtoreth. This false goddess appears throughout the Old Testament (Judg 2:13). Not only does he worship this "sex goddess," but he also worships Milcom (whom some scholars identify as Molech). The worship of Molech involved the incineration of infants (v. 5; cf. Lev 20:2-5; 2 Kgs 23:10; Jer 32:35). Molech had a burning belly with hands reached out, and worshipers would give their children to him, and the child would be consumed. Solomon also builds a high place for Chemosh (v. 7). Solomon accommodates his foreign women's wishes by building them a place for this abominable practice. All of this was "evil in the Lord's sight" (v. 6; this phrase will appear throughout Kings). Verse 8 also implies other gods were involved.

A contemporary example of this isn't hard to find. People may change their theology in order to satisfy their immoral desires. If people don't repent of sin, they will end up changing what they believe to justify their sinful lifestyle. Solomon should have stopped and repented, but instead he practiced syncretism. His downfall was a gateway to apostasy.

His Downfall Caused Devastating Results (11:9-43)

The Lord's response has three parts. First, in verses 9-13, we see the anger of the Lord (v. 9). While God is slow to anger and abounding in love, idolatry provokes God to anger, causing Him to act swiftly and justly (Exod 32–34; Num 20). God blessed Solomon tremendously, but he turned his back on God. Second, God speaks to Solomon and tells him that the kingdom will be torn away from him (v. 11). Third, Solomon and his descendants will keep the throne only because of God's promise to David in 2 Samuel 7:1-17 (vv. 12-13). It's only for David's sake that

Solomon remains king, and it's only for David's sake that his descendants will rule a fragmented nation. Despite this grace the resulting punishment is inevitable and tragic. Division, idolatry, and exile await Israel.

In the following verses we read about adversaries God raised up to oppose Solomon. Verses 14-25 mention neighboring adversaries. Verses 26-40 describe Jeroboam, an adversary from within.

The first of the neighboring adversaries was Hadad the Edomite. He was from the southwest, and he would harass Solomon from below (vv. 14-22). Next we read of Rezon from Damascus in Aram (Syria) who hated Israel (vv. 23-25). He was from the northeast and would harass Solomon from above. These men will pose an ongoing threat to Solomon, one from the north and one from the south.

After we read of the neighboring adversaries, we read of one from within. Jeroboam, who was once Solomon's employee, becomes an agent of God's judgment (vv. 26-40). As a young man Jeroboam impressed Solomon, and Solomon gave power to him. Little did Solomon know that he would be the man who would end the Davidic dynasty's rule over northern Israel (v. 28).

Through the prophet Ahijah, God informs Jeroboam that he will have a kingdom (vv. 29-39). The prophet tears a cloak into 12 pieces, giving 10 pieces to Jeroboam to illustrate that he will have 10 tribes, while two remain for David's descendants (Judah and the unmentioned tribe of Benjamin). Thus the nation will be divided and weak. The reasons are also provided. God will preserve Judah because of His faithfulness to David (vv. 32,34,36), and God will bring judgment because of the idolatry of Solomon and the people (v. 33). Jeroboam is also promised blessing if he walks in the ways of David (vv. 37-38). As a result of the promised split, Solomon seeks to kill Jeroboam, but Jeroboam flees to Egypt until Solomon's death (v. 40).

Prophets begin to appear more often in the story now. One wonders where the prophets went during Solomon's decline. We will soon find them anointing kings, doing miracles, and providing a theological conscience to the people.

After we read of the adversaries that God raised up to oppose Solomon, we read of Solomon's death (vv. 41-42). House says that no one knows the exact contents of the "Book of Solomon's Events," but it probably contained both narrative and chronological materials (*1, 2 Kings*, 173). Like David he reigned for 40 years. His successor is also mentioned: Rehoboam (v. 43). However, Rehoboam's reign will be under a dark cloud, for his kingdom will be smaller because Israel's glory days are over.

What Should We Say at Solomon's Funeral?

We began our tour with Solomon's glory, and now we end at his funeral. What should we say at the graveside? He definitely had positive traits, namely wisdom and eloquence. He used his wisdom to write, organize, develop efficient foreign policy, build the temple, grow the economy, trade, and build great fortresses. He also offered a magnificent prayer to God in chapter 8. We should remember these positive traits about Solomon.

Unfortunately we must also note his flaws: he broke clear commands, like taking many foreign wives; he used oppressive measures to gain wealth; and worst of all, he enabled and committed gross idolatry, which led to national disaster. House states, "At worst then, this wise leader of Israel acts no better than the most foolish of his subjects. He thereby serves as a warning to those who take their God-given gifts for granted or, worse, come to believe they have achieved greatness on their own" (House, *1, 2 Kings*, 174).

Perhaps you have gained it all—wealth, power, sexual pleasure, a big home—but you don't have Christ. Jesus asks this question: "For what does it benefit a man to gain the whole world yet lose his life?" (Mark 8:36). Eternal life is in the balance!

We can die well because our King finished well. For David's sake, God remained faithful to His people (2 Sam 7:14-15). God left a lamp burning (1 Kgs 11:36). He doesn't wipe out Israel, though they will face dreadful consequences. Eventually the One greater than Solomon did come. He is the perfect Mediator, the ultimate Protector and Provider, the perfectly righteous One, the ultimate wise King, and the One with infinite riches.

This King wouldn't turn away from God's law but would keep it perfectly and then die on behalf of idolaters. This King would also go to a grave, but he would only sleep with His fathers for three days. Paul said,

> From this man's [David's] descendants, according to the promise, God brought the Savior, Jesus, to Israel. . . . Through this man forgiveness of sins is being proclaimed to you, and everyone who believes in Him is justified from everything that you could not be justified from through the law of Moses. (Acts 13:23,38-39)

Our hope is this Savior-King whose kingdom is forever. If you aren't a follower of the King, then bow to Him. As the queen of Sheba came and marveled at Solomon, so come to Jesus and experience His salvation. If you have failed Him, then don't let sin go unchecked. Repent of sin and experience His renewing mercies today.

Reflect and Discuss

1. Have you ever felt jealousy or covetousness toward someone far richer than you?
2. Are God's people promised riches if they are faithful?
3. Was it wrong for Solomon to engage in various building projects other than the temple? Why or why not?
4. Why is wealth so appealing?
5. How do godly contentment and godly ambition work together?
6. Describe the Queen of Sheba's response to Solomon's wisdom and wealth.
7. Why was Solomon forbidden to marry women from other nations?
8. What was the result of Solomon's disobedience?
9. How might believers today let relationships with others overtake their relationship with God?
10. Has God ever blessed you with something and then taken it away because you misused His gift?

The Torn Kingdom

1 KINGS 12:1–14:20

Main Idea: The division of the kingdom was accompanied by sad events during this dark period of Israel's history.

I. **Division (12:1-24)**
   A. The assembly (12:1-15)
   B. The aftermath (12:16-24)
II. **Downfall (12:25-33)**
   A. Do you trust God?
   B. Do you love God?
   C. Do you fear God?
III. **Disobedience (13:1-34)**
   A. The Judean prophet confronts Jeroboam (13:1-10).
   B. The Judean prophet gets killed by a lion (13:11-32).
IV. **Death (14:1-20)**
V. **Conclusion**

As in a good television series, allow me to give you a 30-second review of where we are in this Old Testament drama before we move on to the next episode. In chapter 11 God promised that He would tear the kingdom apart because of Israel's sin and idolatry. The prophet Ahijah gave this prophecy to Jeroboam, who was also told that he would reign over 10 tribes of Israel, the northern kingdom (11:26-39). Solomon then sought to kill Jeroboam, but Jeroboam fled to Egypt until Solomon died (11:40). Now Rehoboam succeeds Solomon as king, but we are left to wonder what will happen in light of the prophecy of the torn kingdom and the promised reign of Jeroboam. The glory days of Israel are over, and a sad division of the kingdom is drawing close.

The passage under consideration has it all: political gamesmanship, a stoning, bovine worship, honest preachers, lying preachers, manipulation, deception, stupidity, fear, faith, pronouncements, a withered hand, a destroyed altar, the death of a child, and (oh yeah) a lion mauls a man. Welcome to the part of the Bible few people read! But we should read it, for there's much to learn here. Over it all is the sovereign God of the universe displaying justice and mercy.

We can consider 1 Kings 12:1–14:20 under four headings: division, downfall, disobedience, and death. The kingdom is divided, just as God promised (12:1-24). Downfall happens in every way, most dreadfully perhaps through Israel's worship of a golden calf (12:25-33). Disobedience persists, even in the prophets' lives (13:1-34). Death occurs, most vividly with the death of Jeroboam's child (14:1-20).

Throughout this drama there are many exodus-like aspects. As Moses led Israel out from Egypt's tyranny, so Jeroboam is looked to as the one who will lead Israel out from Rehoboam's tyranny. Just as God hardened Pharaoh's heart to accomplish His will, so Rehoboam's hardness of heart will lead to the schism God promised. When Jeroboam leads the people out, however, things don't go well. Jeroboam actually turns into a new Aaron! He makes two golden calves and says, "Israel, here is your God who brought you out of the land of Egypt" (12:28; cf. Exod 32:4). Such disobedience eventually leads to exile.

Though many years have passed since these golden calf incidents, the sinfulness of the human heart remains. Our sinful nature is drawn toward rebellion and idolatry, and we're in great need of redemption. We're in great need of David's greatest Son. And we find traces of that hope in this dark period of history. We find God keeping His word. We find God ruling over the events of history sovereignly. Because God keeps His word and because Yahweh is the only sovereign God, we have found salvation through the anticipated King. Let's take a look at these events, and let's remember that God is at work, even in this dark season.

Division
1 KINGS 12:1-24

The opening narrative breaks down into two simple parts. First, we find the assembly (vv. 1-15); and second, we see the aftermath (vv. 16-24; Davis, *1 Kings*, 126). At the conclusion of each section, there is a theological note to underscore that God is in charge of this situation. Humanly speaking, stupidity and stubbornness of heart cause the split of the kingdom, but the author makes clear that, divinely speaking, this is the outworking of God's purposes. He says,

> *The king didn't listen to the people, because this turn of events came from the LORD to carry out His word, which the LORD had spoken through Ahijah the Shilonite to Jeroboam son of Nebat.* (1 Kgs 12:15)

This is what the LORD *says: You are not to march up and fight against your brothers, the Israelites. Each of you must return home, for I have done this.* (1 Kgs 12:24)

So before we try to make practical applications from this story, we need to make sure we understand what the writer wants us to see primarily. The focus is on divine sovereignty, not on the lack of wisdom of youth or how older people get ignored (Davis, *1 Kings*, 128). We might rightly note such matters, but the point *in the text* is that God is keeping His word sovereignly. No human beings, regardless of how much authority they have, can compete with His rule and reign. The writer of Proverbs says it like this: "A king's heart is like streams of water in the LORD's hand: He directs it wherever He chooses" (Prov 21:1).

The Assembly (12:1-15)

So Israel set out to make Solomon's son Rehoboam the new king. We're told that Jeroboam, meanwhile, returned from Egypt upon hearing this news. The people, including Jeroboam, tell Rehoboam that his kingship is contingent on responding positively to their demands. They claim Solomon had been too hard on them (cf. Exod 1:14; 2:23), and thus they were looking to the new king to lighten their burdens. Rehoboam tells them he will give them an answer in three days.

At this point the book of Proverbs comes to mind. It's often missed that Proverbs has a royal dimension to it. The first nine chapters, which serve as a unit, have a father speaking to his son about living in relationship to wisdom. Many have noted that one can see Solomon training his son how to rule the kingdom wisely (Prov 8:15-17). Throughout Proverbs there are explicit instructions about ruling the kingdom justly and wisely as well (e.g., Prov 16:12-15; 21:3,15; 25; 31:9). So the questions here in Kings are: Will Rehoboam rule wisely or not? Will he follow the counsel of Proverbs and surround himself with wise people or with fools (Prov 13:20)? Will he speak persuasive words filled with gentleness (Prov 16:21,24)? Sadly, Rehoboam acts foolishly.

He receives counsel from two groups. The older men first instruct him to go easy on the people at the beginning of his reign in order to persuade those on the fence to remain loyal to him. But Rehoboam rejects this counsel. He turns instead to his peers, who will tell him what he wants to hear. The young guns tell him the opposite approach is needed: fear and intimidation.

Rehoboam takes the counsel of the younger men and then gives his speech on the third day to all the people. He says, "My father made your yoke heavy, but I will add to your yoke; my father disciplined you with whips, but I will discipline you with barbed whips" (v. 14). He behaves like Pharaoh, increasing the burdens after hearing a plea for relief (Exod 5:1-21). And with this you can hear the kingdom shredding.

Over it all, however, is God. The writer says, "The king did not listen to the people, because this turn of events came from the LORD to carry out His word" (v. 15). Thus we see divine sovereignty and human responsibility here (cf. Exod 4:21; 7:3-4; 7:13). This event isn't "mechanical" (Davis, *1 Kings*, 128). God didn't violate Rehoboam's will. The young king made his own stupid decision. Yet this whole event happened through a turn of events from the Lord. God isn't surprised. God is actually accomplishing His purposes. We see this sort of dynamic—sovereignty and responsibility—at work in the cross of Christ (Acts 2:23).

In the middle of political and social chaos, we should remember that God sits in the heavens and does as He pleases (Ps 115:3). This should encourage all believers in general and those living under oppressive governments in particular. God will have the last word. God is in charge. We may not be able to answer all of the questions related to divine sovereignty, but that's not the point. The point is, because God reigns supremely, we should humble ourselves before Him and trust Him. The book of Revelation makes this point in high definition for us. We know where the future is headed, and there's only one who will sit on the throne!

The Aftermath (12:16-24)

Following Rehoboam's decision and speech, his actions remain foolish. The people rebel against the new king, disperse, and go home. Then Rehoboam sends his servant Adoram on a special assignment to impose forced labor on the northern groups. Rehoboam wanted them to know that the new king was serious. But Adoram didn't execute his mission; instead Israel executed Adoram, so Rehoboam retreated to Jerusalem. The writer then tells us of the long-term division that ensues: "Israel is in rebellion against the house of David until today" (v. 19).

Because of Rehoboam's folly, Israel calls Jeroboam to be king, which also fulfills God's word (11:35-37). Only the tribes of Judah and Benjamin remain under Rehoboam's rule.

Verses 16-20 contain repeated references to "David" and the "house of David." This emphasis may intend to raise the tension of David's dynasty. Will David continue to have a son to sit on the throne or not? We have the privileged vantage point of knowing that God will keep His promise (2 Sam 7:16) despite Rehoboam's rebellion and the kingdom's division. Thus, in a story about God's judgment, we also see God's mercy peeking out behind the clouds. This theme runs throughout the Kings narrative. A lamp in Jerusalem remains until the ultimate Son of David rules.

In verses 21-24 we find Rehoboam reacting to Israel's decision. He decides to restore the kingdom through warfare. However, a prophet named Shemaiah prevents this by bringing Rehoboam this word: "This is what the LORD says: You are not to march up and fight against your brothers, the Israelites. Each of you must return home, for I have done this" (12:24). Based on Rehoboam's previous decisions, one would expect him to reject this word. But shockingly, he heeds it. The writer says, "So they listened to what the LORD said and went back as He had told them" (v. 24).

We are thus left with Rehoboam actually making a wise decision. God intervenes, speaks His word, and everyone listens. Unfortunately, this story doesn't last long. The northern and southern tribes will have constant wars in the future (see 14:30; 15:6; 16). The division here in chapter 12 has a ripple effect for years to come.

Let us be a people who submit to God's Word, heed godly counsel, and trust in God's comprehensive sovereignty. And let us give humble thanks and joyful adoration to our perfect King, Jesus, who alleviates our burdens, provides for our greatest needs, and rules His kingdom with wisdom and justice.

Downfall
1 KINGS 12:25-33

The next episode bears much similarity to the wilderness journey in the book of Exodus. This "new Moses," Jeroboam, leads the people out from under the yoke of the pharaoh-like Rehoboam. But as in the Exodus narrative, worshiping a golden calf follows deliverance.

Before taking a quick look at that event, we must realize how often this tragic downfall is referenced in the book of Kings. The writer constantly refers to Jeroboam's idolatry as Israel's characteristic sin that eventually leads them into exile (Provan, *1 and 2 Kings*, 109; e.g., 1 Kgs 15:26,34; 2 Kgs 17:20-23). This is a tragic downfall.

Several application questions emerge from this story. We need to consider this account since we too are prone to sink into the pit of idolatry. Three causes of Jeroboam's false worship are his lack of trust in God, his lack of love for God, and his lack of the fear of God.

Do You Trust God?

Jeroboam doesn't trust anyone. Not only does Jeroboam distrust Rehoboam, but he also doesn't trust the people to remain loyal to him (12:25-27). What's worse, he doesn't trust God, who told him he would be the king (11:31-39). To ameliorate his insecurity, he decides to "make" a religion that will prevent Israel from going to Jerusalem.

Have you ever acted like Jeroboam? Have you ever tried to control and manipulate things for your own security rather than trusting in God's Word? Is *security* your god? Do you find yourself walking more by sight than by faith in what God has promised? Are you more logical than spiritual? We should be critical of Jeroboam here, but we also need to admit our likeness to him. We need help to look to God instead of ourselves for security. As the hymn "'Tis So Sweet to Trust in Jesus" puts it, "Oh for grace to trust Him more!"

Do You Love God?

Jeroboam also provides an example of using religion for purely political reasons instead of living with real devotion to the living God. In this account he's worried about losing his subjects to the other political leader. This golden-calf project actually has little to do with religion. He simply decides to use religion for self-gain. Sounds familiar doesn't it? Pandering to people through religious language and ritual.

Many want to use God but not love God. How different are true followers of Jesus! A disciple finds the glory of God *beautiful*, while a vain, religious person only finds Him *useful*. To the latter person God isn't ultimate. God is a means to that person's own twisted end. Don't be a merely religious person. Follow Jesus genuinely. Bow to Him whatever the cost. Love Him. Serve Him. Don't play religious games. Will you die in your devotion to Christ or die in dead religion?

Do You Fear God?

After taking counsel from his pathetic advisors, Jeroboam acts: "Then he made two golden calves, and he said to the people, 'Going to Jerusalem is too difficult for you. Israel, here is your God who brought you out of the land of Egypt'" (12:28). He thus defies God's holy commands (e.g., Exod 20:4) and worships idols. Like the aftermath of the golden-calf incident in Exodus, judgment is coming.

Jeroboam does the exact opposite of what God initially told in him chapter 11.

> *After that, if you obey all I command you, walk in My ways, and do what is right in My sight in order to keep* My statutes and My commands *as My servant David did, I will be with you. I will build you a lasting dynasty just as I built for David.* (11:38; emphasis added)

Instead of revering God and His word, Jeroboam follows his sinful heart.

To secure his position (v. 29), he makes a center of worship in both the far north (Dan) and the far south (Bethel). These locations provided a convenient religion for the people. They also held historical significance. Bethel's significance went back to Abraham (Gen 12:8; 13:3-4) and Jacob (Gen 28:10-22; 31:13; 35:1-16; cf. Judg 20:26-28). Worship took place previously in Dan during the period of the judges (Judg 18). Thus, Jeroboam was able to mask his purposes and perhaps play on tradition and history. The whole plan seems quite subtle.

Finally, we find descriptions of Bethel in particular. Jeroboam makes his own high places, his own altar, and his own priests. To complete the circus, he makes his own festival (cf. Exod 32:5). All of this he does to rival Jerusalem and to secure his position. He violates clear commandments like those in Deuteronomy 12.

Jeroboam lives with absolutely no fear of God. He thinks he can dishonor God with impunity. He considers politics more important than true worship. He thinks his security comes from self instead of God. He lives in total folly, for the handbook for Kings—Proverbs—tells us clearly and repeatedly, "The fear of the LORD is the beginning of wisdom" (Prov 9:10). Jeroboam neither fears God nor has wisdom from God.

Don't play the fool. In our culture the foundational message for individual decision making seems to be "follow your heart." But the Bible teaches otherwise. The message is "fear God" not "follow your heart." Comedian Bill Murray quips, "I followed my heart, and it led me to the fridge." Rehoboam and Jeroboam followed their sinful, selfish hearts, and it led them into idolatry and ruin. Will their prophets do any better? Will they fear God and keep His word? We shall see in the next episode.

Disobedience
1 KINGS 13:1-34

After Jeroboam builds his new temple, he is all set to initiate his false religion. But things don't go as planned. Provan contrasts him with Solomon:

> Solomon's temple was built *in fulfillment of a prophetic promise* about both temple and dynasty (2 Sam 7:1-17), the building of Jeroboam's temple *evokes prophetic threats* (1 Kgs 13:2-3; 14:7-13), which in due course will come to fulfillment in the destruction of both dynasty and temple. (*1 and 2 Kings*, 113; emphasis added)

God intends for His word to be obeyed. Jeroboam violated God's word, and now we're introduced to a story of two prophets who must also heed God's word—first the Judean prophet and then the prophet from Bethel.

The Judean Prophet Confronts Jeroboam (13:1-10)

The man of God from Judah does well at first. While the ceremony at Bethel is going on, this prophet stands up and brings a threat related to the altar. He tells of a descendant of David, Josiah, who will bring judgment on the new priests by destroying them on Jeroboam's altar and profane the altar by putting human bones on it. He also says that an imminent sign would validate his message.

Jeroboam will have none of it, so he reacts immediately. The king stretches out his hand, saying, "Arrest him!" But when he does, his hand withers and he can't pull it back (v. 4). In verse 5 we then read that the altar does in fact split and its ashes pour out.

The whole account shows that God isn't only displeased with idolatry, but He's also not under the control of any other "god." He can split the buildings and the altars today if He wishes. He's also sovereign over rulers.

He can take the finger with which they point and immobilize it. Right now, God gives breath to every atheist who breathes out "There is no god." In God's immeasurable mercy and patience, He doesn't always crush such people instantly but instead offers them an opportunity to repent.

But Jeroboam doesn't repent. He asks for prayer, but this is more like the inauthentic prayers of Pharaoh (e.g., Exod 8:8,28; 9:27-28; 10:17; 12:32) than the prayer of a repentant person. Jeroboam tells the Judean prophet, "Plead for the favor of the LORD your God and pray for me so that my hand may be restored to me" (v. 6). His request gets answered, but his heart doesn't change.

As a pragmatic politician, Jeroboam decides to take a different course of action with the prophet. If he can't capture the prophet, what about inviting him to dinner? He offers the prophet not only a kingly meal but also a kingly reward. But the prophet refuses. He obeys God and says, "for this is what I was commanded by the word of the LORD: 'You must not eat bread or drink water or go back the way you came'" (v. 9). Then we read, "So he went another way; he did not go back by the way he had come to Bethel" (v. 10). God wanted the prophet to stand up, speak up, and get home without being distracted or corrupted. And the prophet obeys. So far so good.

Throughout all of chapter 13, the "word of the LORD" is the primary theme (13:9,17,20,21,26,32; Davis, 148–49). Jeroboam refuses it. The Judean prophet follows it at first (13:1-10) but then abandons it (13:11-24). The prophet from Bethel abuses it (vv. 11-32). What will you do with God's Word?

The Judean Prophet Gets Killed by a Lion (13:11-32)

The following story is filled with surprising and mysterious drama. The writer tells us that an old prophet from Bethel in the south makes an effort to meet up with this Judean prophet. When the old prophet finds the Judean prophet, he invites him over for dinner. As with Jeroboam, he tells the old prophet that he must decline based on God's word. His instructions were not to stop for bread and water and to return home by another way. Not to be refused, the old prophet played the "the Lord told me" card and lied to the Judean prophet. This lying prophet insisted that the Lord told him to show hospitality to the Judean prophet, and his lie proved persuasive, as the Judean prophet "went back with him, ate bread in his house, and drank water" (v. 19).

Be careful whenever someone says, "The Lord told me." Many cult leaders have played this same trick. Be careful around religious people who know how to manipulate others through religious language and schemes. Paul says that false teachers "worm their way into households and capture idle women" (2 Tim 3:6). Such people are deceptively evil. We should also be mindful that yesterday's victories don't ensure today's and tomorrow's victories. The Judean prophet triumphed at Jeroboam's altar, but in the next scene he disobeys God's clear word. This wild story reminds us of our great need for discernment and a daily, resolute commitment to obey God.

The story takes a strange twist. The old prophet actually speaks God's word honestly. God can use all sorts of people. After clearly lying (v. 18), the old prophet now speaks truth:

> This is what the Lord says: "Because you rebelled against the command of the Lord and didn't keep the command that the Lord your God commanded you—but you went back and ate bread and drank water in the place that He said to you, 'Don't eat bread and don't drink water'—your corpse will never reach the grave of your fathers." (vv. 21-22)

Because of the Judean prophet's disobedience, he will not make it home, and he will not die in peace. So a lion attacks and kills this man of God from Judah. A strange scene then follows his awful death. The lion doesn't eat the body or attack the donkey. The lion's unusual behavior magnifies that fact that this death was not an ordinary "man gets mauled by a lion" type of death. This is God's judgment. The strangeness led everyone to talk about it.

When word gets back to the prophet from Bethel, he goes and retrieves the dead body, performs burial rites, and tells his sons that what the Judean prophet actually said concerning Jeroboam will come to pass.

The writer then says that Jeroboam didn't change his evil ways but continued in sin despite the previous prophecy and the miracle at the altar. Due to his hard heart, destruction awaits the king.

As we observe this odd story, we should make one additional, obvious application: everyone must obey God's word—prophets, kings, and everyone in between. In the case of the prophets, we're reminded that those doing public ministry don't get a pass on personal obedience. Just because the Lord uses you to speak His word doesn't mean you can take personal obedience casually. The Judean prophet serves as a warning to us. Our personal lives and our public ministry should be harmonious, not duplicitous. Live with the same degree of commitment to the Lord in your home and neighborhood as you do in a church building and on a platform.

Death
1 KINGS 14:1-20

The next episode in the Jeroboam reality TV show is equally intriguing and sad. Jeroboam is troubled by his son's sickness, so he sends his wife to the clergyman who predicted his ascent to the throne (11:37-38). He wants to know his son's future. He tells her to take some Krispy Kreme doughnuts with her and to disguise herself. But the disguise makes no sense for two reasons. Ahijah is a prophet who already knows about the situation, and he's blind.

Why does Jeroboam try to use this tactic? We aren't told, but it's probably because he was not following Ahijah's original instruction to follow God's word. Jeroboam probably thinks if he approaches Ahijah directly, then bad news will follow. He wants good news. But no one can manipulate God (cf. Acts 8:9-25), and no one is ever out of the eyes of God. No one can sneak away from God's just judgment.

In verse 6 Ahijah dispenses with the games, saying, "Come in, wife of Jeroboam! Why are you disguised? I have bad news for you." He proceeds to give her the unbearable news. Because Jeroboam hasn't acted like David and has worshiped false gods instead, disaster is coming. The Lord is going to bring Jeroboam's dynasty to a disgraceful end:

> *I will eliminate all of Jeroboam's males,*
> *both slave and free, in Israel;*
> *I will sweep away the house of Jeroboam*
> *as one sweeps away dung until it is all gone!*
> *Anyone who belongs to Jeroboam and dies in the city,*
> *the dogs will eat,*
> *and anyone who dies in the field,*
> *the birds of the sky will eat,*
> *for the LORD has said it! (vv. 10-11)*

Ahijah then tells her of the fate of her sick son: he will die. It's tragic indeed, but at least this son will be buried. The wider tragedy is that Jeroboam's house will be cut off. Ahijah tells the king's wife,

> The LORD will raise up for Himself a king over Israel, who will
> eliminate the house of Jeroboam. This is the day, yes, even today! For
> the LORD will strike Israel and the people will shake as a reed shakes
> in water. He will uproot Israel from this good soil that He gave to their
> ancestors. He will scatter them beyond the Euphrates because they made
> their Asherah poles, provoking the LORD. He will give up Israel because
> of Jeroboam's sins that he committed and caused Israel to commit.
> (vv. 14-16)

Provan summarizes, "Jeroboam's disobedience affects not just his own destiny (as the Judean's prophet's destiny had done), nor just that of his own house; it affects the destiny of the whole kingdom" (*1 and 2 Kings*, 119).

When Jeroboam's wife returned and crossed the house's threshold, the boy died according to the prophet's word, and all of Israel mourned.

This story echoes David, who also lost a son due to sin, and the king's sin affected others (2 Sam 12). But of course David's whole house wasn't destroyed. The God of justice is also the God of mercy, who in the fullness of time brought forth the ultimate Son of David, Jesus.

Conclusion

This is where we should end: Jesus. How might we wrap up this dark period of Israel's history of division, downfall, disobedience, and death? The story reminds us that we need a better King and a better Prophet. We need One who can overcome our great problem: death. We need One who can bring about a united kingdom under a perfectly just and wise reign. We have all of this—yes, all of this—in Jesus, the King to end all kings.

The good news of the gospel is that God is merciful to sinners. He forgives idolaters and liars. He offers everlasting life to dying people. This salvation is made possible through the work of the King who took our judgment at the cross, rose from the dead, and opened the way of salvation for all who will heed God's call to repent and believe in Christ. Don't persist in sin. Repent. Look to Jesus as your sin-bearing substitute who alleviates our greatest burden, and embrace the fullness of salvation He offers. Then you can be assured of a place in His coming kingdom. If you have embraced Him as your Savior and King, then rejoice in Him now. Realize that your King has come, your King will return, and peace and righteousness will dwell forever. Live this day in light of that day, as a citizen of Jesus' kingdom.

Reflect and Discuss

1. Describe how God is both faithful and just when He splits the kingdom of Israel.
2. Why is Rehoboam harsh toward Jeroboam and the assembly?
3. How important is godly counsel for believers today?
4. Why did Jeroboam make two golden calves?
5. How might church leaders today lead God's people astray with good intentions?
6. Do people often make pragmatic choices that compromise their beliefs? Give examples.
7. Jeroboam feared that Israel's faithfulness to God would lead them to return to Rehoboam. When faithfulness and self-gain compete in your life, which one wins?
8. Can faithfulness ever lead God's people astray?
9. God uses the prophet to confront Jeroboam but also judges the prophet for his disobedience. What does this teach about God's character?
10. In what ways are you tempted to love yourself more than obedience?

A Lamp in Jerusalem

1 KINGS 14:21–16:34

Main Idea: Several kings in Judah and Israel were corrupt, but God made a faithful promise to bring the ultimate King through the line of David.

I. **Kings of Judah (14:21–15:24)**
   A. 1: Rehoboam, "The Conformer" (14:21-31)
   B. 2: Abijam, "A Lamp for David's Sake" (15:1-8)
   C. 3: Asa, "A Seeker of the Lord (for the Majority of His Life)" (15:9-14)
II. **Kings of Israel (15:25–16:34)**
   A. 4: Nadab, "Like His Bad Dad" (15:25-32)
   B. 5: Baasha, "The Basher" (15:33–16:7)
   C. 6: Elah, "The (Drunken) Frat Boy" (16:8-10)
   D. 7: Zimri, "The Weeklong Warrior" (16:10-20)
   E. 8: Omri, "The Seashell Collector" (16:21-28)
   F. 9: Ahab, "The Atrocious King" (16:29-34)
III. **Final Applications**
   A. See the sinfulness of sin.
   B. See the faithfulness of God.

Occasionally you hear truth in strange places. In an episode of *The Simpsons*, Homer said of the Bible, "All these people are a mess . . . except this one guy." True words! Even the best of men in the Bible fail, like Noah, Abraham, Moses, David, and Peter. Even some of the men who wrote the Bible were murderers (Moses, David, Solomon, and Paul). The whole Bible shows us that we are a mess, and we need a Savior.

The fact that God used men such as these reminds us that God can save and use anyone. It also reminds us that we shouldn't put our ultimate hope in mere mortals. People will disappoint us.

In the book of Kings we see this reality of sin lived out. Many of the individuals in Kings are in fact a mess. But a promised King is coming who will keep God's law perfectly. What keeps Kings from being a depressing book is the promise that God is going to preserve a remnant through the ultimate Son of David who will come and reign forever. God will preserve "a lamp in Jerusalem" (11:36; 15:4). This passage of Scripture reminds us of this divine promise.

I could entitle the message "Eight Wicked Kings and One Mostly Good King" or "A Really Bad Baseball Team" (or "The Astros!"). We basically have a description of nine rulers, three in Judah and six in Israel. One of them, Asa, stands out as a mostly good example. Ahab is the final batter in the lineup, and like a pitcher, he's the worst hitter! Here's the batting order:

Three Kings of Judah (Southern Kingdom):
Rehoboam (14:21-31)
Abijam (15:1-8)
Asa (15:9-24)
Six Kings of Israel (Northern Kingdom):
Nadab (15:25-31)
Baasha (15:33–16:7)
Elah (16:8-10)
Zimri (16:10-20)
Omri (16:21-28)
Ahab (16:29-34)

The writer of Kings follows a consistent pattern in describing these kings. It's sort of like a Wikipedia page. We're given (1) the identity of the king, (2) the length of his reign, (3) his relationship to the king in the other kingdom, (4) the identity of the king's mother (in the case of Judah's kings), (5) occasionally an explanation of the divine point of view, (6) a statement of death, and (7) recommendations for further study.

The reigns of the three Judean kings cover about 60 years (930–870 BC). Thus, this is but a brief survey. Two other "survey sections" appear later, in 2 Kings 8:16–13:25 and 2 Kings 14:1–17:6.

After explaining the latter part of Rehoboam's reign and the short reign of Abijam, the writer recounts the long reign of Asa. He brought stability. As a whole, the southern kingdom of Judah was more stable—nationally and internationally—than the northern kingdom of Israel. It certainly wasn't honorable in every way, but it was more stable. The northern kingdom partook in more idolatry and was exposed to other threatening nations, including Assyria. But the most important detail is God's promise to David. Other matters are important, but this is most important. David set an example (albeit an imperfect one), and God made a promise to him. The other kings are compared to him. How will each king respond to God's covenant? This question lingers throughout the narrative.

We have many lessons to learn as we observe nine kings—especially the lesson not to waste your life on things that don't matter—but we have one overarching word of hope: God will preserve a lamp in Jerusalem. This should encourage us. God was and is faithful. Jesus came. He came to live and die and rise for sinners, and He forever reigns as our King. So let us learn from these nine kings, and let us worship and give ourselves wholeheartedly to the King of kings.

To help us remember a significant detail about each king, I have given each a nickname or tagline. The author has been talking about Jeroboam in Israel, but he switches to Judah in 14:21 and then comes back to Israel's rulers. It's similar to the MLB network that goes back and forth between games.

Kings of Judah
1 KINGS 14:21–15:24

1: Rehoboam, "The Conformer" (14:21-31)

After a note on Rehoboam's famous dad (Solomon), Rehoboam's age, and his 17-year reign, we read of Solomon's folly: namely, his marriage to Naamah the Ammonite. The writer of Kings finds this so important that he bookends this section with a note about this Ammonite mother (v. 31). Bookends are significant in the Bible. They provide a lens by which we can read everything in the middle. Why is it that Rehoboam conformed to the culture and began to worship idols? It was partially due to the influence of his mother, whom Solomon should have never married in the first place.

Rehoboam didn't have to follow his mother, but he did. We will see that all of these kings have a choice to make. Rehoboam made the wrong choice. The Chronicler puts the blame on Rehoboam, saying, "He did not determine in his heart to seek the LORD" (2 Chr 12:14). Rehoboam didn't curb the idolatry. The sin introduced by Solomon and his foreign wives worsens in Rehoboam's reign.

Next, we read about the entire community of Israel. The writer says, "Judah did what was evil in the LORD's eyes" (1 Kgs 14:22). Even though we're examining kings, God's people remain in view. They identify with the king. The writer says the people provoked God to "jealous anger." Modern readers may have trouble with this concept of jealousy, but this is holy jealousy. God isn't careless about His people. Like a husband who wants to protect his wife with a righteous jealousy, God wants to protect His people. God is jealous for His bride and jealous for His glory.

The evil committed by the nation was "more than all that their ancestors had done." It was a dark day in Israel. The writer then outlines some of the dark practices: "They also built for themselves high places, sacred pillars, and Asherah poles on every high hill and under every green tree; there were even male cult prostitutes in the land" (vv. 23-24). High places were altars to pagan deities, often located on hilltops. Asherah poles were wooden representations of a female deity. Such idols were supposed to be destroyed (Deut 12:3-4). Asherah was often seen as the partner of a male god, Baal (more on Baal in 1 Kgs 17), giving an obvious sexual message. In light of the sexual nature of his cult, the presence of prostitutes was common at the shrines. Worshipers would fulfill their obligations to the fertility gods (House, *1, 2 Kings*, 194). The reference to "male cult prostitutes" means ritual sodomy was practiced (Deut 23:17).

These practices were the reasons God drove out the other nations in the first place, but now Judah conformed to their customs. Instead of exclusive allegiance to Yahweh, they adopted Canaanite idolatry.

How could this be? What would attract anyone to male cult prostitution? Rehoboam is simply conforming to the surrounding culture. Paul says, "Do not be conformed to this world" (Rom 12:2 ESV), and John says, "Do not love the world" (1 John 2:15). Just because culture deems something acceptable doesn't mean God approves of it. Some say, "We have progressed. The Bible was written a long time ago." No, God was opposed to these sinful practices then, and He still opposes them now.

The bottom line is, God's people are to live differently. Jesus said that we are "the salt of the earth," and we are no good if we lose our saltiness (Matt 5:13). We're all susceptible to popular sins of the culture like greed, racism, and laziness. But we're supposed to be different.

In verses 25-28 idolatry led to political problems. The nation encountered an enemy from Egypt: Shishak. The Chronicler says this attack was because Rehoboam "abandoned the law of the LORD," which is affirmed by the prophet Shemaiah (2 Chr 12:1,5). Then the Chronicler says the people humbled themselves and God promised to "grant them a little deliverance" (2 Chr 12:6-7). But Rehoboam had to give up treasures from the temple to pay him off. The king then replaced the gold shields he lost with bronze shields. This signifies the fading splendor of the nation.

Besides the idolatry and the political weakness, we also read of Rehoboam's lack of peace. Unlike David he couldn't defeat his enemies, and unlike Solomon he couldn't establish peace (House, *1, 2 Kings*, 195). Rehoboam was at war with Jeroboam "throughout their reigns" (1 Kgs 14:30). In every way the kingdom was in decline because Rehoboam "did what was evil, because he did not determine in his heart to seek the LORD" (2 Chr 12:14).

But even in the midst of decline, we read, "His son Abijam became king in his place" (1 Kgs 14:31). You can read about this genealogy in Matthew's Gospel as he introduces Jesus (Matt 1:7-8). In the midst of darkness, God preserves a light. A lamp continues to burn in Jerusalem. That's grace!

2: Abijam, "A Lamp for David's Sake" (15:1-8)

In the eighteenth year of Jeroboam's rule, we see that Abijam (aka Abijah) reigned in Judah, and he apparently married within the faith. The writer says he married "Maacah daughter of Abishalom [Absalom]" (v. 2). However, he "walked in all the sins his father before him had committed" (v. 3). What does this mean? It means "he was not completely devoted to the LORD his God as his ancestor David had been" (v. 3). Literally, "his heart was not whole with Yahweh his God, like the heart of David his father."

God is after the heart. He wants you to be true to Him. Like the other kings Abijam is compared to David, and the writer says he falls short.

In 2 Chronicles 13 we read a bit more positive story about him. Abijam opposed Jeroboam in Ephraim, and because the men of Judah actually "cried out to the LORD," they prevailed (2 Chr 13:14). Judah took Bethel, Jeshanah, and Ephron, with their dependent villages. Compared to David, Abijam was less faithful. Compared to Jeroboam, he was better. But the Chronicler still agrees with the assessment in Kings since he too notes the idolatrous practice; the Chronicler simply neglects to give an explicit comment on his personal godliness.

Abijam does provide some relief from the north, but he still walked in the sins of his father. Why does God not wipe him out? "But because of David, the LORD his God gave him a lamp in Jerusalem to raise up his son after him" (vv. 4-5; cf. 1 Kgs 11:36; 2 Kgs 8:19).

Lamps are common symbols of God's continuing presence (1 Sam 3:3) and of a ruler's continuity (2 Sam 21:17; also of ancient Near Eastern practice). A burning coal symbolizes family continuity (2 Sam 14:7). Today we can visit the "eternal flame" at Arlington National Cemetery commemorating John F. Kennedy. In our homes the presence of light means someone is home. In Psalm 132:17 God promises to prepare "a lamp for My anointed one." All of these images provide a stunning backdrop to statements made in Revelation: "Its lamp is the Lamb" (Rev 21:23).

The Lord is gracious, and the Lord keeps His promises. God promised to continue David's dynasty. David wasn't perfect, for he sinned in "the matter of Uriah the Hittite" (1 Kgs 15:5), but he was repentant. Though the kings don't keep their promises, God does. Sacrifices continue to be offered for sins. Lambs are slaughtered. Atonement is provided. The light continues to burn as all of this prepares the way for the Savior. Despite the sins of these kings, God was faithful, and consequently we have forgiveness of sins.

3: Asa, "A Seeker of the Lord (for the Majority of His Life)" (15:9-14)

The writer tells of Asa's unusually long reign (41 years) and presents this king as a breath of fresh air. Rehoboam was a conformer, but Asa was a reformer. We read of his personal reformation, as the writer says, "Asa did what was right in the LORD's eyes, as his ancestor David had done" (v. 11). Only Hezekiah and Josiah receive higher praise than Asa.

This is what matters in life: personal godliness. Are you living before the eyes of God with loving faithfulness to Him? You see, Asa chose to live differently from his fathers. Perhaps you grew up in a hard family. Don't let this reality keep you from living for the glory of God. Kings doesn't promote fatalism. God is sovereign, but you're responsible.

The next positive statement refers to his worship reform. Asa puts away the "male cult prostitutes" and "the idols" (v. 12). Asa does physically what we must do spiritually, that is, destroy the idols of our hearts. He opposes Asherah poles so much that he gets rid of his grandmother, Maacah, "the queen mother," because she possessed one of these idols. Asa destroyed it. Asa's reform cost him. And following Jesus will cost us too. You might have to break ties with family members in order to follow Jesus (Luke 12:52-53). While you should be gracious and patient with your family, you must realize that not everyone will approve of your walking in the ways of Christ.

Asa also collects some gold and silver for the temple. He gives attention to this holy place. The only negative point is that he didn't remove the high places completely, indicating some inconsistency. However, in 2 Chronicles we read that the high places were destroyed (14:3-5), at least in Judah. It appears that he destroyed them in the southern kingdom, but those in the north still had non-Jerusalem places for worship. Nevertheless, the text says his heart was true to the Lord (1 Kgs 15:14).

The Chronicler highlights Asa's spiritual leadership saying that he "*told the people of Judah to seek the* LORD . . . and to carry out the instruction and the commands*" (2 Chr 14:4; emphasis added). Asa points the nation in the right direction.

Have you ever been serious about seeking the Lord? If not, follow Asa's example: put away the idols and seek the Lord. James says, "Draw near to God, and He will draw near to you" (Jas 4:8). This happened to me in college. I had been around the church growing up, but I didn't earnestly seek the Lord until then. Perhaps you have some religious practices but no living relationship with the God of the Bible. Let me urge you to follow this model of seeking first the kingdom of God and His righteousness.

We also read of another positive example of Asa's leadership when Zerah the Cushite (Ethiopian) came against him with his massive army. The Chronicler writes that Asa "cried out to the LORD his God: '. . . Help us, LORD our God, for we depend on You, and in Your name we have come against this large army'" (2 Chr 14:11). As a result, "the LORD routed the Cushites" (v. 12). Asa and his men pursued them until "the Cushites fell" (v. 13; a miracle that anyone could exhaust Ethiopian runners!).

Additionally, the Chronicler notes that a prophet Azariah spoke to Asa, saying, "If you seek Him [the LORD], He will be found by you, but if you abandon Him, He will abandon you" (2 Chr 15:2). Asa responded to this message positively (vv. 8-18).

Despite the positive lessons we learn from Asa, we also learn a negative example. Asa falls later in life due to unbelief. Against the Ethiopians, he trusted in God, not human methods, and won the victory. But then we read of the sad account of Asa paying Aram's Ben-hadad to break his covenant with Israel's Baasha in order to protect Judah from Baasha's threat (1 Kgs 15:16-24). When the pressure was on, he abandoned his convictions and made a terrible compromise.

On a purely human level, this looked like a military genius at work. Baasha had fortified Ramah, a strategic economic area just north of Jerusalem, and in response Asa pays off the greedy Ben-hadad with treasures from the temple. As a result of Aram's attack on Israel's cities, Baasha leaves, and then Asa's people cart off all of the construction materials Baasha left behind, using these items to fortify Geba and Mizpah! Great move, right? Wrong. It may look good on paper, but in Chronicles we read of how Hanani the seer rebuked Asa:

> *Because you depended on the king of Aram and have not depended on the LORD your God, the army of the king of Aram has escaped from your hand. Were not the Cushites and Libyans a vast army with many chariots and horsemen? When you depended on Yahweh, He handed them over to you.* (2 Chr 16:7-8)

The seer then describes how God is looking for "those whose hearts are completely His" (2 Chr 16:9). As a result of the stinging rebuke, Asa got "angry with the seer and put him in prison," and "Asa mistreated some of the people at that time" (v. 10).

Finally, his last years included more tragedy as we read that he "developed a disease in his feet," and even with this disease, "he didn't seek the LORD but only the physicians" (2 Chr 16:12). This verse isn't a proof text to argue against using doctors; it's simply a statement of Asa's lack of trust in God in his final years.

Asa, the wonderful king, fails to trust in God, turns against the seer, inflicts cruelties, and doesn't seek the Lord. What a warning to us! A person may seek the Lord and command others to seek the Lord for many years but then fall at the end of life. God is looking for, in the words of Eugene Peterson's book title, *A Long Obedience in the Same Direction.* Every day we must begin afresh with God, repenting of sin, reading His Word, and asking for His help. Let us pursue a life of faithfulness. We also learn that success in the eyes of the world may be unfaithfulness to God. Asa won a victory but not the way God desired.

Nevertheless, Asa did slow the slide of Judah, and we read that his son Jehoshaphat reigned in his place (1 Kgs 15:24). We will study his reign later, in 1 Kings 22:41. God continues to keep the light burning in Jerusalem.

Kings of Israel
1 KINGS 15:25–16:34

As we shift to the northern kingdom, there are many changes in leadership. There are also civil strife, darkness, and political conspiracies. In the midst of this, we read of the prophetic word frequently—old and new predictions coming true (House, *1, 2 Kings*, 198). With the prophetic word, we see how God is in control of history. From Nadab to Ahab, we see that all of the northern kings of this era are evil.

4: Nadab, "Like His Bad Dad" (15:25-32)

I give Nadab this title because the writer says the new king did evil and "followed the example of his father." He has an opportunity to lead a reformation, but instead he continues in the sins of his father.

While Nadab is besieging Gibbethon, Baasha strikes him down. Baasha goes on to wipe out the house of Jeroboam, which fulfilled the word of the prophet Ahijah the Shilonite. Thus, the sins of Jeroboam affected his descendants. House rightly notes, "Persons who lead a nation to embrace empty religious and ethical systems often create an environment of violence, greed, and oppression" (*1, 2 Kings*, 198).

5: Baasha, "The Basher" (15:33–16:7)

Baasha rules for 24 years after he assassinates Nadab. (He isn't the only king that comes into power by killing another king.) He is the first king to reign in Tirzah (although it was previously mentioned as Jeroboam's base; 14:17). Tirzah remained the capital until Omri moved it to Samaria. Tirzah was rich with gardens and groves and abundant water. Reference to Tirzah is made in Song of Songs 6:4: "You are as beautiful as Tirzah, my darling." But Baasha "did what was evil in the LORD's sight and followed the example of Jeroboam" (1 Kgs 15:34), demonstrating that some people, in the midst of beauty, don't worship its Creator. We see plenty of examples of this in our own day—people worshiping creation instead of Creator (see Rom 1).

In 16:1-4 we read of another prophet—Jehu. He comes to bring a word against Baasha. He basically says the Lord gave the king an opportunity to change things, but he acted like Jeroboam, and consequently Baasha will share Jeroboam's fate. It was pretty simple: you live like Jeroboam, you will die like Jeroboam.

In verse 7 a curious statement is made. We read that he will suffer the fate of Jeroboam because of "all the evil he had done in the LORD's sight." Understandable. But then the writer says, "And because Baasha had struck down the house of Jeroboam." In 1 Kings 15:29 we read that when Baasha took out Nadab and all of Jeroboam's family that it was "according to the word of the LORD." So wasn't Baasha acting as an agent of God's judgment? Yes. We see this tension elsewhere (1 Kgs 21:21-24; 2 Kgs 9–10). God accomplishes His purposes through wicked men, but their actions don't remove their moral responsibility. When Peter preached at Pentecost, he said a similar thing: lawless men killed Jesus, yet it happened according to God's plan (Acts 2:22-23).

The problem with these Jeroboam-like kings is their lack of obedience to God's word, not lack of information about God's word. They could never plead, "I didn't know how to rule." God wants His people to obey His Word. Simple, childlike obedience to God's Word is what makes a faithful believer.

6: Elah, "The (Drunken) Frat Boy" (16:8-10)

Still in Asa's era, we read of another king, Elah, who reigned for two years. He isn't viewed positively either. We read that he gets drunk at the home of one of his officials and is killed by Zimri. Up to this point we have read nothing about alcohol abuse, so Elah appears to add to the sins of the previous kings.

His drunken stupor took place while Zimri, his servant, was conspiring against him and apparently while Elah's army was in Philistia (16:15). But Elah wasn't with his army. He was getting drunk. Zimri struck Elah down and killed him. Thus, Zimri follows Baasha's example of assassination to secure the throne. While Nadab died in the context of war, Elah dies a completely dishonorable death.

Next we read that Zimri went on to wipe out the house of Baasha (vv. 11-14). This too fulfilled prophecy (v. 12). Jehu told Baasha, Elah's father, that his house would be like the house of Jeroboam (v. 7).

A few applications emerge from this story, particularly the sin of *drunkenness* and the problem of *diversion*. Drunkenness is prohibited in Scripture (Eph 5:18). It also carries several practical dangers, like impairing one's judgment and diverting one's time and energy away from what matters. In Elah's case it was even more problematic since kings were to set an example of responsibility and maturity (Prov 31:4-5). Instead,

Elah is reigning like a frat boy, getting hammered and neglecting his responsibility.

Elah reminds me of what Darrin Patrick calls a "Ban" (*Church Planter*, 10–12). Patrick describes the problem we have with prolonged adolescence among males in our culture. We have guys who are neither boys nor men. They live suspended between childhood and adulthood; thus he says they are a hybrid of boy and man, a "Ban."

Remember, David told the future King Solomon to "be courageous like a man" (1 Kgs 2:2). We pointed out that what makes a man is obedience to Gods' Word (1 Kgs 2:3; Ps 1). Elah isn't showing himself a man.

Unfortunately, a great number of Bans exist today. We need young men that will grow up, be men. We need men who will get serious about Jesus, study the Bible, serve others, keep their pants on, stop looking at porn, fight injustice, serve the poor, and take the gospel to hard places. Young dudes, don't waste your life playing *World of Warcraft* or inventing drinking games. You're only young once, but immaturity can last a lifetime.

Finally, before we get self-righteous, let's remember that we also can have our attention diverted away from what's important in other ways, with other vices. For some the problem may not be with Jack Daniels but with their favorite sports team. I know some who can name starting line-ups of their favorite college team for the past 10 years but have never taught their kids the basic doctrines of the faith. Elah gets diverted. Let's pray for grace that we don't get diverted. Let's stay focused on the kingdom of God.

7: Zimri, "The Weeklong Warrior" (16:10-20)

Zimri reigns for only seven days. When the pro-Omri army hears of the assassination of Elah, they declare that Omri, the military leader, should be king. Zimri carried out a conspiracy without the army's support, and now he will pay. Omri and the people besiege Tirzah, and when Zimri sees that the city has been taken, he "entered the citadel of the royal palace and burned it down over himself" (v. 18). The writer than tells why he did this: "Because of the sin he committed by doing what was evil in the LORD's sight and by following the example of Jeroboam and the sin he caused Israel to commit" (v. 19). He was just as bad as the previous kings.

What's striking about this comment is that God held him just as responsible for not making appropriate changes, even though he reigned only seven days (Davis, *1 Kings*, 188)! Idolatry needs to be dealt with aggressively and immediately. But Zimri, like the other kings, was more interested in power than in faithfulness to God.

Another lesson we might draw here is about the fleeting nature of success. Zimri probably thought he was on top of the world as he washed Elah's blood off his hands. He had taken out the king and was reigning in the beautiful land of Tirzah. And he was indeed the king—for seven days. But how fleeting his success was. Our life is a vapor; let's make the most of it.

8: Omri, "The Seashell Collector" (16:21-28)

Omri was an important ruler. He reigned for 12 years. He had several challenges, like dealing with division in Israel because some were devoted to Tibni, his rival for the throne. However, Omri takes over after Tibni dies. We don't know how he died. Old age? Illness? Murder? All we know is Tibni had a funeral, and Omri had a coronation (Davis, *1 Kings*, 189).

Omri also had the challenge of dealing with the ruins of Tirzah, which Zimri burned. We read that he reigned for six years there, but then he "bought the hill of Samaria from Shemer for 150 pounds of silver" and called it Samaria, after the previous owner (v. 24). Establishing Samaria as the new capital city of the northern kingdom was one of his most significant achievements. It was a strategic place militarily and economically, overlooking important trade routes. It remained Israel's capital until Assyria plundered it in 722 BC.

Unlike the drunken Elah and the shooting star Zimri, Omri was a real leader. He brought stability to the north. From a worldly perspective, he was an effective king. Foreign armies were kept out, he gave the people the religion they wanted, he made foreign alliances through marriages, and Israel stopped fighting Judah during his reign (House, *1, 2 Kings*, 203). Outsiders recognized him as a great king, for the Assyrian documents refer to Israel as "the land of Omri" (ibid.).

But the biblical writer is unimpressed with his political and military achievements. One can imagine him being praised by the modern media. Surely he would get book deals and be on magazine covers. But the writer of Kings says, "Omri did what was evil in the LORD's sight; he did more evil than all who were before him" (v. 25). He too walked in the ways of Jeroboam. The writer would simply put something like this on his tombstone: "He reigned; he bought a hill; he did evil; he was buried. If you want to know more, watch the documentary." It all amounts to a hill of beans if the leader isn't pursuing faithfulness to God.

Davis points out, "The writer isn't saying he is ignorant of Omri's achievements—he is saying they don't matter" (*1 Kings*, 191). "For what

will it profit a man if he gains the whole world and forfeits his soul?"
(Matt 16:26 ESV). At the end of the day, he was playing *Trivial Pursuit,*
wasting his life and his influence. Don't go the way of Omri. Others may
admire you, but if you don't love God and neighbor, it doesn't matter.
Assyrians had his name in their books, but his name was not in the Book
of Life. Let that serve as a warning to us. What may look like success to
others may actually be a tragedy in the making.

John Piper has a now famous illustration about collecting seashells,
which is where I get Omri's tag line. Piper contrasts the life of a successful American couple with the life of two female missionaries serving in Cameroon. Ruby, over 80 years old, single her whole life, and
Laura, a widowed medical doctor, pushing 80 years old, gave their whole
lives to make Christ known. Their lives were taken in a car accident.
Piper asked, "Was that a tragedy?" Two lives driven by a passion to make
Christ known among the poor, even in their old age? Piper says, "No,
that isn't a tragedy. That is glory. These lives were not wasted." He goes
on to say, "I will tell you what a tragedy is." He then describes an article
about a couple who took early retirement to move to Florida where they
"cruise on their 30-foot trawler, play softball, and collect shells." He says,
"Picture them before Christ at the great day of judgment: 'Look, Lord.
See my shells.' *That* is a tragedy" (Piper, *Don't Waste Your Life,* 45–46;
emphasis in original).

Take a vacation? Yes. Enjoy creation? Of course. Make this your
ambition? Absolutely not! Don't waste your life on things that don't matter. Invest in the kingdom. Don't go the way of Omri.

At this point you might be crying, "This is boring!" All of these kings,
these confusing names, and these different dates that are impossible to
keep track of! Ryken says, "Maybe this is part of the point. These stories
of these bad kings show *the monotony of idolatry*" (*1 Kings,* 429; emphasis
added). He adds, "The people who live the most interesting lives are the
ones who live for God and not themselves" (ibid.).

9: Ahab, "The Atrocious King" (16:29-34)

Ahab actually inherits a relatively stable kingdom. His rule continues for
22 years. While we don't read of any crazy coups, his reign was atrocious.
He was the worst of the kings during Asa's reign in Judah. The writer
says that Ahab did more evil than anyone before him.

Not only does he walk in the sins of Jeroboam, but he also mar-
ries a wicked woman, Jezebel of Tyre. She was a Baal worshiper; her

father's name was "Ethbaal" ("Baal is with him"). Baal was an appealing and influential god in Israel, as we read about him throughout the Old Testament. Some believed Asherah was his female consort. Baal was known as the god of the storm who granted fertility. He was a popular alternative to Yahweh since people were so dependent on the rain. "Holy prostitutes" were given to worshipers in hopes of bringing about fertility in the land and among people.

Atrocious Ahab sets up an altar for Baal in a temple he built in Samaria. He is also the first Israelite king to serve Baal himself. Solomon gave his wives some places to worship; Jeroboam made altars for bulls; Ahab gives official endorsement to Baal worship. What is more, Jezebel, who wore the pants in the house, oversaw 400 prophets for Baal. She evangelized for this false god. She also persecuted and killed God's prophets (18:4,13).

The writer concludes this section by providing a few interesting notes about the rebuilding of Jericho. First, two children die in the process, either because there was a vile religious practice of child sacrifice or as an act of judgment. This happened "in Ahab's day," implying that he endorsed this vile religious practice and that he sponsored the rebuilding of Jericho as a fortress. This brings us to the second note: Joshua had pronounced a curse on anyone who rebuilt Jericho (Josh 6:26). The writer refers to this pronouncement in the last half of the verse. Who would ever want to defy God's word and rebuild Jericho? Ahab, the atrocious king. God promised through Joshua that anyone who sought to rebuild it would lose his or her children, yet Ahab disregarded this word.

What characterizes Ahab's leadership? It's a total disregard for God and His Word. The stage is set for Elijah, God's prophet in the following chapters, to confront him and exalt the true and living God.

Final Applications

How can we sum up all of this history? Let me try to do so by making two final points of application.

See the Sinfulness of Sin

Recognize that sin has short-term and long-term effects. Sin affects you and others, both now and in the future. It leads you into stupidity and bondage. Sin never sleeps. You cannot let your guard down. You never get to an age where temptation isn't a problem. Don't think you will ever reach an age where you can cease fighting sin. Seek first the kingdom of God and His righteousness, and seek the King afresh every day.

See the Faithfulness of God

In the mist of this dark period of history, we can step back and see that God is faithful. Despite the sin, folly, and rebellion we read of in Kings, God kept a lamp in Jerusalem (15:4). "All of these people are a mess" and so are we, "except this one guy," Jesus. Praise God, we have a King who always did right in the eyes of the Father, then died on our behalf— for us who have done evil in God's sight. There is one way to be saved, forgiven, redeemed, and made part of the eternal kingdom: through Jesus Christ, the ultimate Son of David. Embrace Him as your Lord. Then you can know the power of the resurrection that enables us grow in godliness. We don't have to remain stuck in our own sin, doomed to repeat the sins of our ancestors. Through Christ, by the power of the Spirit, we can be made right with God and given strength to live a life that matters. So rejoice in the faithfulness of God, who kept His word, leaving a lamp burning until Christ came. This King has a title I don't need to make up: King of kings and Lord of lords.

Reflect and Discuss

1. How do the pressures of culture lead believers astray?
2. Why do people long to be like those around them?
3. What sort of spiritual compromises do some believers make in order to fit in with their culture?
4. Why is sin so offensive to God?
5. Asa removed his own mother from a position of authority because of her idolatry. What costs might believers pay today to be faithful?
6. How might the sins of one person affect others?
7. How might the faithfulness of one person affect others?
8. How was God faithful to His people while many of these kings went astray?
9. Describe how God's steadfast love has been manifested in your life.
10. In what ways does Jesus show Himself a good king in contrast to Israel's evil kings?

Elijah: A Man like Us

1 KINGS 17:1-24

Main Idea: The writer introduces a central figure in the Kings narrative, the prophet Elijah, whose life of prayer and faith inspires and challenges us.

I. **Meet Elijah.**
   A. A spiritual giant
   B. A man like Moses and John the Baptist
   C. A man like us
II. **Learn from Elijah.**
   A. Believe what God has said (17:1).
      1. Elijah's context: national apostasy
      2. Elijah's background: total obscurity
      3. Because Elijah believes what God has said, he proclaims it.
      4. Because Elijah believes what God has said, he prays it.
      5. Because Elijah believes what God has said, he obeys it.
   B. Trust God for daily bread (17:2-16).
      1. God provides through an unclean raven in the Cherith Ravine (vv. 2-6).
      2. God provides through an unknown Gentile widow in Baal's territory (vv. 7-16).
   C. Rely on the God who raises the dead (17:17-24).
III. **One Greater than Elijah Is Here.**

Two things have me thinking about my personal prayer life: "Insanity" and Elijah. I just finished my seventh week of the max interval workout called "Insanity". Every morning around 5:45, I head to my garage, roll out my mat, turn on my computer, and proceed to "dig deeper." I haven't sweated like this in a long time. My face has been on my garage floor praying for the second coming more than once!

But that isn't the only reason this exercise program has made me think of prayer. My pastor friend, Greg Breazeale, finished the program before I did and sent me an e-mail to instruct and inspire me, both physically and spiritually. He challenged me with this honest admission:

"I wish I could pray 45 minutes a day for nine weeks straight. I'm working on that." Ouch. Paul put it this way: "The training of the body has a limited benefit, but godliness is beneficial in every way" (1 Tim 4:8). Exercise is important, but spiritual exercise is more important.

If you're like me, you will admit that you could and should be spending more time in prayer. What most of us need isn't this reminder but inspiration. That is what we have in Elijah. While Shawn T inspires me to do better switch kicks and plank punches, Elijah's example inspires me in the exercises of *faith* and *prayer*. In the Kings narrative we find some wonderful examples of Elijah's courage and his "insane" prayer life. Spurgeon notes, "What a mighty master of the art of prayer was Elijah the Tishbite!" ("God's Care of Elijah").

Meet Elijah

A Spiritual Giant

Who is Elijah? His name means "my God is Yahweh," an appropriate title for this spiritual giant. His ministry occupies a large section of the Kings narrative (1 Kgs 17–19; 21; 2 Kgs 1–2), and he remains one of the most important characters throughout Scripture. He carries on the prophetic-intermediary tradition of Moses, confronting a Pharaoh-like ruler in Ahab and bringing another exodus-like judgment on the land.

Elijah's ministry dazzles us. Ravens bring him food. God uses a widow to provide daily bread for him in Baal's territory. Elijah prays, and God raises the widow's son from the dead. Elijah wins the showdown against the prophets of Baal at Carmel. He calls down fire from heaven, and he strikes down 450 false prophets. Plus, he was an athlete! He ran 17 miles from Carmel down to Jezreel, outrunning horses and chariots.

God raised up prophets to address rebellious kings early in the narrative (14:7-11; 15:29-30; 16:1-2,12). Ahab, "The Atrocious King," was the worst of all of the kings in Israel and, with his wife, was a big booster of Baal worship. He will meet Elijah, the greatest of all the prophets, during this era.

Elijah performs many miracles, which often troubles modern readers. Liberal theologians are often embarrassed by such stories and seek to explain them away. Should we avoid taking these stories seriously? Should we treat them like McDonald's happy meals—only cherishing them as children but not as adults? Of course not! If you strip away the stories of the Bible and try to hold on to the faith, you have a building with no foundation. These miracles, which often occur during particularly dark periods of redemptive history, validate the ministry of the true prophets. Elijah's stories demonstrate that he was a true prophet, like Moses, who came along in a period of kingdom decline. He performed miracles, had a remarkable prayer life, and spoke God's word accurately and boldly. Further, these miracles point the way to understanding the greater Prophet, Jesus, who would also carry on this tradition in a much greater way (Luke 7–9). And Jesus' miracles were little foretastes of the new heavens and new earth, where there will be no death, starvation, or tears. If you don't take the stories of Elijah seriously, then you shouldn't take the ministry of Jesus seriously. Moreover, Jesus took them as truth, not fiction! He refers to miracles in the lives of Jonah, Elijah, Elisha, and more.

Now, we don't have prophets like Elijah today because the true and greater Prophet Jesus has come, but that doesn't mean these stories aren't true or that they have no relevance. We may not have ravens feed us or serve a poor widow with an inexhaustible barrel of flour, and we may not see the dead raised in this life, but that doesn't mean these stories aren't for our spiritual nourishment. God still takes care of His people, normally through prayer and providence and (at times) miracles. An example of how God normally provides through providence rather than miracles is in the story of how God cared for his prophets in chapter 18. He used an administrator named Obadiah to take food to the suffering prophets (18:4). God miraculously provided for Elijah, but He used ordinary means of providence for 100 prophets. In both cases God is providing.

Further, while God doesn't always save His people on earth from calamity, we know He will ultimately save them and bring them into glory, which is made possible by the miracle of new birth. We who are believers have not been overlooked in the working of miracles. We have received a new heart and will one day be raised forever.

A Man like Moses and John the Baptist

Elijah was like Moses, with whom he later appeared at the transfiguration of Jesus (Matt 17:3). Like Moses, Elijah went eastward for a season after he had confronted a wrathful king (Exod 2:15; 1 Kgs 17:2-6). Moses challenged Pharaoh; Elijah challenges Ahab. Like Moses, Elijah lived on God's abundant provision of bread, meat, and water (Exod 16; 1 Kgs 17:2-6). Like Moses, Elijah goes to Mount Horeb for 40 days and 40 nights to appear before God (1 Kgs 19:8,11). Like Moses, he needs and receives assurance of God's presence to finish his mission (Exod 33:18-23; 1 Kgs 19:13-17). And like Moses, Elijah feels the burden of the failure of the people so much that he desires death (Num 11:14-15; 1 Kgs 19:3-4). Elijah is the prophet like Moses that God raises up to preserve a remnant who won't bow down to Baal (Konkel, *Exodus*, 308–9).

Elijah was also like John the Baptist, with whom he is associated in the New Testament (Luke 1:13-17). Jesus affirms the identity of John the Baptist as the last prophet, the messenger Elijah who was to come (Matt 11:7-15; Luke 7:24-28). Elijah didn't reappear literally as John the Baptist, for that would be something like reincarnation. But their lives and ministry were similar. They both came from obscure places, they dressed similarly (Matt 3:4; 2 Kgs 1:8), both called people to repentance, and both were forerunners to Messiah (Mal 3:1-3; 4:5).

Elijah continues to play an important role in Judaism. At meals he is mentioned in prayer: "May God in his mercy send us the prophet Elijah." He is mentioned at the circumcision of children. He also gets a seat at the Passover meal (Konkel, *Exodus*, 310).

A Man like Us

My brother-in-law, David, currently serves in the army. He and three other soldiers made the team for the baseball Hall of Fame Classic, a game played in Cooperstown, New York, comprising living Hall of Famers. In an effort to honor the military, nearby soldiers were invited to try out for the team, and David was one of the four selected. I was so envious! It was so cool to see his name listed beside Ricky Henderson, Goose Gossage, Rollie Fingers, and more legends. His association with these men fascinated our family because, even though David is a tremendous athlete, he isn't a Hall of Famer! He would say that he is far distant from these Hall of Famers in regards to baseball talent, but in reality he isn't that distant from them because he has a human nature just like them.

We may also try to distance ourselves from Elijah, who is in the Hall of Faith (Heb 11:35), but we must remember James' extraordinary statement: Elijah was a "man with a nature like ours" or "a man like us." We can relate to him. We can look to him.

> *The urgent request of a righteous person is very powerful in its effect. Elijah was a man with a nature like ours; yet he prayed earnestly that it would not rain, and for three years and six months it didn't rain on the land.* (Jas 5:16-17)

The language James uses is the language Paul and Barnabas used in Lystra, when the people wanted to worship them as gods: "We are men also, with the *same nature* as you" (Acts 14:15, emphasis added). While Elijah holds a special place in redemptive history, James wants us to know that every believer, dressed in the righteousness of Jesus, pursuing likeness to Jesus, can have an effective prayer life like Elijah.

So Elijah is like us, and we should seek to be like him. How so? In the next three chapters of Kings, Elijah teaches us about great faith and effective prayer. We find him standing up boldly in the face of opposition, and we find him praying for God to act on His word (1 Kgs 17:1), for God to raise the dead (17:21), and for God's glory to be known and people to repent (18:36-38). In this particular chapter, I want to suggest three lessons on prayer and faith that Elijah teaches us.

Learn from Elijah

Believe What God Has Said (17:1)

As we consider the opening verse of chapter 17, it's important to note a bit of background that highlights the rarity of Elijah's belief in God's word. A physical famine was coming, but there was first a spiritual famine, for the word of God was absent.

Elijah's context: national apostasy. We will read a lot about not only Elijah but also Ahab (1 Kgs 16:29-34), whose family's story continues for many chapters. The unfolding drama of Ahab and Elijah highlights two mega themes: *the righteousness of God* and the *glory of God.* Concerning righteousness, we will have no doubt whether the exile was a righteous judgment after reading of Ahab's evil influence. Concerning God's glory, Ahab's story shows us that God alone deserves exclusive worship and God is passionate about His glory.

With Ahab's reign Baal worship was now state sponsored. Baal was known as the "rider on the clouds," the god of rain and fertility, and because of this, the god of riches. As mentioned, Ahab married Jezebel who "evangelized" for Baal. Baal's followers believed he restored life after the death of summer. In contrast to Baal, the Elijah narratives highlight that God alone gives life and death and controls fertility and infertility. The psalmist portrays Yahweh as the "rider on the clouds" who alone gives rain and provides for creation (Ps 104:3-4).

If there was no rain, Baal followers believed Baal was submitting to the god of death, Mot, until a later date when Baal would be revived. So

Baal was not the only god worshiped. In this polytheistic culture, people wanted a little bit of everything—a little goddess worship, a little Baal worship, a little Yahweh worship, and more. Exclusive worship of God was absent in most places. Indeed, Elijah thought he was the only real worshiper left (1 Kgs 19:10).

We live in a similar time, in which people worship a little bit of everything but not the living God *exclusively*—a little God, a little horoscope, a little TBN, a little pop psychology, a few conspiracy theories, aliens, zombies, New Ageism, naturalism, and more. They may want God at their death, but they live every day as functional naturalists or materialists. As a result of twisted theology, immorality is normalized in our day just like in the days of Elijah. He lived in a day like ours where people call evil "good" and good "evil."

Elijah's background: total obscurity. Immediately after reading of Ahab and Jezebel, we are introduced to Elijah—with no warm-up! We read about all these kings, and then boom! Elijah.

Who is this guy? The writer tells us that Elijah was the "Tishbite, of Tishbe in Gilead" (17:1). Where is this? No one knows where Tishbe is, though some have tried to identify it. Perhaps he is simply a settler in the wild, forested area east of the Jordan in Gilead. God chooses this man from nowhere it seems. Unlike the kings, we don't know who his family is, and we don't know if he has a wife and kids. Does he have any hobbies? We don't know. It reminds me of Paul's words:

> *Brothers, consider your calling: Not many are wise from a human perspective, not many powerful, not many of noble birth. Instead, God has chosen what is foolish in the world to shame the wise, and God has chosen what is weak in the world to shame the strong.* (1 Cor 1:26-27)

Elijah grew up in obscurity (like many of us). Even so, God chose him out of obscurity in order to confront apostasy. That should encourage you. Your family background, or whether you are from Bunn, Dunn, Pumpkin Run, or London, doesn't determine your usefulness to God. God loves to use nobodies.

God proclaims His message to King Ahab through this hillbilly from Tishbe. Can you picture this? Don't think of a suited-up pastor or a "clergy-fied" minister. Picture Braveheart! This guy Elijah is rough around the edges, entering the presence of the king. And then he says, "As the LORD God of Israel lives, I stand before Him, and there will be no dew or rain during these years except by my command!" (17:1). Here we read Elijah's view of God—Yahweh lives! Because he knows Yahweh alone is the living God, he is able to stand fearlessly before Ahab, for standing before Yahweh puts this mere mortal in his place. Elijah has great faith because he has a great God.

Because Elijah believes what God has said, he proclaims it. God keeps His word. We have seen this repeatedly in Kings. Here we see that God will keep His word of judgment that He speaks through Elijah. The drought we read about in chapter 17 was a promise fulfilled. According to God's law, drought was the punishment for pagan idolatry:

> *Be careful that you aren't enticed to turn aside, worship, and bow down to other gods. Then the LORD's anger will burn against you. He will close the sky, and there will be no rain; the land will not yield its produce, and you will perish quickly from the good land the LORD is giving you.* (Deut 11:16-17; cf. Deut 28:23-24)

This makes sense. God's people were to trust God alone for rain. If they turned to another god, then God would withhold rain. This specific judgment is fitting since Baal was supposed to give rain. Not only will it not rain, but also there will not even be dew. No one could claim "bad luck" or a "bad break." No rain *and* no dew clearly demonstrated God's judgment.

Elijah boldly stands up and proclaims what God has already said. God is still looking for courageous prophets who will herald His truth.

Because Elijah believes what God has said, he prays it. Remember what James said? He said Elijah prayed fervently that it would not rain for three-and-a-half years. Although 1 Kings 17 never says Elijah *prayed* for a drought, we do find Elijah praying in 1 Kings 18:42 for the drought to end. Other examples of his insane prayer life exist in the Kings narrative, but James focuses on the famine. Douglas Moo is surely right in saying, "It is a legitimate inference to think that *he prayed for its onset* as well" (*James*, 248; emphasis added).

I think the prayers of Elijah preceded his proclamation to Ahab. Elijah had been before God in the prayer closet prior to being before Ahab in the palace (Ryken, *1 Kings*, 439).

What do we learn from Elijah's prayer for this drought? Surely there are many lessons about faithfulness, persistence, and passion, but I would like to underline one important lesson. Elijah teaches us to pray according to God's Word. Elijah is simply claiming the promise of God's word. Why a drought? It was because this came directly from Scripture.

Elijah knew his Bible. He knew the punishment for idolatry was famine. Elijah's prayers were not rooted in his own imagination. He wasn't asking God to perform neat tricks. He was boldly asking God to act on His own word.

Some think since God has promised something, we shouldn't ask Him. No, the promise should inspire us to pray. Andrew Murray said, "It is on prayer that the promises wait for their fulfillment, the kingdom for its coming, the glory of God for its full revelation" (*With Christ in the School of Prayer*, ii). It's as if the promise awaits a prayer. An example of praying the promises is found in Daniel 9:1-19. The prophet Daniel was reading Jeremiah concerning the end of the exile after 70 years, and he realized it was near. He didn't go dancing into the streets; instead we read, "So I turned my attention to the Lord God" (Dan 9:3).

Here is one of the first ways Elijah schools us in prayer: pray Scripture. How do you pray for 45 minutes (and more!)? Read, pray. Read, pray. Fill your prayers with the Word of God. James says in his epistle, "You have not, because you ask not" (Jas 4:2 KJV). Jesus said, "If you remain in Me and My words remain in you, ask whatever you want and it will be done for you" (John 15:7). As you abide in the Word, ask and keep on asking your Father to act on His Word. Ask Him for provision and the Spirit's power, for wisdom, boldness, and illumination—these things and more are in line with His Word. Let's not fall into prayerlessness or unbelief, but let us cry out to God with passion and understanding of His Word, believing He hears the prayers of His children and loves to answer.

Because Elijah believes what God has said, he obeys it. The word of the Lord came to Elijah and he submitted to it: "So he did what the Lord commanded" (1 Kgs 17:5). "So Elijah got up and went to Zarephath" (17:10). "So Elijah went to present himself to Ahab" (18:2). His life was consumed with obedience to God's word, even though it called for radical actions like "drink from a brook and let the ravens feed you." It sounds simple, but his sensitivity to God's word sets him apart from his culture. He lived by God's word in a culture that rejected it.

Elijah is like us; let's be like him. Elijah teaches us to believe what God has said. God is the living God, and we must be a people who speak, pray, and obey His living Word because we believe it.

Trust God for Daily Bread (17:2-16)

God provides through an unclean raven in the Cherith Ravine (vv. 2-6). Like Moses, Elijah flees to the East after an initial confrontation since he needs protection from Ahab. He goes to this inhospitable area east of the Jordan. While he may be spared from Ahab, it looks like he cannot be spared from death, for there is no food. However, Elijah drinks from the brook and gets fed by a raven.

Notice a few interesting features about this story. First, God controls not only the rain but also the whole natural order (Provan, *1 and 2 Kings*, 133). He even controls the ravens, ceremonially unclean creatures now used for God's purposes of sustaining the prophet's life. We know God provides for the birds of the air, and here He uses the birds of the air to provide for His prophet. Elijah is looking ultimately to the God who reigns over nature for daily food and water, not to the raven or the brook.

Second, the bread and meat are brought in every morning and evening, thus Elijah has a replay of the wilderness meal plan (Ryken, *1 Kings*, 438). God provides "daily bread" (cf. Matt 6:11) and actually provides it more abundantly than in the wilderness, for Elijah eats both bread and meat twice a day (cf. Exod 16:8,12-13).

All of this should encourage us. God controls the natural order. Jesus reminds us to "look at the birds of the sky" and consider how God provides for them; He asks, "Aren't you worth more than they?" (Matt 6:26). He teaches us not to worry about "what [we] will eat or what [we] will drink" (Matt 6:25). You can trust in God to provide for your daily needs. He may not supply you with the finest of meats every day, and He may not provide in such a miraculous way as He did with Elijah, but God provides. No doubt the false prophets of Jezebel ate better than Elijah during this period, but God still provided for him. That too is a good lesson. Even the prophet is suffering from this famine; he isn't immune to suffering. But he has the presence of God and the provision of God, and that is enough. We who receive such daily bread should be grateful and content. Paul reminds us: "But if we have food and clothing, we will be content with these" (1 Tim 6:8). In Charles Spurgeon's sermon "God's Care of Elijah," he reminds us to be grateful for such provision:

> Remember, too, the prayer which I quoted just now—"Give us this day our daily bread." Not, "our weekly bread," not, "our monthly bread," not "our annual stores"—but, "give us our daily bread." God is pleased to give some of His servants in the bulk, but there are many others who only "live from hand to mouth"—and perhaps though not best for the flesh, it is best for faith, for we are apt, when mercies come regularly, to forget from whence they flow! ("God's Care of Elijah")

Let's praise God from whom our daily bread flows! We see His provision in how He provides for Elijah through an unclean raven in the Cherith Ravine.

God provides through an unknown Gentile widow in Baal's territory (vv. 7-16). When the brook dries up, God's provision for Elijah gets more dramatic. He now goes to a little Phoenician town of Zarephath, which is Baal's territory (Jezebel's stomping grounds). Here, God promises to use an unnamed widow to provide for Elijah. Not only can Baal not stop the drought, but Yahweh's provision also extends right into Baal's home turf. God has prepared a table for Elijah in the presence of his enemies. Elijah goes to "stay there" (v. 9) and experience God's power and grace.

It seems that each experience prepared Elijah for the next challenge. We see this in the life of David, who killed a lion with his bare hands and then boldly faced Goliath. We also see this in the life of Jesus, who endured the wilderness test and then faced a more difficult challenge in the garden. Every trial and test prepares us for what is next.

Widows were poor and vulnerable during this period. When Elijah approaches this particular lady, he first asks her for some water. After her favorable response he also asks her for "a piece of bread" (v. 11). Even though she isn't an Israelite, she answers in the name of Elijah's God—"As the LORD your God lives"—and then tells him that all she has is a handful of flour and a little jug of oil, which she planned on using for the last meal before she and her son die (v. 12). Not exactly the best time to show up for dinner!

Elijah tests her faith and asks her to provide for him first, then for herself and her son. He assures her that there will be enough for her and her son and that her flour and oil will last through the drought. She trusts in this promise, acts accordingly, and God provides. Elijah's word is confirmed through this miracle.

Can you imagine this scene? Every day the widow goes over to her barrel of flour and jar of oil and had just enough bread to bake for one more day. Elijah could have testified with the psalmist, "You who are His holy ones, fear Yahweh, for those who fear Him lack nothing" (Ps 34:9).

This passage teaches us some important lessons about the nature of God. It teaches us about God's extraordinary *providence.* It highlights God's *exclusivity,* for only the true and living God could provide. Observe also God's *sovereignty.* God chooses this one, unnamed widow to provide for Elijah. God tells Elijah, "I have commanded a woman who is a widow to provide for you there" (v. 9). But we don't read that God ever speaks to her. Even though she has no prophet to tell her this news, God can ordain it to be so because He is the only sovereign. Proverbs tells us, "A king's heart is like streams of water in the LORD's hand: He directs it wherever He chooses" (21:1), but here we see that God also works sovereignly in the lives of the least of these.

Additionally, we should marvel at God's *compassion*. God shows amazing concern for this weak widow and her son. We know that God is a "father of the fatherless and a champion of widows" (Ps 68:5). Here is just one example of such mercy and care.

We should also underline *God's saving grace to outsiders*. When she says, "As the LORD your God lives," this doesn't seem to be her confession of faith yet. She calls God "*your* God" but not yet "*my* God" (Ryken, *1 Kings*, 449). But here Elijah is an example of a messenger taking the good news to the nations (and later she believes—1 Kgs 17:24). Jesus refers to this widow in Luke's Gospel (a Gospel that has numerous allusions to Elijah):

> He also said, "I assure you: No prophet is accepted in his hometown. But I say to you, there were certainly many widows in Israel in Elijah's days, when the sky was shut up for three years and six months while a great famine came over all the land. Yet Elijah was not sent to any of them—but to a widow at Zarephath in Sidon. (Luke 4:24-26)

After Jesus expounds Isaiah, claiming that His ministry is about bringing good news to the poor and proclaiming liberty to the captives (Luke 4:18), His hometown rejects Him (4:22,28-30). In response Jesus uses this story of the widow of Zarephath, an outsider, to warn them. While there were many poor widows during the three-and-a-half-year drought in Elijah's day, he wasn't sent inside Israel but outside Israel to this widow. ("Three-and-a-half years" is a more specific figure than the rounded "three years" in Kings. Perhaps the figure is used because of its symbolic associations with a period of judgment, as in Dan 7:25; Rev 11:12; 12:14; see Moo, *James*, 248.) A foreign lady, by faith, accepted the word of Elijah and trusted in Elijah's God (1 Kgs 17:24). Jesus is saying that while not everyone in His hometown will accept Him, other outsiders will. He compares those in Nazareth to the apostates in Ahab's day. As for the widow, Bock says it well: "Salvation will open up to all kinds of people" (*Luke*, 418). Jesus then tells how God uses Elisha to heal an Aramean Gentile leper, Naaman (Luke 4:27). God again worked outside of Israel.

We have noted this already: God isn't a tribal deity. He is the God of the nations (cf. Acts 10:45). He will have a people from every tribe and tongue. Let us remember this and rejoice that we have received His grace, and let us proclaim the good news to everyone. The most unexpected people may find saving faith in the most unexpected places.

God graciously provides daily bread to satisfy our physical hunger, and He has provided the bread of life in Jesus, who satisfies our spiritual hunger. Let us, as His beggars, tell other beggars where to find bread.

Rely on the God Who Raises the Dead (17:17-24)

So far the threat of death has been removed by these two miracles, but now a third and more dramatic miracle takes place. The widow's son becomes ill and dies. In response the widow blames Elijah for the tragedy. Elijah, however, takes the boy in his arms and cries out to God, "My LORD God, have You also brought tragedy on the widow I am staying with by killing her son?" (v. 20). Both attribute this event to the Lord, but the difference is that the woman apparently thinks this is the end of the matter, while Elijah will not let it rest (Provan, *1 and 2 Kings*, 134).

Notice in passing another lesson on prayer: the prayer of a righteous person doesn't mean always having the right answers or always understanding God's purposes. Elijah took his anxieties and concerns to God in prayer. He prays in faith and desperation (Heb 11:35). Once again he gives us an inspiring example for prayer. Pour out your heart to the living God in faith.

The writer says, "Then he stretched himself out over the boy three times. He cried out to the LORD and said, 'My LORD God, please let this boy's life return to him!'" (v. 21). Elijah prays fervently and desperately. As a result we read, "So the LORD listened to Elijah's voice, and the boy's life returned to him, and he lived" (v. 22).

Remember Baal wasn't the only god worshiped. Mot, the god of death, was also recognized. Elijah isn't only in Baal's territory, but he's also in Mot's territory. Does Yahweh have to submit to Mot like Baal does? Of course not—God alone reigns over life and death! You can have a dynamic prayer life because our God is the true and living God.

After the boy is raised, Elijah took the child and "gave him to his mother" and said, "Look, your son is alive" (v. 23). The woman then confesses that she believes that the word of God is in Elijah's mouth. At last she believes in the living God. Ryken notes,

The widow of Zarephath shows how faith in the living God is grounded in the factuality of the resurrection. Belief in the resurrection of the body isn't just for super-Christians; it is the foundation for true faith. Resurrection is the proof of the promise of God. (*1 Kings*, 460)

We're reminded of the reality and pain of death in this story. Stories of death are all around us. At any moment, a loved one could breathe his last breath. As in this story, just when things seem to be working out wonderfully, death takes someone. In this case it's a precious child. But there is hope beyond the grave for every grieving believer: God raises the dead. God gives us a little sign of His resurrection power in this Old Testament story.

We should ask God to do what only He can do: most importantly, raise spiritually dead people to life (Eph 2:4-5). This young boy eventually died again. What everyone needs is to be raised up forever by the resurrection power of God.

Paul reminds us that in our present suffering we should also remember the resurrection power of God. He writes,

> *For we don't want you to be unaware, brothers, of our affliction that took place in Asia: we were completely overwhelmed—beyond our strength—so that we even despaired of life. Indeed, we personally had a death sentence within ourselves, so that we would not trust in ourselves but in God who raises the dead.* (2 Cor 1:8-9)

In your trials and in your weaknesses, cast yourself on the mercy of God and plead for His strength and His power. Resurrection truth is truth not only to die on but also to live on.

One Greater than Elijah Is Here

In Luke 7 we read a fascinating story of Jesus that has strong echoes of this scene in Kings:

> *Soon afterward He was on His way to a town called Nain. His disciples and a large crowd were traveling with Him. Just as He neared the gate of the town, a dead man was being carried out. He was his mother's only son, and she was a widow. A large crowd from the city was also with her. When the Lord saw her, He had compassion on her and said, "Don't cry." Then He came up and touched the*

*open coffin, and the pallbearers stopped. And He said, "Young man,
I tell you, get up!" The dead man sat up and began to speak, and
Jesus gave him to his mother. Then fear came over everyone, and they
glorified God, saying, "A great prophet has risen among us," and
"God has visited His people." This report about Him went throughout
Judea and all the vicinity.* (Luke 7:11-17)

There are two widows, one in Zarephath and one in Nain (25 miles
from Capernaum). Consider the similarities:

- Both widows are stricken with grief at the loss of their only son.
- Both Elijah and Jesus perform an unclean act: Elijah lies on a
  dead body, and Jesus touches the coffin (mercy is more important than sacrifice, Hos 6:6).
- Both women witness their sons coming back to life.
- Both receive their sons (the language in Luke 7:15 is the same
  as in 1 Kgs 17:23).
- People believe after the miracle ("A great prophet has arisen
  among us!" and "God has visited us").

However, there is one great difference: Elijah cries out for God's
help in prayer, stretching himself over the boy three times. Jesus just
says the word: "Young man, I say to you, 'arise.'" Kent Hughes points
out, "But when it came to resurrections, he [Jesus] used only his word
(cf. Mark 5:41; Luke 8:54; John 11:43). Clearly, he wanted everyone to
see that resurrection power rests in him!" (*Luke*, 264).

Elijah was great, but Jesus is greater. Speaking about Martha's
brother Lazarus, Jesus said, "Your brother will rise again" (John 11:23).
Then He said, "I am the resurrection and the life. The one who believes
in Me, even if he dies, will live. Everyone who lives and believes in Me
will never die—ever" (John 11:25-26). Then He asks her what He asks
you: "Do you believe this?"

God's power to raise the dead was demonstrated once for all in the
resurrection of Jesus (1 Cor 15:4). He has swallowed up death in victory
(1 Cor 15:55-56). Now God gives life to spiritually dead people (Eph 2:1-
10), and in the future we await the glorious, final resurrection, when the
dead in Christ will rise (1 Thess 4:16-18). We will hear something like
this: "Arise, Tony," or "Arise, Kimberly." Jesus has made the grave like a
bed and the resurrection like waking up.

Elijah was like Moses. He was like John the Baptist. He was like us.
And He was like Jesus. The greater Elijah knew what it was like to live on

every word that proceeded out of the mouth of God (Matt 4), He was called out of obscurity to confront unbelief (John 1:46), He cared for the widow (Luke 7:11-17), He raised the dead (John 11:25), His prayers were effectual (John 17), and He fasted 40 days and 40 nights. Some even thought Jesus *was* Elijah (Matt 16), and one can see why. Elijah was an end-time figure and a miracle-working prophet. Jesus was too, but He was more than that.

Jesus, unlike Elijah, never sinned. Jesus lived and died, finishing His course, taking judgment on Himself instead of pouring it out on those that deserved it. He was raised from the dead and is now interceding for us (Rom 8:34; Heb 7:25).

Yes, Elijah prayed. Yes, we should have an "insane" prayer life like Elijah. But what saves us is Jesus' insane work, and what sustains us now is Jesus' insane prayer life.

May the life of Elijah inspire us to pray biblically and faithfully, and may his life point us to our great source of hope: the true and better prophet, the ultimate mediator, the King of kings, Jesus.

Reflect and Discuss

1. Why might God have sent a famine on the land?
2. Have you ever experienced God's provision in unexpected ways?
3. Have you ever experienced God's blessing through unexpected people?
4. Are there any ways God might bless His people that His people might consider to be beneath them?
5. Why does God choose to use the lowly things of this earth?
6. Why is it difficult to take God at His word during times of difficulty?
7. Elijah rises out of obscurity, and God essentially sends him into the wilderness. Would he have been more productive if God had sent him to a city center? Why or why not?
8. How can Elijah's prayers instruct believers today?
9. God raises people from the dead at various points in Scripture. What can this teach us about God?
10. How is Jesus' ministry similar to Elijah's ministry?

The Showdown at Mount Carmel

1 KINGS 18:1-46

Main Idea: The spectacular showdown between Elijah and the false prophets demonstrates that the God of Elijah is the true and living God.

I.   Elijah and Obadiah: The Preparation for the Showdown (18:1-16)
II. Elijah and Ahab: The Proposal for the Showdown (18:17-19)
III. Elijah and the People: The Purpose of the Showdown (18:20-25)
IV. Elijah and the Prophets: The Prayer-Answering Champion of the Showdown (18:26-46)
    A.   The emptiness of false religion (vv. 26-29)
    B.   The power of the living God (vv. 30-46)
    C.   A mighty master of the art of prayer

I love movies with showdowns. I own a bunch of John Wayne and Clint Eastwood films, and some more modern Westerns like *Tombstone* and *Open Range*. I grew up watching many of these classics with my dad. Many of these Westerns climax with a dramatic gunfight. Sometimes the outnumbered guy or group wins the battle. Sports movies are similar. For example, *Hoosiers* is a classic story of an underdog victory, in which a most unlikely team wins the state championship in Indiana.

The Bible also contains showdowns, and in many cases an underdog triumphs. For example, Moses, a sheepherder, goes up against mighty Pharaoh and triumphs over the evil empire by God's power. When the people cross the Red Sea, they sing, "I will sing to the LORD, for He is highly exalted; He has thrown the horse and its rider into the sea" (Exod 15:1). Other battles occur as history progresses into the story of Joshua's conquest and then into the reign of the judges. Perhaps the greatest underdog story is of Gideon, who with an army of 300 wins a battle over the Midianites because the Lord was with him. The most famous of the showdowns in the Old Testament is David and Goliath. Sportswriters and filmmakers refer to this classic underdog battle all the time. In each of these biblical stories, God raises a leader, a mediator, who represents the people and God and who goes up against the enemies of darkness. Of course, none of these are truly underdog stories since God was with them and for them! But from a human perspective, they were underdogs.

In 1 Kings 18 we have another story of a mediator-leader that God raised up to combat evil: Elijah. After an initial meeting with King Ahab, Elijah went away and was preserved by God's miraculous supply of daily bread during a famine. Now after three years he appears before Ahab again. In this meeting Elijah arranges one of the great showdowns of Scripture. It's a firefight on Mount Carmel between Elijah and the false prophets to prove once and for all who the real God is. Elijah is outnumbered, but he is confident because he is the prophet of the living God. Once again he serves as a mighty example of *prayer* and faith (Jas 5:17-18). In fact, the whole showdown at Mount Carmel was essentially about whose God actually answered prayer.

Let's trace our way through this narrative with four headings: (1) Elijah and Obadiah: The Preparation for the Showdown (18:1-16); (2) Elijah and Ahab: The Proposal for the Showdown (18:17-19); (3) Elijah and the People: The Purpose of the Showdown (18:20-24); and (4) Elijah and the Prophets: The Prayer-Answering Champion of the Showdown (18:25-46).

Elijah and Obadiah: The Preparation for the Showdown

1 KINGS 18:1-16

After the three-year drought, God speaks to Elijah again and says, "Go and present yourself to Ahab. I will send rain on the surface of the land" (v. 1). Once again Elijah follows God's instructions obediently. The writer reminds us, "The famine was severe in Samaria" (v. 2). We can only imagine how bad this drought was. No doubt the people of Israel were drained. Under the leadership of Ahab and Jezebel, they had put their hope in the storm god, Baal, yet they were famished and desperate. They should have looked to Yahweh who alone controls the rain, for He, not Baal, "covers the sky with clouds, prepares rain for the earth, and causes grass to grow on the hills" (Ps 147:8; cf. Pss 68:4; 104:3). Ahab, presumably living royally still, along with his prophets, apparently cares more for his horses than for his people, and in his pride he refuses to turn the people's eyes to the true and living God.

In verse 3 we're introduced to a new character: Obadiah. He serves in Ahab's court as an administrator. We are told that he "greatly feared the LORD." This comment is striking. Why is Obadiah serving wicked king Ahab if he fears the Lord? Some have argued that Obadiah isn't an example to be followed, claiming he lacked courage, that he was a compromiser, that he had divided loyalties, or that he was an ungodly troublemaker (see Wiersbe, *Be Responsible*, 318; and Ryken on Meyer, *Elijah*, n.p.). However, I'm inclined to say that Obadiah is an example worthy of admiration (albeit imperfect like us). I believe he was a risk-taking servant of Yahweh.

Why should we have a positive assessment of Obadiah? Twice he—at great risk to his own life—provided for the prophets of Yahweh when Jezebel was killing them. Obadiah "took 100 prophets and hid them, 50 men to a cave, and provided them with food and water" (vv. 4,13). Obadiah clearly loved Yahweh and His servants.

Obadiah saves prophets, but Ahab saves horses (Davis, *1 Kings*, 229). While Obadiah was fulfilling Ahab's request to look for water for the horses, he meets Elijah. Obadiah calls Elijah "lord" (vv. 7,13), but Elijah apparently takes a negative view of Obadiah, saying Ahab is his "lord" (vv. 8,11,14). Elijah tells Obadiah to tell Ahab that "Elijah is here" (v. 8). Remember Elijah's name: "My God is Yahweh." Tell them "My God is Yahweh" is here. Obadiah waffles at this demand since he fears for his life. Obadiah's allegiance to Yahweh has been quiet, and perhaps he thinks Elijah's confrontational style will end his life and the lives of those he has been protecting.

Obadiah goes on to tell Elijah that Ahab has searched the world over to find the prophet. Obadiah wrongly assumes that if he relays Elijah's message to Ahab, then Elijah will disappear again, and Ahab will kill him. Here Obadiah displays a lack of trust in God's sovereign care. Elijah responds by saying, "As the LORD of Hosts lives, before whom I stand, today I will present myself to Ahab" (v. 15; cf. 17:1). Elijah will do what he came to do. He will take his stand before Ahab, not fearing the king, because he knows he ultimately stands before Someone who is more awesome. In verse 16 we read that Obadiah obeyed Elijah's instructions and told Ahab, and Ahab went out to meet Elijah. While Obadiah was fearful at first, he did obey (cf. Matt 21:28-31).

Before we move to the conversation with Ahab and Elijah, I think it's worth noting that Obadiah and Elijah provide two ways to serve God. Not everyone will be called to formal ministry like Elijah, but many will be called to serve as "secular saints" like Obadiah. Davis says,

> Elijah's ministry is more public and confrontational; Obadiah
> works quietly in behind-the-scenes fashion and yet is faithful

in the sphere where God placed him. The Bible never tells us that there is only one kind of faithful servant (1 Cor 12:4-6); it never demands that you must be an Elijah clone. (*1 Kings*, 231)

Obadiah is like the man or woman working for an unbelieving boss. How should you work in such an environment? Obadiah teaches us to do good work. He was elevated to his position because he apparently did a good job. Christians should be known for good work. Paul says, "Whatever you do, do it enthusiastically, as something done for the Lord and not for men, knowing that you will receive the reward of an inheritance from the Lord" (Col 3:23-24). Obadiah also illustrates how one should use one's influence and resources. Obadiah had access to provisions and made them available to these persecuted prophets. Those who work in professions that allow them to have good salaries and benefits should consider how to use such blessings to advance the kingdom. One might object, claiming that Obadiah was being deceptive, but nothing in the text says that he lied or did anything unethical. He knew about suffering believers, and he used his resources to provide for them. Finally, Obadiah teaches us to be courageous. He ultimately followed Elijah's instructions at great risk to his own life. The lesson here is that if you are ever in a position where it's either obedience to God or obedience to man, choose God (Acts 5:29), even if it might cost you your job—or your life.

Elijah and Ahab: The Proposal for the Showdown
1 KINGS 18:17-19

Ahab meets Elijah and blames the prophet for bringing the trouble on Israel: "Is that you, you destroyer of Israel?" (v. 17). I don't think he simply couldn't recognize Elijah (though his appearance had probably changed over the three-year drought). No, Ahab was making an accusation. He had to blame someone, so why not Elijah? The blame game is as old as the garden. Ahab doesn't want to accept responsibility. God plainly told His people that famine would result if they worshiped idols (Deut 28:22-24). Ahab disregarded God's word and received God's judgment. After three years Ahab still won't change his mind and heart. Instead of repenting, he blames Elijah. For what we don't know. Is he saying Elijah's belief in only one God has aroused the wrath of Baal? Is he blaming Elijah for the criticism he has received from others who are upset by the drought, pointing their fingers at the king? Or has Ahab just grown weary of the drought and wants to blame someone, and Elijah seems like the best candidate? It doesn't really matter. He definitely doesn't welcome Elijah but instead accuses him.

This shouldn't surprise the Bible reader. Prophets are persecuted. Jesus said in the final beatitude,

> You are blessed when they insult and persecute you and falsely say every kind of evil against you because of Me. Be glad and rejoice, because your reward is great in heaven. For that is how they persecuted the prophets who were before you. (Matt 5:11-12)

Paul was accused of stirring up riots (Acts 24:5). James encouraged his suffering believers by saying, "Brothers, take the prophets who spoke in the Lord's name as an example of suffering and patience" (Jas 5:10). So don't be surprised if the world hates you, for they hated the true and better prophet, Jesus, as well (John 15:18-20; cf. Luke 23:3,5). We don't live for the applause of people but for the glory of God, and such allegiance to King Jesus will bring accusations from men of earth.

Elijah retorts by telling Ahab, "I have not destroyed Israel, but you and your father's house have, because you have abandoned the LORD's commands and followed the Baals" (18:18). The prophet is clear as to why Ahab is the real troubler. He points out Ahab's sin. Ahab has committed sins of omission and sins of commission (Ryken, *1 Kings*, 477). Did you catch them? Sins of omission: "abandoning the commands"; and sins of commission: "followed the Baals." He reminds Ahab that it isn't just Israel that has sinned, but "you have." Yahweh, not Baal, must be feared. And nothing here indicates that Ahab has any true fear of God. He apparently cares for his horses because he trusts in his ability through them to protect and provide more than he trusts in Yahweh (cf. Pss 20:7; 33:17).

Next, Elijah proposes the showdown. He says, "Now summon all Israel to meet me at Mount Carmel, along with the 450 prophets of Baal and the 400 prophets of Asherah who eat at Jezebel's table" (v. 19). Elijah wants to settle the question of who is God. He offers to meet these prophets at Mount Carmel, if they could get up from Jezebel's dinner table. Mount Carmel is a mountain range of limestone and flint, containing many caves, off the Mediterranean coast, which at its highest point is 525 meters (1,724 feet). It sits near modern-day Haifa. It's a beautiful place to visit today. Davis tells us of its mention in historical documents. In Egyptian records it was called "Holy Head," suggesting it was a sanctuary. An Assyrian king dubbed it "the mountain of Baal of the promontory." In our day we might call it "Baal's Bluff" (Davis, *1 Kings*, 234). Therefore, this site is the selected battleground, not because it was just a great place to watch a fight but because it was a location of Baal worship. Olley summarizes,

> Its location is favorable to the worship of Baal and Asherah with lush vegetation due to the headland encouraging rainfall. It was also the site of a broken down altar of the Lord (30). (*Message of Kings*, 172)

Yahweh's altar had been pulled down, and Baal was celebrated there in His place.

It was a good place to decide who should be worshiped. Elijah was going to be playing a "road game" since Baal worship was being practiced there. Elijah offered to meet the prophets on their turf. In so doing he wanted there to be no doubt who the real God was. He was not going to be accused of rigging the contest by having people meet on his turf. In the other corner Ahab surely liked the odds. He had 850 prophets playing at home. Those who follow sports know the home team always has the upper hand. I just watched game seven of the 2014 NBA playoffs between the Heat and the Pacers. Since the game was at Miami, the odds were with them. They have great home-court fans, and they showed up with excitement, rallying the Heat to an impressive victory. How would Elijah, the roughneck prophet, do against an army of prophets at their place?

Elijah and the People: The Purpose of the Showdown
1 KINGS 18:20-25

The meeting at Mount Carmel wasn't a circus. The purpose wasn't to entertain but to demand a choice between Yahweh and Baal. Elijah's desire is expressed later in his prayer: "So that this people will know that You, Yahweh, are God" (v. 37). Before we read of this prayer, we see him explaining this purpose in verses 21-24.

Ahab summons all the people to Mount Carmel, where Elijah meets everyone. We can only imagine the scene, but I can picture the rugged Elijah standing there, atop the limestone mountain overlooking the sparkling Mediterranean Sea, with his beard and robe waving in the wind. Israel was there in attendance as well, filled with anticipation and curiosity. There were 450 prophets of Baal and 400 prophets of Asherah, arrayed in their cultic attire, ready to perform their rituals, salivating at the opportunity to defeat Elijah. Ahab surely rolled up to the scene in style, with an entourage in their chariots, arriving to take their special seats.

Elijah addresses the people atop the mount, saying, "How long will you hesitate between two opinions? If Yahweh is God, follow Him. But if Baal, follow him" (v. 21). Elijah's message is plain and simple. You cannot worship Yahweh and Baal or Yahweh and Asherah. This isn't an academic matter detached from real life. He basically says, "Theology leads to discipleship. Commitments have consequences" (Davis, *1 Kings*, 233). He calls the people actually to follow God, not merely assent to an idea or discuss a topic.

Elijah throws down the gauntlet like Moses, who had passionately addressed the golden-calf-worshiping Israelites: "Whoever is for the LORD, come to me" (Exod 32:26); and like Joshua, who had said, "Get rid of the gods your fathers worshiped beyond the Euphrates River and in Egypt, and worship Yahweh. . . . choose for yourselves today the one you will worship" (Josh 24:14-15). Elijah tells them to get off the fence. Jesus said something similar: "No one can be a slave of two masters" (Matt 6:24). If you are still on the fence, you are saying you aren't following Him. Jesus said that if we aren't for Him, then we are against Him (Matt 12:30).

"But the people didn't answer him a word" (v. 21). Not a word! Why? Was it because they were shocked by his message? Surely not. Surely they had heard that Elijah only worshiped Yahweh and rejected all idols. Why silence? Silence is the easiest way to be noncommittal. When I confront my kids over an issue, their default response is stone-faced silence. They try to find a neutral zone. The Israelites couldn't respond because they weren't committed to Yahweh alone. They knew of Yahweh and the Red Sea and the law, but their functional trust had been in Baal, the storm god. Elijah urges them to make a decision. A real decision to follow the living God will lead to people boldly confessing their faith in Him.

In many ways the multitude reflects the postmodern times in which we live. For example, *uncertainty* is held up as a virtue. One of my unbelieving neighbors recently told a seminary student friend of mine, "My job is to try to get people to question everything." I heard of one schoolteacher who said her agenda is to "lead the students into the wonders of uncertainty." However, the faith of God's people is expressed in confidence. The psalmist says, "The LORD is my rock, my fortress, and my deliverer, my God, my mountain where I seek refuge" (18:2). That doesn't sound like uncertainty. There is only one rock, only one God, who alone provides security and comfort.

Others in our culture want to worship on a Sunday, but when it comes to business, politics, or international conflict, they're tempted to defer to conventional wisdom and what's in keeping with the times. Some believe economics and God, or politics and God, should remain separate. Elijah challenged his generation who believed the same thing. They acknowledged Yahweh but believed following Baal was a more practical way for farmers and merchants to live. However, if God is God, then we must submit to Him and surrender every area of our lives to His lordship.

Israel was "hesitating" or "limping" or "wavering" between Baal and Yahweh (v. 21). Ryken says they were like Little League baseball players, who "step in the bucket" when they're afraid of the ball (*1 Kings*, 483). I see this vividly as a coach for the "Coaches Pitch League." A lot of my kids bail out. They have one foot going to the dugout while part of their body tries to stay in the batter's box to hit the ball. Bucket steppers waver between two opinions just like the people in verse 21. They partially want to serve Yahweh, but they also want to embrace false gods. Elijah, however, will not allow it because Elijah's God is the exclusive God who will not share His glory with another.

Elijah breaks the silence in verses 22-24, explaining the rules of the contest and basically giving every advantage to the home team. He reminded everyone that he was greatly outnumbered. He then displayed good sportsmanship by letting the prophets of Baal choose first. They got first pick of the bulls to put on the wood for the sacrifice. Not only does he let them choose first, but Elijah also lets the prophets of Baal go first. He says, "Then you call on the name of your god, and I will call on the name of Yahweh. The God who answers with fire, He is God" (v. 24).

Further, the entire contest played into Baal's strength. Baal was supposedly the god of the sun, so fire should be no problem. He was also the god of the storm, pictured in ancient paintings with a thunderbolt as his arrow (cf. 2 Sam 22:15; Pss 18:14; 77:17; 144:6; Hab 3:11). Surely he can burn up some wood and a bull on top of the hill. The people finally speak: "That sounds good" (v. 24). "Bring it on," they say. "We like this."

Thus, the contest was really about *whose God could answer prayer.* The God who answered was the real God. That was the purpose of the showdown. Though the story is spectacular and miraculous, the application is common and simple. The God of the Bible hears and answers prayer. We have a relationship with a God, by grace through faith in Christ, who invites us to call on Him and promises to answer. While demonic powers are present and people may *feel something* in a false cult or religion, it doesn't mean their god *hears prayer* like our God. No, the test is the same. The only God who answers prayer is the God of the Bible, and He is the true and living God.

Elijah and the Prophets: The Prayer-Answering Champion of the Showdown

1 KINGS 18:26-40

Who is the real God: Baal or Yahweh? The people are about to find out. The prophets of Baal go first, no doubt in dramatic attire and with cultic liturgical practices. There is a stark contrast between how they try to call on Baal and how Elijah calls on Yahweh. We will look at three parts of the prophets' attempt to get "the storm god" to throw a lightning bolt their way to burn up their bull. Then we will see how Elijah approaches God. The story as a whole shows us the emptiness of false religion and the power of the living God.

The Emptiness of False Religion (vv. 26-29)

First, they called on Baal, but no one answered. They cried out, but the writer emphasizes the emptiness of their petition. He says, "There was no sound; no one answered" (v. 26). He says it again emphatically in verse 29: "There was no sound; no one answered, no one paid attention." The lack of response from Baal illustrates the truth of the psalmist's statement:

> *The idols of the nations are of silver and gold,*
> *   made by human hands.*
> *They have mouths but cannot speak,*
> *   eyes, but cannot see.*
> *They have ears but cannot hear;*
> *   indeed, there is no breath in their mouths.* (Ps 135:15-17)

It reminds me of the cell phone commercial, "Can you hear me now?" In this case they never had a connection in the first place. Baal was not on the line because he doesn't exist! They were like kids playing with a banana pretending it's a phone. Folly.

Not only did they call on Baal to no avail, but also they cried out from "morning until noon" (v. 26). Let us be reminded that a long worship service doesn't necessarily imply a powerful worship service. These prophets went on for hours but were wasting their breath and their time. The same is true for prayer. A long prayer doesn't mean a better prayer, especially if you are praying to the wrong god! You can pray nine times a day facing any direction you want, be dressed with religious garb, and have incense and candles and more, but if you aren't praying to the God of Elijah, you are engaging in spiritual futility.

Second, they danced, but they were only burning calories. The writer says, "They danced, hobbling around the altar they had made" (v. 26). While dancing and celebration are fitting in response to the grace of Jesus, the type of cultic ritual going on here is once again empty. Leaping around this altar may have provided an entertaining show, but it accomplished nothing spiritually.

Elijah responds to their lengthy prayers and ritual dances with some holy sarcasm. He mocks them in order to draw attention to the folly of following Baal. He wants everyone to know that Yahweh has no rivals. So he says, "Shout loudly, for he's a god! Maybe he's thinking it over; maybe he has wandered away; or maybe he's on the road. Perhaps he's sleeping and will wake up!" (v. 27). In pagan mythology gods actually performed many human activities, so Elijah uses such silliness to show the vanity of their religion. He says, maybe your "god" had to wander to the restroom! Maybe he went on a journey. Elijah was actually referring to common beliefs. Some believed Baal made journeys, went to sleep, and performed other human activities, including dying. One ancient document says his sister could not find him one day because he had gone hunting (Davis, *1 Kings*, 236)! The prophetic sarcasm is meant to expose the uselessness of Baal worship.

Elijah's sarcasm draws attention to the opposite of these remarks. Yahweh "is God." Yahweh never sleeps (Ps 121:3-4). He needs no air or food, and He is never "away." God's people can always reach their Father. Elijah exposes Baal's impotence by allowing them to go first and attempt to get an answer from Baal. Soon, Elijah will display the omnipotence of Yahweh.

Third, they cut themselves and raved, but their frenzy produced no fire. The prophets "cut themselves with knives and spears, according to their custom, until blood gushed over them" (v. 28). Then he adds, "They kept on raving until the offering of the evening sacrifice" (v. 29). House states, "Baalists cut themselves and practice frenzied prophesying, not unlike self-hypnosis" (*1, 2 Kings*, 220).

Here's an illustration of some common activities in false religions. Some religions engage in activities that bring bodily harm. They may slap themselves with whips while walking through the streets, cut their flesh during a ritual, or abstain from certain pleasures, adopting an ascetic lifestyle. All of these actions are intended to get their god's attention and rid themselves of guilt and shame. It was useless for these worshipers, and it's still useless. Masochism has no place in Christian worship.

While many Americans are more civil than this, the thought is present. People still try to perform religious activities to merit God's approval and blessing. They want to do something to absolve the guilt. Praise God, we don't have to cut ourselves, beat ourselves, or deny ourselves food and drink and marriage in order to get God's attention. Blood has already been spilled: Jesus' blood. His blood and His activity alone allow us to come into God's presence. By His work, not our work, we're able to commune with God and be free from condemnation. That news should make you dance and sing and pray!

Regarding "raving," the Baalists remind us that we don't need to "check our brains at the door" in worship. While emotion definitely is important in worship, mindless emotionalism isn't part of true Christian worship. We bring our minds with us when we become Christians. True worship involves mind and heart, "light and heat." We must respond to God's revealed truth in worship. We must be earnest, but we don't need to be frantic, and we must not substitute actions for spiritual life.

Clearly in these four short verses we see the emptiness of false religion. In contrast to this emptiness, in the verses that follow we will see the power of the living God.

The Power of the Living God (vv. 30-46)

In this section we find Elijah, "a man like us," teaching us about our "prayer-answering God."

Elijah's preparation (vv. 30-35). Now it's Elijah's turn. He calls all the people to him. He then repairs the altar, which actually signified Israel's spiritual condition (vv. 30-32). He built the altar properly (cf. Exod

20:25; Lev 1:6-8) with 12 stones. He was reminding them of the faith of their fathers and saying he isn't proposing something new. Elijah was calling them to return in repentance to the covenant God. He then prepared the altar with the wood and the bull.

Then Elijah shocks everyone. Three times he has them pour four jars of water on the offering and on the wood. It was enough water that it "ran all around the altar; he even filled the trench with water" (v. 35). Elijah wants everyone to know for sure that what is about to happen can only be explained by the power of God. He wants them to know that this handicap is no problem to the living God.

Elijah's petition (vv. 36-37). Elijah prays that God would burn the wet wood and the sacrifice. In contrast to the lengthy prayers of Baal's prophets, consider how short Elijah's prayer is! Take out your watch, and time it. Ready? Here it is:

> *Yahweh, God of Abraham, Isaac, and Israel, today let it be known that*
> *You are God in Israel and I am Your servant, and that at Your word*
> *I have done all these things. Answer me, Lord! Answer me so that this*
> *people will know that You, Yahweh, are God and that You have turned*
> *their hearts back.*

It takes less than 30 seconds! The prophets of Baal had ranted and raved from morning to noon. Here is another lesson from the "mighty master of the art of prayer." Prayer isn't about the length, volume, or eloquence. It's about praying to the right God with sincerity.

Later the greater Prophet-Mediator, Jesus, teaches us the same truth about prayer:

> *When you pray, don't babble like the idolaters, since they imagine*
> *they'll be heard for their many words. Don't be like them, because your*
> *Father knows the things you need before you ask Him.* (Matt 6:7-8)

Jesus goes on to describe in the model prayer how one might pray God-centered, comprehensive prayers to the Father.

The differences in Elijah's prayer and those of the false prophets are obvious. "Baal's boys" had home-field advantage, but that didn't matter, for God isn't bound to a place. They prayed longer prayers, but that was of no consequence either. God responded instead to a 30-second, heartfelt prayer. They "worked themselves into a feverish pitch in a cacophony of noise and a trail of blood" (House, *1, 2 Kings*, 237), but God was not impressed by this bedlam. You cannot manipulate God with gimmicks.

He was drawn instead to the humble, heartfelt prayer of Elijah. Don't buy into the practices of Baal's boys. Believe that God really does hear the prayers of His children when they pray in sincere faith.

Let me summarize some application points from Elijah's prayer. First, **have a relationship with the living God**. Elijah prays to the God of the covenant, the God of Abraham, Isaac, and Israel/Jacob. God had a relationship with these individuals. He called Abraham "God's friend" (Jas 2:23). We can call on God and even call him "Father" (Mark 14:36) if we know Him by grace through faith in Christ. If you have a relationship with the Father, you can be sure He hears you.

Second, **seek the Glory of God**. Elijah's prayer is blatantly God centered. He wants people to recognize the glory of God. Pray like this! Jesus taught us this type of praying in the model prayer, saying, "Our Father in heaven, Your name be honored as holy. Your kingdom come. Your will be done on earth as it is in heaven" (Matt 6:9-10). Before He taught us to pray for things like bread, holiness, and forgiveness, He taught us to long for God's name to be glorified and God's kingdom to cover the earth. Are you praying for God's glory to be made known?

Third, **pray for rebels to turn to God**. Elijah prayed that God would turn the people's hearts back to the living God. He prayed that they would know truth (that "I am Your servant, and that at Your word I have done all these things," v. 36), and respond to it with repentance and faith. Are you praying for conversions? C. S. Lewis said,

> I have two lists of names in my prayers, those for whose conversions I pray and those for whose conversions I give thanks. The little trickle of transferences from List A to List B is a great comfort. (*Collected Letters*, 2:948, quoted in Ryken, *1 Kings* 513)

Let us pray for God to turn idol worshipers into Christ worshipers (1 Thess 1:9-10).

Elijah's brief, God-centered prayer stands in great contrast to the empty prayers of Baal's boys. Let us follow Elijah's example.

God's power and grace (vv. 38-40). In verse 38 we read of how God answered Elijah's prayer: "Then Yahweh's fire fell and consumed the burnt offering, the wood, the stones, and the dust, and it licked up the water that was in the trench" (v. 38). The fire fell. Despite the soggy wood, God consumed everything. It was no problem for the God who is "a consuming fire" (Deut 4:24; Heb 12:29). God can light wet wood!

Previously in Israel's history, God sent fire at the inauguration of the tabernacle worship (Lev 9:24). It signified Yahweh's acceptance of the sacrificial system. Later, David sacrificed as ordered by God at Ornan's threshing floor, and Yahweh answered with fire, signifying His acceptance of the offering (1 Chr 21:26). David then said that this particular spot would be the place for the future temple (1 Chr 22:1). Finally, when Solomon completed and dedicated the temple, fire again fell, showing God's acceptance of their worship.

Here in our story, the fire from heaven is a sure sign that God accepted Elijah's sacrifice. God proved to everyone that He alone answers prayer, and He must be approached in a particular way. Yahweh provided a way for the people to approach Him, but the people abandoned "the old rugged altar" (Davis, *1 Kings*, 240). Therefore, this story shows us not only *God's power* in answering prayer but also *God's grace* for inviting us to approach Him through blood. Praise God, today we get to approach Him through a better means, through the "old rugged cross," by the perfect sacrifice of the spotless Lamb of God, Jesus Christ. God reconciles sinful rebels to Himself, forgives their sin, and invites them to call on Him by the blood of Jesus. Let's never stop thanking God for the cross.

In verse 39 we read of the proper response to God's power and grace: "When all the people saw it, they fell facedown and said, 'Yahweh, He is God! Yahweh, He is God!'" True worship isn't about doing religious aerobics and slicing an artery; it looks more like this: prostration. The people bow before this awesome God, confessing their belief in Him. To be clear, many postures are appropriate for worship, but this is certainly an appropriate posture for those in awe of God.

Those who limp between two opinions never fall on their knees in humble adoration of Yahweh. Uncertainty will never lead you to deep intimacy. Divided affections will never lead you into devoted worship to God. Who is God? If Yahweh is God, then worship Him.

Based on the next action, it seems that Israel finally decided they would follow Yahweh. Their action seems severe to some readers. Then Elijah ordered them,

> *"Seize the prophets of Baal! Do not let even one of them escape."* So they seized them, and Elijah brought them down to the Wadi Kishon and slaughtered them there. (v. 40)

Some think Elijah acted wrongly here. Was this an act of vicious revenge? No. The reason we don't understand it is because we forget that Israel was a theocracy. Elijah was calling the people to act in accordance with Deuteronomy 13:12-15. God said that if someone led Israel into idolatry, then that person should be put to death with the sword. Don't forget how seriously God took idolatry. It was the great danger to Israel. God was preserving Israel, through whom God would ultimately bring forth the Messiah. When you understand this, then you can see how this judgment on the false prophets was actually an act of God's love for the world that shows us both the severity and grace of God. Because God wouldn't allow idolatry to persist, Messiah came, and we who are believers will be raised from the dead.

The church today is not a theocracy, and God doesn't call us to kill others who worship false gods. Instead, we are called to put to death idolatry in our own hearts. Don't waver between two opinions! "Put to death the deeds of the body," Paul says (Rom 8:13). Don't allow functional saviors to rule your heart—money, success, pleasure, peer approval, beauty, politics, control, or sex. These counterfeit gods cannot satisfy your heart, and they cannot answer prayer. Let your heart say, "Yahweh, He is God!" in humble, heartfelt adoration, and live your life out of the overflow of that confession.

True and vibrant worship is possible because there was another showdown on another hillside. Jesus Christ crushed the enemies—Satan, sin, and death—through His cross and resurrection. He was the ultimate Prophet, Mediator, and Victor, showing us once and for all who the real God is. We marvel at Elijah and learn from his prayer and faith, but we realize that what save us and sustain us are the power and grace of Jesus. One greater than Elijah has come.

God's provision and grace (vv. 41-46). Following the fire, God graciously provides the rain. Elijah tells Ahab, "Go up, eat and drink, for there is the sound of a rainstorm." This command to go up and eat is probably an exhortation to celebrate the passing of the drought. Elijah confidently expects the rain to fall. Then Ahab actually does something positive when he listens to Elijah and "went to eat and drink."

Prior to reading of the ensuing rain, we find Elijah praying again. He gets alone on the mountain and bows down. What was Elijah doing on his knees? The posture suggests intense prayer. Remember when James said Elijah prayed that first it would not rain, and then he prayed that it would rain (Jas 5:17-18). Here we seem to find the second part of that verse: Elijah praying for God to end the drought with rain. We're reminded that Elijah wasn't a superhero or a magician; he was a helpless man like us, who desperately sought the living God.

Elijah prayed in line with the living God's promises, for God promised to send rain on the earth (see the specific promise in 18:1 and a general promise in 8:35-36). Elijah realized that God's promises are invitations to prayer (see the previous section). Elijah could hear the rain: "Elijah said to Ahab, 'Go up, eat and drink, for there is the sound of a rainstorm'" (v. 41), but he didn't stop praying until the promise was fulfilled.

God still works through the prayers of His people. And He invites us to pray according to His Word, for He delights to answer such prayers (John 15:7). However, God doesn't always act immediately when we pray. Elijah's prayer for fire was answered immediately, but his prayer for rain required persistent prayer. Elijah told his servant to go look for the rain seven times, until a cloud was visible. Then the heavens grew black, and a "downpour" came on the earth. Ahab went down to Jezreel as Elijah had ordered, which seemed like a step in the right direction for this wicked king.

God sends the fire, bringing people to faith in Him, and now God sends the rain, providing food and drink. God alone stands as Creator and Redeemer. Stop and thank Him for His amazing provisions of grace.

Verse 46 reminds us of the secret to Elijah's ministry: "The power of the LORD was on Elijah." This phrase also describes God's rescuing Israel from the clutches of Egypt (Deut 4:34; 5:15; Ps 136:12) and Ezekiel's being transported from place to place (Ezek 3:22; 33:22; 37:1). While recognizing that there are differences between us and these prophets, my heart still longs for God's hand on my life. We need His grace and favor as we labor!

Elijah was a man of great passion, power, and faith-filled prayer, but verse 46 also illustrates his humility. Elijah "tucked his mantle under his belt and ran ahead of Ahab to the entrance of Jezreel." What should we make of this verse? It seems strange to the modern reader, though we find it interesting that Elijah was the Vince Coleman of the prophets (super fast)! He runs some 17 miles to Jezreel out in front of Ahab's chariot. Why? Ralph Davis puts it this way:

> We should consider Elijah and Ahab here primarily in terms of their respective offices, i.e., as prophet and king. . . . The fact that Elijah runs before Ahab suggests that Yahweh's prophet

may be a servant rather than an opponent to the king. The
kings and the prophet could work together in ongoing
reform. . . . The king could have the prophet as his willing
servant instead of his glowering adversary. (*1 Kings*, 250)

Ryken agrees, saying that Elijah ran ahead of the king to "identify himself as one of Ahab's servants . . . one of the king's footmen, or heralds" (*1 Kings*, 518). Such a practice was common. Near Eastern kings
had heralds go before them to announce their approach (Esth 6:11;
2 Sam 15:1; 1 Kgs 1:5). Elijah's joining of the royal escort demonstrates
remarkable humility. He submitted to the authority of the king by going
before him.

But such an act of humility on Elijah's part was also an invitation to
king Ahab. Would Ahab submit to God's word? Would he repent and
lead the nation back to repentance? It seems Elijah thought the king
and the people were turning their hearts back (v. 37), but his hopes were
soon crushed (see ch. 19). Nevertheless, one stands amazed at God's
grace to Ahab. God still hasn't destroyed him but has instead given him
a gospel opportunity. Davis says, "Ahab has an offer of grace in his hand,
but his feet will soon stand in the devil's bedroom" (*1 Kings*, 252).

A Mighty Master of the Art of Prayer

Before concluding, let's collect some application from this prayer warrior, Elijah. We have already noted some from his "fire prayer." We need
to (1) have a relationship with the living God, (2) seek the glory of God,
and (3) pray for rebels to turn to God. Now, in verses 41-46, we may add
the need to (4) get alone with God, (5) pray with the promises of God,
and (6) keep on asking to receive from God.

Elijah gets alone on Mount Carmel with no one except his servant.
When he prayed for the fire to fall, he prayed in the presence of many
others, but here Elijah illustrates for us Jesus' words: "When you pray,
go into your private room, shut your door, and pray to your Father who
is in secret. And your Father who sees in secret will reward you" (Matt
6:6). Do you have a place where you can get alone with the Father and
cry out to him?

His specific prayer for rain once again is tied to the promise of God.
Fill your prayers with Scripture as you ask God to meet specific needs.

Finally, he persists in prayer until the rain falls, reminding us of
Jesus' words, "Keep asking" (Matt 7:7-10). Pray persistently! Paul says to

pray constantly (1 Thess 5:17). Don't stop praying for your lost friend or family member. Don't stop praying for the fire of revival to fall on your city. Don't stop praying for God to grant you wisdom, boldness, and faith. Sometimes God answers immediately, but often we must persist in prayer until we see the clouds forming.

How this chapter should encourage our souls! God answers prayer! We see the living God responding to the prayers of His people throughout the Bible until the very end. In Revelation we see a final example of this "promise-prayer" dynamic. Jesus makes this promise: "Yes, *I am coming quickly.*" And then John writes the following prayer based on that promise: "Amen! *Come, Lord Jesus!*" (Rev 22:20; emphasis added).

John then concludes with a final note, "The grace of the Lord Jesus be with all the saints. Amen" (Rev 22:21). Yes! May the One greater than Elijah come quickly, and may He give us grace to live faithfully until we see this promise fulfilled.

Reflect and Discuss

1. Obadiah protected God's prophets during times of persecution. How might God's people protect one another today?
2. How can God's people honor those who preach God's Word?
3. How do people today despise those who preach God's Word?
4. What are some of the Baals of your culture?
5. Elijah admonishes the people to choose between Baal and Yahweh and then "follow Him." What can this logic teach us about discipleship?
6. In what ways is Elijah bold before the prophets of Baal?
7. Why did Elijah command so much water to be poured on the altar?
8. In what ways are you tempted to doubt God's faithfulness in your life?
9. Does God answer prayers today like He did Elijah's prayers?
10. Is it significant that God defeated the "storm god," then sent rain immediately afterward? Why or why not?

God's Grace for a Depressed Servant

1 KINGS 19:1-21

Main Idea: Following the events at Mount Carmel, Elijah gets extremely discouraged, but God graciously renews His servant.

I. **Elijah's Spiritual Depression (19:1-4)**
   A. The course
   B. The causes
II. **God's Gracious Response (19:5-21)**
   A. Bread in the wilderness (vv. 5-8)
   B. A voice on the mountain (vv. 9-13a)
   C. A vision for the future (vv. 13b-21)

'm going to Disney World!" Phil Simms, the quarterback of the Super Bowl champions, the New York Giants, first uttered this advertising phrase in 1987. Other famous athletes (and some winners of nonsporting events) have appeared on commercials echoing Simms. The phrase is so popular that you can hear Little League coaches jokingly say after a win, "We're going to Disney World!" Champions normally celebrate but normally not at Disney World, which makes this expression funny and memorable. We're used to seeing champagne poured on heads in the locker room, parades in the city, and much more.

Elijah just won the "Super Bowl" at Carmel. He would make a great candidate for a Disney World commercial! But we don't see him going to Disney World, having a parade, or riding off into the sunset in triumph.

Chapter 19 doesn't begin the way we expect at all. We expect to see Israel turning their hearts back to God (18:37). After all, in response to God's burning up the soggy altar, they fell on their faces and confessed, "Yahweh, He is God! Yahweh, He is God!" (18:39). But do we see national revival? Nope. We hope to find wicked King Ahab returning to the palace to remove Jezebel for her idolatrous influence in the land. After all, we left him in chapter 18 obeying Elijah's word (vv. 42,45). But is that what Ahab does? No, he doesn't. His repentance was false, and his spine was like a jellyfish. He runs back and tattles on Elijah to the Baal-promoting Phoenician queen. We wonder if Jezebel will surrender her false theology and repent. Instead, she seeks to put Elijah to death. We at least expect to find "Mr. My God is Yahweh" standing tall in the midst of this rebellion. After all, "the power of the LORD was on Elijah" (18:46). But is that what happens? No, it doesn't. We find our brother Elijah depressed, throwing a pity party, running from Jezebel, and asking God to take his life.

We have read of Elijah's mountaintop experience at Mount Carmel, but now we see Elijah down in the valley under a broom tree. He previously ministered to others but now is focused on himself. Elijah confronted Ahab and the false prophets courageously, but here we find him running like a coward from a lady. Previously, Elijah moved at God's word, but now we see him fleeing apart from God's word. In the previous chapters we see him praying for rain and fire, but now we find him praying for God to take his life.

Elijah's faith and prayer life have challenged us, but now Elijah's spiritual collapse serves as a warning and provides wise counsel.

Elijah was a man like us (Jas 5:17), which means he experienced the same temptations and struggles we face, including spiritual discouragement and despair. I have struggled with what to call his condition here. Alistair Begg's exposition is called "Down in the Valley," Charles Spurgeon titled his exposition "Faintness and Refreshing," Sinclair Ferguson's exposition is titled "Experiencing Spiritual Depression," and Steve Brown also called this condition "Spiritual Depression" (each sermon found online). Paul House calls Elijah a "prophet drained of strength" in a "pit of fear and depression" (*1, 2 Kings*, 224). Faucett and Brown call this "an extraordinary depression of mind" (*Commentary Critical and Explanatory*, Logos Software). Provan says Elijah is a man who "has had enough" (*1 and 2 Kings*, 144). Hughes and Laney call it "discouragement and deep despair" (*Tyndale*, 136). Phil Ryken says Elijah "has descended into the blackness of spiritual despair" (*1 Kings*, 516). Bimson says, "In the depths of depression and despair, he prayed that he might die" ("1 and 2 Kings," 360). "Spiritual depression" seems to be a good description of Elijah's condition.

My hero, Spurgeon, knew of spiritual depression. In his classic book, *Lectures to My Students*, he has a chapter titled "The Minister's Fainting Fits," in which he addresses this matter:

> Fits of depression come over the most of us. Usually cheerful
> as we may be, we must at intervals be cast down. The strong

aren't always so vigorous, the wise not always ready, the brave
not always courageous, and the joyous not always happy. I
know by most painful experience what deep depression in
spirit means. (*Lectures*, 154)

Others in church history have suffered periods of discouragement and
despair. D. Martyn Lloyd-Jones, Martin Luther, William Cowper, Mother
Theresa, Henry Nouwen, Martin Luther King Jr., and many others experienced what some call "The Dark Night of the Soul."

After Hurricane Katrina, I myself suffered, trying to deal with my
despair with four scoops of Moose Tracks ice cream every night! Of
course, many pastors feel despair every Monday! That's why many counsel pastors to mow their yard or steam clean their carpet on Monday, for
at least they will have some sense of accomplishment after feeling like a
failure from the previous day.

I heard Mark Driscoll use the phrase "Bread Truck Mondays" to
describe the Monday blues. He reported that sometimes he dreams
on Mondays about what he could do other than pastor, like driving a
bread truck. He said he imagines the bliss of only being responsible for
bread, not people. Bread doesn't commit adultery, lie, have unpredict-
able giving patterns, or gossip. Driscoll liked the idea of driving around
listening to sports talk radio instead of enduring the mental strain that
goes along with pastoring. I've never forgotten that illustration because
I have had my own Bread Truck Mondays.

So we can understand a person's struggle in this area. We shouldn't
be surprised by spiritual depression, but we shouldn't want to remain
there either. Why? Lloyd-Jones says, "It is very sad that anyone should
remain in such a condition . . . and such people are very poor representatives of the Christian faith" (*Spiritual Depression*, 23). Yes! We need
to learn from Elijah's struggle so we may avoid it or at least not become
mired in it. And we need to consider this subject so that we may present
the gospel in a way that is compelling and makes Jesus look glorious. It's
hard to communicate this way when we are downcast. It's like we are saying, "My life stinks. Do you want to be a Christian too?" We believe that
a fruit of the Spirit is joy! When you read Acts, you find a happy group
of witnesses. Their joy was attractive and contagious.

Before moving on, let me qualify the matter. I don't mean that
we should go around smiling all the time. There are many psalms of
lament in the Bible. Not all brokenness is negative; indeed, it's often

appropriate. We should grieve over our lost neighbors, injustice, poverty, and other effects of this fallen world. Further, sometimes being down is a natural, physical experience. Spurgeon said,

> Certain bodily maladies, especially those with the digestive
> organs, the liver, and the spleen, are the fruitful fountains of
> despondency. . . . As to mental maladies, is any man altogether
> sane? Are we not all a little off balance? (*Lectures*, 155)

Indeed we are! Sometimes the reason many pastors are down on Monday is simply a matter of adrenaline depletion. You only have so much, and you must rest and be restored. You cannot keep stretching the rubber band, using adrenaline when you don't need it, never taking a break. Eventually the rubber band will break. You will inevitably pay for not resting.

However, sometimes we're down for no good reason, and we must look away from ourselves to the finished work of Jesus in order to be free from this downcast demeanor and to commend the gospel to others. Derek Thomas puts it this way:

> There are various kinds of depression, to be sure, and some
> are the result of complex physical and psychological disorders.
> But there are times when we are spiritually depressed for no
> good reason. There are times when the best thing to do with
> our feelings is to challenge them: "Why are you cast down,
> O my soul, and why are you in turmoil within me? Hope in
> God; for I shall again praise Him, my salvation and my God"
> (Ps 42:11). ("A Light in Dark Places")

This passage reveals some of the causes of Elijah's spiritual depression and how God tenderly responded to him. My goal isn't to address all of the complicated matters related to depression but instead to attempt to talk about the spiritual dynamics associated with it (recognizing that we are complex creatures, with the physical and spiritual always affecting each other). Olley summarizes the overarching application well:

> Depression has been known for years; "burn-out" is a
> recently named phenomenon. The narrative is brief, but
> it provides encouragement to people experiencing such,
> and is an example of God's compassionate, understanding
> response. Throughout, Yahweh meets Elijah's depression and

resignation with gentle and patient understanding and quiet revelation, and an expression of trust in giving a task that is new. (*Message*, 181)

Let us find encouragement from this chapter by considering it under two headings: Elijah's spiritual depression and God's restoring grace.

Elijah's Spiritual Depression
1 KINGS 19:1-4

Before we note the causes of Elijah's despair, consider its course, that is, what actually happened in the story. We can trace the course in five sections.

The Course

Elijah lost perspective. He lost sight of the fact that a short-term victory doesn't mean the war is over. He had been triumphant at Carmel, but he would be engaged in a battle until his life was over. He had a relentless foe in Jezebel. She was not just a lady with an attitude. She had tremendous resources at her disposal, and she was angry at the defeat. When this Baal-promoting queen saw the rain, she was probably ready to attribute that to her "storm god." However, Ahab comes back to relay the news and tells her that not only did Yahweh send the rain but also Elijah slew Baal's prophets (17:1). A poor loser can be vicious. Jezebel is determined to take out Elijah.

For the believer the battle never ends. Yesterday's victory doesn't ensure today's success. Every day we must rely on God's power to overcome our challenges. Without God's strength Elijah was a weak man. In the words of Jesus, "You can do nothing without Me" (John 15:5). We must take the long view on the Christian life. Until you see Jesus, you are engaged in a war.

Elijah lost his commitment to follow God's word. Elijah didn't allow God's word to direct his path. After Jezebel's threat, "Elijah became afraid and immediately ran for his life. When he came to Beer-sheba that belonged to Judah, he left his servant there" (v. 3). In chapters 17–18, "the word of the LORD came to Elijah," and "he went" (17:2,5,8,10; 18:1-2). But now there is no word from the Lord, and Elijah seemingly departs on his own. The "word of the LORD" doesn't appear again until verse 9. Elijah seems to put God's word behind his back and lives as his own master. He has lost his spiritual bearings and drifted from his routine of depending on God's word to determine his steps. He is AWOL.

We will face the same temptation. Will we order our lives by God's authority, or will we do what we want, when we want, how we want? When we get away from the simple discipline of regularly reading and applying God's Word, we will drift into ungodliness and spiritual darkness. If you aren't in God's Word, the question isn't whether you will drift away from God's will, but when, and how far will you wander?

Elijah lost his vision of the greatness of God. Elijah "became afraid" (v. 3). The word can be translated "saw." He saw and ran for his life. How could the mighty Elijah be afraid? He was gripped by fear because he took his eyes off the greatness of God. We previously read of how Elijah stood before Ahab declaring, "As the LORD God of Israel lives" (17:1). But here he drops his elevated concept of God and panics.

Some argue that he didn't leave out of fear of his own life but as a purposeful withdrawal as a judgment on Israel and as an intentional journey to the mountain where Yahweh first made the covenant with Israel. I find this hard to believe. I see a more human, frail picture of Elijah running for his life. House says, "For whatever reason—fatigue, lack of faith, or a sense of resignation at the prospect of never having peace—Elijah flees" (*1, 2 Kings*, 222). I think all three conditions probably contributed to Elijah's flight, but the purpose was not to allow judgment to fall on Israel. His fleeing in chapter 17 appears to be a different experience from that here in chapter 19. The first was positive, but this one is negative. I agree with Provan who writes that Elijah runs "as far away from Jezebel as he can get." He adds, "The journey south was certainly not on God's agenda" (*1 and 2 Kings*, 144).

We must maintain a high view of God as we journey through the challenges of this life. Even the best of saints, like Elijah, can lose sight of who He is and what He can do.

He lost his fight. This results from his losing perspective, bearings, and vision. He fled. But notice where he flees. He goes all the way to Beer-sheba! As you read through the Old Testament, you will see the phrase "from Dan to Beer-sheba" representing the northern and southern extremities of the promised land. Elijah heads to the deep South, abandons his servant, and then goes "a day's journey into the wilderness" (v. 4). When faced with the question of "fight or flight," Elijah had previously responded to conflict with "fight." But now he runs away.

While we may not have a lady named Jezebel who wants to kill us, we're engaged in a spiritual battle. We must address those issues that are threatening the kingdom of God in our lives. When we fail to tackle the most pressing spiritual issues before us, we discover that we are unable address smaller matters well. You cannot work around your challenges for long. You have to fight them.

Elijah lost his desire to live. We are stunned by the writer's words: he "prayed that he might die. He said, 'I have had enough! LORD, take my life, for I'm no better than my fathers" (v. 4). Elijah was not the first person to despair of life, and he was not the last. Moses told God, "Kill me right now" (Num 11:15). Job wished that he would have never been born (Job 10:18-19). Jeremiah cursed the day of his birth (Jer 20:14). Jonah asked God to take away his life because death was better than life (Jonah 4:3). These men longed for death, but they didn't actually take their lives. Instead, God sustained and restored them. The good news for Elijah is that God brought him out of it. We should consider it a good sign that we have this story. There was no eyewitness other than Elijah who could have reported it. God brought him through it. And interestingly, he was the one prophet who never died at all but was instead taken up into heaven (2 Kgs 2:11).

Have you ever said, "I've had enough, Lord"? If so, then you can identify with this struggling saint. Whether you are tempted to leave your spouse, your job, or this life, there is hope in this story. God deals with Elijah with amazing grace and patience.

The Causes

But what led to this course? How did Elijah despair of life itself? Surely there are numerous factors leading to this situation. As noted, there were natural and spiritual factors, and these two aren't unrelated. Let's consider them in four categories. Some are plainer in the text than the others.

Elijah was drained. This is clear. **Physically**, he had been a man on the run for three years, living by God's miraculous provision of bread. When he sent Ahab to Carmel to eat and drink (18:41-42), Elijah went to pray. Then he ran 17 miles ahead of Ahab to Jezreel. But he wasn't done running. The distance from the top of Mount Carmel to Beer-sheba is about 120 miles. It would take a traveler about six days unless he ran part of the way. Then we read that he went another day into the wilderness. Later he would travel all the way to Mount Horeb (v. 8).

That all adds up to about 300 miles! When we're physically tired, we're spiritually vulnerable as well.

Emotionally, he was also drained. He presumably had a letdown after his victory at Carmel. We can relate to this. We are vulnerable after a victory. We need manna every day. We cannot live on yesterday's victories.

Sometimes God wants to humble us with trials to teach us to depend on Him. After describing his great experiences, including being caught up into the third heaven, Paul says, "Therefore, so that I would not exalt myself, a thorn in the flesh was given to me, a messenger of Satan to torment me so I would not exalt myself" (2 Cor 12:7). Twice Paul says he was afflicted with this irrevocable thorn in the flesh (v. 8) in order to humble him, and he goes on to say that it taught him to rely on God's sufficient grace and power (vv. 9-10). In other words, Paul couldn't stay up on the mountain continuously, and God in His infinite wisdom chose to humble him through trials. When afflicted, we must follow Paul's lead and not slip into depression but rather rely on God's grace and power.

Spiritually, Elijah was drained. He was the object of intense spiritual opposition. Surely, this drained him. Evil opposition takes its toll on us, and we will be tempted to give in and not rely on God's strength.

Ministerially, he may have felt like he had nothing left to give. He was a worn-out servant. In his book *Leading on Empty*, Wayne Cordeiro says, "Those whose vocation is all about *giving* out are *wearing* out" (24). He tells the story of how he went for a run before a leadership conference in California and later found himself on a curb weeping uncontrollably (ibid., 13). He asked, "What in the world is happening to me?" He learned that he had been leading on empty. Cordeiro writes, "The only way to finish strong will be to first replenish your system. If you don't, prepare for a crash" (ibid., 26).

I have learned that replenishing is a spiritual discipline. I was on a panel recently with some other pastors. The question was asked, "What do you do to recover?" Two of the three said they take Monday off. Another had a different answer but still had a plan for personal renewal. I told them, "I'm working on it. I think I'll give Monday a try this fall." The fact is I have always struggled to do this. But I don't want to cry on a curb someday because I have not taken care of myself. Beside that, I believe we're best with a combination of work, rest, and play. I need to execute my own philosophy and rest!

As I have been doing the "Insanity" workouts, I have noticed how much they promote recovery. We have a recovery day each week and a recovery week in the middle of the nine-week workout. We also have "recovery formula" that is recommended. Gatorade also has a drink now, to go along with their pre-workout and workout drink, that is a recovery drink. We have to allow our bodies and souls to recover and be replenished. Elijah needed to recover, and so do we.

Elijah was disappointed. Though we don't read this explicitly in the text, I think it's a safe assumption that the "result at Carmel was not what Elijah expects" (Olley, *Message*, 178). Elijah probably thought revival would come to the land as people turned their hearts back to God, and even king Ahab would repent. His hopes were sky high, but then they were dashed when he heard Jezebel's threat. This dejection had to crush him.

Elijah was isolated. We have followed Elijah in chapters 17–18, and he has been a man virtually alone. If he is indeed "a man like us," that means he needs fellowship. In chapter 19 Elijah leaves his servant behind and departs by himself, not for prayer but for a pity party in which he is the host and the only guest.

Ryken notes, "Depression isn't only caused by the absence of community; it also perpetuates it" (*1 Kings*, 523). If you are tired and discouraged, isolation isn't what you need. You need others to encourage you and lift your spirits. We cannot go without human relationships very long. We are made for community. This reality was illustrated in the movie *Castaway*, in which Tom Hanks is alone on an island, and after a while he invents a friend out of a volleyball, whom he names "Wilson." We weren't made to be on an island by ourselves; we were made to be in community. And God has met that need physically in family and spiritually in the church.

Elijah believed half-truths that triggered feelings of self-righteousness, self-pity, and self-importance (Ryken, 533–34). Elijah mentions that he isn't any better than his fathers (v. 4). This is a **self-righteous** attitude. Did he previously think he was the best of all time? Sure, he had been a great prophet, but what was he currently doing? He was running away. He also states,

> I have been very zealous for the LORD God of Hosts, but the Israelites have abandoned Your covenant, torn down Your altars, and killed Your prophets with the sword. I alone am left, and they are looking for me to take my life. (v. 10)

Part of this statement was true. The majority of the people did forsake the Lord, but it seems some turned back. What of the altar? It was rebuilt. What of the prophets? Was it not the prophets of Baal who were destroyed in the previous chapter? In mixing truth and falsehood, he goes on to note that he was zealous for the Lord. True, but look at him now. What is he doing? He is running from Jezebel. Did he have reason to boast? No. The Lord has to question him, "What are you doing here, Elijah?"

Instead of repenting and asking for grace, Elijah turns to the comparison game to make himself superior. That's what self-righteous people do. They compare themselves to other people, just like the Pharisee with the tax collector praying in Jesus' parable (Luke 18:11). "Lord, I'm glad I'm not like this man" is the way their self-righteous prayers begin. Do you think you are superior to others? Do you think you are the only zealous one out there? Be careful of the blinding sin of self-righteousness. Only One is totally righteous, and that person isn't you.

Notice also his feeling of **self-importance**. He stated that he was the only one serving God presently (vv. 10,14). He says, "I alone am left" (v. 10). In the age-old battle between the seed of the woman and the seed of the servant, Elijah thought he was the last in the line, and if he throws in the towel, then God loses. He has forgotten some things about the line of David, and he has forgotten some other things. Like what about the 100 prophets Obadiah was serving? Sure, they were hiding in a cave, but look at Elijah! Further, God tells him that He has "7,000 in Israel" (v. 18). What is Elijah doing? He is exaggerating how important he is. Was he important? Most definitely, but he was not the only servant in Israel.

This feeling of self-importance can easily arise in our hearts. You might think you are the only one who cares about prayer, justice, discipleship, or evangelism, or that you are the only one ever preparing the fellowship, or giving to missions. If that is your feeling, your pride will eventually turn to despair. You must keep a sober assessment of yourself.

Next consider Elijah's **self-pity**. He stated that others wanted to take his life. This was simply inaccurate. Jezebel wanted to take his life, but we don't read that the whole nation of Israel was trying to do so. What do you call this? It's called self-pity. Self-pity happens when you exaggerate the problem. Depressed people do that; they make things sound worse than they really are.

Believing half-truths is a temptation for us all. Exaggerating our righteousness, our importance, and our problems feeds our flesh, and we must fight it. How? Quite simply, we must believe the pure truth of the gospel. Spurgeon said,

> I find myself frequently depressed—perhaps more so than any other person here. And I find no better cure for that depression than to trust in the Lord with all my heart, and seek to realize afresh the power of the peace-speaking blood of Jesus, and His infinite love in dying upon the cross to put away all my transgressions. ("The Secret of Happiness")

Similarly, Elyse M. Fitzpatrick writes,

> The depressed don't simply need to feel better. They need a Redeemer who says, "Take heart, my son, my daughter; what you really need has been supplied. Life no longer need be about your goodness, success, righteousness, or failure. I've given you something infinitely more valuable than good feelings: your sins are forgiven." ("The Gospel Cure")

In the words of Lloyd-Jones, we spend too much time "listening to ourselves" and not enough time "talking to ourselves" (*Spiritual Depression*, 20). What does it look like to preach to yourself? He writes,

> Would you like to be rid of this spiritual depression? The first thing you have to do is to say farewell now once and for ever to your past. Realize that it has been covered and blotted out in Christ. Never look back at your sins again. Say: "It is finished; it is covered by the Blood of Christ." That is your first step. Take that and finish with yourself and all this talk about goodness, and look to the Lord Jesus Christ. It is only then that true happiness and joy are possible for you. What you need isn't to make resolutions to live a better life, to start fasting and sweating and praying. No! You just begin to say: "I rest my faith on Him alone who died for my transgressions to atone." (*Spiritual Depression*, 35)

Are you drained? Are you disappointed? Are you isolated? Are you believing half-truths that trigger feelings of self-righteousness, self-pity, and self-importance? What we need is this: heavy doses of grace and truth that are in Jesus.

God's Gracious Response
1 KINGS 19:5-21

How did God minister to His depressed servant? He ministered to him with patient grace and tender compassion. The three means of grace God used for Elijah were bread in the wilderness, a voice on the mountain, and a vision for the future.

There are several echoes of the story of Moses and the wilderness journey here. These parallels highlight God's faithfulness, patience, and grace. Such faithfulness and grace and patience should encourage us also.

Bread in the Wilderness (vv. 5-8)

God's first response to Elijah wasn't rebuke. It was "eat." He had fed him with a raven and with a widow, and now He uses an angel to feed him. After Elijah slept under the broom tree, he awoke to an angel who touched him and said, "Get up and eat." Elijah looked and there was "a loaf of bread baked over hot stones, and a jug of water." Elijah "ate and drank and lay down again." This happened a second time, and then "on the strength from that food, he walked 40 days and 40 nights to Horeb." That's some good bread! (It actually reminds us of another mediator in the wilderness besides Moses who could go 40 days and 40 nights: Jesus; see Matt 4; Luke 4.)

How encouraging is it that God feeds His runaway prophet instead of actually answering Elijah's prayer for death? I find this remarkably encouraging. John Piper has written a deeply edifying poem on Elijah. In part three of it, he says,

> Elijah fled to Judah, then
> Beyond Beersheba's well full ten
> More miles, and fell exhausted there
> Beneath a spreading broom tree where
> He sat and asked the Lord that he
> Might die. Instead he slept. The tree
> God made to give him shade, then sent
> An angel down with food, who went
> And woke the prophet thus: "Awake!"
> Instead of death, God gives you cake.
> By this you will walk forty days
> And forty nights until you gaze
> Like Moses on the majesty

> Of God. Nor am I sure that He
> Will ever grant your wish to die.
> Come now, Elijah, eat and fly. ("Elijah, Part 3")

Instead of death God gave him cake. Oh, the tenderness of God here! He will rebuke him later, but first we find gentleness and care.

Are you drained and dejected like Elijah? Consider also the ministry of Jesus, who tells us, "Come to Me, all of you who are weary and burdened, and I will give you rest . . . because I am gentle" (Matt 11:28-29). What you need is **spiritual rest** in Christ, the bread of life (John 6:35). There we find forgiveness and joy, knowing that "no condemnation now exists for those in Christ Jesus" (Rom 8:1). When you have had enough and you look to Him, you find He is enough.

Perhaps you also need **physical rest**. Good food and good sleep are wonderful cures to spiritual depression. Sleep and food, after all, are gifts of God (Pss 104:14-15; 127:2). Look at what kind of God you have. When you run away like Elijah, He says, "Have breakfast." Remember when Peter denied Jesus, Jesus made him breakfast (John 21)! He renewed him physically and spiritually.

Elijah is being renewed by the grace of God. The scene here illustrates Isaiah's words, which say we must trust in the Lord and renew our strength, then we shall "run and not grow weary . . . walk and not faint" (Isa 40:31).

It may be a stretch, but I wonder if the angel didn't also provide some **companionship** for this lonely servant. Elijah needed a companion, and he received a fresh touch from this angel. Later he will receive a wonderful companion in Elisha. Elijah is a man like us, and that involves the need for company. Maybe you need some companionship. Don't run from this need. Seek a local body of believers with whom you can fellowship. Perhaps God wants to use you to minister to lonely, depressed servants. Take them a cake and spend some time with them.

A Voice on the Mountain (vv. 9-13a)

Now Elijah goes to the mount of God. What will happen here? Will we find him still wallowing in self-pity and complaining, or will he respond with fresh vigor?

We find him railing against the Israelites. Elijah's memory is selective (Provan, *1 and 2 Kings*, 145), as demonstrated when he says the Israelites "have abandoned Your covenant, torn down Your altars, and killed Your prophets" (v. 10). Again, he believes half-truths and wallows in pity.

With the bread in the wilderness, God reminded him of the past. But Elijah is still depressed, so God will now remind him of His power once again. This time Elijah will hear God's voice at the mount. At this mount Israel met with the Lord and discovered what God required of them (Exod 19–20). Now God's presence and God's voice will awaken Elijah and sustain him.

In verses 11-12 Elijah stood before the Lord, and the Lord "passed by," and a great wind tore through the mountains. Then there was an earthquake, then a fire. But the Lord was not in these powerful displays. Instead, after a fire, Elijah heard a "soft whisper." On hearing this, Elijah "wrapped his face in his mantle and went out and stood at the entrance of the cave" (v. 13).

Previously, God showed up with fire, consuming the drenched altar. People marveled. But this passage emphasizes God's quiet ways. God often appears not in the spectacular but in the gentle whisper. Provan says, "Elijah needs to remember the past, but he also needs to realize that there is more to the Lord than fire" (*1 and 2 Kings*, 146).

This phrase "a soft whisper" only appears two others times. It appears in Job 4:16 and Psalm 107:29. It is used in both passages in the context of rest and refreshment in the midst of pain, distress, and fear.

Let's remember that God often works in quiet ways. David wrote, "Your gentleness made me great" (Ps 18:35 ESV). Sometimes the fire does fall in corporate gatherings, but God also works quietly through His written Word and His Spirit in the hearts of His people. Don't always seek controversy and drama or major conferences. Seek the God of grace in the quiet place. Get alone with Him and listen to His Word. Think on His gospel.

A Vision for the Future (vv. 13b-21)

Ryken notes, "Spiritual depression is hard to shake. It isn't a twenty-four hour virus. Getting over it takes more than a pastor saying, 'Take two Bible verses and call me in the morning'" (*1 Kings*, 530). After bread from an angel and the quiet voice of God on the mountain, Elijah is still rehearsing his speech when God asks him, "What are you doing here, Elijah?" It's as if God says, "Let's try this again." But Elijah is inflexible. He responds with his same rehearsed speech. He's slow to understand and change, perhaps because he doesn't want to understand and change.

But in the midst of his depression, Elijah is at least talking to God. If you ever sink this low, remember to keep speaking to God.

We see here that God is "compassionate and gracious, slow to anger and rich in faithful love" (Ps 103:8). God's mercy is demonstrated here in that He gave Elijah a new vision for the future. This vision involves an assignment and a word of assurance.

His **assignment** is to anoint Hazael, Jehu, and Elisha (vv. 15-17). This may in fact be what the gentle whisper was about (Provan, *1 and 2 Kings*, 146). The ultimate victory over Baal worship will not be solved by the victory at Carmel, instead it will come through a slow political process that will extend beyond Elijah's life. The defeat of Baal will not happen by Elijah alone, nor will it happen in his lifetime.

Elijah's job wasn't just to fight well in the present but to prepare others for the future. We will read of Elijah's instructions being lived out for many chapters to come (2 Kgs 8:7-15; 9–10). God teaches Elijah (and us) that no one is indispensible.

A new assignment often lifts us from the ashes. Such an assignment may involve preparing others for service. We must fight well in the present, but we must also prepare others for the future, as did Jesus, who fought victoriously and trained up others to take the good news to the nations after His ascension.

We read of Elijah anointing Elisha, God's chosen prophet, in verses 19-21 (Provan thinks Elijah is not enthused about this assignment [*1 and 2 Kings*, 147]; I'm not sure). Who was Elisha? His name means, "God saves." He was a farmer and apparently a wealthy one since he had "twelve teams of oxen" (v. 19). Elijah put his mantle on him, symbolizing the transference of prophetic power. Elisha's commitment is evidenced in what follows: "He left the oxen, ran to follow Elijah" (v. 20). But then Elisha requests, "Please let me kiss my father and mother, and then I will follow you." Elijah permits him to do so. Then we read of Elisha's total abandonment of all things for God's will. Elisha not only kisses his family good-bye but also kisses the world good-bye. He destroyed all of his old means of sustenance in verse 21. He tells everyone publically that he's following God's will. What's more, he seems to be throwing a party to tell everyone. He isn't reluctant; he's excited. Here's a picture of one saying, "You can take the world, but give me Jesus!"

Elisha's devotion to God's call gets echoed in Jesus' call to discipleship. In Luke 9 Jesus calls a man to follow Him, and the man says, "I will follow You, Lord, but first let me go and say good-bye to those at my house" (Luke 9:61). He seems to say the same thing Elisha says, but instead of allowing it like Elijah did, Jesus says, "No one who puts his hand to the plow and looks back is fit for the kingdom of God" (Luke 9:62). The reference to the plow sounds like 1 Kings, and so does this call. But Jesus doesn't grant this request. Why? Jesus is greater than Elijah, and His call takes precedence over everyone and everything. Jesus demands immediate obedience and wholehearted allegiance. Elisha is being asked to follow a prophet, but we have been called to follow the Son of God. Follow Him at once, and then deal with these other details later.

So God gives Elijah a fresh vision, which includes an assignment. Part of Elijah's assignment involved a new partner. Notice the last sentence of the chapter, "Then he left, followed Elijah, and served him" (v. 21). Here God not only gives Elijah an assignment but also gives him companionship. How this young apprentice must have given Elijah fresh strength! In 2 Kings 2:12 Elisha calls Elijah "father," indicating the intimacy the two shared. Elisha was like an intern who apparently did some menial tasks like washing Elijah's hands (2 Kgs 3:11).

God's vision included not only a new assignment but also a word of **assurance**. We skipped over it. In verse 18 God tells Elijah, "But I will leave 7,000 in Israel—every knee that has not bowed to Baal and every mouth that has not kissed him." Paul recalled this principle of God's sovereign grace:

> God has not rejected His people whom He foreknew. Or don't you know what the Scripture says in the passage about Elijah? . . . I have left 7,000 men for Myself who have not bowed down to Baal. In the same way, then, there is also at the present time a remnant chosen by grace. (Rom 11:2,4-5)

In the words of Paul, "God's solid foundation stands firm, having this inscription: The Lord knows those who are His" (2 Tim 2:19). The doctrine of God's electing grace should give encouragement to depressed servants.

Elijah wasn't the only one left in Israel following the living God. He wasn't the only seed to survive. God had a remnant. And God preserved His people until the ultimate seed, Jesus, appeared. Jesus was the slain seed, who was put into the ground, lying there silently, only to rise again triumphantly. Now Jesus has a people, not just from Israel but also of every tribe, who have been chosen by grace. God's saving grace was a word of assurance to Elijah, and it should be a wonderful word of assurance to us as well. Look away from yourself and look to Jesus, who said, "It is finished."

Elijah would stand on a mountain again. And he would stand there with Moses. We read of it in the Gospels. This time it isn't Mount Horeb but the Mount of Transfiguration. Jesus took with Him Peter, James, and John. They saw Jesus talking with them as the dazzling glory of Christ was unveiled for a moment. A voice from heaven was heard, "This is My Son, the Chosen One; listen to Him!" (Luke 9:35). Until we gaze on the face of Jesus, let's feast on the Bread of Life, let's listen to His voice, and let's be spurred on by a glorious future that awaits all of His suffering saints.

Reflect and Discuss

1. Why might Jezebel have disbelieved Yahweh after such an extraordinary display of His power?
2. Is it surprising that Elijah doesn't remain steadfast when Jezebel threatens his life, especially after Baal's defeat at Mount Carmel? Why or why not?
3. Elijah says he is no better than his fathers. Is this a true statement? Did God choose Elijah because he was better or worse than his fathers?
4. How is God compassionate toward Elijah?
5. Has God ever shown you compassion in dark moments?
6. Has God ever sustained you through nearly impossible situations?
7. What do the strong wind, earthquake, fire, and whisper teach us about God?
8. Do you ever feel like you are the only faithful one left? Explain.
9. In what ways can fellow believers and gospel laborers encourage one another in the faith?
10. Why is fellowship important in the Christian life?

Warlords and the Word of the Lord

1 KINGS 20:1-43

Main Idea: Ben-hadad and Ahab go to battle twice, but the Lord is the true victor.

I. Prebattle Trash Talk (20:1-12)
II. First Battle: The Lord Defeats Aram with the JV Team (20:13-21)
III. Debriefing and Preparing (20:22-25)
IV. Second Battle: The Lord Defeats Aram with Two Little Flocks of Goats (20:26-30)
V. Postbattle Drama (20:31-43)
VI. Application

A re you ready to rumble? In chapter 20 we will read of two battles between Ben-hadad and Ahab. But the battles actually fail to exalt either lord as victorious. Instead, these events exalt the sovereign Lord, who wins the battles for Israel. Yahweh's unlimited power, sovereign rule, astonishing grace, and perfect justice are on display here.

In this war-saturated chapter we also read of many strange events. A king (Ben-hadad) gets drunk with 32 other kings, a wall falls down and kills 27,000 Arameans (Syrians), and a lion kills a prophet because he refuses to punch a fellow prophet! Seriously. That's right: we have another lion killing a prophet (cf. 1 Kgs 13:24). Welcome to 1 Kings 20.

Based on the Lord's instructions to Elijah in 1 Kings 19:15-18, we expect to see God's plan carried out. Elisha has been recruited. But what about Hazael and Jehu? It will actually be a while before these characters are introduced—well into 2 Kings. Hence, we find here an amazing illustration of God's sovereignty. God is working out His plans in His own timing.

Instead of Hazael, we read of king Ben-hadad (presumably the son of the previous Ben-hadad, 1 Kgs 15:18-20). He is as worthless as Israel's king, Ahab. Why is it appropriate to call them both "worthless"? It's not difficult to see. Ahab repeatedly rejects God's word. He doesn't fear God (Deut 17:19). He doesn't rule with wisdom and justice, as kings were supposed to lead (Prov 8:15-16). Ben-hadad is also a self-centered, self-indulgent king. His lifestyle is totally out of step with the responsibilities of a competent leader (Prov 31:1-9).

In the midst of these warlords, we meet a number of prophets. Elijah (who reappears in chapter 21) wasn't the only one serving God during this time, nor was he the only prophet willing to bring a message to Ahab. We read of unnamed prophets here in chapter 20 and of Micaiah in chapter 22. All of these chapters show Ahab's repeated failure to submit to God's word, which ultimately leads to his death.

Let's have a look at the two battles described in chapter 20, and let's pay attention to God's word throughout the narrative. The whole chapter should cause us to fear God, marvel at His grace, and make us grateful for His Word.

The chapter describes two battles: the first over Samaria and the other at Aphek. Each battle has the same basic outline, as stated below:

The Battle over Samaria
    1. Aramean Threat (20:1-12)
    2. Prophetic Intervention (20:13-15)
    3. Israelite Victory (20:16-21)
    4. Aftermath (20:22-25)

The Battle at Aphek
    1. Aramean Threat (20:26-27)
    2. Prophetic Intervention (20:28)
    3. Israelite Victory (20:29-30)
    4. Aftermath (20:31-43)

We could examine the passage with this structure (which Davis helpfully provides, *1 Kings*, 280), but I found it more memorable to understand it with some contemporary terminology, in five total parts, emphasizing the Lord's victory. God predicts each victory through a prophet. Before the first battle, God declares, "I am handing it [the Aramean multitude] over to you today" (v. 13). Before the second battle, He declares, "I will hand over all this great army to you" (v. 28). Clearly God is the hero of both battles, as evidenced by the obvious human inability of Israel on both occasions. Therefore, the outline at the head of this section gives the main points of this chapter as I see them.

Prebattle Trash Talk
1 KINGS 20:1-12

Ben-hadad formed a strong alliance with 32 kings in order to attack Ahab's Samaria. He first lays out his terms to Ahab. He demands silver and gold and the best wives and children Ahab has to offer.

So the nations are raging against Israel (cf. Ps 2). The Aramean coalition has penetrated Israel's border, closing in on Samaria. The phrase "horses and chariots" emphasizes the human power of this coalition. But God's people have been told that battles are won by the Lord, not by horses and chariots (Ps 20:7). Ahab's confidence should have thus been in the Lord. But as a cowardly king, he caves into Ben-hadad's demands.

Here's an example of one listening to the wrong voice. When Ben-hadad's messengers said, "This is what Ben-hadad says," Ahab should have countered with, "This is what the Lord says," but he didn't. He chose to allow things that clearly violated God's word, like intermarrying with pagans, giving up God-given resources, and handing over their own children. He even tells the Aramean king, "I am yours" (v. 4). What an awful picture of Israel's king.

Why does Ahab compromise? He obviously has fear-of-man issues. But before we criticize him, we should examine ourselves. How easy is it for us to play Ahab? It takes Spirit-filled courage to stand up against bullies who want us to compromise biblical truth. The spirit of Ben-hadad is at work in the world. We will be tempted not to view sin as wickedness, to be silent in evangelism, not to treat marriage as a holy covenant, not to insist that Jesus is the only way to salvation. In moments of timidity, let us look to God, who alone is Sovereign, for strength and power to do and say what is right.

As a greedy king, Ben-hadad wasn't content with the first demands. He actually countered by making his demands more severe. These demands are more *extensive*, more *intrusive*, and more *immediate* (Provan, *1 and 2 Kings*, 141). Ben-hadad is going beyond forming a vassal relationship. He's picking a fight. He's looking to attack Ahab.

Ahab's compromising heart only goes so far, though. He refuses this second round of demands. After a meeting with the elders, he sends a message back that he will submit to the first demands (which he shouldn't have done), but he won't submit to the second demands.

Then the trash talking begins. I like Eugene Peterson's paraphrase of the exchange. Ben-hadad says: "May the gods do their worst to me, and then worse again, if there'll be anything left of Samaria but rubble" (20:10 MSG). Like a kid at recess, Ahab snaps back at the Aramean bully, "Think about it—it's easier to start a fight than end one" (20:11 MSG). In modern-day talk, he says something like, "Don't count your chickens before they hatch, big boy" or "Do your talking on the field." One can almost hear the crowd saying, "Ooh. It's on!" And it is. With his bottle of "Aramean Ale" in his hand, Ben-hadad says, "Take your positions" (v. 12).

First Battle: The Lord Defeats Aram with the JV Team
1 KINGS 20:13-21

Ben-hadad and Ahab had their messengers, but now we read of Yahweh's messenger. God intervenes by sending His prophet to Ahab promising an Israelite victory:

> A prophet came to Ahab king of Israel and said, "This is what the LORD says: 'Do you see this entire great army? Watch, I am handing it over to you today so that you may know that I am Yahweh.'"
> (v. 20:13)

Consider the grace of God here. The word of God came to Ahab. Did he deserve such a gift? No. This was grace. And how will the battle be won? Yahweh will hand him the victory. Could Ahab have defeated such a multitude on his own? No. This is grace upon grace.

One often struggles with the so-called problem of evil, which asks, "How could a good and powerful God allow evil into the world?" But here we must face the "problem of grace," which asks, "How could a holy God be so kind to such an evil king?" Few people actually struggle with the problem of grace. We tend to think we deserve God's favor and blessing, but we need to see afresh how unspeakably kind God is to unjust people. Peter tells us that God is patient with unrepentant people because He wants them to be saved (2 Pet 3:9). We should thank God for such mercy and grace.

Notice also the purpose of God's grace: "That you may know that I am Yahweh." This phrase is a featured phrase in the books of Exodus and Ezekiel (e.g., Exod 6:7; 7:5; 10:2; 14:4; 16:12; Ezek 5:13; 6:7; 7:4; 11:10; 12:15). In Joshua–Kings the phrase only appears in this story here and in verse 28 (Olley, *Message*, 188). God is going to win the battle and make His glory known. This too is a wonder of grace: that God would reveal His power and glory to sinners.

Ahab wants to know specifically how the battle will be won. He's surprised by the answer. God is going to use the "JV team" to win the battle! The prophet says, "This is what the LORD says: 'By the young men of the provincial leaders'" (v. 14). God is going to use a young, inexperienced, Gideon-like army to defeat the Aramean coalition. Why will God not use the typical army? Simple. He wants to reveal His own surpassing glory and power, so that everyone will know that He alone is Lord.

Ahab then asks, "Who is to start the battle?" The prophet replies, "You" (v. 14). Ahab follows the instructions, grabs these 232 lads, but also drafts a back-up army of 7,000.

While God's grace is on display, something else is on display: Ben-hadad's foolishness and arrogance. "They [Israel] marched out at noon while Ben-hadad and the 32 kings who were helping him *were getting drunk in the tents*" (v. 16; emphasis added). Ben-hadad is acting more like a foolish college student on spring break than a responsible king in war. He probably thought an Aramean victory was certain, so why not get the party started, open the champagne, and enjoy some laughs with the boys? But the only one laughing was the sovereign Lord (cf. Ps 2:4).

When Ben-hadad is told that Israel is on the move, he can't even utter a sensible reply. He spouts out drunken gibberish: "If they have marched out in peace, take them alive, and if they have marched out for battle, take them alive" (v. 18). The latter half of this statement makes no sense because Ben-hadad is apparently wasted. He must have meant, "If they come for war, take them dead or alive."

Here's one of many reasons you should abstain from drunkenness: you lose control of your sensibilities. People do stupid things and say stupid things when they're under the influence of alcohol (Prov 23:30-35).

Some in modern America would have probably produced a reality TV show of Ben-hadad. They would celebrate his lifestyle. But a mark of a genuine, Spirit-filled Christian is self-control (Gal 5:23), not this type of self-indulgence. When under pressure, learn to rely on the Spirit's power, not on a substance (Eph 5:18).

When Ben-hadad implements this inane plan, the Aramean frontline forces are struck down. Ben-hadad and the remainder of the force flee. Israel, by the grace of God, enjoys this victory over the bully, Ben-hadad: "Then the king of Israel marched out and attacked the cavalry and the chariots. He inflicted a great slaughter on Aram [Syria]" (v. 21). Yahweh provides another example of how the kings on earth are no match for His sovereign might. Proverbs says, "A horse is prepared for the day of battle, but victory comes from the LORD" (21:31).

Before going further, we should stop and ponder the wonder of the gospel. The gospel is good news for sinners. Previously, Ahab had only received opposition from the prophets. But in this passage he hears good news. He hears of the promise of victory. And what did he do to solicit such news? Nothing. The prophet simply appears. What did Ahab do to experience victory? Nothing (cf. Rom 4:3-6). Throughout Scripture we find that "salvation is from the LORD" (Jonah 2:9). Give God thanks for sending a gospel messenger to you. Give God thanks for doing the work *for* you, through Jesus Christ. While we were perishing, God intervened and won the most important victory in the most unlikely way—through a cross (Col 2:13-15). Sadly for Ahab, he still refused to place His faith in this gracious God.

Debriefing and Preparing
1 KINGS 20:22-25

Though the battle was won that day, the war wasn't over. The same prophet comes back and gives the following word about round two:

> Go and strengthen yourself, then consider what you should do, for in the spring the king of Aram will march against you. (v. 23)

This time the word of grace comes in the form of a warning. Ahab must prepare for a springtime battle with Ben-hadad. Spring was a common time for kings to go to war (2 Sam 11:1). Thus Ahab's celebration over Aram is short-lived. It's time to get ready for the second battle.

Once again the prophet comes totally unsolicited. God's grace to Ahab is astonishing in its nature and its frequency.

In the Aramean headquarters another discussion was taking place. The king's servants gave their "half-time speech," as they debriefed and prepared for another battle. The king's servants decide to do some theology and offer some military strategy. Unfortunately, they offered *bad* theology. They claim that Israel only won the battle because their "gods" are "gods of the hill country." Perhaps they had the story of Elijah in their minds, in addition to this most recent battle. Of course, it wasn't the "gods" who gave the victory but the *only* God. And He's the God of *heaven and earth,* not simply the hills (Pss 121:2; 123:8). Nevertheless, they advise the king to replace the destroyed army with another army and fight Israel on the plain. Ben-hadad heeds the counsel, and we're all set for another battle.

This polytheistic thinking of the Arameans is still common today. Many around the world believe in a god over this and a god over that. But the God of the Bible is Lord over all things, and we should seek to place the totality of our lives underneath His rule (Col 3:17,23-24). We shouldn't live with a distinction between our *secular lives* and our *spiritual lives.* Submit your private life, public life, church life, dating life, financial life, family life, work life, and recreational life to the Lord Jesus Christ and seek to glorify Him in every way (1 Cor 10:31).

Second Battle: The Lord Defeats Aram with Two Little Flocks of Goats
1 KINGS 20:26-30

Now picture something like a grade school basketball team going up against the San Antonio Spurs. No contest, right? Well, think again. The Lord puts His power on display in this war through a greatly over-matched Israelite army.

The Arameans (Syrians) march against Israel. This time the show-down is at Aphek. Aphek was farther north of Samaria, located east of the Sea of Galilee. Once again Aram has a vast army compared to Israel. The odds are against Israel. In the first battle Israel won with their JV team. Now they are going to battle with "two little flocks of goats" (v. 27). This weak little army is no match for Aram. But this is just the type of war Yahweh likes. It all sounds familiar, doesn't it? Yahweh often uses such scenarios to show off His glory. He often uses the weak to shame the strong so that everyone can only boast in Him for the victory (1 Cor 1:26-31). We could line up a host of people to testify to this fact. Moses, Joshua, David, Gideon, Elijah, Paul, Peter, Timothy, and more could all testify that God loves to use ordinary people, and even "weak" people, to do extraordinary things so that people will glorify and rejoice in Him.

Now enter God's prophet. This is the third time so far that God has sent His messenger to Ahab. Once again grace is present. Once again God's word is sure. The prophet gives the following assurance to the king:

This is what the LORD says: "Because the Arameans have said:
Yahweh is a god of the mountains and not a god of the valleys, I will
hand over all this great army to you. Then you will know that I am the
LORD." (v. 28)

The prophet informs the king that God will correct the theological nonsense of the Arameans and show everyone that He is the God of both the mountains and the valleys. And in granting Israel victory, the Lord will show that He alone is God.

In confronting the Arameans' faulty theology, God was actually showing grace to the Arameans also. God is, after all, a missionary God. God saves people from all nations out from under their polytheistic worldviews. If the Arameans had eyes to see, then they could rejoice in Yahweh as the only God and Redeemer (2 Kgs 5:1-14).

But there's an additional missionary application here. God's unlimited power means we can go to the hardest places on earth today and proclaim the gospel with confidence (Acts 18:9-10). God can change the hardest of hearts. Do you think some places on the earth are more likely to experience God's salvation than others? Oh, I know that some places are dangerously dark and hostile to the gospel. But God is the God of both the mountains and the valleys, of America and Afghanistan, of Canada and North Korea. Do we really believe in His all-encompassing power, or are we functional Arameans? This text beckons us to recognize the scope of God's power. Jesus will have a people from every tribe and nation, and many of them may look unreachable to us. But we need to reconsider the breadth of God's mercy and power.

The summary of the battle actually sounds a lot like the battle at Jericho (Josh 6, especially 6:15). Consider the casualties here. The Israelite "goats" killed 100,000 Aramean soldiers in one day. That's astonishing! Then, like the battle at Jericho, a wall fell down. This collapsed wall killed 27,000 soldiers. Remarkable! The victory could only be attributed to the hand of Yahweh. God has no real threats to His throne.

Postbattle Drama
1 KINGS 20:31-43

Every battle or sporting event has postgame drama. What will happen now in the aftermath of this Israelite victory? The ensuing verses are intriguing.

Twice-defeated Ben-hadad is now out of options, so he goes with plan C: beg for mercy. The defeated king follows his advisors' instructions and tries to weasel out of his deserved punishment. He pleads, "Please spare my life" (v. 32). Ahab, surprised that Ben-hadad is alive, declares, "He is my brother," and spares him.

In the following chapter Ahab will allow a faithful Israelite to be murdered, but here he shows leniency to his enemy. This is the same enemy who threatened to enslave Israel's women and children, carry them off into a foreign land, and lead them to idol worship. In the "King's Handbook," Proverbs, we read, "Wicked behavior is detestable to kings, since a throne is established through righteousness" (16:12). Ahab favors wickedness instead of righteousness. He refuses to wisely execute justice, even though "a wise king separates out the wicked and drives the threshing wheel over them" (Prov 20:26). The sage also says, "Justice executed is a joy to the righteous but a terror to those who practice iniquity" (Prov 21:15). Ahab could have sent a message to other potential threats by giving Ben-hadad a just judgment, but he prefers to satisfy his greed.

A deal is struck between the two warlords. The previous arrangement is reversed, and Ahab is given trading privileges in Damascus. Following the deal, Ben-hadad, the bitter enemy now a brother, is freed. Thus, Ahab reveals much of his own idolatry. He's not a king leading justly; he's a self-indulgent, covetous, and cowardly king.

The peace that ensued from these agreements, however, only lasted three years (1 Kgs 22:1-5). More war will come. More importantly, Ahab's compromise with his enemy didn't please God, who loves justice (Ps 99:4). In spite of recurring grace, Ahab continues to rebel against God's ways.

The writer provides more details of the aftermath in verses 35-43. We have a vivid illustration of the seriousness of God's word.

Once again a prophet appears (v. 35). He is one of the "sons of the prophets" mentioned elsewhere in association with Elisha (2 Kgs 2:3,5,7,15, etc.). This prophet pulls out a play from the prophet Nathan's "Primer for Prophets" manual in an effort to confront the king for his failure to deal appropriately with Ben-hadad.

When the prophet Nathan confronted David over his sin with Bathsheba, he told the king a story about a rich man with many flocks and herds and a poor man with nothing but a little ewe lamb he raised and cherished. In the story the rich man needed to prepare a lamb for a guest, and instead of taking one of his many lambs, he made the wicked decision to take the precious lamb from the poor man. After Nathan tells this story, David exclaims, "As the LORD lives, the man who did this deserves to die! Because he has done this thing and shown no pity, he must pay four lambs for that lamb"; then the bold prophet replies, "You are the man!" (2 Sam 12:5-6). By using the storytelling approach, Nathan was able to get the king to confess his own guilt and pass his own judgment.

The anonymous prophet in 1 Kings 20 not only tells a story but also acts it out in order to have the same kind of effect on Ahab. One has to admire the prophet's work. You probably didn't hear this story growing up in Sunday School, but it's fascinating! Let's summarize the events. Through the grace and power of God, Israel defeated Aram twice. After the second defeat Ahab had the Aramean king, Ben-hadad, in his hands. But in Ahab's wickedness and cowardice, he freed Ben-hadad. In so doing he actually put Israel at risk and dishonored God (cf. Josh 7:25).

So the unnamed prophet dresses like a servant returning from battle. In order to look like a soldier, he asks a fellow prophet to punch him. He makes this strange demand in obedience to Yahweh's word. I know—it's crazy. When the fellow refuses to strike the prophet, he's informed that a lion will kill him. And so it happens—the lion kills the fellow prophet. That's the second time this sort of thing has happened to disobedient prophets (cf. 1 Kgs 13).

The prophet finds another potential punching prophet. This time his fellow strikes him and wounds him. Now looking the part, bruised and bandaged, the prophet approaches king Ahab. He tells the king the story, "I've just come home from the battle. I was supposed to guard a prisoner, and if I failed then I would have to give my life in exchange, or come up with an unrealistic amount of money. But I got distracted, and the prisoner escaped" (v. 39a, paraphrase). The king replied, "So shall your judgment be; you yourself have decided it" (v. 40 ESV). Boom. Nathan would be proud. The prophet removes the bandage, reveals his identity, and rebukes Ahab for letting Ben-hadad go free. Ahab's disobedience will cost him his own life, just as he said it should.

When Ahab heard these words, he went home "vexed and sullen" (v. 43 ESV), an attitude that carries over into the next chapter (21:4). He's resentful and angry, and his death is getting closer. Interestingly enough, he will try the disguise method later, but it doesn't work out for him (1 Kgs 22:30).

Application

What on earth should we learn from this story? Obviously, it's not that we should walk around and ask people to punch us. Consider four transferable principles.

Avoid the Folly and Rebellion of These Two Kings

Ahab and Ben-hadad are living illustrations of *how not to live*. They show us what "the fear of the Lord" doesn't look like. Drunkenness, greed, violence, injustice, and faithlessness may get you a reality TV show, but it's not how you should live your life. The saddest part of the chapter is that God actually showed grace to these men, yet they still refused to see the Lord for who He is and submit to Him. We have a better King, Jesus, who lived a sinless life, who gave His life for sinners like these men. Look to Him for salvation. Look to Him as your example of how to live a humble, others-oriented life. Look to Him for power to do justice and show mercy.

Marvel at God's Grace

Grace is amazing because God shows it to wretches. Why should we be shown God's unmerited favor? Why should sinners hear the good news of the gospel when they aren't even seeking it? Grace! Respond to God's grace in gratitude and with a life of faithfulness. Respond to God's grace by reflecting His kindness to others.

Live in View of God's Unlimited Power

The Lord's two victories in this chapter should give us greater confidence in God's ability to do more than we could ask or imagine (Eph 3:20-21). Are you trusting in God's power to overcome the hard heart of your neighbors and friends? Are you seeking Him as you endure a particular physical challenge? Are you looking to Him for strength as you parent your children? Are you trusting in God's unlimited ability to provide for you as you live on mission? He's God of both the hills and the valleys.

Take God's Word Seriously

We learn this lesson throughout the chapter. God's word is sure. What God declared, He did. We see this from the story of the dead prophet who refused to obey Yahweh's command to strike the Lord's messenger. His story was a preliminary paradigm of Ahab (Davis, *1 Kings*, 290), who also refused to take God's word seriously. He chose compromise and self-indulgence instead of submission to God's word. Prophets and kings must obey God's word. Obedience to God's word will look strange to casual observers, but we must take it seriously.

In chapter 21 we find Ahab continuing his wicked deeds. We also see him become somewhat moved by God's word, but ultimately he refuses to submit to God completely. We should learn from his tragic life. We have received grace upon grace. Why on earth should God extend grace to Ahab? We need to ask, why should he extend it to us? God has not only given us a *second chance* but has also given us a *second Adam*. Jesus Christ, the perfect King, the obedient Prophet, who always did what pleased the Father, lived a sinless life and died the death we deserved to die. Why should we benefit from His perfect life and substitutionary death? It's grace. The question is, will you respond in genuine repentance and faith toward God, or will you play games like Ahab and go your own way? The only wise response is the former. Don't take this decision lightly. Those who refuse to respond to Christ with saving faith will face something worse than a hungry lion. Flee to Christ and escape the irreversible word of eternal judgment on those who choose sin, folly, and rebellion over the everlasting joy of Christ's presence. The psalmist summarizes the appropriate response:

> So now, kings, be wise;
>   receive instruction, you judges of the earth.
> Serve the LORD with reverential awe
>   and rejoice with trembling.
> Pay homage to the Son or He will be angry
>   and you will perish in your rebellion,
>   for His anger may ignite at any moment.
> All those who take refuge in Him are happy. (Ps 2:10-12)

Reflect and Discuss

1. What are some ways the world celebrates greediness and drunkenness?
2. What are some ways greediness and drunkenness can lead a person into conflict and trouble?
3. Why might the Arameans believe Yahweh is a God of the hills?
4. Are there areas of your life where you believe God is unable to reign?
5. Discuss any personal experiences of God's victory in unexpected circumstances.
6. Why did Ahab allow Ben-hadad to live?
7. What are some ways believers today sacrifice righteousness for fellowship with the world?
8. The unnamed prophet goes to great lengths to speak the word of the Lord to Ahab. Are you ever tempted to think proclaiming God's Word is too much trouble? How so?
9. What does Jesus' life teach us about the cost of righteousness?
10. Do you ever find yourself sullen over the consequences of sin? How so?

"Payday Someday"

1 KINGS 21:1–22:53

Main Idea: In greed and wickedness, Ahab and Jezebel seize the vineyard of a faithful servant named Naboth, but the couple's sin doesn't go unnoticed by the all-seeing Judge, who will have the last word.

I.   **Be Prepared to Suffer for the Sake of Righteousness (21:1-16).**
    A.   Ahab's covetousness (vv. 1-2)
    B.   Naboth's righteousness (v. 3)
    C.   Ahab's sullenness (v. 4)
    D.   Jezebel's sliminess (vv. 5-7)
    E.   Collective wickedness (vv. 8-14)
    F.   Temporary happiness (vv. 15-16)
II. **Be Willing to Sacrifice for the Sake of the Oppressed (21:8-16).**
III. **Remember: There Will Be a Payday Someday (21:17–22:53).**
    A.   The prophet Elijah appears (21:17-29).
    B.   The payday train arrives (22:1-53).

The heading in your Bible for chapter 21 might say something like "Naboth's Vineyard." At first glance the title may not interest you unless you like gardening, enjoy grapes, or your name is Naboth. You might assume this story has little relevance for modern readers. However, that assumption would be incorrect. This chapter makes my blood boil because of its tragedy and relevance. This isn't a story about grapes; it's a story about the injustice of man and the justice of God. We learn what it's like to suffer injustice, what it costs to do justice for the sake of the oppressed, how much we long for God's justice, and how we can be made right with God the Judge.

Chris Wright tells the story about a young man from India who read the Bible for the first time. For whatever reason the first passage he read was the story of Naboth's vineyard. Wright met this young man at a conference where Wright was teaching on the Old Testament. The young man told Wright that he became a Christian by reading the Old Testament, and he was particularly thrilled that they would be studying the Old Testament in the sessions. Wright tells how this young reader was drawn to the God in the story of Naboth's vineyard:

He grew up in one of the many backward and oppressed groups in India, part of a community that is systematically exploited and treated with contempt, injustice and sometimes violence. The effect on his youth was to fill him with a burning desire to rise above that station in order to be able to turn the tables on those who oppressed him and his community. . . . He was contacted in his early days at college by some Christian students and given a Bible, which he decided to read out of casual interest, though he had no respect at first for Christians at all.

It happened that the first thing he read in the Bible was the story of Naboth, Ahab, and Jezebel in 1 Kings 21. He was astonished to find that it was all about greed for land, abuse of power, corruption of the courts, and violence against the poor—things he himself was all too familiar with. But even more amazing was the fact that God took Naboth's side and not only accused Ahab and Jezebel of their wrongdoing but also took vengeance upon them. Here was a God of real justice, a God who identified the real villains and took real action against them. "I never knew such a God existed!" he exclaimed. He read on through the rest of Old Testament history and found his first impression confirmed.

He then went on, he told me, to read the books of the law, and his amazement grew. "God!" he cried out, even though he didn't know who he was talking to, "You're so perfect! You think of everything!" . . . He found himself praising this God he didn't know. "God, you're so just, you're so perfect, you're so holy!" he would exclaim, believing this was the kind of God that answered the need of his own angry struggle.

Then he came upon Isaiah 43:1, and came to an abrupt halt. "But now, says the Lord." It is a beautiful word in Telugu, apparently. It means, "yet, in spite of all that." The end of Isaiah 42 describes Israel's sin and God's just punishment. But suddenly, unexpectedly, God is talking about forgiveness and pardon and love. "I couldn't take that," he said. "I was attracted to the God of justice and holiness. I ran away from a God of love." But he couldn't. For as he read on he found such a God more and more—still in the Old Testament! It was about then that the Christian friends came and explained more about the fullness of God's justice and love on the cross, and he came at last to understand and surrender to the God he had found in the Old Testament and his life was transformed through faith in Christ. . . . "I never knew such a God existed." But he does—not just in the past of ancient Israel, but in today's world. Are we afraid to discover him? (Wright, "I Never Knew," 3)

I love that response: "I never knew such a God existed." Let us rediscover this awesome God in this Old Testament story.

There are four main characters in chapter 21: Naboth, Ahab, Jezebel, and Elijah. We read of Ahab's coveting and sulking and of Jezebel's manipulation and destruction. R. G. Lee, who preached a sermon from this passage titled "Payday Someday," introduced Ahab as "the vile human toad who squatted upon the throne of his nation—the worst of Israel's kings," and he called Jezebel a snake "coiled upon the throne of the nation" ("Payday Someday").

We also have Naboth, the faithful Israelite who models obedience. Remember when God told Elijah he had "7,000 in Israel" who had not bowed to Baal (1 Kgs 19:18)? Here is one of them—living just outside the palace of this evil king. He has a little vineyard that he cherishes, which had been in his family for years. Finally, we have a *rejuvenated* Elijah appearing before Ahab (cf. 1 Kgs 19), reminding the vile human toad that he can hide nothing from God's sight and that his sin will surely find him out (Num 32:23).

As we move through the narrative, consider three particular applications: be prepared to suffer for the sake of righteousness, be willing to sacrifice for the sake of the oppressed, and there will be a payday someday.

Be Prepared to Suffer for the Sake of Righteousness
1 KINGS 21:1-16

We see in Naboth an example of a person being persecuted for righteousness's sake. In Ahab and Jezebel we see the nature and destiny of those who inflict such injustice on them.

This story also reminds me of the last part of the Sermon on the Mount (esp. Matt 5:11-12) and of a parable Jesus told about a vineyard (Matt 21:33-46). Concerning the latter, that particular parable served as an allegory of the whole history of Israel, a nation who persecuted their prophets (the servants tending the vineyard) and rejected and killed Jesus. In the parable such persecution didn't go unnoticed by the owner of the vineyard, who inflicted miserable punishment on the unrighteous ones. Such is the story of Naboth. The unrighteous kill the righteous, but the true Owner of the vineyard is aware and will have the last word.

Ahab's Covetousness (vv. 1-2)

Had he been alive today, Ahab would have subscribed to *Better Homes and Gardens* and enjoyed *House Hunters* on HGTV. His own palace may have been on *MTV Cribs*. He loved building his palaces, and he loved enlarging his gardens. He had a summer palace in Jezreel. After having some hard years of drought, now things were going pretty well for him in many ways. Rain could water his plants. Desiring now to expand his comforts and add to the beauty of his palace, he took an interest in the vineyard of Naboth. He makes an offer. Even though it was a nice vineyard, Ahab wants to turn it into a vegetable garden. So he offers him a sweet deal. He offers Naboth "a better vineyard." Or, if Naboth is finished with the vineyard business, he says he will just pay him what it's worth. Sounds generous, right?

But there are problems with this offer. Consider his desire to turn it into "a vegetable garden." This proposal would have been significant for an Israelite. We read about a "vegetable garden" in the same chapter of Deuteronomy where we read about the famine being a punishment for idolatry (Deut 11). God told His people,

> For the land you are entering to possess is not like the land of Egypt, from which you have come, where you sowed your seed and irrigated by hand as in a vegetable garden. But the land you are entering to possess is a land of mountains and valleys, watered by rain from the sky. It is a land the LORD your God cares for. (11:10-12)

The vegetable garden was a reminder of Egypt. It required human care, whereas the promised land relied on God's care. Add to this the fact that Israel was known as a vine under God's care (Ps 80; Isa 3:13-15; cf. Mark 12:1-12; John 15:1-17), and you can see that Ahab's desire is to turn Israel back to Egypt. Israel's kings had already turned the people back to Egypt with their foreign wives, and here Ahab continues this trend by making this proposal.

This is more than a little story about a vineyard. It's a battle of the kingdom of God versus the kingdom of darkness.

Further, Ahab falls into the sin of covetousness. This sin is committed when you desire something that isn't yours, like someone else's possessions, wife, success, or body, just to name a few. It's often associated with possessions, as in this case. Ahab has so much, but now he wants someone else's property. God gives him a land with milk and honey and vineyards, but he wants more. He surely knew this property was off limits since the land belonged to God and the families were not to sell their land, but Ahab wants it anyway. His appetites were beastly. To paraphrase R. G. Lee, Ahab was like a bear looking to lick a bit more honey, a lion looking for a piece of cheese, or an overstuffed bull looking for a bit of grass outside his own pasture ("Payday Someday").

Ahab's course of action illustrates James's words on the nature of sin's progress: "Then after desire has conceived, it gives birth to sin, and when sin is fully grown, it gives birth to death" (Jas 1:15). Ahab's desire gives birth to sin and eventually leads to death.

Ahab's story isn't new. He's like David, who desired someone else's wife and then murdered an innocent man (2 Sam 11–12). Ahab is like Cain, killing his brother.

Covetousness (or "greed") begins in the heart, and it leads to other sins. Idolatry always leads to further sins: "But those who want to be rich fall into temptation, a trap, and many foolish and harmful desires, which plunge people into ruin and destruction" (1 Tim 6:9). Is this verse not expressed in Ahab's tragic story? Sinful desire leads to harmful desires and destruction. Is it not also seen at the crucifixion of Jesus? Covetous men testified falsely against Him, betrayed Him for 30 pieces of silver, and ultimately nailed Him to the cross.

Don't take covetousness lightly. We must watch out for greed in our hearts (Luke 12:15; Eph 5:3; Col 3:5). Jesus said one of the reasons the word doesn't take root in hearts is that the "seduction of wealth" and the "desires for other things" choke the word (Mark 4:19). Therefore, guard your heart. Put sin to death. Give generously. And find your ultimate joy in the Savior, not in things of this world.

Naboth's Righteousness (v. 3)

Enter the faithful Israelite. Oh, the difference between Naboth and Ahab! Naboth responds to Ahab's proposal, saying, "I will never give my fathers' inheritance to you." Naboth is theologically motivated, not financially motivated. His God was not money but Yahweh. Naboth knew the Old Testament understanding of land—that land ultimately belonged to God, who gave it to the families. He knew God brought Israel into the land, fulfilling His word to Abraham (Gen 17:8), driving out the previous residents, and through Joshua allocating it to the tribes as their inheritance (Josh 13:1ff.). Naboth knew that selling the land wasn't an option and that established laws kept the land in the families (Lev 25; Num 36:7-9). Under certain emergencies an Israelite might sell land (Lev 25), but that didn't apply to Naboth's situation here. We read later how the prophets spoke against the neglect of property laws, saying, "Woe to you" (Isa 5:8; Mic 2:1-2). We read of Ezekiel's looking forward to the day in which the rulers wouldn't oppress but would allow the rightful people to posses the land according to their tribes (Ezek 45:8).

What a picture of righteousness! Think about it: Naboth could have been richer. He could have perhaps negotiated a bit more and worked his way up the royal ladder. But Naboth lives by the word of God and for another world. This is the only time we hear him speak. He simply says, "The Lord forbid that I should give you the inheritance of my fathers" (v. 3 ESV). Righteousness involves saying, "The Lord forbid." Even though the culture might accept something, that doesn't mean the Lord favors it. To paraphrase Paul, Naboth detests what is evil and clings to what is good (Rom 12:9). When presented with some unrighteous temptation, may the Lord give you power to say, "Absolutely not!" (Rom 6:1-2).

Your theology determines your biography. What we believe drives what we do. These men have two different theologies, and consequently, they have two different biographies.

Ahab's Sullenness (v. 4)

Ahab responds like a spoiled child who throws a fit when being denied a trinket while having a room full of toys: "Ahab went to his palace resentful and angry, because of what Naboth the Jezreelite had told him." This seems to be a common attitude of Ahab (cf. 20:43).

Look at this picture of a king: crying and refusing to eat because he didn't get what didn't belong to him! Lee says he is whining like a sick hound ("Payday Someday"). He probably had servants trying to cheer him up, musicians playing music, and entertainers trying to put him in a better mood. He was the pouting potentate.

Sulking isn't just childish. It also exposes something more than greed. Sulking exposes this about your heart: you aren't content with the providences of God. In the heart of the disciple is a deep trust that God is in control, and while things may not be going super well, you can go on without throwing a fit and refusing dinner.

This story is also sad when you consider that Ahab and Jezebel had God-given abilities. Their minds and skills, however, were used for evil and not for good. Look at how quickly Jezebel could devise a plan to kill Naboth! She could have put her skills to use for the kingdom—for the poor, the orphan, or the widow. How tragic it is to see people who are blessed by God using their gifts for the things of this world instead of the kingdom of God. Ahab should have been out caring for the nation; instead, he is crying in his bedroom over a little vineyard. How small his vision was; how cold his heart was. Beware of the self-centeredness of Ahab.

Jezebel's Sliminess (vv. 5-7)

Throughout Ahab's reign we have observed his weak passivity and Jezebel's snake-like influence. Here Jezebel asks Ahab what is wrong, and he proceeds to tell her of Naboth's refusal. Only Ahab doesn't report the story correctly. Naboth didn't say, "I won't give you *my* vineyard" (v. 6; emphasis added). The whole point was that the vineyard was *not* Naboth's to sell in the first place. He actually said, "*The Lord* forbid that I should give you the inheritance of my fathers" (v. 3 ESV; emphasis added).

Jezebel then tells Ahab, "Now, exercise your royal power over Israel. Get up, eat some food, and be happy. For I will give you the vineyard of Naboth the Jezreelite" (v. 7). With this sarcastic exclamation she seems to call Ahab a wimpy crybaby. She decides to take care of the matter herself since her weak husband cannot demonstrate power.

Perhaps she compared her weak husband to her father and thought, "King Ethbaal would never allow his subjects to refuse him." Such a thought would have probably enraged her. She had influenced Ahab to act like pagan kings, but he was not demonstrating their force in this particular episode, so she decides to take over. She will get the land without paying a dime.

Jezebel, like Eve in the garden, has no regard for God's authority. She will do what she wants, taking forbidden fruit, while her docile, Adam-like husband stands by passively.

Instead of using royal power to bless others, we have an example of using power to mistreat others (cf. Deut 17:14-20). This is a classic case of injustice, which can be understood as the abuse of power. Sadly today the powerful often manipulate, abuse, and torture the weak through bribery, corrupt legal systems, intimidation, and force. Land grabbing remains a serious matter around the world. In many places the vulnerable have their land and livelihood violently taken from them and have no place to turn.

If God ever gives you influence, remember why you have it. It isn't to satisfy your selfish desires. It isn't to trample on others or glorify yourself. You have influence so you can bless others in general and those with no influence in particular (Prov 31:8-9). Such godly character is nowhere to be found in Ahab and Jezebel, and sadly it was not found in the leaders of Naboth's town either.

Collective Wickedness (vv. 8-14)

Jezebel goes to work. She writes letters with the king's letterhead to those in charge of Naboth's town. She gives specific instructions (vv. 9-11). Each line was like another stone with which to execute an innocent man. Such a plan sounds familiar: an innocent man, falsely accused by false witnesses being killed outside the city (cf. Matt 26:57-68).

Then we read the cold story. The men of the city follow Jezebel's plan (vv. 11-13). They took him outside the city and stoned him to death.

So corrupt judges submit to Jezebel's wicked demands. Here's an example of a legal system becoming a tool for devilish politicians. Notice how easily this passes through the system. Such a process shows how corrupt this collective group of leaders was.

They send word back to Jezebel that Naboth is dead. All of this injustice is done in the name of religion. A day of prayer was observed on the same day this faithful Israelite was executed. They also followed the law of having two witnesses (Deut 17:6-7; 19:15; Num 35:30), and the appropriate penalty was then applied for cursing God (Lev 24:13-16).

Ahab and Jezebel had no interest in following God's word, but when it allowed them to get what they wanted, then they considered it. They used God to get what they wanted. And they apparently thought they could get away with it.

Temporary Happiness (vv. 15-16)

It appears the game is over. Jezebel tells Ahab that Naboth is dead. Then she tells him to take possession of the vineyard. If you glance over to 2 Kings 9:26, you see that Naboth's sons were also taken out in order to remove any other interferences with family rights of the land. Perhaps she laughed and mocked her husband: "Look what I've gotten you for free." Her conscience seems unprovoked by this innocent man's death. Perhaps this incites righteous indignation inside your heart. It does mine. If so, you can resonate with Psalm 73 as the psalmist laments over the "prosperity of the wicked" (v. 3). He talks about all they enjoy, while he is "punished every morning" (v. 14). Then we read, "When I tried to understand all this, it seemed hopeless until I entered God's sanctuary. Then I understood their destiny" (vv. 16-17). In other words, the psalmist realized the happiness of the wicked is temporary. It will not last long. For the unbeliever this life is as close to heaven as he will get. There will be a "payday someday." Don't envy the wicked. Instead, place your faith in Jesus and live for another reward. Say with the psalmist, "Who do I have in heaven but You? And I desire nothing on earth but You" (73:25). Ahab will enjoy his little vineyard for a brief time, but he didn't kill the true Owner of the vineyard.

As we stand over the grave of Naboth, we can find encouragement and instruction on being faithful in the midst of suffering. His story reminds me not only of the Beatitudes but also of Peter's words in 1 Peter 4:12-19. Peter reminds us that we should be prepared to suffer when we decide to follow Jesus. He says we shouldn't be surprised by persecution. We should rejoice in the midst of it. We should remember the spiritual blessing of suffering for Christ. We should glorify God through the suffering. We should remember that suffering for righteousness is sanctifying and temporary, while the unrighteous's suffering will be horrific and eternal. And finally Peter tells us to entrust our souls to God during the whole trial.

Jesus modeled suffering for righteousness and what it looked like to entrust one's soul to God in the midst of it. Peter says earlier in his letter,

> *He did not commit sin, and no deceit was found in His mouth; when*
> *He was reviled, He did not revile in return; when He was suffering,*
> *He did not threaten but entrusted Himself to the One who judges*
> *justly.* (1 Pet 2:22-23)

We have a Savior who understands human suffering, for He was the ultimate righteous sufferer. The story of an innocent scapegoat isn't on the periphery of the Bible; it is the central message of it (Leithart, *1 and 2 Kings*, 157). As Jesus endured such suffering, He was making a way for us to escape God's ultimate judgment and empowering us to live in the present as believers in Him. Peter says, "He Himself bore our sins in His body on the tree, so that, having died to sins, we might live for righteousness; you have been healed by His wounds" (2:24).

Be Willing to Sacrifice for the Sake of the Oppressed
1 KINGS 21:8-16

Not only should we be willing to suffer for the sake of righteousness, but we should also be willing to sacrifice for the sake of the oppressed. I draw this point from the inactivity of the people in Naboth's city. Where are the protesters? Nowhere. Not one single person steps up to defend Naboth. The leadership of Naboth's city does nothing, the people do nothing, and that is exactly the reason injustice goes on today. It has been said, "All that is necessary for the triumph of evil is that good men do nothing." I don't want to call these "good men," but I am sure injustice prevailed because the people did nothing.

The reason they complied with Jezebel's wishes was that they were afraid of the consequences of refusing her. We can understand their fear, but we cannot condone their actions. They do nothing to stop the death of a faithful Israelite and apparently allow the death of his sons to happen without raising their voices. Like Jesus, Naboth was killed by "lawless people" (Acts 2:23).

As noted previously about Ahab's and Jezebel's lack of concern for blessing others, especially the weak, as kings were obliged to do, so here is another example. The leaders in Naboth's town should have used their influence to protect the weak. Instead, they crumbled under pressure. They feared a woman and her mafia more than they feared God (cf. Matt 10:28).

But we shouldn't just shake our heads at the people in Naboth's city. Let us beware of our own passivity and indifference to the great problems of our day. What are you doing about poverty, land grabbing, abuse, trafficking, and the spiritual lostness of our world? We must repent not only of our sins of commission but also of our sins of *omission*. It has been said, "The opposite of love isn't hate; it is indifference." Are you unmoved by the Naboth-like stories of our world?

Serving in Jesus' name will inconvenience us. It will cost us. But love acts. Are you using your influence, time, and talent for the sake of those in need? Don't confuse sympathy with love. Feeling sorry for the orphan, the widow, the abused, and the lost doesn't help them. Love acts. If God gives you any influence, use it to protect and bless those in need. Sacrifice by spending time in prayer for victims of injustice. Give financially for the good of others. Go to the nations to speak the gospel to those who have never heard it. Do it knowing that though suffering awaits you, Jesus is with you, and He will bring you safely into His heavenly kingdom.

In the 2013 movie *42*, about baseball hero Jackie Robinson, Harrison Ford gives a stellar performance as general manager Branch Rickey. I was moved by how Rickey gave a glimpse of what it looks like to suffer on behalf of another. Obviously, Robinson endured unimaginable mockery and criticism, but so did Branch Rickey, who defended Robinson. Near the end of the movie, Robinson presses Rickey as to why he submitted himself to the whole painful ordeal. Rickey explains that earlier in his life he had the opportunity to stick up for the best player on his college team, who was a black man, but he did nothing. Then Rickey said, "There was something unfair about the heart of the game I loved, and I ignored it. But a time came when I could no longer do that. You let me love baseball again. Thank you."

Rickey was unhappy with his past apathy and indifference and sought to do something about it. Maybe you have stood back long enough from fighting on behalf of the oppressed. Let me encourage you to play ball. Speak up. Get involved. Act.

Remember: There Will Be a Payday Someday
1 KINGS 21:17–22:53

Following Ahab's deception, we learn of Ahab's imminent death. Two particular prophets will predict his death, and then 22:29-40 describes this death.

The Prophet Elijah Appears (21:17-29)

Ahab is enjoying the herbs from his vegetable garden, and Jezebel is probably planning her next scheme. But then someone appears. It's the "Hillbilly from Tishbe!" Elijah is back!

We read that familiar phrase again: "Then the word of the LORD came to Elijah" (v. 17). God says, "Get up and go to meet Ahab king of Israel, who is in Samaria. You'll find him in Naboth's vineyard, where he has gone to take possession of it" (v. 19). Twice we read where Jezebel told Ahab to "get up" (21:7,15); now God tells Elijah to "get up." For every Jezebel who tells an Ahab to get up and do injustice, God has an Elijah to whom He says get up and speak justice.

Because of Ahab's murder and wrongful acquisition of land, the Lord tells Elijah to say, "In the place where the dogs licked Naboth's blood, the dogs will also lick your blood!" (v. 19). God will step in to defend the defenseless. Ahab will reap what he has sown. God was not unaware of these events. Proverbs says, "The eyes of the LORD are everywhere, observing the wicked and the good" (Prov 15:3).

Elijah obeys and goes to meet Ahab. The king asks, "So, you have caught me, my enemy" (21:20). Previously, Ahab called him a "destroyer" (18:17), but now he calls him "my enemy." Elijah was Ahab's enemy because Ahab had become an enemy of God.

Elijah responds that God will destroy Ahab's royal dynasty because he has provoked the Lord to holy anger, and Ahab will suffer the same fate as Jeroboam and Baasha (21:22). Elijah tells Ahab that God will also execute judgment on his serpent-wife, Jezebel.

These prophecies were fulfilled eventually. Jezebel's execution is described in 2 Kings 9:30-37. Years after Elijah's prophecy an army captain named Jehu, obeying God's word, had all of Ahab's descendants killed. He also gave an order to have Jezebel, who had put on her makeup in anticipation of Jehu's arrival, thrown down from an upstairs window. She died from the fall. When Jehu sent men to bury her, they found only traces of her body, which had been eaten by dogs, thus fulfilling Elijah's prophecy

The Lord delayed judgment, but it came. And when it came, it came swiftly and sovereignly. Perhaps Ahab thought Elijah was not telling the truth. Perhaps Jezebel mocked her husband every time they ate out of Naboth's vineyard, and mocked Elijah, sarcastically asking, "Did he not say judgment was coming? Where are the dogs?" But R. G. Lee was probably right in saying that Ahab jumped every time a dog barked ("Payday Someday").

The wicked may prosper for a short time in this life, but the arrow of God's judgment will strike, and God, the righteous Judge, will have the last word. Ahab may have been able to manipulate corrupt judges, but he could not manipulate the ultimate Owner of the land of Israel and the Judge of all the earth.

This passage gives suffering believers great comfort. Though Christians may suffer around the world today, not one single unjust action goes unnoticed by God. No one had to report this event to God.

Davis says, "Jezebel's letters had already been put through the shredder at city hall; none of the shady details came out in the papers. Elijah himself apparently didn't know until Yahweh told him. . . . Yahweh didn't let it pass. He saw and intervened (cf. Ex 3:7-8a)" (*1 Kings*, 304). Just as in the Exodus narrative: God heard, saw, and knew about His people's suffering, and He brought judgment on Egypt.

The question we might have in the story is, why did God wait so long? Naboth is already dead. We like the fact that God pronounces judgment, but what of Naboth? The mystery of God's timing in judgment appears throughout Scripture. Moses is spared, but others die at the hands of wicked Pharaoh. The toddler Jesus is spared though others die at the hands of Herod. John the Baptist is put to death by the heartless king Herod Antipas (Mark 6:14-29). Herod Agrippa kills James, but Peter experiences an amazing jailbreak (Acts 12). How can we make sense of these stories? While we will never understand the mysterious ways of God, the text still stands as a great comfort for us (as the opening story of the young man from India interpreted it). The flow of the story is intended to show us that God defended Naboth. As Davis says:

> The Naboth episode, we can say, is no guarantee of immunity, only of justice—and that not necessarily this October. But come it will, for 1 Kings 21 is a preview of 2 Thessalonians 1:6-7. We have the narrative in 1 Kings 21; we have the doctrine in 2 Thessalonians 1. God will intervene to bring justice to his wronged people. We mustn't allow our quandary over the timing of Yahweh's justice to eclipse our comfort over the fact of it; indeed, the way Yahweh takes up the cudgels here for his wronged people is what, in part, makes him such an attractive God. (*1 Kings*, 304)

God defends the weak. God knows. God sees. God will judge the unjust in His own timing.

What we read in verses 25-29 after the Elijah encounter surprises us. We might expect Ahab to respond to this message with more evil deeds or for God to act immediately. Instead, we read that Ahab "tore his clothes, put sackcloth over his body, . . . and walked around subdued" (v. 27). This act was a sign of repentance. God then speaks to Elijah:

> *Have you seen how Ahab has humbled himself before Me? I will not bring the disaster during his lifetime, because he has humbled himself*

before Me. I will bring the disaster on his house during his son's lifetime. (v. 28)

Though Ahab will die violently in battle, his dynasty will go for a while under the reign of his sons. Judgment is delayed but not canceled.

There is a difference between a rain delay and a cancellation. In Scripture God often delays judgment when people repent. The prophecy of Huldah to Josiah is an example of this principle (2 Kgs 22:8-20).

Was Ahab's repentance authentic? He did humble himself, and God granted him delayed judgment, so there seems to be reason to accept it as genuine. But then again, true repentance involves restoration. We don't read of any actions of King Ahab in trying to restore what he broke. He doesn't give the vineyard back to Naboth's family or admit his wrongdoing. True repentance looks like Zacchaeus, who after coming to Jesus returned fourfold what he owed to others (Luke 19:8). I would call this scene a merciful act of God but not true repentance. In the midst of wrath, God remembered mercy. God's display of mercy was an invitation for Ahab to go deeper into repentance, that is, to live a life of repentance and obedience to Him. It was an invitation to "produce fruit consistent with repentance" (Matt 3:8).

What kind of God could show such mercy? He is the God who has shown us mercy. For you see, we deserve to be punished for our sins, also. While we may not sin exactly like Ahab, we are guilty of sinning against God. Jesus likens anger to murder in the Sermon on the Mount. Only One is perfectly righteous: Jesus. And there will be a payday someday for everyone. How can we escape God's just judgment? R. G. Lee says,

> . . . the only way I know for any man or woman on earth to escape the sinner's pay-day on earth and the sinner's hell beyond—making sure of the Christian's pay-day on earth and the Christian's heaven beyond the Christian's pay-day—is through Christ Jesus, who took the sinner's place upon the Cross, becoming for all sinners all that God must judge, that sinners through faith in Christ Jesus might become all that God cannot judge. ("Payday Someday")

We need a substitute. And that's what we have in Jesus. God provided the righteousness we need in Him. Judgment will fall. Either Jesus takes your judgment, or you will face it. We cannot hide from God. He knows our sins—in thought, word, motive, and deed. We have one solution: we must be hidden in Christ. In Christ we are safe. In Christ we're righteous. In Christ we're loved. In Christ we don't have to fear impending judgment. In Christ we have power to stand up for the oppressed, and we look forward to future reward in His kingdom.

This great salvation is made possible by the greatest story of the innocent sufferer, Jesus. For Naboth's story calls our attention to Jesus' story in Matthew 26:59-68. Jesus' enemies conspired against Him too. They falsely accused Him of blasphemy, mocked and beat Him, and eventually took Him outside the city to kill Him (Heb 13:10-13). Jesus' blood speaks a better word than the blood of Abel and the blood of Naboth (Heb 12:24), for their blood cries out for vengeance, but Jesus' blood cries out with forgiveness to everyone. Jesus is the innocent scapegoat offering salvation to the world and promising that one day the cries of the martyrs will be heard and their blood will be avenged.

The Payday Train Arrives (22:1-53)

Ahab's doom is sure. Even though God's wrath has been delayed, it is surely coming. His death has been foretold by two different prophets (20:41-42; 21:19). In chapter 22 we find yet another prophet, Micaiah, foretelling Ahab's disaster as well.

Peace existed between Aram (Syria) and Israel for three years. Despite a previous Israelite victory, Aram still has control of an important city: Ramoth Gilead in the Transjordan. Wishing to reclaim this city, Ahab decides to form a partnership with the king of Judah, Jehoshaphat.

If we jump over to verses 41-50, we learn a bit more about Jehoshaphat. The Chronicler spends much more time describing his reign than the writer of Kings (2 Chr 17:1–21:1). In addition to his peaceful relationship with the wicked king of Israel (1 Kgs 22:44), we also read about some commendable qualities of this 25-year-long king of Judah (vv. 41-42). He followed the ways of Asa, and he did what was right in God's eyes (v. 43). He also removed the male cult prostitutes from the land (vv. 45-46). Unfortunately, though, he didn't completely remove the high places. Despite his failures he was one of Judah's better kings, strengthening the nation militarily and spiritually. His life of prayer and faith is displayed vividly in 2 Chronicles 20. The writer of Kings notes that he controlled Edom, who became a supporter of Judah later (2 Kings 3). Why would Jehoshaphat go to war alongside Ahab?

Perhaps it was for political reasons, or perhaps because his son married Ahab's daughter (2 Kgs 8:18: 2 Chr 18:1).

While Jehoshaphat does some unwise things, he at least seeks to know God's will before battle. So he seeks an authentic prophet (1 Kgs 22:7). Ahab had gathered up 400 "yes-men" prophets. The story is read well against the backdrop of Elijah and the false prophets in 1 Kings 18 (Provan, *1 and 2 Kings*, 162). We meet one prophet saying something entirely different from the majority once again. Ahab only wants to hear "good" (22:8; cf. 2 Tim 4:3). Consequently, he doesn't like the idea of calling the prophet Micaiah, who is captive to the word of God.

Due to Jehoshaphat's influence, Ahab calls Micaiah. All the prophets appear before the kings and prophesy. One prophet, Zedekiah, uses horns to act out his message, declaring that Ahab will gore the Arameans like an ox (22:11; Ezek 4:1–5:4). All the other prophets agree with Zedekiah. When Micaiah enters, he's told to follow suit. However, this prophet will only speak what the Lord gives him to speak. Sarcastically, though, Micaiah begins his speech by confirming the words of the prophets. Ahab smells the sarcasm and requests the truth. Micaiah then delivers the news: "I saw all Israel scattered on the hills like sheep without a shepherd. And the LORD said, 'They have no master; let everyone return home in peace'" (22:17). The Lord has decreed Ahab's disaster. This is now the third prophet to tell him of his future.

Micaiah goes on to tell Ahab about the means God, who is seated on the real throne, will use to bring about his death. The plan involves God's using these lying prophets to entice the king to go off to war (vv. 19-23; cf. 1 Sam 16:14-15). Before one jumps to question God's method, we need to see that God doesn't deceive Ahab; He actually tells Ahab what He's doing. Yet Ahab still listens to the lying prophets despite having this knowledge.

Micaiah is struck in the face, seized, and punished. It's not the last time that a truth-telling prophet will be punished (cf. Matt 5:10-12; John 18:22; Acts 23:2-3; Jas 5:10). Micaiah stands as a hero of the faith, speaking God's word courageously and faithfully.

Ahab then arrogantly goes off to war. We aren't told about how the decision was reached, but Jehoshaphat went along with it. Stupidly, Ahab decides to disguise himself in the war, as if a disguise can thwart God's stated purposes.

The Arameans are looking to take out Ahab but only find Jehoshaphat, whom they let go. Then an unnamed archer shoots "without taking special aim" (22:34). The arrow strikes Ahab between the scale armor and the breastplate. The writer gives every impression that this took place under the sovereign Lord's power. Ahab gets propped up in his chariot and eventually dies, and his blood flows into the bottom of the chariot. When his body gets brought back to Samaria, as his servants are washing the blood off the chariot, "the dogs licked up his blood, and the prostitutes bathed in it" (v. 38). The mention of prostitutes reminds the reader of the whole idolatrous life of Ahab (e.g., 14:24; 15:12). Provan says, "He has fed the people idolatry, and now he is consumed by it" (*1 and 2 Kings*, 164).

God's triple prediction came to pass (20:42; 21:19; 22:17,23). Now the reader anticipates the fulfillment of the rest of the prophecies concerning his house. But Ahab's son Ahaziah reigned in his place and continued in the evil ways of his wicked father.

In six plus chapters about Ahab, we learn the incredible folly of rejecting God's Word and the absolute certainty of God's judgment. Allow his story to lead you to repentance. Trust in Christ before payday comes for you. Love Christ, who is the perfect King and who will avenge the blood of every Naboth one day. Anticipate the day in which the King greater than David appears in glory to establish His kingdom, filled with *shalom*, where peace and righteousness dwell forever. When you suffer like these faithful prophets, fill your mind with this glorious future. Someday the wicked will be justly punished. Someday those who are in Christ will see the Savior in glory. Let us think of the next world as we live faithfully in this one.

Reflect and Discuss

1. Why did Naboth value his vineyard so much?
2. What do you have of spiritual value that isn't worth trading for goods or money?
3. Do any other passages in the Bible speak to the question above?
4. Jezebel manipulates and abuses others to get what she wants. What are some sins that are so bad that even unbelievers repudiate them?
5. Why are the powerless people of the world, like Naboth, of such value to the Lord?
6. God relents some of His wrath when Ahab repents. What does this teach us about God's character?
7. Do you ever feel that someone is too evil to receive God's mercy?

8. Ahab despises Micaiah because he criticizes him. Do you invite or despise criticism?
9. How can believers today value the Word of the Lord in their lives?
10. Ahab attempts to escape the judgment of God by disguising himself. In what ways are you tempted to try to escape the consequences of sin?

2 Kings

Chariots of Fire

2 KINGS 1:1–2:25

Main Idea: In this transitional section of the narrative, Elijah denounces idolatrous Ahaziah and later gets carried up to heaven; Elisha takes up the prophetic mantle in the spirit of Elijah.

I. Background
II. Elijah Confronts a Sick King and Kingdom (1:1-8).
III. Judgment and Mercy (1:9-18)
IV. Elijah's Ascension: He Finishes His Race (2:1-12).
V. Elisha's Ascension (2:13-25)
  A. A new Joshua (vv. 13-18)
  B. A glimpse of Eden (vv. 19-22)
  C. To kill a mocking boy (vv. 23-25)
VI. Conclusion

In life we are faced with massive questions: Why am I here? What is my purpose? What job will I pursue? Whom will I marry? However, the most important is, To whom will I entrust my life? When the end of life has come, where will I turn?

We live in a world that turns everywhere. Our world often says all roads lead to the same place, but what if that isn't true? What if there is only one way? To whom will you entrust your life when you are on your deathbed? Allah? Buddha? Joseph Smith? Yourself? Whom will you seek on the final day?

The main question in this text is, Is there a God in Israel? Whom will they seek? Who will they turn to with their questions and problems? We will see that the king and the mocking boys look elsewhere besides Yahweh. We discover there is one true God we should seek, and He continually provides prophets and His word to turn His people back to Him.

Background

The contemporary mind may object to the miracles in this text. Some people would say we are too sophisticated for the supernatural events that occur in this story. However, if there is a God, then miracles are possible. He has power over nature and can step outside the natural order. In this text we see God operate outside the natural order to validate His message, endorse His man, and bring judgment on those that show derision toward Him.

Second Kings continues the events and narrative of 1 Kings. The conclusion of 1 Kings isn't a pronounced climax, considering the two kingdoms are in decline and folly. Ahab is dead and gone. We have seen him to be a fool, standing on a shaky foundation, building his whole life on things that pass away and gods who cannot hear or act.

We observe overall that Jehoshaphat was a good king compared to others. He walked in the ways of the Lord, but he wasn't the long-expected King. Jehoshaphat didn't tear down the high places, he had bad alliances, and he married one of his sons to Ahab's daughter (this will have massive repercussions, putting David's line in jeopardy).

Ahaziah is depicted as an idolatrous train wreck like his father Jeroboam, doing evil in the sight of the Lord. Second Kings picks up right here, with the kingdom spiraling downward toward exile. God's people are being removed from God's place because they will not submit to His rule and keep His commandments. This nation, brought into the promised land to be a light to the nations, instead coveted the gods and kings of those nations. So God essentially says, "You love the neighbor's gods so much, why don't you go live with them outside the land of promise!?"

Elijah Confronts a Sick King and Kingdom
2 KINGS 1:1-8

In an act representative of his kingdom, King Ahaziah essentially falls over a banister and is seriously injured to the point that he doesn't know whether he will live or die. Ahaziah is living out what was said of him in 1 Kings as he walks in the ways of his father by serving Baal. The king, like his kingdom, is now hurting.

Ahaziah decides to look outside of Israel for an answer. The confrontation on Mount Carmel hadn't convinced him that Yahweh is strong and Baal is impotent and sleeping, so he seeks another god. Oddly he seeks a localized version of Baal in the land of the Philistines. This is the group that was soundly defeated—their bitter enemies. Ahaziah is seeking out Goliath's god for an oracle. Even though Yahweh's prophet

Elijah has shown the ability to raise the dead, Ahaziah looks elsewhere. The downward spiral of the kingdom has gotten worse. At least Jeroboam sought out a prophet of God when his son was sick, but not so with the wicked line of Ahab.

The author likely uses a derogatory term *Baal-zebub* instead of *Baalzebul* (v. 6). It's a play on words, insulting him as the "Lord of Flies" instead of "Baal the Exalted"—the author looks with disdain on this deity that Ahaziah seeks.

The king believes his hope rests in a pagan, enemy, territorial god whom Elijah embarrassed. Ironically, according to the law in Israel, turning to a pagan god is worthy of death. Exodus 22:20 says, "Whoever sacrifices to any gods, except the LORD alone, is to be set apart for destruction."

Here we see the sins of the fathers manifested in the son. Ahaziah had seen the gracious and harsh acts of God toward Ahab, yet he follows in the evil path of his father. When parents detest God or minimize Him, they shouldn't be surprised when their children do the same. When we passively and implicitly teach our children that God isn't important, our children will live it out. Parents who inadvertently teach their children that the world revolves around them by regularly skipping corporate worship to play on a travel baseball team (because their son is "so good") shouldn't be surprised when later in life he doesn't see connection to the local church as that big of a deal. Children will be influenced by what they have been taught, whether it is explicit or implicit.

When you are staring your own mortality in the face, it's no time to play games with a mute, impotent god. Whom will you seek? This idea of one true God flies in the face of our tolerant culture, but if there is indeed *only one* true God, then the tolerance of mute, impotent gods is unwise and unloving. Some people are turned off by this idea, saying the exclusive claims of Christianity are intolerant, but what if there is indeed only one way? Is tolerance of the wrong path wise or loving? If you have a heart attack, is the doctor intolerant, unwise, and unloving when he points out that *only* surgery will save your life?

We can all be tempted to look elsewhere. It could be overt, like horoscopes and palm readers. Or it can be less clear, like trusting Freud for counseling, prosperity teachers for theology, or alcohol or drugs or food as a coping mechanism. It could be turning to work for satisfaction and meaning or to weightlifting because we are obsessed with our looks. It could be turning to immoral sex for fulfillment. We live in a world that will turn almost anywhere for relief but doesn't want to turn to a God that deserves and demands our all.

God takes violation of the first commandment seriously. Ahaziah has belittled Yahweh, essentially suggesting that there is no God in Israel, or that He is impotent and less powerful than Baal-zebub. This is our idolatry as well: when we seek idols, we are saying either that Yahweh cannot help or that He's not good enough to handle our problems and desires.

Amazingly, God sends Elijah to deliver a message. God isn't done pursuing Israel or her wayward kings, and this is an act of mercy, like a doctor telling someone the truth about their sickness. The death notice is issued as the messenger returns to the sick king—what will Ahaziah's response be?

Judgment and Mercy
2 KINGS 1:9-18

Tragically, Ahaziah responds by sending his army to detain the prophet and, like his father, seeks to control the prophet's word. Their intended goal is foolish, as they try to bring the word of God under human control. Yahweh will again send fire to validate His prophet and judge the idolaters.

Ahaziah has rejected mercy through God's prophet and instead has shown reverence to a mute god. He now sends captains to arrest Elijah. Throughout the narrative there has been a showdown between Yahweh and Baal, and this is represented in fire (which Baal is supposed to control). However, Baal is an impotent god, and now 100 men will die because of Ahaziah's ineptness and hubris as Elijah sends fire to judge Israel.

The first captain of 50 asks, and the second captain of 50 demands. Messengers had the authority of the one who sent them. Neither the captains nor King Ahaziah respect the One who sent Elijah. Through judgment, they would learn that they don't make demands of Yahweh or His man.

The seemingly harsh treatment of the captains and soldiers must be seen not only as judgment but also as an act of protection. It isn't like the 50 are headed toward him because they want to bring him down to play golf with Ahaziah. Yahweh is choosing to protect His prophet.

These groups are coming to liquidate Elijah. The fact that a regiment is coming shows Ahaziah's hostility toward the prophet and his hope to silence the prophecy by getting rid of him. He believes he can control the oracle by putting the prophet under his authority. In doing so he has refused to seek Yahweh or listen to His word. Deuteronomy 18:13-15 says,

> You must be blameless before the LORD your God. Though these nations you are about to drive out listen to fortune-tellers and diviners, the LORD your God has not permitted you to do this.
> The LORD your God will raise up for you a prophet like me from among your own brothers. You must listen to him.

Elijah, like other prophets, calls the king back to covenant faithfulness—a covenant made by the gracious God who delivered them out of Egypt. But Ahaziah will not listen.

The third captain of 50 acts as the king and nation should: he gives a gospel response, demonstrating how we should seek One to whom we can entrust our lives. The third captain comes humbly and reverently. He seems truly to believe that Elijah is a man of God. This is a great example of gospel confession and response, a bowing before God and a cry for mercy. He, unlike Ahaziah, recognized that mercy might be available, and it was. The same is true continually for the believer: we daily must fall on His mercy through the gospel.

If the king and nation would respond in the same manner, then they would live and stay in the land (no exile). Ahaziah's attitude, however, doesn't change when he comes face-to-face with Elijah, and neither does Elijah's. Rather, Elijah confronts idolatry and tells the king why his life is demanded. And not surprisingly, the word comes true: Ahaziah dies.

So whom will we seek? Idols? False gods? Functional saviors? Or will we entrust our whole being to Yahweh? To whom are we crying out in times of trouble and distress? Whom will we seek for salvation? The wages of sin is death, and so it is for this one who showed such derision for Yahweh, but mercy is available, as the third captain found out.

Elijah's Ascension: He Finishes His Race

2 KINGS 2:1-12

As Elijah's earthly ministry draws to a close, a scene ensues where Elijah will go town to town trying to shake Elisha (vv. 1-6). Two of the towns are places known as centers of pagan worship. Bethel was where Jeroboam set up the golden calf, instituted non-Levitical priests, and appointed a feast. Jericho had been cursed by Joshua. In these towns we're introduced to "the sons of the prophets," who are pupils of the prophets and part of a prophetic community. The sons of the prophets seem to have been set up strategically in these cities that are deeply entrenched in idolatry. In places of great darkness, we need Bible-preaching and -teaching believers.

Elisha will not let Elijah shake him. Most scholars believe the point of his not leaving Elijah's side is to test whether Elisha will count the cost of discipleship, probably a final test to see if he will persist. We see something of our own call here—to forsake all for the glory of the Name. The question for us, like Elisha, is, will we persist and persevere? This is the sign of the true disciple: we bring the Word near, and we delight in God above all else. Elisha is a true disciple, for he had forsaken all, burning the plows, to follow Elijah. This won't be the last time disciples forsake all to follow a great prophet!

Elisha doesn't want to hear that Elijah is being taken up. A deep bond has probably developed—imagine 18 years of apprenticeship. Elijah, the new Moses, now parts the Jordan, as described in language reminiscent of the exodus, and they cross on dry land. The sons of the prophets witness from a distance this passing of the torch. Elijah has crossed the Jordan and is about to enter the most precious of promised lands.

Once they cross, Elisha asks for "two shares," referring to the double portion the firstborn inherits (Deut 21:17). In this case it isn't wealth but prophetic power. Thus, Elisha is essentially saying he will count the cost and dedicate his whole life to continue Elijah's work as though he is his firstborn. Elisha asks this, not unlike Solomon, realizing he will need great help as God's representative to complete the task to which he is called.

Now a war vehicle comes for God's prophet—a "chariot of fire with horses of fire" (vv. 11-12). These aren't fluffy, cotton candy clouds but a war instrument. Elijah is called the "chariots and horsemen of Israel." The appearing of the chariot of fire symbolizes that these prophets are the power of Israel, and it is because the power of Yahweh is in them. The chariot was an instrument of military might, and the author is essentially saying Elijah is like the army of God, the true defense of Israel, because God is with him.

Elijah goes on to his eternal reward without tasting death because God is in control of death and can overrule it. Elisha is saddened and shows signs of sorrow over losing a mentor. The text leaves us with some questions: Will we count the cost? Will we persist? Will we seek the glory of God over our own? Will we rely on God's power to speak God's Word faithfully in places of darkness?

Elisha's Ascension
2 KINGS 2:13-25

A New Joshua (vv. 13-18)

We learn some important lessons about Elijah in this passage. First, Elijah points us back to Moses. Both called Israel to covenant faithfulness and then died outside the promised land, leaving behind disciples to take up the work. We now see in Elisha a new Joshua with a similar name—*Joshua* means "Yahweh is salvation" and *Elisha* means "my God is salvation." Elisha comes through the Jordan to Jericho, and he comes to root out Canaanite worship.

Second, Elijah points forward to John the Baptist, a prophet who would wear the same kind of clothes as Elijah. John the Baptist—crying out in the wilderness against a national power, with a woman at the center of it seeking his life—would be a forerunner of Joshua's fulfillment, Jesus. Like Elijah, John would anoint his successor at the Jordan and see his successor as the firstborn receiving the promised inheritance. God is orchestrating a plan to save His people.

At this moment it may have seemed that Israel's defense system was gone because the one who had stood in the gap calling the Baal lovers to turn and repent is gone. However, God will not cease to have a man calling Israel to faithfulness. Elijah may be gone, but Yahweh isn't. The God of Elijah is still here, which is what Elisha is saying when he strikes the river and says, "Where is the LORD God of Elijah?" Elisha believes God has certainly not abandoned them, and he relies on Yahweh for power. The new man is here!

This passing of the mantle to Elisha will be validated in **three signs**. The new Joshua **parts the sea** and heads toward Jericho and then to Bethel to root out the pagan worship.

The company of prophets realizes that Elijah has passed his prophetic work on to Elisha with their words and actions. They revere him as the new representative of God for Israel. Elisha gives in to peer pressure here when he first tells them not to seek for Elijah but then gives in to their request. After a fruitless search for Elijah, Elisha basically says, "I told you so." This validates Elisha as the one who bears not only the power of Yahweh but also His wisdom.

A Glimpse of Eden (vv. 19-22)

Another miracle validates Elisha's work. The men of the city seek Yahweh's help. The men essentially say the city is pleasant but something lethal in the water is causing humans and animals to miscarry. Historically, Joshua had cursed anyone who would try to rebuild Jericho, and during Ahab's day someone did, paying the price of the curse. The city that was under a curse now receives a blessing from Yahweh. Elisha **heals the water** and assures them it will no longer cause death. Here we glimpse what miracles do. They don't invade the natural order but restore it.

In miracles you taste the past and the future. We glimpse of Eden where there was no foul water, and we glimpse the future when there will be streams of water that bring life and there is no death. We see grace here! Elisha restores the water to its original design, and the curtain of history is pulled back ever so briefly, and the curse is lifted.

It isn't just human beings who await the return of the King; the earth itself does. The earth is groaning, Romans tells us, and just briefly those groans stop in Jericho, of all places. This will not be the last prophet with power over water and the curse.

To Kill a Mocking Boy (vv. 23-25)

I have often quoted this passage in response to sarcastic statements about my bald head! It seems to be a favorite text among follicly challenged men like me. But what exactly is going on here?

As you consider everything behind this account, you realize this act involves more than just teenagers joking with their teacher. It's a serious offense. These guys are mocking the prophet of God. They ridicule this new Joshua who has come into pagan Bethel to root out Canaanite worship.

Bethel is the town Jeroboam used to house the golden calf, so it isn't shocking that teens here would mock and ridicule God's prophet. They're like their fathers. Elisha had proven who he was, yet he still is mocked. This won't be the last prophet who is mocked.

"Go up, baldy! Go up, baldy!" they say. Even though Elisha probably had his head covered, they apparently knew he was in fact bald, so they decided to mock his physical features as well as his God and his office. In saying, "Go up," they essentially mean "get out of here; we don't want anything to do with you." So they show total derision toward him.

Evil mockery in general is ridiculing those made in God's image and thus deriding the One who made them. James 3:8-10 says,

> . . . but no man can tame the tongue. It is a restless evil, full of deadly poison. We praise our Lord and Father with it, and we curse men who are made in God's likeness with it. Praising and cursing come out of the same mouth. My brothers, these things should not be this way.

In their mockery these guys are showing contempt and hostility toward Yahweh and His representative. Something more sinister yet is going on. If pagan worship persists, the coming of the Messiah could be compromised. This is Satan's plan: to compromise the line of the coming One through intermarriage with pagans so God's people cease to exist as a nation. However, Elisha is the new Joshua protecting the promised Seed by protecting the line that will bless the nations.

The word for "small boys" here could be steward or servant. It's likely these are officials at the shrine to the golden calf, so the new Joshua is beginning a holy war against the shrines of the Canaanites and their central places of worship set up in Israel.

Elisha **brings on God's judgment**, and she-bears attack the boys. The warning in Leviticus 26:21-22 comes to mind:

> If you act with hostility toward Me and are unwilling to obey Me, I will multiply your plagues seven times for your sins. I will send wild animals against you that will deprive you of your children, ravage your livestock, and reduce your numbers until your roads are deserted.

We should remember that God will not be mocked. Galatians 6:7 simply says, "Don't be deceived: God is not mocked. For whatever a man sows he will also reap." God will have the last word.

We aren't sure if the boys are actually killed because the word literally means "mauled," so they may not have died. Whatever the case, covenant infidelity has brought on a curse. This curse on the boys was a warning to the nation. If they persist in mockery, disdain, disobedience, and apostasy, then there will be dreadful consequences. This episode was a vivid sign to the people. Soon a great bear would come maul them and take them to exile.

Conclusion

Elisha, the new Joshua, is on a crusade. He has been shown as a true successor who brings both blessings (for those who cry out to God) and curses (for the mocking enemies of God). Elijah is gone, but everything is OK because Yahweh is present. Elisha is carrying on with power, wisdom, judgment, and grace.

The judgment of both chapters is clear: those who seek and call on the Lord (the third captain and Jericho) will get Him and His grace (restored waters and new creation), and those who don't will suffer the loss of all things through fire and judgment.

So, in a world where there are many paths to choose, where do the Scriptures tell us to turn? They tell us to seek and entrust ourselves to a greater Prophet. This is a Prophet who will call everyone to turn from false gods. This is a Prophet who judges by fire like Elijah but One who takes the fire on Himself before He pours it on unrepentant sinners. On the last day a fire will come for all who have not fled to Him. This Prophet will set His face like flint toward Jerusalem, saying He has a baptism of fire that He must undergo and how He is anxious to undergo it (Luke 12:50). This Prophet is greater than Elijah; He doesn't have to escape death by ascension but goes through death so He can defeat it before He ascends.

Another Prophet will be anointed for service at the Jordan River. On that day He will not just get the double portion of the firstborn; He will actually be the firstborn Son of God, in whom God is well pleased. Another Prophet has command over the water; in fact the water will rage against Him, and He will say, "Be still!" And the water will listen! "Who is this man?" people will ask.

Another Prophet will be mocked and have His hair pulled out. Thorns will be put on His head, and He will not be told to go up, but He will be mocked while He is on a cross and be told to come down. This Prophet, even in the midst of persecution, will show that He is a gracious Prophet who would tell one of the mockers who turns and repents that He will be with this Prophet-King in paradise.

This Prophet can pronounce blessing and roll back the curse by crushing that ancient Serpent. This One will share the name of Joshua and Elisha. His name will be Jesus.

One greater than Elijah and Moses is here, the God-Man Jesus Christ. He doesn't just call us back to covenant faithfulness. He actually bears the penalty that covenant breaking deserves and is lifted up on an instrument of torture so that, if you will seek Him, His judgment will be your judgment, and His resurrection will be your resurrection.

This is the most important question today and on that final day: Whom will you trust? Yourself, Baal-zebub, or this Messiah/Prophet/King? He will come again to judge the world that has rejected Him, and on that day fire will fall. Your judgment can already have been taken at the cross if you will be like the third captain, repenting and saying, "Let my life be precious in Your sight." We should look to this One: His ministry to the nations has now been mediated to us. We too had brothers standing and seeing the better Prophet taken up, and He like Elijah left His Spirit for us to carry out the tasks given us as successors, heirs, and sons so that nations would delight in Yahweh. Let's do this work with hope because death cannot touch us; we will ascend one day like our King

You see, this chapter isn't the last we hear from Elijah. He will make one more appearance with Moses and the two prophets who had been permitted to see the glory of God on a mountain. This time they will once again be on a mountain seeing the glory of God but this time in a face. The question is, Do we see that glory? Or are we looking in Philistine territory? Whom will we trust? Whom will you set your gaze on? Look to Jesus.

Reflect and Discuss

1. Why does God oppose Ahaziah?
2. Why is the sin of idolatry so offensive to God?
3. What is it about Baal that might have appealed to Ahaziah? How might worldly ideas and values appeal to believers today?
4. Compare and contrast the attitudes of the three captains of 50 as they approached Elijah.
5. Was God harsh in responding to the two captains and their men? Why or why not?
6. Why does Elijah lead Elisha around town to town?
7. Do the two scenes where Elijah and Elisha part the Jordan River remind you of any other biblical passages? Are these scenes important? Why?

8. What do the "sons of the prophets" seem to be concerned about? They honor Elisha, then reject his first counsel. Why?

9. How might people today pay lip service to the Word of God yet disobey it?

10. How might people today, like the small boys, mock the Word of God and the people of God?

Elisha: Mighty in Word and Deed

2 KINGS 3:1–4:44

Main Idea: Elisha the prophet proves to be mighty in word and deed as he speaks in a time of war and performs miracles in times of desperation.

I.   **Elisha Speaks God's Word (3:1-27).**
   A.   The need for God's word
   B.   The messenger of God's word
II. **Elisha Shows God's Compassion (4:1-44).**
   A.   Oil for a desperate widow (vv. 1-7)
   B.   A child for a barren woman (vv. 8-37)
   C.   Food for the hungry (vv. 38-44)
III. **One Greater than Elisha Is Here.**

Our kids have been reading several small biographies. I love debriefing them after they finish each volume. One evening Joshua was so excited to teach me about Abraham Lincoln. With serious and childlike happiness, he said, "Papa, I've been reading about Abraham Lincoln. He was the sixteenth president. He was against slavery. But then he got shot and died. Now he's a statue." My drink came out of my nose! After cleaning myself up, I commended him for his reading and his confidence, but I tried to correct the last part of his lesson, reminding him that when you die, you don't turn into a statue. He explained what he meant, however. He said, "People make a statue of you when you do something important. They want to remember you." We went on to talk about Lincoln's presidency and how his influence continues to be remembered in America.

We just finished the biography of Elijah in 2 Kings 2. The larger-than-life prophet died—well, sort of. He was taken up into heaven in a blaze of glory, and he reappears in the New Testament. Nevertheless he is gone, but his ministry isn't gone. It continues on, particularly through the life of his successor, Elisha. Elijah passed the prophetic mantle to him. In the opening chapters of 2 Kings, the sons of the prophets affirmed Elisha's ministry, and now Elisha will prove his ministry to Israel's King Joram and others in 2 Kings 3–4. From these chapters we see how Elisha, like Elijah, was God's special agent, sent to speak truth and to display God's power.

But Elisha not only reminds us of his mentor. As the privileged readers of the Old and New Testaments, we also see how he foreshadows the ministry of Jesus. Elisha's ministry is a Messiah-like ministry. In fact, Elisha's ministry is closer to the ministry of Jesus than Elijah's ministry was in some ways, particularly in the degree of compassion that he demonstrates (though Elijah too demonstrated compassion). Wiersbe overstates it, but he points out the difference, saying that Elijah was "a prophet of fire," but Elisha was a "pastor" and "minister to the people" (Wiersbe, *Be Responsible*, 329). Like Jesus, Elisha has compassion on those in need: a widow, a barren woman, a dead son, a hungry multitude, a leper, and those in difficulty (4:1–6:7).

Of course, Jesus' ministry was much greater than Elisha's ministry, so while we should look closely at the events recorded in 2 Kings, we shouldn't stop there. We should go on to look to the greater Prophet-Savior, Jesus. The Elisha narratives make us love this heroic prophet. But these chapters should make us love Jesus even more—our truth-speaking, bread-providing, compassion-showing, sickness-healing, death-defeating Savior.

Many Bible teachers treat chapter 3 by itself and group 4:1–6:7 together. This makes sense. The mighty acts of Elisha are told in rapid-fire succession in 4:1–6:7, much like Mark's Gospel shows the mighty acts of Jesus (Mark 4:35–5:43). However, I have chosen to include chapter 3 with this section and treat half of the miracle stories of 4:1–6:7. While recognizing some discontinuity between chapter 3 and 4:1–6:7, I think there are some connections in the story of the Moabite revolt in chapter 3. Most relevant is that the point of chapter 3 seems to be to validate the *word* of the prophet Elisha. The following chapters go on to show *deeds* of Elisha. I prefer to see these two sections together. Like Jesus, Elisha was mighty in word and deed (Luke 24:19). So let's look at Elisha's word and deed ministry by considering four ways his ministry points us ahead to the ministry of Jesus.

Elisha Speaks God's Word
2 KINGS 3:1-27

King Joram of Israel, King Jehoshaphat of Judah, and the king of Edom will go up against King Mesha of Moab in this unfamiliar and puzzling story.

The Need for God's Word

The chapter opens by stating that Joram is the new king in Israel. (The HCSB consistently spells Israel's king "Joram" and his counterpart in Judah "Jehoram." In Hebrew the two names are spelled identically.) His reign lasts for 12 years. He was the son of the wicked king Ahab and the brother to Ahaziah, who died in an accident. Joram is an awful king too but not quite as awful. While he did evil in God's sight, "he removed the sacred pillar of Baal his father had made" (v. 2). This doesn't mean that Baalism ceased to exist. Joram tolerates the Baal cult, though he apparently doesn't participate in it. This sacred stone remains in the land until the reign of Jehu (10:26-27). He turns away from the pillar of Baal, but he doesn't turn away from the sins of Jeroboam. In other words he deserves judgment though he was not as evil as his dad. To say, "I am more righteous than Ahab," isn't anything to boast in. That is like saying, "He is the tallest hobbit," or "That team is better than the Cubs." God's Word reveals that the standard of holiness is God, and because of that, we're in great need.

We need God's Word **to point out essential gospel truths** like the reality of our sinfulness. The doctrine of sin isn't popular, but it's fundamental. While a person may not be as bad as they could be, no one is as righteous as they should be. We have failed to worship God alone and have been led astray to false gods. We have done evil in the sight of a holy God and need to be made righteous by Him. Only through Christ can we receive righteousness and be accepted by God. Don't rely on your own efforts to be accepted by God. Sure, you may not be Ted Bundy, but you aren't Jesus. Though you might have given up robbing banks or cheating on your taxes or committing adultery, you still haven't earned salvation. You have sinned in thought, word, deed, and motive. The good news of the gospel is that Christ died for sinners like you and me, and He alone makes us holy and acceptable in God's sight. The gospel says, "Tony did evil in God's sight, but then he trusted in Christ, and now Tony is accepted in God's sight."

We need God's Word not only to point out essential gospel truths but also **to give us personal guidance**. The story goes on to tell of Moab's revolt against Israel (mentioned in 2 Kgs 1:1). After the death of Ahab, Mesha decides to stop being a vassal of Israel. He was a sheep breeder who paid tribute in lambs and wool, but he decides to do so no more. In response Joram decides to exert his authority. He asks Jehoshaphat to go with him. The story echoes 1 Kings 22:4, where Ahab called on

Jehoshaphat help him. Jehoshaphat may be kind, but he isn't wise. In the case of his connection with Ahab, though his alliance was questionable, at least Jehoshaphat sought counsel from the Lord (1 Kgs 22:5). Here in 2 Kings, Jehoshaphat partners again with Israel's king but doesn't inquire of the Lord until they get desperate—after the decision to go to war was already made. We're surprised by his failure to seek God first.

Let this serve as a reminder to us. We will be tempted to live by our impulses rather than by God's Word. We need to seek God's Word for all matters of life. Don't rush off into life without the essential resource: God's Word. The psalmist reminds us of its necessity when he says, "Your decrees are my delight and my counselors" (Ps 119:24).

The war strategy involves marching through a wilderness in Edom, approaching Moab from the south. The king of Edom joins them (probably another vassal of Israel), they all make an "indirect route for seven days," and they run out of water (3:9). The account echoes both holy wars, like the battle of Jericho, and the wilderness experience. Because the kings decide to march out without any divine instructions, it shouldn't surprise us that they will encounter disastrous results even before the war begins. No water. Complaining. Blaming God. It sounds like the exodus.

Joram blames God. He didn't seek God's counsel in the first place, but he deems it appropriate to blame God for the result. "It wasn't *my* fault" was the attitude. Sinful humanity has been following this pattern of blame shifting since the garden (Gen 3:12; Jas 1:13-15). Joram may be "religious," but he doesn't love Yahweh. That's evidenced by his lack of submission to Him.

Eventually Jehoshaphat asks, "Isn't there a prophet of the LORD here? Let's inquire of Yahweh through him" (v. 11). Elisha is then mentioned as the one who "used to pour water on Elijah's hands" (meaning that he was a servant to Elijah), and he is sought out (v. 12). Surprisingly, Joram concurs in going to Elisha, unlike Ahab who resisted calling on the prophet Micaiah.

The Messenger of God's Word

Elisha responds to king's inquiry, "We have nothing in common. Go to the prophets of your father and your mother!" (v. 13). Elisha is offended by the king's sudden interest and responds sarcastically and harshly. Joram is seeking God's counsel because of an emergency, not out of wholehearted loyalty to Yahweh. Joram is like today's pluralists: they don't acknowledge Christ's exclusive lordship, but in an emergency they may try anything, including the Bible.

Don't treat God's Word like an airbag in your car—only there in case of an accident. God calls us to lifelong submission to His Word, not to temporary, sporadic moments of interest. We need His Word in the normal days of life, not just when we are dying of thirst in a wilderness. Are you really interested in a path of discipleship or just escape from trouble (Davis, *2 Kings*, 45)?

Surprisingly, instead of pronouncing doom, Elisha announces God's salvation. Behold again the goodness of God to undeserving people. Elisha first tells the king that the only reason he will speak the word is because Jehoshaphat is present. Then he asks for a musician, and while one played, Elisha proceeded to speak. The prophets received their messages in a variety of ways, including through music (1 Sam 10:5). Elisha reports the good news. A double promise is presented: God will provide water for the army and the livestock, but He will also provide them with a victory. Can God give us water? Of course! It is "easy in the LORD's sight." Elisha also reports that God can do the heavy lifting as well. He says God, in His abundant generosity, will provide a victory for them. What a gracious God, who can do "above and beyond all that we ask or think" (Eph 3:20).

Can God provide for your daily necessities? Of course! It is an easy thing! You can cast "all your care on Him, because He cares about you" (1 Pet 5:7). Seek Him for your provision. But He can do more than give you groceries. God has provided for your greatest need, namely salvation from your enemies of sin and death and the grave. God lavishes His grace on us. He gives us bread to eat, and He gives us eternal life in Christ.

Perhaps you feel no need to ask God for "easy" things because you are so immensely blessed with food and clothing. You should stop and thank Him for such provisions. So what about your heavy things? How will you deal with your sin problem? Look to Jesus, who carried the cross for sinners and died in their place, giving them life. God alone can deliver us from our greatest enemies.

Water came just as Elisha promised; then the victory is described just as Elisha predicted. When the Moabites see the water, they are fooled into thinking it's blood (more exodus echoes) and the kings have decided to fight each other. But when they come into the Israelite camp, the Israelites drive them back and carry out Elisha's instructions.

Observe how God saved Israel in this story. The prophet tells of the promise of salvation to Joram. How will salvation come? It will come *by God's grace* (for Joram didn't deserve it). And it will come *because Joram is with the Davidic king,* Jehoshaphat.

We're in the same position. We can be saved by God's grace alone, through our union with the ultimate Davidic King, Jesus. If we are in Him, then we have received grace upon grace. How kind of God to grant sinners salvation!

Just when we think this story looks just like other victory stories, we read of the surprising twist. Mesha responds to his initial defeat in two ways. He first tries to break through the enemy lines, but he and 700 swordsmen could not get through. His second attempt involves him offering up his own son (and heir to the throne) as a sacrifice, probably to the pagan god Chemosh in an apparent attempt to receive divine help. Then we read that his sacrifice actually brought relief. The Israelites retreat to their own land and fail to get complete victory over Moab. Why? After the child sacrifice, "great wrath was on the Israelites" (v. 27). Puzzling.

Whose wrath/fury was this? Was it "against" or "on" Israel? Some suggest it refers to divine wrath (either Chemosh's or Yahweh's), but the text never says it was God's wrath explicitly. I have a hard time believing Chemosh brought relief. Some suggest that Yahweh was angry because this war was never on His agenda; He simply gave them a partial victory. Others suggest it was human wrath, either referring to the Moabites' fury or the Israelites' indignation at the gruesome scene. House summarizes this strange ending well:

> Given the nature of the author's theology, however, it is much
> more likely either that the action inspired Moab's army to
> fight more fiercely or that it caused Israel such indignation
> and sickness of heart that they lifted the siege. Though
> the exact meaning is unclear, the result is the same: Israel
> withdraws without further disaster yet also without control of a
> former vassal. (*1, 2 Kings*, 264)

As House says, while the meaning of the phrase is difficult to interpret, the result is at least clear: Israel doesn't achieve total victory. This seems to be another picture of Israel's decline.

The story's ending highlights at least two applications for us. First, **God is the God of surprise endings**. Just when we think we know how this story is going to end, we meet something unusual. God does as He pleases (Ps 115:3) and does more than we can imagine (Eph 3:20-21). Just look at the story of Jesus. He was the innocent One who cared for those in need and spoke God's word, yet the King of kings is crucified horrifically at the climax of the story. Not the ending most would expect—a King, crucified. But the story doesn't actually end there. In three days the Son of David vacates the tomb in triumph. I don't mean we don't know how the story will end (for we can read it in Revelation!); I simply mean God doesn't always work the way the world expects, and we will see some surprising things as believers, both in this life and in the next (like which persons get greatly honored in the coming kingdom). We don't always know what God is doing in this life (especially in hard times), but we know He is good, and therefore there is one thing to do: trust Him (Leithart, *1 and 2 Kings*, 183). He is in control. He is good. Trust Him.

Second, **we must look to Christ**. We should point out from this story the difference in following gods like Chemosh and following Christ. Jesus said,

> *Come to Me, all of you who are weary and burdened, and I will give you rest. All of you, take up My yoke and learn from Me, because I am gentle and humble in heart, and you will find rest for yourselves. For My yoke is easy and My burden is light.* (Matt 11:28-30)

Dead religion doesn't offer you liberty; it gives you burdens and bondage. No one but Jesus can offer you an easy yoke. When you submit your life to Jesus and His Word, it actually frees you. When you follow pagan gods, or simply today's cultural idols of money, sex, power, or fame, they enslave you, they crush you. The Word of God is liberating. Jesus said His "truth will set you free" (John 8:32). You don't have to live enslaved, sacrificing a child, cutting yourself in attempt to get rid of guilt and shame; you don't have to live an oppressed life, trying to pay God back for your sins. You can come to Jesus and experience His grace. We don't have to offer blood, for the blood of Jesus has saved us.

While Joram doesn't really improve the situation with Moab, he now knows God's word is with Elisha. He has seen Elijah's successor's word fulfilled in this partial victory.

Elisha Shows God's Compassion

2 KINGS 4:1-44

Elisha isn't just a truth-speaking prophet; he is also a compassionate servant of the people. Let's consider three displays of God's compassion.

Oil for a Desperate Widow (vv. 1-7)

Elisha's ministry continues to echo the ministry of Elijah. This story and the following one remind us of 1 Kings 17, with some differences. Here a widow is desperate because of debt, not because of famine. She is an unnamed widow, the wife of one of the sons of the prophets. But he died, and she is in serious financial trouble. Since she cannot pay off her debts, her sons are to be taken as slaves (cf. Isa 50:1; Neh 5:4-5).

Her *faithful desperation* and Elisha's *compassion* stand out first. She cries out to Elisha. This is important. She isn't turning away from God in crisis but seeking God. Elisha responds, "What can I do for you?" Notice the compassion of Elisha. This response is different from his response to the inquiry made by Joram. There Elisha said, "We have nothing in common" (3:13). Here Elisha shows us that God cares about nameless, ordinary people. You don't have to be high and mighty to seek God's help. The widow cries out to him, and he is eager to help. She prays like Jehoshaphat: "For we are powerless. . . . We do not know what to do, but we look to You" (2 Chr 20:12).

Elisha responds like Jesus responded to blind Bartimaeus: "What do you want Me to do for you?" (Mark 10:51). Elisha's kindness as a mediator points the way to our Savior, who stands ready to offer grace in times of need. Are you seeking Him in your need? Are you answering the question, "What do you want Me to do?" I'm not advocating prosperity theology; I'm simply encouraging you to present your needs (not your greed) to God. God cares about big stuff and little stuff. He knows the plots of North Korea, and he knows about your car problem in North Carolina. Do you believe He cares and can help? If so, then follow this nameless widow to the throne of grace.

Next we observe her *insufficiency* and God's *sufficiency*. Elisha asks her, "What do you have in the house?" Her modest response: "Your servant has nothing in the house except a jar of oil" (v. 2). Notice the way God often works: it is good for us to consider our inadequacy, for we see our great need for Him. We may have little, but God is the all-sufficient Provider who loves to take what we have and multiply it (2 Kgs 4:38-44; Mark 6:40-44).

Then we read about her *obedience* and God's *miraculous provision*. Elisha gives her specific instructions about how the problem will be solved. She is told to gather up vessels, go inside, shut the door, and pour her little jar of oil into the vessels. After each one is filled, she is to pour oil into the next one. She does everything the prophet says. As in the Elijah encounter with the widow of Zarephath (1 Kgs 17:7-16), her small amount is turned into abundance. God chooses to provide for a lowly widow through a miracle. Does God always do this? No. But He can. Regardless of whether through a miraculous provision or God's "ordinary providences," He is still the one who provides for our daily bread.

Consider how this episode takes place in secret. Even though the neighbors would have known about the vessels, no one knows about what happened when she closed the door. God often does His great work in secret. Jesus told us to pray in secret, and "your Father who sees in secret will reward you" (Matt 6:6). He said the same thing about giving to the needy (Matt 6:2-4). He said you don't need to blow a "trumpet before you" every time you do a righteous act. While a lot of the Christian life is public, we need to remember that not everything we do for the King needs to be on social media. You may couch your words with "to God be the glory," but much done in the name of "sharing your testimony" is self-exaltation. Love God in secret.

She tells Elisha when the jars are filled, and he says, "Go sell the oil and pay your debt; you and your sons can live on the rest" (v. 7). Take in these simple instructions and the amazing kindness of God. Not only can she pay off her debts, but she also has an abundance left over to live on.

God's faithful people matter to Him, even if they are unknown to the vast majority of the world. Here is one little lady being cared for by Yahweh. Truly, He is "father of the fatherless and a champion of widows" (Ps 68:5).

A Child for a Barren Woman (vv. 8-37)

This story is filled with acts of *kindness*. First, we read of yet another nameless lady who displays kind hospitality to Elisha. She is a woman of means who uses her wealth to bless others. Elisha accepted her hospitality whenever he passed through her area, like Jesus who accepted the hospitality of others. She asks her husband to build a modest guest room for the "holy man."

Jesus had something to say about welcoming prophets. He told his disciples, "The one who welcomes you welcomes Me, and the one who welcomes Me welcomes Him who sent Me" (Matt 10:40). He then added that the gracious host would receive a reward: "Anyone who welcomes a prophet because he is a prophet will receive a prophet's reward" (Matt 10:41).

We need to remember the significance of hospitality ministry. Gracious hospitality is a trait of the righteous throughout the Bible (Gen 18; 47; Ruth 2:15; 1 Sam 25; Neh 5:14-19; Job 31:32; Acts 16:11-15; 1 Tim 3:2; Jas 2:25). Of course, Jesus didn't teach that we should only show hospitality to prophets. He also said that we should invite "those who are poor, maimed, lame, or blind" to our parties (Luke 14:13). While they can never repay us, Jesus said, "You will be repaid at the resurrection of the righteous" (Luke 14:14). We welcome all people because we have received God's gracious hospitality. He has welcomed us (Rom 15:7). Jesus told His disciples that He is "going away to prepare a place for [us]" (John 14:2).

We must welcome others, and when we do, we need to know that this is no small act. Let's practice hospitality as individual families, and let's welcome others as a church family (Rom 12:13; 1 Pet 4:9; cf. Luke 10:9-10). Christians often neglect this biblical ministry because of ignorance (unaware of the biblical teaching on hospitality), carelessness (failure to plan on it), greediness (people often want to pamper themselves instead of serving others), or fear (being intimidated by it). Follow this barren lady's example, if at all possible, and host people regularly.

Have you thought about how you can use your home to bless others? Adoption? Foster care? Itinerant ministers? An elderly widow? Welcoming that functionally fatherless kid down the street?

In response to her kindness, Elisha wants to return kindness (more reward is coming, it seems—see 2 Kgs 8:1-7). He serves as an example of accepting hospitality. He treats their care for him as a big deal and wants to thank her. He doesn't say, "Oh, I'm a prophet. They *should* care for me."

But what do you give the lady who has everything? Gehazi offers a suggestion: "She has no son, and her husband is old" (v. 14). Nothing is more valuable than a human life. Elisha likes the idea, so he calls the Shunammite lady and tells her, "At this time next year you will have a son in your arms" (v. 16). She tells Elisha not to get her hopes up, but sure enough she conceives and gives birth to a son just as Elisha said.

This isn't the only Bible story of a barren woman giving birth. Sarah, Rebekah, Rachael, Mrs. Manoah, Hannah, and Elizabeth all experience God's amazing provision. This story is different, however, in that the children of those other ladies were essential for the continuing of the covenant people, or their child becomes a significant leader in a time of crisis. But here we don't even know the child's name, and there are numerous other children in Israel. So why does God act? One reason could be that He is pointing to the authenticity of Elisha's ministry. Elisha is a kind, miracle-working prophet. But perhaps God simply wants to show off His own goodness. Maybe He just wants to bless this lady (Davis, *2 Kings*, 63). It may be that simple. God is good, and He does good things. Paul says that God "richly provides us with all things to enjoy" (1 Tim 6:17). Though God is high and lofty, His exaltation doesn't remove Him from His children; it simply means He has unlimited power to bless them. The psalmist says,

> *Who is like Yahweh our God—*
> *the One enthroned on high,*
> *who stoops down to look*
> *on the heavens and the earth?*
> *He raises the poor from the dust*
> *and lifts the needy from the garbage pile*
> *in order to seat them with nobles—*
> *with the nobles of His people.*
> *He gives the childless woman a household,*
> *making her the joyful mother of children.*
> *Hallelujah!* (Ps 113:5-9)

God is swift to bless, but don't get the wrong idea. If you show hospitality, you will not necessarily be blessed with a child! Get the major idea: God rewards biblical hospitality. God will ultimately reward every act of obedience for the kingdom of God because it demonstrates that you have welcomed the gospel (Matt 10:14,42; Luke 14:13-14).

Thus, we have a story of the kindness of this lady, the kindness of Elijah, and the abundant kindness of God. Let us "praise God from whom all blessings flow."

But the story isn't over. Next we read of *mysterious sorrow*. After her son is grown, he dies tragically in her arms (vv. 18-20). She isn't willing to accept this tragedy, though. She lays his body on Elisha's bed and prepares to confront the prophet. Her husband appears to be somewhat skeptical, maybe because he has not been told of the child's death. He objects at the timing of her venture, but she goes off anyway, some 15 miles to Mount Carmel. When Elisha sees her coming, he sends his servant to meet her, but she dismisses the inquiry with the same type of evasive response she gave to her husband. She finally reaches Elisha and grabs his feet and proceeds to pour out her heart to him. She refuses to leave him.

While she is upset and mystified by this tragedy, one should stop and commend her for heading to the right person in time of crisis (as in the previous story). Elisha was God's ambassador, and she knows that. She is essentially clinging to God. What do you call it when you are dumbfounded by the difficult providences of God, but you still cry out to him? Faith! (Davis, *2 Kings*, 65). Faith says, "The LORD gives, and the LORD takes away. Praise the name of Yahweh" (Job 1:21). She doesn't have the answers; she is grieved, but she has not turned away from God.

This lady isn't the only one with limitations in this story. Did you notice what Elisha said? "The LORD has hidden it from me. He hasn't told me" (v. 27). Elisha has limited knowledge of the event. (Could he have also had limited knowledge of the events in chapter 3? I think so.) He has limited power. When he sends Gehazi to lay his staff on the head of the child, nothing happens. Now, Elisha was God's prophet, but he was not God. He has limitations. The only thing he can do is pray (Davis, *2 Kings*, 66). When Elisha came to the house, "he went in, closed the door behind the two of them, and prayed to the LORD" (v. 33). Even though Elisha performs physical actions in verses 34-35, the whole episode illustrates his desperation in prayer.

While we hold some people up as marvelous Christian leaders, we are reminded that even the most gifted servants are limited. If Elisha is desperate, how much more are we? Recognize your limitations and pour out your heart to God, who is unlimited in power. We will fail to pray when we do the reverse. When we think we are powerful enough to handle problems and God is small, then we will not pray like this. Rather, we are powerless but God is powerful. Seek Him.

The child eventually sneezes seven times (a sign of complete restoration perhaps) and opens his eyes. Elisha then calls the mother and gives her son to her, similar to the story of Elijah and the widow's son (1 Kgs 17:17-24).

Thus, another miracle has been performed in secret. Elisha is shown to be an agent of God's compassion and power who can raise the dead like Elijah. And the recipient of this gift bows to the ground in gratitude.

There's a similar story in Luke 7, concerning a widow of Nain. Jesus "had compassion" on her and raised the child. The difference is that the Old Testament prophets *pray*, but Jesus simply *speaks*. "Young man, I tell you, get up!" He says. Jesus is greater than Elijah and Elisha. He's our ultimate hope of resurrection. Perhaps you wonder why God doesn't raise the dead today. Well, in these cases, these children would eventually die again. God has done something greater for us. He has promised that everyone in Christ will be raised permanently (1 Thess 4:13-18). Elijah and Elisha were giving a sneak preview of the resurrection power of Christ. When Christ was on earth, He was giving us a sneak preview of the ultimate resurrection to come. This lady looked to Elisha in desperate trust, but we look to Jesus, who has triumphed over the grave.

In two stories we have two unnamed ladies receiving daily bread, two children, and a sneak preview of the resurrection power of Jesus. Elisha is putting the compassion of God on display. Prophets were not just brash speakers of truth; they were also agents of God's mercy. How much more so with the Savior. John says He was "full of grace and truth" (John 1:14).

Food for the Hungry (vv. 38-44)

Elisha displays God's compassion next to the sons of the prophets. During a famine Elisha instructs his servant to prepare a large pot of stew. This story reminds us of the earlier Elijah narrative, where God provided for the prophets during famine (1 Kgs 17:1-24; 18:1-15), and of chapter 2, where Elisha purifies the water (2 Kgs 2:19-22).

A problem emerges when one of the men goes looking for some herbs and decides to add some wild gourds to the stew, not knowing what they were. The result is disastrous. The men take a bite of these vicious vittles and cry to Elisha, "There's death in the pot, man of God!" (v. 40). It's hard to know if the wild gourds could have literally killed them or if it only tasted horrible. Perhaps it was both. Elisha responds in compassion and wisdom. He knows what to add to the pot to cure it. He says, "Get some meal" (v. 41). They do so, he throws it into the stew, and "there was nothing bad in the pot" (v. 41).

Should we take as our application the need to know how to cook? Was Elisha a miracle worker *and* a master chef? While I do recommend learning how to cook, I think the simple application, once again, is that

God provides daily bread for His people. "Give us each day our daily bread" was and is a desperate and regular prayer for those living in agrarian cultures and in poor regions. Some of us in prosperous places may have a hard time identifying with this prayer. When we need food, we go to the grocery store. We complain if we have to stand in line longer than three minutes! In agrarian cultures it wasn't easy and simple. Starvation and hunger were real problems. Furthermore, this was a time of famine. The people were thus doubly desperate. Yet God takes care of them.

God isn't distant and remote. He's involved in our lives. He takes interest in a pot of soup, not just ruling the solar system. God is interested in providing poor students with washing machines and furniture. God understands us. God loves us. God is near to us. God is real to us. God is good to us. God faithfully provides for us. Bless the Lord. Don't forget His benefits (Ps 103).

This same application continues in the next episode. God's faithfulness shines as Elisha multiplies 20 loaves of bread and feeds 100 people. The food comes from an unnamed man from Baal-shalishah. He brought Elisha what was to be offered to the priests: "20 loaves of barley bread from the first bread of the harvest" (v. 42; cf. Exod 23:19; Lev 23:20; Num 18:13; Deut 18:4-5). Why does he not give the bread to the priests? Apparently it was because of the corruption in the priesthood in northern Israel. He bypasses them and gives it to the man of God instead. You might say he was a separatist. God had a remnant of loyal followers, and he was one of them (cf. 1 Kgs 19:18).

Gehazi does the math and says that such provision is impossible. Feed 100 people with 20 loaves of bread? That's either some tiny people or some big bread! However, Elisha insists, "Give it to the people to eat, for this is what the LORD says: 'They will eat, and they will have some left over.'" So what happens? Yahweh fulfills His word: "So he gave it to them, and as the LORD had promised, they ate and had some left over" (v. 44). God does what He promises. God multiplied what they brought Him (cf. 2 Cor 9:10).

Being a Christian doesn't exempt you from trouble or even from starvation. God may choose not to provide for some people for His own sovereign reasons. But when provision comes, we should bless His name. And we need to remember that God always keeps His word. Those who are in Christ will one day enjoy the new heavens and the new earth, where all the needs of God's people are met gloriously, fully, and eternally. Praise God for daily bread, and rest in His eternal promises.

One Greater than Elisha Is Here

We are left to admire Elisha. He speaks truth in an evil day. He cares for a widow in great need. He provides a child to a barren woman. He raises the dead. He feeds a multitude. He's a compassionate prophet who points us to Jesus.

Jesus was in Elisha mode on several occasions. He fed 5,000 (Mark 6:30-44) and 4,000 (Mark 8:1-10) and had food left over. The feeding of the 5,000 appears in all four Gospels. In John's Gospel Andrew reflects the concern of Elisha's servant. After finding the young lad with five loaves and two fish, Andrew says, "What are they for so many?" (John 6:8). While Andrew has his doubts, Jesus commands the people to sit down in groups. Then Jesus multiplies fewer loaves than Elisha had and fed a greater number of people (Mark 6:39-44). Some in the audience surely reflected on this Elisha story. John says that some said, "This really is the Prophet who was to come into the world!" (John 6:14). Surely, some thought, "One greater than Elisha is here."

The problem in Jesus' day was also like the problem of Elisha's day. Some looked to Jesus only for miracles, not for true spiritual transformation. The miracles should have sent people to embrace Him by faith as Lord; instead they simply looked to Him to help them in a temporary emergency. Jesus said, "Don't work for the food that perishes but for the food that lasts for eternal life, which the Son of Man will give you, because God the Father has set His seal of approval on Him" (John 6:27). He told them that if they come to Him by faith they will never be hungry again (6:35). He called them to believe in Him for eternal life and receive the assurance that He will "raise them up on the last day" (6:40). But sadly, when Jesus finished His discourse, many turned away. A faithful few received Jesus, but many rejected Him. Elisha experienced a similar result. While he was able to provide for the faithful remnant, his ministry didn't lead to an overall change in the nation. Many ignored or rejected him, as others later did with Jesus and as many do today.

What will you do with Jesus? Will you embrace Him as Lord? Or will you turn away from the One who has had His body torn like bread and His blood poured out like wine in order to grant hungry sinners forgiveness, freedom, eternal life, and joy? May God open your eyes to embrace the One "powerful in action and speech" (Luke 24:19), who conquered death, fulfilling everything written of Him in "the Law of Moses, the

Prophets, and the Psalms" (24:44), and who now grants grace to sinners and clothes them with power to tell the world of His salvation (24:48-50).

Reflect and Discuss

1. Why does Elisha oppose Joram?
2. The coalition succeeds because of Jehoshaphat. What does this teach about God's character?
3. The author says God's provision of water for the coalition is "easy." What "easy" things might God provide to His people today?
4. Should it be a priority to ask God for "easy" things (i.e., mundane needs)?
5. What does God's provision for whole armies, lonely widows, distressed mothers, and hungry prophets teach about God's character? How is each story significant?
6. Is it important to live under the Word of God and among the people of God? Why?
7. Why might God have given the barren woman a son and then allowed him to die?
8. Does it seem unjust when bad things happen to good people?
9. Discuss ways God gives simple gifts to His people today.
10. The miraculous provision of food and water, barren women giving birth, and dead sons coming back to life—do these stories sound similar to any other biblical stories?

Cleansed Lepers and Floating Axe Heads

2 KINGS 5:1–6:7

Main Idea: In a show of His power and grace, the Lord (through the ministry of Elisha) first heals an outsider of leprosy and then provides for the needs of His servants through an unusual miracle.

I. God's Saving Grace (5:1-15)
   A. A great man with a great need (v. 1)
   B. A great evangelist (vv. 2-5a)
   C. A great word (vv. 5b-13)
   D. A great transformation (vv. 14-18)
II. God's Supplying Grace (6:1-7)

A few years ago some guys from our church went to Nigeria on a mission trip. The trip included medical missions, orphan care, theological training, and a visit to a leper colony. I will never forget the day we pulled into the isolated place where a group of lepers was living. We spent our initial time visiting with them. We went hut to hut, sitting down with these wonderful individuals, hearing their stories, and asking them about their faith. Some of them had no toes or fingers. They dwelt in sad-looking huts, trying to survive on limited food resources. The locals wouldn't allow the lepers' kids to leave the colony, so the colony was filled with kids also. Of course, the kids latched on to us and celebrated as we handed out candy. The sights, sounds, smells, conversations, and touches caused us all to be emotional.

I wasn't prepared for what happened next. A local chaplain gathered everyone to the center of the village and said, "Now pastor Tony will preach." That was news to me! I didn't know I was preaching. I didn't even have a Bible. And what on earth can you say to a group of dying lepers? I decided simply to quote Romans 8:18-31 as best as I could and encourage these individuals, many of whom were followers of Jesus. As I spoke about suffering and future glory, the people began to worship. I have a picture of a lady standing behind me with her arms lifted up in the air as I told the villagers that all of us are dying, lepers and non-lepers alike. But soon Jesus will come to make all things new, and this fallen world will give way to indescribable glory. We had a powerful time of worship, and Romans 8 came with fresh application to us all.

Presently the Ebola outbreak in West Africa has brought great fear to people across the world. Health professionals and international leaders struggle to stop this deadly disease that has reportedly taken over 700 lives (and growing as I write). This outbreak has rightly caused many to grieve and pray. It has also brought to mind—at least for some—that we're made for another world where there is no more sickness, fear, or tears.

While Jesus was on earth, He demonstrated His messianic reign in many ways, including the healing of sick people, like lepers. When John the Baptist had a crisis of faith, he sent a question to Jesus, asking about the Savior's identity. Jesus replied with a mild rebuke:

> *Go and report to John what you hear and see: the blind see, the lame walk, those with skin diseases are healed, the deaf hear, the dead are raised, and the poor are told the good news. And if anyone is not offended because of Me, he is blessed.* (Matt 11:4-6)

Jesus' words were intended to leave no doubt that He was indeed the Holy One, of whom all the prophets spoke. His clear proofs included His miraculous healings and His powerful gospel preaching.

Jesus' miracles were foretastes of the kingdom to come. His miracles weren't the *violation* of the laws of nature but the *restoration* of the laws of nature. Jesus gave an early viewing of the ultimate restoration to come. Jesus will one day reverse the curse of this fallen world triumphantly, fully, and finally. Now we groan with longings for that day (Rom 8:18-31). We wait with groanings that are at times too deep for words (Rom 8:26). But our groanings should be mingled with confident hope, for hope has come in a person, Jesus, and He will come again to make all things new.

Elisha's ministry included "previews of Jesus." We have already noted that their ministries have numerous similarities. Once again we see that to be true. In 2 Kings 5 we read of the prophet Elisha healing a leper. His healing points us to the ultimate Prophet and Great Physician, who on one particular occasion healed 10 lepers, giving a sign of the ultimate restoration that will one day come fully.

Naaman's cleansing provides a vivid illustration of the power of the gospel. His physical healing is only part of the whole story. What we witness here is an amazing conversion of one who had been outside the faith. God graciously saves a leper from a deadly physical condition and ultimately from eternal judgment. Naaman eventually confesses, "I know there's no God in the whole world except in Israel" (2 Kgs 5:15). So now you see, this isn't simply an encouraging tale for sick people. This is a story that we can all identify with. As believers, we were spiritual lepers until Christ cleansed us from sin.

Indeed, this story reminds us that no one is too bad to come to Christ for salvation. There is real gospel hope in this dusty old story. My good friend and colleague Nate Akin illustrates this glorious gospel truth with the following story. One Sunday, in the response time following a pastor's sermon, a lady began to weep as she filled out a response card at the front of the worship center. The pastor went and sat next to her in order to learn more about her situation. She took the card she had filled out and said, "You see my name?"

"Yes," the pastor said.

She replied, "You see that 'Mrs.' in front of my name?" The pastor affirmed. She went on, "I'm no 'Mrs.' I've never been married. I write 'Mrs.' in front of my name on account of my little baby boy. When he was born, I said in my heart, 'I'm going to raise him in that wonderful First Baptist Church in Dallas.' So I began bringing him into the nursery, and I began attending the services, and I've been listening to you preach, and today I felt I wanted to become a Christian and become a member of the congregation."

"But," she said, "Since I have come and since I've been seated here, I've been thinking about my life as a prostitute. I've been thinking about what I've done, and if you knew me, and if these people knew me, you would not want the likes of me in this church."

Of course, the pastor told her otherwise. The truth is, we aren't unlike this woman. We have a fundamental problem. We are all unclean. Paul puts it like this:

> There is no one righteous, not even one. There is no one who understands; there is no one who seeks God. All have turned away; all alike have become useless. There is no one who does what is good, not even one. (Rom 3:10-12)

This story in 2 Kings 5 reminds us that God powerfully, sovereignly, and graciously can overcome the effects of the fall and save sinners like Naaman—and like us.

But that's not all. God's sovereign grace is on display in the story that follows the Naaman incident, as God works through Elisha to recover a floating axe. This whole section is a marvelous testimony to the amazing grace of God. We will look at this chapter in two parts—God's saving grace and God's supplying grace.

God's Saving Grace
2 KINGS 5:1-15

The account of Elisha's miracles not only points us ahead to Jesus, but it also points us back to Elijah. Here's another account of how God was at work in the prophet to impact those outside the nation of Israel. We find here a great man with a great need, a great evangelist, a great word, and a great transformation.

A Great Man with a Great Need (v. 1)

Naaman is quite an impressive individual. He is a commander of the Aramean (Syrian) army. He's a successful man with high standing. Most interestingly, he's a man who had gained victory with the help of Yahweh. His success was due to Yahweh's sovereign will.

This is a remarkable illustration of God's total sovereignty. Yahweh controls Aramean politics and all "foreign affairs" around the world. God was not merely the God of Israel. He was and is the God of the nations. The psalmist says, "The earth and everything in it, the world and its inhabitants, belong to the LORD" (Ps 24:1). Davis says, "Yahweh is both the God of the church and Lord of the world. Yahweh draws near to his people but that doesn't mean he allows pagans to run around unsupervised" (*2 Kings*, 86). Indeed, it shouldn't surprise us that Naaman's success came at Yahweh's pleasure.

But this great man had a great need: "he was a leper" (v. 1 ESV). Bible commentators point out that technically this "skin disease" (HCSB) was probably not modern-day leprosy, that is, Hansen's disease. Naaman's patchy disfigurement appeared "white as snow" (5:27). Hansen lesions aren't white. Naaman's disease seems to be something like psoriasis (Leithart, *1 and 2 Kings*, 193). Whatever the exact condition was, we know it was serious enough to bring fear and elicit concern from others. Most importantly, this skin disease would have rendered Naaman ritually unclean (Lev 13–14) and under God's judgment (Num 12:1-15; 2 Kgs 15:5). Thus, Naaman was *a double outsider*. He was an Aramean, and he was a leper. He was a great man, but he had a great need. He needed to be cleansed in every way.

Naaman's story, however, isn't unique. We all need to be cleansed. But before we can find true cleansing, we must realize our own need. This is hard for some to admit, especially successful people and especially "religious" people. In Luke 4 Jesus retells the story of Naaman:

> *And in the prophet Elisha's time, there were many in Israel who had serious skin diseases, yet not one of them was healed—only Naaman the Syrian.* (Luke 4:27)

After hearing these things, they wanted to kill the Savior. Those listening to Jesus describe His mission didn't receive Him. They rejected Him like Israel rejected the prophets. We must not make the same mistake. Grace is available for all who admit they're spiritual lepers in need of Christ's cleansing.

A Great Evangelist (vv. 2-5a)

God's sovereignty is displayed in His involvement not only in big foreign affairs but also in the small details of seemingly "unimportant" individual's lives. Enter the "young girl" (v. 2). How will Naaman ever hear the "great thing" (v. 13) of the prophet Elisha? God uses means to accomplish His purposes. One of those means is human beings testifying of God's saving power, like this unnamed servant girl. We know little about her, but she proves to be tremendously important.

She had been taken away after an Aramean raid. Perhaps her parents were dead. She probably had no hope of returning home. She was living out her days in the service of a foreign person in a foreign land. Yet she stands as a wonderful example to us. She's aware of Naaman's condition. Concerned for his welfare and confident in God's work through Elisha, she tells her mistress that someone can cure the commander. This word was passed up to Naaman, who then went and received permission to go to Israel in hope of being cured.

Never underestimate the power of words. Never think God can't use you where you are. Point people to Jesus within the ordinary rhythms of your workweek. You never know who might respond and how God may be glorified. That's the legacy of this little evangelist.

Today this might look like something as simple as giving a Christian book to someone at your school or in your office. It might involve simply inviting someone to corporate worship with you on a Sunday. It might involve your simply asking if you could pray for your sick neighbor or taking the family some soup. If you want to do great things, great! But most Christians need to start with small things. This small girl did the small task of telling someone about Elisha, and it made a huge difference. Don't think you need a position in a church or in a corporation to be used of God. God loves to use ordinary people to accomplish His extraordinary purposes. Live every day with gospel intentionality.

A Great Word (vv. 5b-13)

In contrast to the faithful servant girl, we now meet a pathetic servant. This time the servant has position, influence, and power, but he's useless. Naaman goes off to Israel with an official letter from Aram's king and a lot of goods, clothes, and gold. Presumably the Aramean king thought that there would be a close relationship between the prophet and the king's court. But Israel's king (Joram? 2 Kgs 3) is no help whatsoever. He responds with mourning and panic. His assumption is that Aram wants to fight again. The slave girl has faith, but the king of Israel doesn't.

Israel's king doesn't seek out the prophet, but when Elisha hears about the situation, he responds: "Why have you torn your clothes? Have him come to me, and he will know there is a prophet in Israel" (v. 8). Following this invitation, "Naaman came with his horses and chariots and stood at the door of Elisha's house" (v. 9).

Isn't it interesting that this man Naaman is coming to the country where Yahweh's chosen people live, but the king in the country doesn't even truly know Yahweh? How similar is this to people who grow up in religious environments but never become real Christ followers? Proximity doesn't always lead to salvation. Your name may be on a church roll, but what matters is whether it's in the Book of Life (Phil 4:3).

Now for the great word of Elisha. His word is a word of salvation, but like the gospel this word can offend.

Elisha sends his messenger to Naaman instead of going himself. Imagine this scene. A royal entourage is at your door, and you stay at your desk, sending someone to speak for you! The writer doesn't interpret Elisha's actions, but surely this act was a bit humbling to Naaman. But if this didn't humble Naaman, Elisha's instructions surely did. In fact, they disturbed him. Naaman anticipated a faith-healing event, like the waving of the hand, an incantation, and boom—leprosy gone! But that's not what happens. Elisha tells him to go to the Jordan and wash seven times. Elisha treated this man like any other leper who needed to be healed, and Naaman didn't like it (Davis, *2 Kings*, 90).

The gospel must first humble us before it heals us. Everything about the gospel humbles us. It crushes our pride and our cultural assumptions. You must first humbly admit that you're a desperate sinner. Proud, morally relativistic people don't want to recognize this fact. You must humbly accept that Jesus, the One hung on a tree 2,000 years ago, is the *only* way of salvation. Proud, intellectual people don't want to embrace this fact either. You must also humbly acknowledge that you can't do anything—anything!—to earn salvation. Proud "self-made" people don't want to admit this either. They want to justify themselves. They want to work out their own self-salvation projects. Indeed, everything about the gospel humbles us. But for all those who do humble themselves, they will find grace and be exalted (1 Pet 5:5-6).

Naaman is being humbled in this account. He's bothered by Elisha's dogmatism and "narrow-mindedness." He's bothered that he has to go into the Jordan, Israel's major river, instead of some other body of water, maybe one in his own country. Will Naaman stumble over this message, or will he submit to this message?

Paul tells us that many stumble over the cross, but others find salvation in it (1 Cor 1:23-24). Some *scoff* at the message of a bloody cross while others *sing* about it. Scoffers find it too embarrassing, too uncivil, too stupid, too simple, and too narrow. Believers find it altogether glorious, infinitely wise, hope giving, and powerful. The cross of Christ divides the human race into two categories, and it unites all believers. To sing about the wonders of the Savior, one must first humbly submit to the word of the Savior.

Naaman eventually submitted to the prophet's word. His servants tell him that instead of scoffing at the message, he should rejoice in its simplicity and experience the promise of responding in faith. By God's grace, we then read of his conversion.

A Great Transformation (vv. 14-18)

After washing in the Jordan, Naaman's skin is transformed. He's healed instantly and fully. It's a beautiful picture of his new status and his new identity. The miracle wasn't due to any magical powers in the Jordan River, either. His transformation can only be attributed to the power and grace of God.

Bible teachers disagree over whether or not one should see this account as having some baptismal significance. While we should avoid making this story a key text for an argument regarding baptism views, it's hard not to see some similarities. Even those who practice a different mode of baptism than me see this text as saying something about it. Leithart goes so far as to say, "The story of Naaman is the richest Old Testament story of baptism and anticipates Christian baptism in a number of specific ways" (*1 and 2 Kings*, 192). One could argue that Naaman's "baptism" anticipates the baptism of thousands of future Gentiles. Naaman's baptism, like Christian baptism, also identified Him with God and His people. And his baptism was a picture of *death to life*, like Christian baptism.

In verse 15 we see that Naaman's skin wasn't the only thing that changed. His mind and heart changed also. What an awesome confession of faith and change of heart! Naaman confesses that Yahweh alone is God. He also calls himself a "servant" of Elisha. Finally, he wants to give an offering as a sign of his love and loyalty. That's quite a shift from his initial reaction.

But there's even more evidence of his transformation. The next part of the passage might puzzle you, but I think it makes sense. Naaman essentially explains that he's not adding Yahweh to his already existing pagan gods, but rather he's turning from all false gods and replacing them with Yahweh. The situation he describes in verses 17-19 might not first appear to say this, but I think that's exactly the point. Naaman says that he's committed to worshiping Yahweh exclusively, but he wants pardon in advance because he knows that he will be going to the pagan temple with his master. Is Naaman, then, not committed to Yahweh? No, I think the opposite is true. This was simply part of Naaman's job description. Naaman is implying with the "soil sample" that even though he will be in the temple with his master, he will not worship his master's idol. Because of his work expectations, he asks for pardon.

So I don't think we should take this negatively. Elisha takes it as no big deal, saying, "Go in peace." He simply leaves it at that. Davis rightly says that verse 18 actually shows a mark of conversion, namely, a "sensitive conscience" (*2 Kings*, 94). Naaman is bothered by his workplace expectations. Too bad more Israelites weren't as sensitive as Naaman. Naaman lost not only his leprosy but also his paganism (ibid.).

A real conversion involves turning from idols to the living God exclusively (1 Thess 1:9-10). It involves a change of status. It involves new desires. It involves a sensitive conscience. It involves generous giving. All of these things are expressed in this remarkable conversion story. Leithart summarizes it well:

> The story of Naaman's conversion is one of the most detailed and one of the most sociologically and psychologically rich conversion stories in the Bible. Almost for the first time, the Bible depicts the change of mind and heart, as well as the change of status, that occurs when a sinner turns to the God of Israel. (*1 and 2 Kings*, 193)

Indeed, everything changed for Naaman, and everything changes for anyone else who truly repents and believes in Christ.

Paul told the formerly unclean Corinthians, "Therefore, if anyone is in Christ, he is a new creation; old things have passed away, and look, new things have come" (2 Cor 5:17). Becoming a Christian isn't about becoming a nicer person. It's not about turning over a new leaf. It's about becoming a new person. That's the change Christians have experienced, and that's the message we hold out to the world. So, like this little slave girl, let's keep telling everyone about the One greater than Elisha that can make them new and clean.

Unfortunately, the whole story of Naaman's conversion doesn't end positively for everyone. While Naaman experiences the wonder of God's gracious salvation, Gehazi experiences a negative transformation. In the first story Naaman is healed from leprosy; in the second story Gehazi, because of his great sin, is struck with the same disease. We read of Gehazi's greed and lack of gospel understanding and appreciation in verses 19-27. This whole account is sad. Elisha refuses to receive anything from Naaman, but Gehazi is looking to cash in on the matter, reminding us of the sin of Achan (Josh 7) and Simon the Magician (Acts 8:18-24).

Gehazi makes up a story about Elisha. His lie is carefully told, for it doesn't come across as excessive but believable. Naaman had previously offered much more. Naaman agrees and hands over the goods to Gehazi.

Motivated by greed, Elisha's servant lies and takes what doesn't belong to him. Then he lies again when Elisha asks him where he has been. Elisha informs Gehazi that he knows what has happened. Elisha then informs him that such great sin has consequences, and in this case it results in leprosy.

What's probably most deplorable in this episode is that Gehazi distorted the gospel. God's grace was coming free of charge to Naaman, yet Gehazi tried to put a price on salvation. Davis says, "Gehazi's greed implied that Yahweh was a 'taker' like all the other deities that littered the Near East. . . . This explains why Gehazi's punishment is so severe, why God deals so harshly with him" (*2 Kings*, 97-98).

Grace is free. We must not distort it. Paul warned the Galatians about adding anything to the saving grace of God. The apostle taught that if anyone distorted the life-changing gospel of grace, they should be under a curse (Gal 1:8).

Stand in joyful awe of Naaman's conversion; stand in fear of Gehazi's greed and distortion. Celebrate the gospel. Preach the gospel. Believe the gospel. Don't use the gospel for your own selfish gain. Don't communicate false ideas about the living God. God really is gracious and sovereign, and He really delights in saving people. May everything we do and say commend the Redeemer to the nations.

God's Supplying Grace
2 KINGS 6:1-7

The "God of all grace" (1 Pet 5:10) not only saves us by grace but also graciously supplies all our needs. God's power is at work in Elisha, and God cares about supplying the smallest of needs for all His servants.

At first glance this story seems unnecessary. Who cares about a floating axe head? Someone cared about it! We aren't given his name, but one particular prophet would never forget this story about God's miraculous provision. God cares about world events, and He cares about giving us daily bread . . . or an axe head. Be encouraged by this fact. This was a simple need, but it was a real need.

These seminary students really needed more space. They needed tools. After the axe falls into the water, the student cries out for help because of his need. The fact that he didn't own an axe probably meant he couldn't afford one. Losing the axe would only add to his financial burden, since they were probably expensive (Davis, *2 Kings*, 105). So God in His mercy works a miracle. Elisha strikes the water. The iron rises to the surface, and the student picks up his tool and presumably goes back to work.

I love this story. I think it teaches us that we can take every care to God as we seek to fulfill His will for our lives. He is a God you can call out to in your emergencies and trust that He provides for His children. He may provide in *mundane* ways or *miraculous* ways, but either way, it comes from our good and gracious God. Trust Him. Seek Him. Believe He responds to our cries. God's servants can rely on Him to supply their needs.

As we wait for the day that God makes all things new, let us keep our eyes on the One greater than Elisha, Jesus Christ. Soon we will dwell with Him forever, where all the redeemed from every tribe and tongue will sing praises to His name. On that day there will be no more lepers. No more Ebola sufferers. No more pain. No more tears. All the redeemed, who experienced God's saving grace and who lived on God's supplying grace, will exalt the One who rescued them. Former lepers will be able to lift their new hands in praise to the King. Like the little girl, let's tell everyone of this good news. A Savior for all nations has come, and He will come again.

Reflect and Discuss

1. Discuss any personal experiences where God used seemingly insignificant people to extend His significant grace.
2. Why did God use a little girl to call Naaman instead of someone well known and powerful?
3. Why did the king of Aram send gifts to the king of Israel? Can God's blessing be procured through diplomacy?
4. Why did Naaman become enraged when Elisha told him to wash in the Jordan?
5. How might people today reject God's blessing because it doesn't suit them?
6. How do pride and humility function in the story of Naaman's healing?
7. Discuss any personal experiences with God extending grace in surprising ways.
8. Which is the most significant part of the story of the floating axe head, the miraculous physics or the mercy shown to an unnamed prophet? Why?
9. Are there any needs today that a person might consider too small to ask of God?
10. How might the stories of the little girl, Naaman, and the floating axe head offer comfort to someone in need?

Four Types of Hearts

2 KINGS 6:8–8:29

Main Idea: As the Elisha narrative continues, the writer describes four types of responses to God's Word.

I.   The Rebellion of a Stubborn Heart (6:8-24)
II. The Impatience of a Superficial Heart (6:25-33)
    A. Famine (vv. 24-29)
    B. False repentance (vv. 30-33)
III. The Cynicism of a Skeptical Heart (7:1-20)
    A. Deliverance promised (vv. 1-2)
    B. Deliverance provided (vv. 3-7)
    C. Deliverance proclaimed (vv. 8-15)
    D. Mercy and judgment experienced (vv. 16-20)
IV. The Obedience of a Soft Heart (8:1-6)
    A. Elisha's word (v. 1)
    B. Her obedience (vv. 2-3)
    C. God's providence (vv. 4-6)
V.   The Brokenhearted Prophet and the Decline of Judah (8:7-29)
    A. A new Aramean king: Hazael (vv. 7-15)
    B. Kings in Judah (vv. 16-29)

The following section of Kings contains some fascinating, tragic, and somewhat comedic stories. You were probably not told about these stories in Sunday school! And I doubt anyone ever used the flannel graph to teach you about people eating donkeys' heads.

Perhaps you have heard skeptics say things like, "You Christians only teach the feel-good stories and easy verses. If you really believe the Bible is God's Word, then why don't you teach on the stories about cannibalism?" Maybe they have asked, "Why does no one teach the 'bloodthirsty stories' in the Bible—like when Joram's assistant was killed violently because of unbelief, or the story of Jehu's bloody purge?" Such questions exist today.

We're attempting to deal with such stories in our exposition of Kings. We're dealing with lesser-known (and sometimes graphic) stories and trying to make sense of them.

Many of the stories in Scripture are difficult to understand and stomach, but that doesn't mean we need to avoid them or that we cannot make sense of them. All Scripture is God breathed and profitable (2 Tim 3:16), and even these puzzling stories are for our good (1 Cor 10:11). We simply need to try to understand them.

What exactly are we looking at? First, Elisha humiliates the Aramean (Syrian) raiders with superior wisdom, with blindness, and with kindness. Then an awful famine was so severe that people were eating children in desperation. Next, Elisha predicts the end of a famine and the death of an assassin. Within this larger story we find an encouraging tale of how God used four lepers to tell the good news of deliverance to famished Israel. After this story the context shifts from national events to God's faithfulness to the same Shunammite woman we read about previously. Finally, the overarching story of Kings is carried on at the end of chapter 8. We read of Hazael rising to power by killing the Aramean king. We witness the decline of Judah and sense the coming end of Ahab's house.

How might we tie all these stories together? Some of the main questions we should ask in studying a passage of Scripture are: What does this passage teach me about God? What is God doing in this passage? God is protecting His people (8:8-23); extending mercy to the Arameans (8:20-23); speaking His word, which involves predicting and controlling the future and interpreting the events of history (7:1,16-17; 8:10,13); using the unclean and unnamed people to declare His salvation (7:3-10); defending the needy (8:1-6); and executing justice (8:7-15).

Another question to ask is, What does this passage teach me about humanity? Here's where we can really sink our teeth into personal application. We have examples of people responding differently to God's revelation. God reveals Himself in word and deed in the ways noted above, yet not everyone responds in repentance and faith. Three individuals illustrate *unbelieving hearts*: the Aramean king (6:8-24), Israel's king (6:25-33), and the Israelite messenger/captain/assassin/officer (7:1-20). We have one example of *belief* in the Shunammite woman (8:1-6). She responds to God's grace and His word with a soft, obedient heart. We might include the four lepers as a positive example as well.

Let's look at the four types of hearts displayed in these people (I'm indebted to Sinclair Ferguson, "2 Kings 7," for the idea of these headings). As we look at them, we need to remember that we're called to respond appropriately to God's Word while we can. The day of grace will one day be replaced by the day of judgment.

The Rebellion of a Stubborn Heart

2 KINGS 6:8-24

God displayed His grace to the Arameans (Syrians) in several ways, yet the Aramean king did not respond with faith in Yahweh. Instead Aram is warring with Israel again. Debate exists about who was king of Aram at this time (and there is debate about the chronology of this section). No name is given in verse 8, but verse 24 names Ben-hadad. Is this the same Ben-hadad? It's possible, but it may also be Ben-hadad II. In either case the point remains. The Aramean king (or kings) had witnessed God's grace yet refused to respond with repentance and faith in God.

How exactly did God extend grace to the king and the Arameans? First, *God blessed them with success.* Notice 5:1: "Naaman, commander of the army for the king of Aram, was a great man in his master's sight and highly regarded because through him, the LORD had given victory to Aram." Did you catch that? God gave them victory! This is an amazing statement of monotheism. Another nation, who worshiped other gods, is given victory—not by the power of their gods but by the power of Yahweh. God isn't a small god who influences only one group of people. He rules His people, the nations, and the cosmos.

Sadly many are blessed by God but refuse to acknowledge Him as Lord and God. Every gift and success a person has comes from the hand of God, Maker of heaven and earth. In response to God's revealing grace, Paul says people sinfully exchange the glory of the Creator for the created things. Because they intentionally suppress the truth revealed to them, they're without excuse (Rom 1:18-25).

Second, *God blessed them with salvation.* In chapter 5 we read of the spectacular healing of Naaman, the Aramean commander. Naaman made the great confession of faith, "I know there's no God in the whole world except in Israel" (5:15). He believed. He was humbled under the mighty hand of God. His story demonstrates that God saves people from every tribe and tongue if they will believe.

Despite seeing Naaman's obvious transformation, the king of Aram doesn't seek Yahweh for himself. Perhaps the reason they are at war now is because of Naaman's transformation. Were they provoked to anger by his testimony praising "Israel's God"? We don't read of Naaman again. Maybe he was killed. I imagine he was at least removed as commander.

Third, *God blessed them by crushing their pride.* In this passage we find three humiliating acts that should have made the king and the

Arameans recognize the supremacy of God and bow to Him. But that doesn't happen. After these three humiliating acts, Ben-hadad besieges Samaria (v. 24). The war intensifies. He never trusts in God but rebels against God because his heart is stony. We then read of his sad death in chapter 7. God graciously humbled this king in various ways; He dealt with him, but the king hardened his heart against Him.

Do you know that God humiliates people in order that they may respond to Him in faith? Jesus humbled the disciples when He told them to cast their net on the other side of their boat for a catch (Luke 5). Peter responded in awe, saying, "Go away from me, because I'm a sinful man, Lord!" (5:8). When Jesus calmed the storm, the disciples said, "Who then is this? Even the wind and the sea obey Him!" (Mark 4:41). God humbles us that He might save us and use us for His glory. However, some respond negatively. The Aramean king goes the way of Pharaoh and Judas instead of the way of Naaman.

How did God humble the Aramean king? **God humbled the king by frustrating his plans**. In verses 8-14 we read the humorous ordeal of Elisha's telling the king of Israel the plans of Aram's king. (Notice the grace extended to Israel's king.) The Aramean king would make his attack plans, but then somehow Israel would find out about it and avoid defeat. This happened more than once. The Aramean king thinks he has a leak in his administration. He asks, "Tell me, which one of us is for the king of Israel?" (v. 11). His aide tells him that he doesn't have a traitor on his team; instead, it's Elisha, who "tells the king of Israel even the words you speak in your bedroom" (v. 12). He accuses the prophet of being the proverbial "fly on the wall." From many miles away God granted Elisha the secret counsels of the Aramean king and was thereby protecting His people. The psalmist said it well: "The LORD frustrates the counsel of the nations; He thwarts the plans of the peoples" (Ps 33:10; see also Ps 44:21).

In this frustration we see that God is dealing with this foreign king. Would this have shaken you? How would you have responded? Sadly, instead of seeking Elisha to learn more, the king grows angry. He says, "Go and see where he is, so I can send men to capture him" (v. 13). His servants obey. They go to Dothan, where Elisha was staying, and surround the city at night in order to capture the prophet. One wonders why he didn't assume Elisha would know of this plan also. Is pride not the reason for this action also?

God humbled the king by protecting His prophet and humiliating the Arameans. God protects His people. The Aramean army frightens Elisha's assistant the next morning, and he cries out, "Oh, my master, what are we to do?" (v. 15). Elisha replies, "Don't be afraid, for those who are with us outnumber those who are with them" (v. 16). Elisha sees what the assistant cannot see. The assistant must have thought, "Just how do we have more soldiers than that massive army?" Elisha then prays, "LORD, please open his eyes and let him see." God opened the eyes of the lad and he saw "horses and chariots of fire all around Elisha" (v. 17). The servant now sees and embraces the reality of God's unseen protection.

God opens eyes for people to see His grace (Ps 146:8). He is also the God who *gives unseen protection to His people* (cf. Ps 91:9-11). Though Jesus didn't use God's unseen protection in Gethsemane, He was aware of it. He rebuked Peter, saying, "Or do you think that I cannot call on My Father, and He will provide Me at once with more than 12 legions of angels?" (Matt 26:53). There were 72,000 spirits ready to fight on His behalf, but they didn't act because the cross was God's will. Jesus knew and lived under the unseen protection demonstrated here in 2 Kings 6:8-23 (Davis, *2 Kings*, 115).

God is a refuge for His people. He delivers His people (Pss 50:15; 107). Elisha tells his servant, "Don't be afraid." We need to hear this. God protects His people. We can say with the psalmists:

> *The LORD is my light and my salvation—*
> *whom should I fear?*
> *The LORD is the stronghold of my life—*
> *of whom should I be afraid? . . .*
> *Though an army deploys against me,*
> *my heart is not afraid;*
> *though a war breaks out against me,*
> *still I am confident.* (Ps 27:1,3)

> *The one who lives under the protection of the Most High*
> *dwells in the shadow of the Almighty.*
> *I will say to the LORD,*
> *"My refuge and my fortress,*
> *my God, in whom I trust."* (Ps 91:1-2)

> *Jerusalem—the mountains surround her.*
> *And the LORD surrounds His people,*
> *both now and forever.* (Ps 125:2)

Indeed, Christian history is filled with stories of God delivering His servants in remarkable ways. It isn't always His will to protect us in this life—the blood of martyrs reminds us of this—but God is always with and for His people. Because of this truth, we can live in peace, not in fear. Are you living in fear because of finances, illness, or relocation? Find refuge in God's promises and His presence.

Next we read of how God *humiliated the Arameans*. Elisha prays next for God to deal with the enemy's sight. He says, "Please strike this nation with blindness" (v. 18, probably not total absence of sight but visual confusion; cf. Gen 19:11). God strikes them with blindness according to Elisha's prayer. Elisha assures them that they will find the person they are looking for (which is himself!). Then he takes them on a 10-mile hike to Samaria.

Elisha prays again in verse 20, this time for Yahweh to open their eyes once they all reach Samaria, and the Lord does so. When the king of Israel (still King Joram, it seems) sees them, he is ready to attack. But instead of a striking them down, Elisha instructs the king to sit them down, feed them, and send them home. He illustrates Romans 12:18-21 and Matthew 5:43-45. So they prepared a "great feast" for their enemies (v. 23). They didn't kill them with the sword but with kindness.

What an embarrassment this must have been to the king! One can only imagine what he thought when they returned. "Did you slay Elisha?" They would have to answer, "No, he fed us a great meal! And we still have some pecan pie in our pockets."

God was slaying the pride of Ben-hadad. He was showing him of the folly of opposing the real King of all the earth. Psalm 2 captures this idea. God laughs at the earthly kings who make plots against him (vv. 1-4). The psalmist urges the reader to

> *Serve the LORD with reverential awe*
> *and rejoice with trembling.*
> *Pay homage to the Son or He will be angry*
> *and you will perish in your rebellion,*
> *for His anger may ignite at any moment.*
> *All those who take refuge in Him are happy.* (Ps 2:11-12)

One can either bow the knee to Jesus and serve the true and living God or perish in rebellion.

Finally, **God humbles him by extending mercy to him**. In this humiliation there is also hope. What kind of God would treat His enemies like this? Only Yahweh. The God who protected Elisha and His servant and Israel would have protected Aram also if they had sought refuge in Him. The shelter of God is available to all who will turn to Christ. As Davis says, one could sing Hart's old hymn like this:

Come, ye Syrians, poor and wretched,
Weak and wounded, sick and sore.
Jesus, ready, stands to save you;
Full of pity, joined with power.
He is able, He is able;
He is willing; doubt no more. (*2 Kings*, 117)

God gave Ben-hadad living examples of His supremacy, power, and transforming grace. Despite the military victories, Naaman's transformation, and these humiliations, the king didn't bow to Yahweh.

How have you responded to God's gracious revelation of Himself? How does God humble us today? He gives us His Word (Isa 66:2). He reveals His glory in creation. Look at a little baby or a majestic sunset over the ocean. Does that not move you? He also changes people's lives, which should make us glorify God (Gal 1:23). Additionally, sometimes we're humbled under the weight of a crisis, a crisis that should make us cry out to God—perhaps death, illness, calamity, or the discovery that life is meaningless apart from God. Sometimes the consequences of living in ongoing sin humble people, which leads them to bow to God in repentance (Ps 107:12). Finally, God may also use the kindness of other Christians to humble the unbeliever. These are all acts of grace intended to move us to faith. Don't sin away the day of grace. Respond to God while you can.

The Impatience of a Superficial Heart
2 KINGS 6:25-33

The next type of heart is illustrated in the life of Israel's King Joram. As we analyze his life, we learn to beware of the impatience of a superficial heart.

Famine (vv. 24-29)

The context of the story involves war and famine, which probably is the result of Israel's unfaithfulness. Aram (Syria) had raided Israel (5:2) and sought to capture Elisha in 6:8-23, but now things escalate:

they execute a full invasion on Israel. Because their siege lasted for an extended period of time, the conditions were terrible in Israel. This famine reminds us of what we may see on the news or what we may have personally observed in some impoverished countries. The poor are poorer, and the rich are reduced to emptiness. It was so bad that people were selling donkey's heads and dove's dung (pigeon manure) for ridiculously high prices. We can only imagine the awful situation. People were eating scraps and viscera and using dung either as fuel or possibly for food. But this seems to be what the rich are reduced to eating. The poor are so driven to desperation that some are eating human beings.

In this fallen world such awful things happen. This story reminds me of the Great Famine in 1932–33 in Ukraine. It too was a man-made famine. Stalin removed food by military force. An estimated three-million-plus people died as a result. Ukrainians called this *Holodomor* ("murder by hunger"). Some report how babies were eaten alive during the famine, and sometimes children would just disappear, but villagers knew what was happening (Eswine, *Preaching to a Post-Everything World*, 32).

In the midst of this sorry physical plight, the writer gives one story illustrating the sorry moral plight: a lady crying out to the king to administer justice. Like the story in 1 Kings 3, this story involves two ladies, two children, and the death of a child. Joram throws a shot at Yahweh, saying, "If the LORD doesn't help you, where can I get help for you? From the threshing floor or the winepress?" (v. 27). He was saying (sarcastically) that he could do nothing since the normal food supply was exhausted (grain and wine) and that was God's job not his. Nevertheless, he asks them, "What is the matter?" (v. 28). One of the ladies responds that they had agreed to consume each other's sons. They would eat one (already dead?) child one day and eat the other son the next day. However, after eating the first son, the mother of the other son was accused of not keeping her agreement; she hid her son. Other ancient documents report similar situations during sieges, and elsewhere in Scripture we read of instances of cannibalism stemming from a long siege (e.g., Lam 2:20; 4:10; Ezek 5:10). This particular story isn't only pitiful physically, but it's also pitiful morally. The women accept the eating of a child as reasonable under the circumstances, but they are quibbling about the failure to keep an agreement.

Unfortunately, it had been a long time since Israel had been under a wise king who administered justice. Solomon demonstrated kingly wisdom in 1 Kings 3:16-28 as he sorted out a dispute between two ladies. Joram was no such king.

False Repentance (vv. 30-33)

In response the king is distressed. He apparently renders no verdict. In anguish he tears his clothes. When he does, everyone sees that he is wearing sackcloth, a symbol of repentance, underneath. His father Ahab wore sackcloth in "repentance" previously (1 Kgs 21:27). Elisha may have called Joram to repentance. Yahweh told Israel they would experience such curses if they were unfaithful to Him (Lev 26:27-29; Deut 28:52-57; Lam 2:20; 4:10). Thus, this is a story of divine judgment. It was right for the king to repent. However, Joram doesn't have a real heart for repentance. He doesn't patiently trust in and wait on God for deliverance. He acts like his mother, seeking to kill the prophet. He may have worn sackcloth, but it doesn't cover up his unrepentant heart.

His impatience is clearly revealed in the next scene. God gave Elisha wisdom to know that Joram wanted to kill him. Before Joram's assassin (or captain, 7:2) arrived, Elisha already told the elders about the king's plan and told them to block him. The captain says, "This disaster is from the LORD. *Why should I wait for the LORD any longer?*" (v. 33; emphasis added). The unrepentant, impatient, superficial heart of Joram is exposed. Why wait on the Lord? Why trust in the Lord? Why seek Him any longer? Joram is turning from his only source of help.

Joram embraced a utilitarian view of religion: "I tried it for a little while, but it didn't work." He thinks politics will solve this problem instead. But how wrong he is (Ps 146:3-4). He doesn't demonstrate the heart of a believer. This is the heart of a believer: "No one who waits for You will be disgraced" (Ps 25:3). "I waited patiently for the LORD, and He turned to me and heard my cry for help" (Ps 40:1). "Like a servant's eyes on his master's hand, like a servant girl's eyes on her mistress's hand, so our eyes are on the LORD our God *until* He shows us favor" (Ps 123:2; emphasis added). This song of ascent beautifully captures the soft, repentant heart of a believer:

> *Out of the depths I call to You, Yahweh!*
> *Lord, listen to my voice;*
>   *let Your ears be attentive*
>   *to my cry for help.*
> *Yahweh, if You considered sins,*
> *Lord, who could stand?*

> *But with You there is forgiveness,*
> *so that You may be revered.*
> *I* wait *for Yahweh; I wait*
> *and put my hope in His word.*
> *I* wait *for the Lord*
> *more than watchmen for the morning—*
> *more than watchmen for the morning.*
> *Israel, put your hope in the* LORD.
> *For there is faithful love with the* LORD,
> *and with Him is redemption in abundance.*
> *And He will redeem Israel*
> *from all its sins.* (Ps 130; emphasis added)

This is a soft, repentant heart—crying for forgiveness; waiting on God; hoping in God. My friend, beware of a superficial heart. Beware of having an outward show of religion but not having a truly repentant, worshiping heart on the inside. Jesus called out the Pharisees for such masquerades: "In the same way, on the outside you seem righteous to people, but inside you are full of hypocrisy and lawlessness" (Matt 23:28).

Have you felt that God has been working too slowly recently? Have you been tempted to doubt God's Word because you have not seen Him remove a particular problem? Keep seeking Him and His Word, and wait on Him.

The Cynicism of a Skeptical Heart
2 KINGS 7:1-20

Deliverance Promised (vv. 1-2)

Now we turn to our third illustration of how *not* to respond to God. Israel's King Joram and his assassin illustrate an unbelieving, skeptical heart.

In the previous passage Joram sent his captain to assassinate Elisha. Astonishingly, Elisha actually proclaims good news of deliverance to the king. God promises some relief in 24 hours. Things would slowly improve. Six quarts of flour would still cost about one month's wage. That was still outrageous. But relative relief was promised. Barley instead of dove's dung is an improvement.

In response to the good news, the captain sarcastically says, "Look, even if the LORD were to make windows in heaven, could this really happen?" (v. 2). His cynicism expresses his skeptical, unbelieving heart. He wonders where this abundance of food will come from. It would take an exodus-like miracle. In his skepticism he mocks the prophet, which is to mock the Lord himself (see 2 Kgs 2:23-25). Elisha tells the mocker, "You will in fact see it with your own eyes, but you won't eat any of it." This is a word of judgment. The people will eat, but this unbelieving captain will not taste it; he will be killed. What this skeptic cannot fathom is precisely what God does. This is vintage Yahweh.

We often fail to believe predictions. My family just returned from the Outer Banks of North Carolina. Many years ago, before the Outer Banks were developed into what it is today, someone told Kimberly's grandmother that she should purchase some land there. She responded, "Why would I want to pay $500 for a bucket of sand!?" Kimberly's dad says, "She wasn't a woman of great vision."

Of course this prediction in Kings was much more important, and it was coming from a more reliable source. Elisha was God's representative. He had a perfect track record. But the cynical skeptic is never satisfied.

What kind of faith does God require? He doesn't tell us to believe just anything. He tells us to *believe His promises*. We are to believe promises like these:

> *The one who believes in Me, even if he dies, will live.* (John 11:25)
> *The one who has the Son has life.* (1 John 5:12)
> *No one will snatch [My sheep] out of My hand.* (John 10:28)
> *I will raise [believers] up on the last day.* (John 6:40)
> *Everyone who calls on the name of the Lord will be saved.*
>   (Rom 10:13)
> *Therefore, no condemnation now exists for those in Christ Jesus.*
>   (Rom 8:1)

God calls us to believe what He says, even though it may sound unlikely at times. But remember: God has a flawless record of faithfulness. Not one word has ever failed! The psalmist said, "God—His way is perfect; the word of the LORD is pure. He is a shield to all who take refuge in Him" (Ps 18:30).

Deliverance Provided (vv. 3-7)

How would God deliver His people? Four men with a "skin disease," traditionally called "lepers," are sitting outside the city gate, unable to enter because of their condition (cf. Lev 13:45-46). These unnamed lepers use some logic. They realize that if they enter the city, then they will face death or famine. If they remain outside the gate, they will also die. If they head to the Arameans, they will *probably* be executed, but they *may* find refuge. The only glimmer of hope was found in deserting to the Arameans. They choose that option.

But when they get there, they find no Arameans. Notice how this happens. We read that the lepers "got up at *twilight*" to go to the Aramean camp (v. 5), but the Lord made the Arameans hear the sound of a great army (v. 6), so that they "fled at *twilight*" (v. 7; emphasis added). Who's responsible for this mighty deliverance? God Himself. Salvation involves receiving what God has done. "Some take pride in chariots, and others in horses, but we take pride in the name of Yahweh our God" (Ps 20:7).

Deliverance Proclaimed (vv. 8-15)

As a result, the lepers find a treasure trove of food, silver, gold, and clothing. In tent after tent they find treasures. But then the lepers have a moral crisis. Their conscience provokes them as they say, "We're not doing what is right. Today is a day of good news. If we are silent and wait until morning light, our sin will catch up with us. Let's go tell the king's household" (v. 9). Does this not sound like a missionary text? How can we keep the good news to ourselves? Evangelism has been described as one beggar telling another beggar where to find food. That's the picture here. Off the finders of food go to the gatekeepers of the city and report the good news. People who know of God's deliverance should proclaim it (Ps 40:9-10).

When the king hears the report, he doesn't believe. He thinks it's a trap. Though Elisha promised deliverance and though Elisha had never failed in his predictions, Joram still refuses to believe.

Are you believing the good news? Perhaps you think you could believe if you saw a miracle? That logic may make sense at one level. But Jesus said it isn't true. In a parable of the rich man and Lazarus, Jesus said,

> They have Moses and the prophets; they should listen to them. . . . If they don't listen to Moses and the prophets, they will not be persuaded if someone rises from the dead. (Luke 16:29,31)

In other words, the problem isn't insufficient reason to believe. You have something sufficient, called God's Word. The book of Kings was in the "Prophets" category Jesus mentioned. God's miracles and promises are contained here. In Scripture we read of the hero of the story, Jesus, crucified and risen, who says, "Believe." The problem isn't with a lack of proof but with a skeptical, unbelieving heart.

The lepers aren't the only unnamed instruments of deliverance. One of the king's servants proposes a reasonable solution. Take five men and check it out. The king sends them off on what he probably considered a suicide mission. However, they find the lepers' story to be true and come back and report the good news to the king. We don't know the names of these five men either.

God often uses nameless missionaries to bring salvation to the nations (1 Cor 1:26-29). We have greater news to pass on to the world than deliverance from any military invasion. We tell the world how death has been defeated and victory is ours through Christ.

Mercy and Judgment Experienced (vv. 16-20)

The people hear the news, and they are ready to go. They head off and plunder the camp of the Arameans. Elisha's word comes to pass regarding the flour and barley. What about his word to the skeptical assassin? It comes true as well. The rushing mob "trampled him in the gateway" and he dies. It's stated twice in case we miss it (vv. 17,20). It happened according to God's word through Elisha, whom he previously mocked.

God takes unbelief seriously. Do you think you can look in unbelief at the evidences of God's grace and not provoke Him? Think again. The author of Hebrews says it well: "Watch out, brothers, so that there won't be in any of you an evil, unbelieving heart that departs from the living God" (Heb 3:12). And later, "Make sure that you do not reject the One who speaks" (Heb 12:25). To mock God's prophet was to mock God because he was speaking God's word. This assassin's death serves as a warning to everyone.

Because of our soft, tolerant culture, we don't like to hear that God punishes those who reject Him. Even in a church culture tempted to believe that the only attribute of God is love, we ignore His holiness, truth, and wrath. But the fact remains, you will be judged if you don't respond in faith to God's Word. Jesus said that at the end of the age, angels will gather up evil people "and throw them into the blazing furnace. In that place there will be weeping and gnashing of teeth" (Matt 13:50). Paul told the Galatians, "Don't be deceived: God is not mocked. For whatever a man sows he will also reap" (Gal 6:7). In Kings we see that God gives people opportunities to repent, but they refuse. They want God to leave them alone. They essentially get what they want.

The Obedience of a Soft Heart
2 KINGS 8:1-6

Elisha was God's special agent who brought salvation not only to Israel in general but also to individuals in Israel and other nations. One of those individuals was this Shunammite woman who showed him hospitality, as we noticed in 2 Kings 4:8-37.

Elisha's Word (v. 1)

Elisha tells her that a seven-year famine is coming and that she should stay somewhere temporarily until it's over. Provan tries to place the timing of this famine:

> We are presumably to understand, therefore, that this warning
> cited here was given to the woman around the same time
> that Elisha restored her son to life. We should distinguish this
> general state of famine from the famine in the city of Samaria
> (6:25 and 7:4),·which seems to be a result of, rather than a
> circumstance preceding, the siege. The implication is that
> before the siege the city itself had not been suffering hunger
> to the same extent as the rest of the country. (*1 and 2 Kings*,
> 207)

If this famine and Elisha's instructions occurred around the time of his raising her son (4:18-37), then Elisha's words to the woman back in 4:13 are particularly relevant. Elisha had asked her, "Can we speak on your behalf to the king or to the commander of the army?" to which she responded at first, "I am living among my own people." She didn't need such help at the time; she had friends and family. However, now, because of a famine, she will be instructed to live away from her people and will be in need of a word spoken to the king on her behalf. That is exactly what happens in 8:4-5. Once again we see this woman being rewarded for caring for God's prophet (cf. Matt 10:40-42).

Her Obedience (vv. 2-3)

She did exactly as Elisha said, demonstrating a soft heart. She believed he was God's messenger. While others in the land would not believe

Elisha (like Joram and his assassin), she believed him and obeyed. She illustrates Jesus' fourth type of heart in the parable of the four soils, "who hear[s] the word, welcome[s] it, and produce[s] a crop: 30, 60, and 100 times what was sown" (Mark 4:20).

She lived in the land of the Philistines for seven years. In contrast to Joram, she patiently waits on the Lord. During that time God protects her. Unfortunately she loses her house and land during her sojourn. Joram may have acted like his land-grabbing father and taken it (cf. 1 Kgs 21). She is in need of help and a defender. She possibly lost her husband as well, making her more desperate.

God's Providence (vv. 4-6)

Providentially, when she arrives at the royal court to beg for her property, Gehazi is telling the king about this lady at the same time. (What is Gehazi doing here? Was he not struck with leprosy in 5:27? Yes, but those events seem to have happened after this event.) The king is curious about the work of Yahweh and His prophet but certainly not committed to Yahweh. As Gehazi is telling the king all about how her son was raised from the dead, she walks into the room (perhaps even with her child). Gehazi advocated for the defenseless in this story, and it proved successful, as God providentially used this encounter to move the king to restore not only all that was hers but also all the income from her land that she would have received if she had not left the country.

This lady received a simple word and she obeyed. Many, like King Joram, received more messages from Elisha than her yet refused to believe. Joram was *charmed* by the truth at times but never *changed* by the truth. Davis says it well: "The men of Nineveh will likely stand up at the judgment and condemn Joram and his heirs, for [the Ninevites] repented when they had only a simple word of judgment but no catalogue of grace" (*2 Kings*, 135). Who are you like: the king, hearing gospel truths regularly but not responding, or this simple lady who takes God's word as truth, obeying it?

The Brokenhearted Prophet and the Decline of Judah
2 KINGS 8:7-29

The rest of chapter 8 fills in some important details for us. We learn about the fulfillment of God's instructions to Elijah. If you remember, he was to anoint Elisha, Hazael, and Jehu (1 Kgs 19:15-17). He did anoint Elisha (1 Kgs 19:19-21), but we never heard of him anointing the other two men. The writer seems to intend for us to see that this is now going to happen through Elisha (Davis, *2 Kings*, 136). Elisha will set apart Hazael as God's instrument of judgment on Israel (8:12). Also, the kingdom of Judah is beginning to look more and more like the kingdom of Israel. After some decent kings—Asa and Jehoshaphat—we read of Jehoram and Ahaziah, who lead the country downward. All the while, we are still waiting for the house of Omri/Ahab to be eliminated. We have had a king from Omri's family since 1 Kings 16:23, despite Elijah's prophecy in 1 Kings 21:21-24. We can feel the tension as we wait. We are just one chapter away from the coronation of Jehu (2 Kgs 9:6), who will execute judgment on that house.

A New Aramean King: Hazael (vv. 7-15)

Ben-hadad is ill, and he sends Hazael to find Elisha, who is residing in Damascus (cf. 1 Kgs 19:15). The king wants to know whether he will live. The foreign king sends for Elisha's prognosis, unlike Ahaziah of Israel who inquired of Baal-zebub in his sickness (2 Kgs 1:2). In an attempt to persuade Elisha to grant a favorable prophecy, a humongous gift is given to him—40 camel loads. Imagine that scene! The sad reality is that the king only inquires as to whether or not he will recover. His vision is shortsighted.

If I may use another beach illustration, my youngest son Joshua and I were out in the ocean. I was holding him as these big waves were coming at us. He said, "Oh Papa, don't drop me. Don't let me drown. I want to eat supper." I laughed because he obviously missed the bigger issue of drowning. If you drown, you have something more significant to think about than supper. Ben-hadad was worried about "supper" when he should have been thinking about eternal life.

Elisha tells Hazael more than he wants to know. He gives him a bit of a riddle. He says, "Go say to him, 'You are sure to recover.' But the LORD has shown me that he is sure to die" (v. 10). This puzzle basically means that Ben-hadad is in fact going to die. However, it isn't going to be from his illness but from something else (for more on this, see Provan, *1 and 2 Kings*, 207).

Jeremiah is called "the weeping prophet," but here we read of another weeping prophet: Elisha. He stares down Hazael and then breaks down in tears. Hazael asks Elisha why the tears. He answers, "Because I know the evil you will do to the people of Israel" (v. 12). When Hazael questions this, Elisha tells him, "The LORD has shown me that you will be king over Aram" (v. 13). This prediction takes place: Hazael brutally inflicts great suffering on Israel (Amos 1:13; Hos 13:16; 2 Kgs 9:14-15; 12:17-18; 13:3-7; 15:16). He rises to power by killing Ben-hadad. We read that he relays the message, "You are sure to recover" (v. 14), but then he apparently proceeds to smother Ben-hadad to death.

Elisha's brokenheartedness reminds us of God's other compassionate messengers. Ezekiel says on behalf of Yahweh, "I take no pleasure in the death of the wicked" (33:11). Jeremiah said, "My eyes will overflow with tears, for the LORD's flock has been taken captive" (13:17). Paul said, "For I have often told you, and now say again *with tears*, that many live as enemies of the cross of Christ. Their end is destruction" (Phil 3:18-19; emphasis added; see also Rom 9:1-5). Jesus Himself wept over the city of Jerusalem (Luke 19:41). God must judge sinners, but He is slow to anger and full of mercy. When judgment comes, there is an element of divine sadness in it. Tears fall with the fire and brimstone. Elisha knew judgment was necessary, but it was sad (Davis, *2 Kings*, 137). He was a brokenhearted prophet.

If people are going to refuse to believe and head off into destruction, then let them do so by walking through a puddle of our prayerful tears. Are you broken for those who don't know the King? Let us learn from Elisha to weep over the unrepentant and to remember, "God seldom blesses a tearless ministry" (Quarles, "Paul: A Model for Ministry").

Kings in Judah (vv. 16-29)

It has been a while since we have read of Judah. In 2 Kings 3 King Jehoshaphat was part of an unsuccessful attack on Moab. Now we learn of his son, Jehoram. (The HCSB consistently spells Israel's king "Joram" and Judah's king "Jehoram." In Hebrew, the two names are spelled the same way.) King Jehoram of Judah was first mentioned in 1 Kings 22:50 and again in 2 Kings 1:17.

Judah begins to look more and more like Israel. Not only do their kings have the same name (in Hebrew), but they also begin practicing the same idolatry. Jehoram "walked in the way of the kings of Israel, as the house of Ahab had done, for Ahab's daughter was his wife. He did what was evil in the LORD's sight" (8:18). He apparently was given to the worship of golden calves, like Jeroboam, and also to the worship of Baal. This would mean he was "worse" than the King Joram of Israel (2 Kgs 3:2-3). He has intermarried with Ahab's daughter (Athaliah, v. 26), and the idolatrous practices of that family have now infected Judah. They are all "one big evil family" (Davis, *2 Kings*, 140). Because of His promise to David, God doesn't eliminate them (v. 19; cf. 2 Sam 7:12-16; 21:17; 1 Kgs 11:36; 15:4). By God's grace a lamp remains in Judah. It would shine, ever so dimly, until the coming of King Jesus. "The LORD was unwilling to destroy Judah." These kings will fall, but God will keep His kingdom.

Edom fails to submit to King Jehoram. Gone are the days of Solomon, who could rule over the nations. Jehoram faces the same kind of problem his northern counterpart faced when they failed to subdue Moab (2 Kgs 3). Judah is forced to flee from the battlefield. Even cities in Judah, like Libnah, are experiencing unrest. The picture is of great decline in Judah. We are told of Jehoram's death in verses 23-24, and we read that Ahaziah is the new king of Judah.

Judah's King Ahaziah (not to be confused with Israel's King Ahaziah in 1 Kgs 22:51–2 Kgs 1) follows in the sins of his father Jehoram and the sins of the family of Ahab/Omri. He reigns a whole year! He went to war with Israel against Hazael (probably sending troops, not going himself). In the battle Israel's King Joram gets wounded. Ahaziah went down to visit Joram, but that was the last visit he would make, for now the stage is set for judgment. King Joram of Israel is in Jezreel, and King Ahaziah of Judah is visiting him. They didn't know what was coming (peek ahead to 2 Kgs 9:14-16).

We are left to marvel at the nature of God. From these accounts it's clear that God is

> *a compassionate and gracious God, slow to anger and rich in faithful love and truth, maintaining faithful love to a thousand generations, forgiving wrongdoing, rebellion, and sin. But He will not leave the guilty unpunished.* (Exod 34:6-7)

For all who call on Him, from Aram to Israel to Bangladesh to Omaha, there is salvation. "You are a forgiving God," Nehemiah prayed (Neh 9:17). But for those who refuse to embrace Christ as Savior and Lord, judgment will come. A day of grace is here now, so respond before the day of judgment comes. You can have a stubborn heart like Ben-hadad, a superficial heart like Joram, or a skeptical heart like his assassin. But you will wish you had believed like the Shunammite woman.

God's divine mercy and justice have been most gloriously displayed in the cross of Jesus. There the sinless One bore our judgment so that we may experience everlasting mercy and grace. Look to Him, and flee the wrath to come—a wrath worse than anything we read of in Kings. In Christ you are safe. In Christ you are free from condemnation.

Reflect and Discuss

1. In what ways does God's mercy extend even to those who reject Him today?
2. What can be learned from the vision of the invisible "chariots of fire all around"?
3. Discuss any personal experiences of trusting God without a vision of invisible chariots of fire.
4. The king of Israel scoffs at the Lord and intends to kill Elisha. What has caused his hardness of heart?
5. In what ways might God communicate His good news through unlikely messengers today?
6. What types of people might be considered unworthy, like the four lepers, of carrying the good news?
7. The miraculous provision of God to His people turns out to be a rod of judgment for the unbelieving captain. How do God's mercy and justice function in this story?
8. How do God's mercy and justice intertwine for people today in the cross of Christ?
9. Discuss the Shunammite woman's obedience and the role it played in her life.
10. How does God bless His people when they are obedient today?

Fast and Furious

2 KINGS 9:1–10:36

Main Idea: Jehu was an imperfect instrument of God, in contrast to the perfect obedience, love, and justice demonstrated by the ultimate instrument of God, Jesus Christ.

I. Context
II. Things That Differ
III. Things That Matter
    A. Justice matters (9:1-10).
    B. God's Word matters (9:11-16).
    C. Worship matters (9:17-22).
    D. God's suffering saints matter (9:23–10:11).
    E. Your heart matters (10:12-36).
    F. The coming of Christ matters.

Playing off a popular commercial, a friend of mine dubs his dad as "the most interesting man in the world." His dad was an Army Ranger and a Green Beret. He was also a trial lawyer. Now he's a professor. This most interesting dad has taught at three intuitions in the area of Old Testament/Hebrew. He speaks nine languages. He learned Russian in one month so he could give a speech in Leningrad at a university. They responded by giving him a standing ovation. I think he tops the Dos Equis man.

As I looked at our main character, Jehu, I thought he might be called the most interesting man in the world. He drives like the actor Vin Diesel, he wipes out people like the Terminator, and he's as cunning as Jack Bauer. Liam Neeson could play him well should Hollywood try to make an action-packed movie based on these two chapters. It's indeed filled with swift drama.

So who is Jehu son of Nimshi? This isn't the prophet Jehu, son of Hanani, whom we met previously (1 Kgs 16). This Jehu was a military commander whom God appointed as His agent of judgment. Unfortunately, not everything about Jehu is commendable, but he's definitely interesting.

We're actually dealing with a difficult story as we consider King Jehu's bloody purge. I suppose some may wonder why anyone would even bother with such a story. Why would anyone preach from a book of the Bible like this? Would this not shrink the church? Good question. I suppose there are many answers, but I might offer three.

To begin, we should teach the whole Bible, even hard passages, because **God builds His church through His Word**, not through gimmicks or great personalities. There's a difference between building a church and building a crowd.

Additionally, I think **people are actually interested in such passages**. Several articles have been written recently about how to keep millennials in the church. One author, Rachael Held Evans, wrote an article for CNN's religion blog titled "Why Millennials Are Leaving the Church." In it she says they are leaving not because of style but for lack of "substance." She says, "Having been advertised to our whole lives, we Millennials have highly sensitive BS meters, and we're not easily impressed with consumerism or performances." While you may not agree with her whole article, I think people long for something deeper than mere performance. They're longing for truth, meaning, and community, which are found through knowing Christ.

Finally, passages like this are important because **we need to know how to answer the skeptics of our day**. Many argue that the Bible's holy wars are just like Islamic jihads, but that shows a lack of good interpretation of hard texts. How do we answer the militant atheists of our day who say that "God is a moral monster" and that Christians should stop trying to persuade people to believe in such a deity? We can only respond well when we have studied diligently.

This passage is about judgment and eliminating those *within* the leadership of Israel. These leaders disregarded all the warnings and refused to repent. Hence, we see God's mercy here. Further, the leaders turned people away from the living God and committed atrocities. Yet they were never brought to justice. Shouldn't those who kill the innocent be held accountable? Of course! Consequently, we see God's justice. This story, therefore, doesn't make God out to be a moral monster but a God of mercy and justice.

Context

To understand this story, you need to know the story of King Ahab. This king from the house of Omri was the worst of the kings of Israel. He married the foreigner Jezebel, who brought with her the idolatry of Baal along with all of its perversions. She basically evangelized for Baal and persecuted the prophets of Yahweh. One particular episode is important for the text at hand: the story of Naboth's vineyard (1 Kgs 21), in which Ahab and Jezebel murdered Naboth, a righteous Israelite.

Ahab wanted Naboth's vineyard, but Naboth refused to sell it or trade it because he knew the land was not his to sell—to do so would be unrighteous. He knew his land was God's, and he was just a steward of it. Ahab then pouted like a spoiled kid. Jezebel decided to take matters into her own hands. She wrote letters to the men of Naboth's city instructing the leaders to stone Naboth (1 Kgs 21:10-11). They obeyed.

Jezebel and Ahab enjoyed their new garden for a while, but then God sent his prophet Elijah to confront Ahab. God was on the side of the oppressed. He was aware of the situation, and He would act on Naboth's behalf. How so? God's prophet Elijah promised Ahab, "In the place where the dogs licked Naboth's blood, the dogs will also lick your blood!" (21:19). That was fulfilled in 22:38, but that was not the end. Elijah also promised that disaster would fall on Ahab's house and on Jezebel. We were told, "The dogs will eat Jezebel in the plot of land at Jezreel" (21:23). More than 12 years have passed now. Ahab is gone, but the house of Ahab (the dynasty of Omri) still reigns. But that comes to an end here in 2 Kings 9–10. God raises up a new king, Jehu, as his instrument of judgment. Elijah had previously been told to anoint him (1 Kgs 19:16-17). Now the time of reckoning has come. God appoints Jehu to clean Ahab's house.

So let's take a look at God's agent of judgment in these two chapters. We left off with the kings of Judah and Israel together. There was a battle in which Israel and Judah fought against Aram. King Joram of Israel was wounded and went back to Jezreel to take care of his wounds. King Ahaziah of Judah went to visit him. At this point the kings of Judah are rebelling in that they have intermarried with Ahab's house, thus leaving the southern kingdom in a corrupt state (2 Kgs 8:27).

It's an easy section to outline, but for some it's a hard section to read because it's bloody. It's divided into three parts: the anointing (9:1-13), the avenging (9:14–10:27), and the assessment (10:28-36). If you scan these sections, you can see the breakdown. A young prophet anoints Jehu, who serves as God's avenger. Jehu eliminates Joram, Ahaziah, Jezebel, Ahab's descendants, and the worshipers of Baal. In the final verses of chapter 10, we are left to ponder the assessment of Jehu's reign.

While this structure covers the story itself, I have chosen to go with a bit different outline: Things That Differ and Things That Matter (Terry Johnson, "The Lord's Justice 2"). We need to make some distinctions between the situation in this story and in our time period, but we also need to take some things seriously that are still true for us.

We have to be careful in interpreting and applying stories like this, in which there's great violence and bloodshed. Should we just dismiss these chapters as morally repulsive and practically irrelevant? No. Do they serve as another argument against religion? No. While many use religion as an excuse for violence, we cannot make such a sweeping assessment of this story. It's true that Jehu is a flawed instrument of judgment, and we cannot hold him up as a perfect example. But God initiates the action and commends Jehu for some actions (10:30) because he did what was according to God's word (9:25-26,36-37; 10:10,17,30). How is this situation different from ours, and what should we learn from this story?

Things That Differ

Briefly we need to make three distinctions.

We must distinguish between Israel and the nations. What happened in Israel was in many ways unique. God placed His name on this nation. They were special. Because of this reality, the judgment on those who led the nation into wickedness was unique in its severity. In addition, because of Israel's specific role, many of Israel's enemies were driven out of the land. This was for a unique purpose, that is, to preserve God's people and to bring the Messiah so the nations could be saved. We aren't like Israel in these ways. We aren't driving out all the people in America who don't believe in Jesus. We aren't going to go wipe out nations. We are going to love the nations. Israel had a unique, specific, limited calling in the Old Testament. There is continuity and discontinuity between the testaments, and we need to remember that.

We must distinguish between God's special revelation and self-deception. Special revelation is what God said—what He has revealed to mankind. Many will say that God "told them" to kill and conquer, but that is self-deception. Few men have been instruments for God's judgment (e.g., Moses, Joshua, Elijah, and Jehu). We await the ultimate One, Jesus. If anyone today says they are killing in the name of God, don't believe them. They are deceived. Many fruitcakes can say that—from Jim Jones to David Koresh to Osama Bin Laden. They think God is on their side for a path of violence. God does grant civil authorities the sword, but that isn't the same as God's calling to these particular representatives in Scripture. This was limited to a few who received God's special revelation.

We have to distinguish between the agent's assignment and the actual execution of the assignment. Jehu isn't a role model in every way because he doesn't follow God's word totally. He has his own interests in mind at times. He was not wholly devoted to Yahweh. Yet God does use him, as broken as he is, but that doesn't mean God approves of everything he does.

Things That Matter

Having noted the things that differ, allow me to identify some timeless truths that really matter as we walk through the passage. Things do matter here! The bloodshed should illustrate this. Christianity isn't something to be lukewarm about. Six particular applications emerge: justice matters, God's word matters, worship matters, suffering saints matter, your heart matters, and the coming of Christ matters.

Justice Matters (9:1-10)

In Psalm 99 the poet exults in God's justice:

> *The mighty King loves justice. You have established fairness; You have administered justice and righteousness in Jacob. Exalt the* LORD *our God; bow in worship at His footstool. He is holy.* (99:4-5; emphasis added)

Then, regarding Old Testament leaders, the psalmist writes, "You were a forgiving God to them, an avenger of their sinful actions" (99:8). God is forgiving and God is just. He will not sweep sin under the rug. In response we should "tremble" at our holy God (99:1) and worship Him.

We should stand in awe of God's sovereignty in His justice. God's sovereignty is over human history. We see this fact in how His word is carried out in the anointing of Jehu.

Elisha carries out the command given to His predecessor, Elijah, and anoints Jehu the commander as king, but He doesn't do it himself. He sends one of the "sons of the prophets" to do so (9:1). Who were these guys? Ira Price summarizes in his biblical survey of the prophets:

> In conclusion, we have found in this brief discussion that the sons of the prophets 1) were collected together in bands

or schools; 2) in six different localities, viz., (a) Ramah,
(b) Bethel, (c) Gilgal, (d) Jericho, (e) Carmel, (f) Samaria;
3) under the tuition of (a) Samuel, (b) Elijah and (c) Elisha;
4) with instruction in (a) prophesying-worship, (b) sacred
music, (c) practical matters of their day; 5) with their time
wholly occupied in (a) study and worship, (b) doing errands
for their masters and God, (c) performing the regular duties
of a prophet; 6) largely dependent for their support upon the
charity of the people. (Price, "The Schools of the Sons of the
Prophets," 249)

Elisha instructs him in verses 2-4. It may have seemed a bit bizarre. He
was to anoint army commander Jehu in Ramoth-gilead, where they were
fighting against the Arameans. Despite the awkward timing the young
"seminarian" goes to the front. God can intervene and intrude when
He deems it appropriate. He is sovereign. When the seminarian arrives
there, he asks to speak with Jehu, who is sitting with his men. He meets
with Jehu, pours the oil over his head, and delivers the message from
Yahweh. Immediately after delivering the message, the young man obediently "opened the door and escaped" (v. 10, see v. 3). Jehu is anointed.
God sovereignly appoints His king. The psalmist says that God stands
men up and sits them down. "Exaltation does not come from the east,
the west, or the desert, for God is the Judge: He brings down one and
exalts another" (Ps 75:6-7). God sovereignly exalts Jehu to this position
and abases Joram.

We should also stand in awe of God's vengeance. Notice the clarity
of this declaration in verses 6-10. The house and Ahab and Jezebel are
to be put to death. Though Jehu is the human instrument for this plan,
God is clearly the primary One responsible for executing judgment.
The messenger reports Yahweh's words, saying, "I may avenge" (v. 7), "I
will eliminate" (v. 8), "I will make" (v. 9). This is God's plan and action.

Paul reminds Christians, "Friends, do not avenge yourselves; instead,
leave room for His wrath. For it is written: Vengeance belongs to Me; I
will repay, says the Lord" (Rom 12:19; see Deut 32:35). You and I aren't
Jehu. We aren't God's chosen instruments for judgment. But we're to
trust that God is totally committed to seeing justice done. The psalmist
says, "Righteousness and justice are the foundation of Your throne" (Ps
89:14). God must and will judge sin. Sinners will be eternally judged
unless they repent and turn to the cross, where Christ paid the debt for
sinners. Forgiveness doesn't mean an absence of punishment. Justice

demands that payment be made for sin. God forgives sinners by putting Christ forward as the substitute for sinners. Let's stand in awe of His vengeance.

We should also stand in awe of His timing. An interesting feature of this story is that it seems to have taken a long time since the prophecy of Elijah. Then it seems like a strange time to execute the plan—while Israel is at war with an ongoing opponent. But this story illustrates God's merciful patience. His judgment is mingled with mercy. Peter says, "The Lord does not delay His promise, as some understand delay, but is patient with you, not wanting any to perish but all to come to repentance" (2 Pet 3:9). It seems like He's slow, or delayed like a flight leaving the airport. But Peter says God is giving unbelievers an opportunity to repent before final judgment. But the day of reckoning will come. When? Peter goes on to say, "But the Day of the Lord will come like a thief" (3:10). We're instructed in the New Testament to "be ready" for the coming of Jesus (Matt 24:36–25:13). We should stand in awe of the fact that the King will come. Are you ready? Have you responded to the gospel in faith? Are you using your days wisely? Many wonder when this will be, but we don't know. Some have charts to speculate. You don't need to be concerned with charts; you better be concerned with your heart.

God's Word Matters (9:11-16)

Jehu's men wonder what happened. They call the young prophet a "crazy person" (v. 11). Prophets were often viewed as mad. Today pastors are viewed the same way by a certain segment of society. But they are in good company. Paul was perceived as being out of his mind, and Jesus was the object of mockery (Matt 26:29; Acts 26:24; 2 Cor 5:13). But we're reminded in this story that God will fulfill His word, though it may seem crazy to people.

After the officers anxiously inquire, Jehu tries to downplay the event for some reason (perhaps testing them, or thinking this was their idea?). He says, "You know the sort and their ranting." But they press him for an answer: "That's a lie! Tell us!" When he tells them that the prophet said, "This is what the LORD says: I anoint you king over Israel" (v. 12), they immediately submit to that word and crown him king. They give a spontaneous, secretive coronation for the new king.

But what is done in secret would soon come out in public. Jehu says that it's time to mount up and go to Jezreel, where the kings of Judah and Israel are staying (vv. 14-16). The news will be told, as the hour of judgment has come for Joram and Ahaziah.

What matters in this story? Truth. God's word takes precedence over national politics, a war, and popular opinion. God's word was also the catalyst for human history. Even though people may laugh at God's message and messengers, His Word will stand forever.

Take a cue from this young man. Speak God's Word to people even if they consider you a crazy person. Paul told the Corinthians, "For the message of the cross is foolishness to those who are perishing" (1 Cor 1:18). We believe a crucified Galilean who lived 2,000 years ago can take away our sin and give us eternal life. We believe He will one day return, as a King better than Jehu, to establish His kingdom forever, where we will live in total peace. We believe those who don't bow down to Christ in this life will do so later, but it will be too late. And this message is the most important message available today. Just remember that you may be considered crazy, but you're in good company (1 Cor 4:13). The prophets and Jesus were considered crazy. When you're opposed or persecuted, remember that God's truth matters more than your comfort. Great is your reward in heaven. We must never allow our sin to be a stumbling block for people, but we must remember that many will struggle with embracing God's "crazy" truth. Such a problem has existed since the garden of Eden. Follow the example of this lad and speak God's truth faithfully.

Worship Matters (9:17-22)

As Jehu approaches Jezreel, Joram sends two different men to meet Jehu and ask, "Do you come in peace?" (vv. 17-19). Jehu retorts each time, "What do you have to do with peace?" (vv. 18,19). This wasn't the day for peace. Each messenger is told to join King Jehu and get behind him. After these two episodes, the watchman says, "He reached them but hasn't started back. Also, the driving is like that of Jehu son of Nimshi—he drives *like a madman*" (v. 20; emphasis added). Jehu felt the need for speed. We might compare him to a skilled tank commander. Apparently he had a reputation for amazing maneuvering in warfare.

Joram doesn't know what's going on, which is why he asks, "Do you come in peace?" (or, "Is all well?"). He may have thought that Jehu was bringing news from the battlefield, of either victory or defeat. But his messengers never returned. So he's alarmed, but he doesn't know what it's about; as a result, he goes out to meet Jehu. Fittingly, they meet at the property of Naboth. Joram asks the same question, "Do you come in peace, Jehu?" Jehu's response revealed that he wasn't coming with news about the battle with the Arameans. He was coming to clean house. Notice carefully what he says: "What peace can there be as long as there is so much prostitution and witchcraft from your mother Jezebel?" (v. 22).

Let's pause here and point out another important matter. "Prostitution" refers metaphorically to worshiping other gods (Exod 34:16; Lev 17:7; Deut 31:16). Since Baalism involved sexual perversion, this was a particularly apt description (House, *1, 2 Kings*, 289). "Witchcraft" probably refers to cultish practices. Idolatry has taken the place of true worship, and there is a relationship between idolatry and judgment. The reason Jehu was told to strike down Ahab's dynasty wasn't because Joram was a Republican or Democrat; it was because these leaders had led Israel into false worship. Israel had been instructed as they came into the land not to follow the practices of the nations (Deut 18:9-14). God was preserving this people and using them to bring the Messiah so that the nations might be saved. Remember that the problem with intermarriage with the Canaanites wasn't race but idolatry (1 Kgs 11:1-2).

Jehu was obedient to God here as he eliminated false worship, but he did not continue to obey God's instructions. At the end of the chapter, we see that he led Israel into sin because he failed to remove the golden calves. "He did not turn from the sins that Jeroboam had *caused Israel to commit*" (10:31; emphasis added; see 1 Kgs 16:33; 22:52). The problem was similar to what Jesus warned against:

> But whoever causes the downfall of one of these little ones who believe
> in Me—it would be better for him if a heavy millstone were hung
> around his neck and he were thrown into the sea. (Mark 9:42)

Jesus was condemning those who sought to lead others away from God's law and those who sought to destroy the faith of believers.

God takes worship seriously. All of us worship something or someone. "Who is my God?" is the most important question you will answer. How can we make sure we are worshiping rightly? Note the repeated emphasis on "peace." This Hebrew word *shalom* occurs nine times in chapter 9, more than in any other chapter in the Old Testament (Olley, *Message of Kings*, 261). How do you get peace? Peace comes from God. Jehu knew there could be no peace while idolatrous practices were present (9:22). Why? It's because peace can only come through a right relationship with God. The problem is that removing those who support idolatry from a place doesn't remove the idols from the heart. Jehu never took his revolution far enough or deep enough.

We need a peace deeper than mere removal of external threats to peace. We need a purging from within the heart. We need internal peace. Jesus came to bring us peace right now, and He promises peace in the future when He returns. Do you want peace? Look to Jesus. Paul says, "We have peace with God through our Lord Jesus Christ" (Rom 5:1). Turn from idolatrous practices and experience the satisfying peace of knowing Christ as your Lord and the supreme treasure of your heart. Jesus said, "My peace I give to you. I do not give to you as the world gives" (John 14:27). Only one King could bring the peace we need.

God's Suffering Saints Matter (9:23–10:11)

Jehu proceeded to eliminate Joram, Ahaziah, Jezebel, and the sons of Ahab. God is avenging the blood of His "servants the prophets and of all the servants of the LORD" (9:7) and, of course, the blood of Naboth.

Joram tries to flee, but Jehu shoots him between the shoulders, piercing his heart, and Joram sinks in the chariot. The irony continues. Jehu says, "Pick him up and throw him on the plot of ground belonging to *Naboth* the Jezreelite" (v. 25; emphasis added). He then quotes the prophecy of Elijah, given over 12 years previously.

> *"As surely as I saw the blood of* Naboth *and the blood of* his sons *yesterday"*—this is the LORD's declaration—*"so will I repay you on this plot of land"*—this is the LORD's declaration. So now, according to the word of the LORD, pick him up and throw him on the plot of land. (v. 26; emphasis added)

Who is Naboth? He was nobody to Ahab. He was garbage to Jezebel. Apparently they had slain not only him but also his sons. But now judgment has come full circle because God's suffering saints matter to Him. God will avenge the blood of His people. This truth is echoed throughout Scripture. When Israel was mistreated in Egypt, God said to Moses,

> I have observed the misery of My people in Egypt, and have heard them crying out because of their oppressors, and I know about their sufferings. I have come down to rescue them (Exod 3:7-8)

Psalm 10 illustrates the cry of the oppressed. While evil men afflict God's people, "payday someday" is coming (2 Thess 1:5-9).

Ahaziah also tries to flee but suffers the same fate as Joram. He flees south. Jehu's men wound him in between Jezreel and Samaria, he dies in Megiddo, and he receives a burial in the city of David. He was killed either because Jehu viewed him as a threat or, more likely, because Jehu believed he deserved judgment for marrying Ahab's daughter. Others say it was because Jehu thought Ahaziah would try to avenge the death of Joram. We don't read of this being "according to God's word." What are we to make of this? The Chronicler seems to help us by saying, "Ahaziah's downfall came from God when he went to Joram" (2 Chr 22:7).

Jezebel decides she will go out in style. She hears that Jehu is coming, so she gets all dolled up. She wants to die as an evil queen. But it will be her last day to put on makeup. She asks the same question: "Do you come in peace?" and then insults Jehu by calling him Zimri (v. 31). Do you remember him? He was a commander who took Elah's throne by force and reigned for a whole week. Jezebel is comparing Jehu to him since Jehu had assassinated Joram. The difference of course was that God never told Zimri to start a revolution. Though she may have looked like she powerfully controlled everyone around her, she's betrayed by two or three eunuchs who throw her out of the window. As with the deaths of Joram and Ahaziah, Jehu has acted swiftly.

When she fell, her blood splattered on the wall, and the horses trampled her. Jehu demonstrates his reign then by going in to eat and drink in her palace. As an afterthought he orders her burial, but the servants discover that there was not much left of her. They found nothing but "her skull, her feet, and the palms of her hands" (v. 35). Dogs had consumed the rest of her. The men realize that this fulfilled Elijah's word (1 Kgs 21:23). Naboth's death has now been avenged. Once again Naboth had meant nothing to Jezebel, but God's suffering saints matter to Him. The only remaining act is to eliminate Ahab's descendants.

The book of Revelation promises that God will avenge the blood of His righteous servants. Evil men may prosper on earth for a short time, but God will have the last word. Dogs may not consume modern-day Jezebels every time, but their future judgment is certain. God will avenge the blood of His persecuted people eventually and finally (Deut 32:43; Isa 59:17; Nah 1:2; Rev 6:10; 19:2). The persecuted church really exists. Brothers and sisters around the world are being kidnapped and martyred. Some burned alive. Others tortured for months. But even if we don't know about all of them, God does.

In Revelation 6:9-10 those who had been slain for the word of God and for the witness they had borne cry out, "Lord, the One who is holy and true, how long until You judge and avenge our blood from those who live on the earth?" Then they are told to rest and wait (Rev 6:11). In Revelation 19:2 we read, "His judgments are true and righteous, because He . . . has avenged the blood of His slaves that was on her hands." God knows His saints and those who kill them. Judgment is coming. A sure and severe judgment is coming.

Joram is dead, but "Ahab had 70 sons in Samaria." Part of the prophesied punishment of Ahab was the execution of his descendants. Jehu issues a challenge to the men of the city. He tells the rulers, the elders, and the guardians to pick the best of the sons of Ahab and to sit him on the throne to fight for Ahab's house. Despite the offer and despite their having access to military resources, Jehu intimidates them, so they decline the offer. They tell Jehu, "We are your servants, and we will do whatever you tell us. We will not make anyone king. Do whatever you think is right" (v. 5). Next, Jehu says that "heads will roll"—literally. He tells the men of the city to bring the heads of Ahab's sons to Jezreel the next day. They act swiftly and send the heads back to Jehu in Jezreel. Jehu puts them out by the entrance of the city and uses them as an object lesson in his morning speech.

When the people gather for Jehu's speech, he uses the heads as evidence of God's approval of his rise to power (House, *1, 2 Kings*, 292). He isn't totally honest in his statements, but his words gain him what he wants, namely, the support of the people. Again we have an example of the flaws of Jehu, but he has nevertheless secured Jezreel. This leads us to the next point.

Your Heart Matters (10:12-36)

Jehu needs to go to Samaria where the other stronghold remained. He sets out for Samaria, but on the way some important meetings happen that shed light on Jehu's heart problem. After these meetings and the wiping out of the Baal worshipers, we read in the final analysis, "Yet Jehu was not careful to follow the instruction of the LORD God of Israel *with all his heart*" (v. 31; emphasis added). He was a man with obvious "zeal for the LORD" (v. 16), but that zeal seems often to be for himself and not for the glory of God.

On this journey Jehu first meets Ahaziah's relatives, who were apparently unaware of the current happenings. Jehu slaughters all 42 of them mercilessly without any stated reason. Perhaps his reason was that Ahaziah's house had intermarried with Ahab's house and must be wiped out or that they had some claim to the throne. But this would be a stretch it seems. House says that these murders "cause Hosea to condemn what occurs in Jezreel (Hos 1:4 5). The prophecies of Elijah and Elisha say nothing about the killing of *David's* descendants" (House, *1, 2 Kings*, 293; emphasis in original). So this is at least questionable.

Jehu then meets a new character, Jehonadab. Jehu asks him, "Is your heart one with mine?" Jehonadab responds, "It is" (v. 15). In response Jehu brings him up into the chariot. His new assistant will be with him as he cleanses the temple of Baal. Who is this Jehonadab? Drawing from Jeremiah 35:6-7, we find out about him from his descendants. We read that he promoted fanatical support for Yahweh that involved living an ascetic and a nomadic lifestyle. They would have rejected all that Ahab's house valued. Jehu tells this man, "Come with me and see my zeal for the LORD" (v. 16). Such an invitation would have been attractive to one like Jehonadab. We will ponder Jehu's zeal in a moment.

Having secured the conservative wing of Israel, Jehu proceeded to wipe out the remaining group of Ahab's house in Samaria, "according to the word of the LORD spoken to Elijah" (v. 17). The writer confirms the eradication of the Ahab loyalists. So while the death of Ahaziah's descendants is questionable, this act seems appropriate.

One may question the nature of the judgment of God in this story. Heads rolling; dogs eating Jezebel; Jehu, a flawed man, exercising judgment—does it have to be this way? Davis points out two good responses to this question (*2 Kings*, 163). First, God has no sterilized instruments. He does all His work through imperfect people. Throughout the Bible, God has used not-so-good and even wicked men (like Judas!) to carry out His sovereign plan. Second, it's difficult to make judgment pleasant. I suppose Ahab's descendants could have died in their sleep, but it was done this way. Either way, God's word is fulfilled. Remember that Jesus' death on the cross wasn't sanitary. There was blood and agony. At His second coming there will be something more frightening than any story in the Old Testament. When we read of God's judgment, we should stand in fear and turn to Jesus for salvation. It's right to feel the gravity of these stories. It is an awful thing to fall into the hands of a holy God. Be hidden in Christ, who took the judgment that we deserve.

Jehu isn't done. He will finish what Elijah started in wiping out the worshipers of Baal. Verse 18 doesn't look like zeal for Yahweh. Jehu says,

"Ahab served Baal a little, but Jehu will serve him a lot." But we should know better by now. Jehu wants to eliminate anything associated with Ahab. So we should catch the play on words in the next verse: "Now, therefore, summon to me all the prophets of Baal, all his servants, and all his priests. None must be missing, for I have a great sacrifice for Baal. Whoever is missing will not live" (v. 19). His idea of a sacrifice for Baal was a bit different from what the Baal worshipers called a sacrifice, for "Jehu was acting deceptively in order to destroy the servants of Baal." All of the Baalists arrive and fill the temple wearing their vestments, making them identifiable. Jehu threatened to kill them if they didn't show up, but ironically he was going to kill them when they did show up. He then searches the place to make sure no Yahweh followers were present. With everyone in the temple, Jehu offers sacrifices. Meanwhile, he has 80 snipers stationed to execute them all at his command. After the sacrifices are made, Jehu gives the order, and the Baal worshipers are eliminated. They also destroyed the sacred stone of Baal, which symbolized the presence of Baal, and they destroy the temple itself. This was the temple built by Ahab (1 Kgs 16:32). To complete the demolition, he turns the temple into a toilet.

Should we commend Jehu for this purging? It wasn't part of the prophetic mandate, but if we consider Deuteronomy 13:1-11, we could make a biblical argument in defense of this action, as we did in 1 Kings 18. But is that *why* Jehu did it? I tend to agree with Davis who says, "Wiping out the Baal cult had more to do with Jehu's zeal for Jehu than his zeal for Yahweh" (*2 Kings*, 165). If he had done this out of a pure zeal for Yahweh, then we would not find what we read in verses 28-29: Jehu basically traded apostasy for syncretism. He wiped out Baalism but didn't turn aside from Jeroboam's practice of worship. These "gold calves" would not have remained in Bethel and Dan if Jehu had desired a true, God-centered reformation. We seem to find mixed motives again.

We are left to evaluate the work of Jehu. As we have been pointing out, there is a qualified commendation of him. The writer says he wiped out the Baal cult, but he didn't turn away from Jeroboam's cult. He's given a limited reward of four generations of leadership for wiping out Ahab's house, but the writer states again that he didn't turn from the sins of Jeroboam. So Israel has returned to where they were before Ahab, but they have not returned fully to the Lord.

What will be the result of Jehu's failures over his 28-year reign? In verse 32 we read, "In those days the LORD began to reduce the size of

Israel." Hazael defeated them throughout the territory of Israel. As a result of Israel's ongoing decline and Jehu's failure to bring true reformation, the Lord began to reduce Israel. God wasn't pleased. Jehu is held accountable for his actions. Even though he was used by God to fulfill particular roles, his sins were not swept under the rug. One section of Israel after another is broken off. And who does it? It's Hazael, the Aramean king. He was another instrument of God's judgment, and he was also deficient. One instrument was used for *scourging* (Hazael) and the other for *purging* (Jehu) (Davis, *2 Kings*, 167).

God uses all kinds of people throughout history to fulfill His purposes, but they are responsible for their actions. Peter said the same about the death of Jesus. It happened at the hands of wicked men, who were accountable to God, but it was according to God's eternal plan (Acts 2:23). Just because you have been used by God to fulfill a role in His grand plan doesn't mean you are acceptable to Him (Matt 7:21-23). You must be found in Christ.

What should we make of Jehu's zeal? You might call it "twisted zeal," or in the words of James, he was "double-minded." Here's a guy who wipes out the prophets of Baal and is used as an agent of judgment against Ahab's house, but then we see him bowing to the golden calves in Dan. We see him throughout this story going after personal gain and securing political power. What a warning to examine our hearts!

What are some modern-day examples of twisted zeal? You might be zealous for religion, but you have never experienced regeneration. You may have zeal to attend worship gatherings but be addicted to pornography. You might think you are zealous for ministry but really have zeal to be known and admired by others. You might claim to have zeal to grow a church but be doing it for all the wrong reasons. You may have zeal for morality but turn into a legalistic Pharisee and know nothing of the grace of God in Christ. You might claim to have zeal for truth but actually have hatred toward those who disagree with you. You might have zeal to preach but actually be driven to please people or be famous. You might be busy with churchy things but have no devotion to Christ, doing everything in the energy of the flesh. You might be into social causes but have no desire for Jesus. Paul says there are some "holding to the form of godliness but denying its power" (2 Tim 3:5). Jehu says, "Come see my zeal." Jesus says, "Let Me examine your heart." That is what matters. Jehu purged Israel, but he still needed purging on the inside.

How can we avoid Jehu's sin? We must experience the transforming grace of Jesus. Paul was formerly "zealous" for a form of religion that led him to persecute Christians (Phil 3:6), but then he experienced conversion to Jesus Christ, leaving him to pursue nothing but Christ. That is what we need: zeal for Christ above all things. May all our sermons be aimed at pleasing Him! May our ministry to kids be about pleasing Christ! May our parenting, our small groups, and our finances be about Him! May our church planting, orphan care, and care for the poor and oppressed be done out of the overflow of a heart for Jesus. Let your heart burn for Christ, not self.

The Coming of Christ Matters

We don't have space to tease this out fully, but we must mention that Jesus is the better Jehu. He's the Anointed One; the One who walked over a carpet of garments on His way to Jerusalem (Leithart, *1 and 2 Kings*, 223); the One who the cleansed the temple, whose zeal for God's house consumed Him (John 2:17). He was the faithful and just Israelite. He lived a sinless life and died a substitutionary death, receiving the judgment of God on our behalf, making it possible for us to escape the just judgment of God. And He's the coming King who will judge the earth.

At His first coming, He taught us to love our enemies and showed us what that looks like. By following His teaching, emulating His example, relying on His power, and entrusting to Him the role of final Judge and Avenger, we don't have to live with constant anger against those who wrong us or hurt us in this life. We can wait on Christ to judge. We can live as Paul says: "When we are reviled, we bless; when we are persecuted, we endure it" (1 Cor 4:12). The certainty that Christ is coming frees us to love the world, including our enemies. (I'm not implying, however, that the guilty shouldn't receive just consequences.) John Piper illustrates this fact beautifully in a sermon he preached on Romans 12:16-20 titled, "Don't Avenge, But Give Place to Wrath."

> In 1974, as many of you know, my mother was killed in Israel. The story, as I was able to piece it together from others who were with her, is that a VW Minivan full of drunken Israeli soldiers swerved out of their lane and hit the bus in which my mother and father were sitting near the front. The death certificate that I read ten days later, when her body arrived in Atlanta from Tel Aviv, said, "lacerated medulla oblongata."

Unless you understand the circumstances of my growing up, you can't know what a loss that was to me at age 28.

But as a tribute to the mighty mercy of God I bear witness from my heart: I don't hate those soldiers. I don't wish them evil. In fact, it has occurred to me that they are probably today about my age or a little younger, and if any of them were reached with the gospel and believed in Christ, I would count it a great joy to be with them in heaven forever. "Vengeance is mine, I will repay," says the Lord. I am happy to leave it with him. This, I commend to you, is a wonderful way to live. This is freedom. And in this freedom there are great open spaces for love. (Piper, "Don't Avenge")

Jehu was God's agent of judgment, but he was imperfect. The perfect conquering King is coming. Revelation 19 gives us this awe-inspiring picture that should motivate us not to waste our lives and to love the world in view of His coming judgment:

> *Then I saw heaven opened, and there was a white horse. Its rider is called Faithful and True, and He judges and makes war in righteousness. His eyes were like a fiery flame, and many crowns were on His head. He had a name written that no one knows except Himself. He wore a robe stained with blood, and His name is the Word of God. The armies that were in heaven followed Him on white horses, wearing pure white linen. A sharp sword came from His mouth, so that He might strike the nations with it. He will shepherd them with an iron scepter. He will also trample the winepress of the fierce anger of God, the Almighty. And He has a name written on His robe and on His thigh: KING OF KINGS AND LORD OF LORDS.* (Rev 19:11-16)

This King, Jesus, is faithful and true. He judges and makes war in righteousness. An army of angels marches at His command. He is the King of kings and Lord of lords. Do you know Him? Have you submitted to His kingship? Are you ready to see Him? Let's tell the world about Him.

Reflect and Discuss

1. Why is God's judgment so strong against Jezebel and Ahab's descendants?
2. What can God's judgment of Jezebel teach us about His character?

3. Jehu destroyed the house of Baal and its prophets, but he accomplished the task by lying. Does God often use imperfect people to accomplish His purposes?
4. How can believers today avoid ignorance while being zealous for the Lord?
5. In this story God is an avenger. Should that strike fear or hope into the hearts of men?
6. How might God avenge His character and His people today?
7. Many of the servants of the Lord (like Naboth) never saw their blood avenged. Should God's people expect to see wrongs done to them immediately avenged?
8. How can believers today have hope that God will do justice?
9. How do God's love and judgment function in this story?
10. Can love and justice coexist in the same person, even in the same acts?

Is There Hope for the Rebellious?

2 KINGS 11:1–16:20

Main Idea: God extends grace, patience, and steadfast love toward His rebellious people.

I. **We Thirteen Kings (14:1–16:20)**
   A. Five kings in Judah
   B. Eight kings in Israel
II. **Grace to the Rebellious**
   A. God preserved the Davidic pipeline in Judah (chs. 11–12).
      1. Joash protected (11:1-3)
      2. Joash proclaimed (11:4-16)
      3. Joash's people (11:17-20)
      4. Joash's problems (12:1-21)
   B. God's power, compassion, and truth provided hope to Israel (13:14-25).
      1. Hope in God's power over the grave (vv. 20-21)
      2. Hope in God's compassion (vv. 22-23)
      3. Hope in God's trustworthy word (vv. 24-25)
III. **The Son of David**

Parents often struggle with mercy and patience. My wife sometimes jokes, "I was never tempted to cuss until I had kids!" Sleep patterns, eating habits, and homework are just a few issues that can drive moms and dads crazy. As I was working through this passage of Scripture, I was reminded of my need for fatherly patience. I was watching the kids at home while my bride attended a meeting. That seemed easy enough. But one of my nicknames in seminary was "Task-mode Tony." I get locked in on things, and I don't like being interrupted. And with ear-buds in, I was focused on finishing a message on this section. This particular week I was tired, weak, and stressed. So after about the third time my kids interrupted me about an issue over a movie, I lost it. I slammed down my commentary and said, "I'm trying to study the Bible! Leave me alone! I have a sermon to prepare!" It wasn't one of my best moments.

Later, I walked downstairs, paused the movie, and told my kids I needed to apologize for being quick-tempered. I asked for their forgiveness, and they graciously forgave me. I gave them a hug and went back upstairs. I returned to my study of 2 Kings 11–16 and marveled at the amazing patience and grace of God to the children of Israel. I was reminded of what a good God we have, who invites us into His presence, and how I often fail to display His character. It was a teachable moment for me. Here I was losing my temper while preparing a sermon on God's patience!

In chapter 17 we see Israel eventually going off into exile. Why has God not already turned His back on them? Commenting on chapter 17, Paul House summarizes, "God's grace alone has delayed the fall this long" (House, *1, 2 Kings*, 340). God was so gracious to His people.

Though they received abundant grace, they were a "rebellious" people. We could also call them an "idolatrous" people or a "worthless" people (17:15). The question is, Is there hope for this rebellious, idolatrous, worthless people? Yes. There's hope because Psalm 145 is true. This psalm, along with other passages, emphasizes how God is "gracious and compassionate, slow to anger and great in faithful love" (v. 8; cf. Exod 34:6; 2 Chr 30:9; Neh 9:17; Pss 86:15; 103:8; 111:4; Joel 2:13; Jonah 4:2). The words "all" or "every" occur 17 times in this particular psalm to emphasize the scope of His compassion and mercy. Here's hope for the rebellious! Christopher J. H. Wright points out, "The only exception in this litany to the universality of God's love are the wicked who choose, in their wickedness, to refuse it (Ps 145:20b)" (Wright, *The Mission of God*, 235). So yes, there is hope for all who turn to Yahweh in repentance. Yahweh is patient and merciful, but don't sin away your day of grace. Seek him while He may be found.

In the midst of the disobedience and decline of chapters 11–16, there are whispers of this hope. We will focus our attention on these whispers while not ignoring the tragic cries of the darkness. We will confine our attention to the reigns of two particular kings: Joash in Judah (chs. 11–12) and Jehoash in Israel (13:10-25). (The HCSB consistently spells Israel's king "Jehoash" and Judah's king "Joash." In Hebrew the kings' names are both spelled both ways.) From these stories I have two gigantic expressions of God's grace to point out, but first let's scan the material in these six chapters.

We Thirteen Kings

Chapters 11–16 mention 13 different kings. Five kings are from Judah and eight are from Israel. I don't think it's necessary to tease out every detail of each king. In fact, in chapter 15 alone the author flies through five kings of Israel over a 30-year period. Ralph Davis says the writer has his finger on the fast-forward button through this chapter, and to slog through it slowly ruins the impression the writer is trying to give (*2 Kings*, 221). Allow me to press the fast-forward button on chapters 11–16 and then hit rewind to go back and examine Joash and Jehoash.

Five Kings in Judah

Joash: the surviving seed of David (chs. 11–12). His rise to the throne is fascinating, filled with warning and example, and should lead us to worship the God of all grace. More on this king in a bit.

Amaziah: the arrogant thistle (14:1-22). Amaziah was a decent king who followed the Law of Moses at times. Sadly, after he defeated the Edomites, he worshiped their gods (2 Chr 25:14-16). This combination of idolatry and pride led him to pick a fight with Israel. Jehoash talked trash to Amaziah. He referred to himself as a "wild animal" that would stomp Amaziah like a little "thistle." He told him to "stay at home" (v. 10), but Amaziah left home around 793 BC, and he fared about as well as Robin Ventura when he left home plate to charge after Nolan Ryan in AD 1993. He got thrashed. Amaziah was captured by Jehoash, who destroyed part of the land and plundered the temple, giving Judah a taste of the coming exile.

Azariah/Uzziah: long-reigning leper (15:1-8). This king, called by two different names, sought the Lord and experienced many victories for the majority of his reign, leading the nation to great peace and prosperity. His reign lasted 52 years! However, the latter part of his life ended shamefully. The Chronicler gives that chilling word: "But when he became strong, he grew arrogant and it led to his own destruction" (2 Chr 26:16). When he tried to burn incense in the temple, an act reserved for the priests, the Lord struck him with a skin disease (2 Chr 26:16-21).

The prophet Isaiah received his call at the time of Uzziah's death (Isa 6:1-8). Amos also prophesied during this time (Amos 1:1). Both Amaziah and Uzziah illustrate the proverb, "Pride comes before destruction, and an arrogant spirit before a fall" (Prov 16:18).

Jotham: a glimmer of light (15:32-38). After already exercising power during his father's reign (because of his skin disease), Jotham becomes the king. He's a relatively good king who "didn't enter the LORD's sanctuary" like his father (2 Chr 27:2). We're told he "did what was right in the LORD's sight" but didn't remove the high places. He does improve the defenses in Israel.

During Jotham's reign a crisis emerges. Aram (Syria) and Israel try to force Judah to align with them against Assyria. This is the Syro-Ephraimite war that features so prominently in Isaiah 7–9. Micah begins his prophetic ministry during Jotham's reign (Provan, *1 and 2 Kings*, 244).

Ahaz: the awful (16:1-20). Ahaz's apostasy is described in the first few verses: he followed the kings of Israel (a phrase used of Jehoram, who married Ahab's daughter), he behaved like the cursed Canaanites, and he burned his own son (an offering to Molech). The Chronicler adds that he made pagan sacrifices in the Valley of Hinnom (2 Chr 28:3; cf. 2 Kgs 23:10; Matt 23:15). When threatened by Aram and Ephraim, he faithlessly looked to Assyria instead of trusting Yahweh for help.

Ahaz was unlike his son Hezekiah, who is remembered for his trust in God (2 Kgs 18:5). Ahaz paid the Assyrians with treasures from the temple. He then corrupted worship by replacing the bronze altar with an altar like that in Damascus, and he also rearranged some of the temple furnishings. He looked to Assyria for salvation and to Damascus for his liturgy (Davis, *2 Kings*, 236).

The only good note about Ahaz is the last sentence: "His son Hezekiah became king in his place." The Davidic line still holds despite this awful king. Such grace will be explained below. Isaiah prophesied during Ahaz's reign, including his fascinating word about the sign of Immanuel (Isa 7:13-14).

Eight Kings in Israel

Jehoahaz: rescued but unrepentant (13:1-9). This king was the first son of Jehu to reign. He did "evil in the LORD's sight," and God was angry with Israel, so He gave them into the hand of Hazael. Surprisingly, we read that Jehoahaz "sought the LORD's favor" and God "heard him" and gave Israel a deliverer (who is unnamed, vv. 4-5). Why did God do this? It was because He saw "the oppression . . . on Israel" (cf. Exod 3:9). God is acting as He did in the exodus, showing pity to the people in distress. But

despite this display of God's mercy, we find an ungrateful people persist-
ing in sin. We then read of the military's powerlessness.

Jehoash: lost opportunity (13:10-25). Jehoash's 16-year reign is briefly
summarized. His most crucial moment is the meeting with Elisha, in
which he received a golden opportunity to defeat Aram completely but
failed to do so.

Jeroboam II: prosperous but not pleasing to God (14:23-29). We find
another whisper of God's mercy in this brief description of another
Jeroboam, the longest-reigning Israelite king. His life was prosperous
but not pleasing to God. His reputation was mixed in that he "did what
was evil in the LORD's sight" (v. 24) yet "restored Israel's border" as
spoken by the prophet Jonah, who predicted a military recovery (v. 25;
Jonah 4:2). Is it possible to have a booming economy and a strong military but be wicked? Yes. Some say these days were similar to the power
of Solomon (Davis, *2 Kings*, 216n16). But Jeroboam's achievements are
barely listed. He wasn't faithful to God. Nothing else really matters.

Why did God show Israel such favor during this time? The writer
tells us: God's magnificent compassion.

> *For the LORD saw that the affliction of Israel was very bitter. There was
> no one to help Israel, neither bond nor free. However, the LORD had
> not said He would blot out the name of Israel under heaven, so He
> delivered them by the hand of Jeroboam son of Jehoash.* (vv. 26-27)

As with Jehoahaz, the God of the exodus was the God of the kings, being
rich in mercy to them. God is patient and merciful despite their hard-
heartedness. If a person fails to turn to God in repentance and faith, it
isn't because of a lack of compassion in God.

Five kings and four coups (15:8-31). After some peace and stability, and
after the long reign of Jeroboam II, Israel goes through five kings in some
30 years: Zachariah (six months, the end of Jehu's dynasty), Shallum
(one month), Menahem (10 years), Pekahiah (two years), and Pekah
(20 years). Four of them die as a result of conspiracy (vv. 10,14,25,30).
The nation is in great decline, and signals of the coming judgment are
present both internally and externally.

Grace to the Rebellious

Let us now consider how God showed grace to a rebellious people, as we
examine two kings in particular: Joash of Judah and Jehoash of Israel.

God Preserved the Davidic Pipeline in Judah (chs. 11–12)

God promised that the line of David would continue until the coming of
the Messiah (2 Sam 7:16). With the kingdom divided, that hope rested
on the line of kings in Judah. This "lamp in Jerusalem" (1 Kgs 15:4)
continues to burn throughout the Kings narrative. In chapters 11–16 we
read of the continuation of this line (see 2 Kgs 15:7,38; 16:20). Later,
Matthew records some names in his genealogy that should be familiar
to us by now (Matt 1:1-17, esp. vv. 7-11; curiously he omits Joash, his
father, and his son), highlighting the faithfulness and grace of God. But
around 840 BC this Davidic promise/covenant was hanging by a thread.
It was one infant away from extinction.

Joash protected (11:1-3). Consider the situation. The Chronicler tells
us that King Jehoram had all his brothers killed (2 Chr 21:1-4). Then
the Philistines and Arabians invaded Judah and carried off and killed all
Jehoram's sons except for Ahaziah/Jehoahaz (2 Chr 21:16-17). Ahaziah
gets caught up in Jehu's purge and is killed after a one-year reign, along
with 42 relatives (9:27-28). The Davidic line has been severely decimated
(Davis, *2 Kings*, 172–73). Now in chapter 11 we meet a new "Jezebel,"
Athaliah, the daughter of Ahab (2 Kgs 8:18,27), grandmother of Joash,
who "ruled" for six years (11:3). (We are reminded of Jehoshaphat's
tragic choice: making a marriage alliance with Ahab of Israel, giving his
son Jehoram of Judah to Ahab's daughter, Athaliah. See 2 Kgs 8:16-18;
2 Chr 18:1.) She is another evil, Baal-worshiping queen mother who
viciously sets out to eliminate what is left of David's descendants in
Judah. However, one of Ahaziah's sons remains: Joash. He is referred to
in the story as "the king's son" (11:4,12).

Athaliah's desire to eliminate the seed of David reminds us of the
Genesis 3:15 trend. The evil one continues to attack any hopes of the
coming seed of the woman who would crush his head. This trend begins
in Genesis 3 but continues throughout history, as evidenced in examples like Cain killing Abel, Pharaoh killing Hebrew children, Saul seeking to kill David, and Herod seeking to kill Jesus (Matt 2:13-18). We too
shouldn't be surprised that enemies of the kingdom of God oppose us
as we seek to bear witness to Christ (1 John 3:13). There will always be a
struggle of light versus darkness, righteousness versus wickedness, and
truth versus error—until the coming of Christ.

Jehosheba, Joash's aunt (sister to Ahaziah, daughter of Athaliah
and Jehoram, wife of Jehoiada the priest), acts heroically and saves the
child and his nurse. She's the true mother of Judah, who for the sake

of the kingdom protects the royal seed, reminding us of other important women in Scripture (Exod 2:1-10; Josh 2) (Leithart, *1 and 2 Kings*, 225). Apparently, Joash's mother, Zibiah (12:1), had been put to death already. Athaliah probably had her killed because she would have been a threat to her queen-mother status. Joash is hidden for six years in the temple, a safe place to hide the prince because Athaliah could not enter since she was a foreigner.

We have much to ponder here. Consider Jehosheba. You have heard about *How the Grinch Stole Christmas*; here is the story of "The Lady Who Saved Christmas." If it weren't for the action of this faithful servant, humanly speaking, there would be no Christmas, no Messiah. We need to recognize the importance of faithful servants in the kingdom of God.

What characterizes this lady? She's marked by a deep **commitment to Yahweh**. When forced to decide between her mother and Yahweh, she chooses Yahweh. She also **values human life**. Granted this was a special child, but can we not draw the application here to protect the lives of all children? What can you do to protect life and fight for the good of the oppressed? Most people will not recognize the name of Jehosheba. Have you ever heard of anyone naming their daughter after her? Probably not. Most people will not recognize our names either, but the Judge of all the earth takes notice of every seemingly small act of obedience. Her **obedience** was a quiet, hidden obedience. That's how the kingdom of God normally grows and advances, not by showy performances. Finally, I think we must hold up her impressive **courage** and boldness. Without her courage we would not rise from the dead. Let's follow the example set by Jehosheba, as we set out to defend the unborn, care for the oppressed, and take the gospel to the nations boldly.

Consider also the subversive presence of the king, Joash. Does this not remind you of our day? Athaliah is on the throne, but the real king is present. Davis notes, "The usurper rules, but the chosen king secretly reigns, unknown to Athaliah" (*2 Kings*, 174). God preserved the Davidic line by using these faithful servants until Joash's greatest descendant arrived. After His death, resurrection, and ascension, He sat down at the Father's right hand, where He rules and reigns (Eph 1:20-22), despite the fact the earthly leaders are unaware of His reign. The presence of our King should give us peace and hope in this troubled life.

In these three verses we have gospel and example. We have a godly example of a faithful servant and the reminder of the grace of God. Jehosheba gives us an example; God preserved the Davidic line by His grace. We aren't left to our own power and strength to live just and merciful lives like Jehosheba's. The King is with us, over us, and for us, and the Spirit of God is in us, empowering us to advance the kingdom of God in the face of the enemy's opposition.

Joash proclaimed (11:4-16). When the prince turns seven, the priest Jehoiada orchestrates a meeting in the temple complex. Jehoiada serves as another example of risk-taking boldness, crowning Joash as king. Later we read about his tremendous influence on Joash (see 12:2). Verses 5-10 record in detail his plan leading to the coronation. He designates the time for action at the end of the Sabbath, when the changing of the guard would involve double the number of soldiers (Olley, *Message of Kings*, 270). The guards take their weaponry and their stations and prepare for the coronation. In verse 12 we read that they "brought out the king's son, put the crown on him, gave him the testimony, and made him king. They anointed him and clapped their hands and cried, 'Long live the king!'" The *testimony* refers to God's covenant law (25:21-22; 26:23; Exod 38:21). Joash received a copy of the testimony, reflecting Deuteronomy 17:18-20. The king was to rule and live by the law of God.

When Athaliah hears all the commotion, she rushes into the temple. The king is standing by the pillar at the temple entrance (v. 14; cf. 23:3). She cries out, "Treason!" but she has no authority. Jehoiada has her taken out of the temple to be executed.

This drama has numerous messianic images. The final Davidic king was also at the temple at an earlier age, being about His Father's business. John says in Revelation 5 that the King, the "Root of David" (v. 4), is "standing" (v. 6; 2 Kgs 11:14), surrounded by heaven's host, and being praised for His salvation.

> Then I saw One like a slaughtered lamb standing between the throne
> and the four living creatures and among the elders. . . . I heard
> every creature in heaven, on earth, under the earth, on the sea, and
> everything in them say: Blessing and honor and glory and dominion
> to the One seated on the throne, and to the Lamb, forever and ever!
> (Rev 5:6,13)

Joash is just a flicker of the glorious light that was to come in Christ, a better King, who would be slain for the salvation of the nations. Jesus is truly worthy of endless praise.

Joash's people (11:17-20). In a covenant-renewal ceremony the people pledge themselves to the commitments of Exodus 19:1-8 and 24:1-8

(House, *1, 2 Kings*, 299; Davis, *2 Kings*, 178). But there was more. This covenant renewal involved destroying the house of Baal and the priest of Baal, Mattan. This temple of Baal (in contrast to the "LORD's temple") was probably the work of Athaliah, who built a place in Judah for the storm god like Jezebel did in Israel. Joash finally "sat on the throne of the kings" (v. 19), and there was rejoicing and peace in the land.

Consider these powerful pictures. First, following the living God involves **smashing idols and following God's Word**. Jesus told His disciples that each must renounce "all his possessions" in order to be His disciple (Luke 14:33). If anything is keeping you from wholeheartedly submitting to the lordship of Christ, then you must throw it away.

Look also at this picture of the people **covenanting together**. Together they're committing to be a people of God's own possession, dedicated to living for His glory. Is this not a great reminder to us about the importance of biblical community? Christianity isn't a lone-ranger religion. It involves covenant relationships. Many today want benefits of a local church (use of facilities, occasionally receiving some teaching, etc.) without committing to a covenant people. It's like dating versus marriage. Following Christ involves belonging to a people, covenanted together, who care for one another and live on mission together.

We should also observe the picture of **the seated king and the quietness of the city**. When I was a kid, my father would come home from work and sit on his recliner. If my friends and I were getting too loud (normally playing Nerf basketball!), then my father would say loudly, "Tony Clifford." That's all it took. Just his voice (and my middle name) caused the house to get quiet. My dad has transferred that seat to me now. When I am studying in my recliner, I often have to speak to my kids with a loud voice to produce silence. Normally, I just say, "Quiet!" and it works. The author of Hebrews reminds us that we now have a king, the Son of David, seated on the throne, who controls the universe "by His powerful word" (Heb 1:3). What comfort to know this.

Just last week I had my Bible open to this verse when we were video chatting with our missionary friends in East Asia. Since they were going through a difficult time, I thanked God that we have the King on the throne and because of that we can rest in His strength and assurance as we face the challenges of this life.

Joash's problems (12:1–21). In the opening verses we read that Joash reigned for 40 years. He receives a qualified commendation for doing "what was right in the LORD's sight" but failing to remove "the high places." This is his first problem: **high places**. There are other mixed aspects of the reign of Joash. The writer speaks of the slow pace of his unspectacular temple renovations. At the close of the chapter, we read of his submission to the Arameans, which involved giving away the treasures from the temple. He has good intentions and a good start, but his reign is mingled with failure, poor decisions, and eventual wickedness. Verse 2 mentions the influence of Jehoiada, who instructed him. Unfortunately, Joash wasn't as faithful as his mentor. Once his mentor died, things fell apart (2 Chr 24:15-27).

Joash's second problem had to do with **repairing the temple**. We haven't read of the temple since 1 Kings 15:18. After the reign of Athaliah, it surely needed some repair. A collection of money was taken up for the renovations from the census (cf. Exod 30:11-15), in fulfillment of vows (cf. Lev 27:13), or brought voluntarily. His appeal echoes the building of the tabernacle in Exodus:

> Everyone whose heart was moved and whose spirit prompted him
> came and brought an offering to the LORD for the work on the tent of
> meeting, for all its services, and for the holy garments. (Exod 35:21)

Those with a generous and willing heart brought their goods as an offering (35:5,22,26,29). There is also an echo from Exodus in that the skilled workers performed their work unto the Lord (Exod 36; 2 Kgs 12:11-12).

However, the pace of the rebuilding is puzzling. They moved at the pace of a snail. In the twenty-third year (he would have been 30), the priests had done no repairs. It reminds me of a quip from my father-in-law. He used to work at the Pentagon. I once asked him, "How many people work there?" He said, "About half!" There were lots of priests, but they made no progress in the temple. Eventually the king took the job out of their hands. (That would have been an interesting meeting!)

Why the delay? Davis says they were probably not being dishonest, for if they were, the high priests wouldn't have been given the new role to collect. He says they were "more slow than slick" (Davis, *2 Kings*, 186–87). Another option is that Jehoiada didn't deem Joash old enough for such an initiative. Handing over leadership to a younger person is extremely difficult for some and so is submitting to younger leadership (Olley, *Message of Kings*, 276). Joash wouldn't be the last one to face this conflict if this were the case. Paul told Timothy, "Let no one despise your youth; instead, you should be an example" (1 Tim 4:12).

Perhaps it was solely a financial issue. Their budget was obviously tight, as suggested by the failure to use any money for temple items, and budgetary decisions are hard for people to justify, especially if it means it will hurt them personally.

The whole matter also speaks to the human limitations of leaders. One may lead a movement to crown the new king but not be any good at administering the vision to repair the temple, like Jehoiada. One may also be able to initiate a fund-raising campaign but be out of touch with the whole project, like Joash (Olley, *Message of Kings*, 276–77)! The whole body of Christ, with all of its various gifts, is needed to do the work of God.

Joash's idea was to have a chest dedicated for receiving the needed funds. This allowed monies to be divided for the priests and for the building project (Davis, *2 Kings*, 187). Money was collected publically and counted and distributed by the secretary and the high priest, with supervisors being trusted to handle things honestly. The priests retained their customary income.

A third and final problem is found in verses 17-21. After telling us of the drama of the temple repair, we read of **depleting the temple** out of fear of the Arameans. For whatever reason Joash gives away sacred objects and gold in submission to Hazael. Others unfortunately gave away temple treasures for political and military security. See: Rehoboam (1 Kgs 14:25-26), Asa (1 Kgs 15:18-19), Joash, Ahaz (2 Kgs 16:8-9), and Hezekiah (2 Kgs 18:13-16). All of these are previews of what the Babylonians will do (Davis, *2 Kings*, 188).

The Chronicler gives more information about the king's reign, including how things changed dramatically after the death of Jehoiada (2 Chr 24). Judah abandoned the house of the Lord and took up fertility worship and idolatry (2 Chr 24:18; cf. 24:2), and wrath came on them. Then Joash executed Jehoiada's son, Zechariah, who by the Spirit of God spoke out against their idolatry (2 Chr 24:20-22). While the writer of Kings reports his assassination (12:20-21), he simply leaves an impression of disappointment. The Chronicler tells more of the wickedness of Joash (Davis, *2 Kings*, 188–89).

What a sorry picture of a young man who had received wonderful instruction from a godly teacher, only to turn his back on God later. He reminds us of Judas, who received superior instruction but turned his back on Christ; and Demas, who learned from Paul but deserted him for the things of the world (2 Tim 4:9). Having the best Christian education doesn't immunize you against apostasy and unfaithfulness. In his excellent book, *A Dangerous Calling*, Paul Tripp says,

> So seminary students, who are Bible and theology experts, tend to think of themselves as being mature. But it must be said that maturity isn't something you merely do with your mind. . . . No, maturity is about how you live your life. (25)

Tripp goes on, saying Adam and Eve "didn't disobey because they were intellectually ignorant of God's commands. . . . The battle was fought at a deeper level" (*Dangerous Calling*, 26). How do you avoid this? You must cultivate a deep relationship with Jesus and cultivate an insatiable desire for the Word of God personally.

Despite the tragic collapse we still read of God's grace in that "his son Amaziah became king in his place" (12:21). Is there hope for the rebellious? Yes, there is hope because God preserved the Davidic pipeline until the King came to save us. It was not due to the goodness of the kings but the goodness of God.

God's Power, Compassion, and Truth Provided Hope to Israel (13:14-25)

God displayed His grace to sinners in preserving the Davidic line in Judah, but what about Israel? Was there any hope for this people who were headed into captivity? Through this fascinating interaction between Elisha and Jehoash of Israel, we find the answer is yes.

We last read of Elisha in 2 Kings 9, as he appointed a son of the prophets to anoint Jehu. Now Elisha is about to die, and the king of Israel goes to visit him, crying out and complimenting the prophet, "My father, my father, the chariots and horsemen of Israel!" (v. 14). The first phrase honors him ("My father"), and the second phrase acknowledges that the king needs the prophet's help, for Elisha's prayers and works were more powerful than horses and chariots. Elisha echoed these same words about Elijah previously (2 Kgs 2:12). Now Elisha is dying. Who will replace him? To whom will they look for divine help?

In an effort to encourage the king, Elisha gives him an object lesson (or an "acted oracle"). He has him take a bow and arrows, he places his hands on the king's hands, and they both shoot the arrow out the east window. The picture is that God is with the king. Elisha then explains this act. The arrow signified how Israel would defeat Aram (Syria).

Though he is sick, the prophet still speaks with authority. What a wonderful picture of God using a weak vessel to communicate His word.

Elisha tells the king to strike the ground with the arrows. I think this means shooting the arrows out the window into the ground. If the arrows represent victories, then what should Jehoash do? He should empty his quiver! He should shoot every arrow he has. Elisha was saying, "Trust me. Shoot all your arrows, and you will have total victory over Aram." However, the writer says the king struck three times and "stopped" (v. 18). The writer didn't have to say he "stopped." This is a note of sadness. The writer could have said the king shot three times, and we would have known he didn't shoot four or five times. But he says he "stopped." Elisha grows angry, telling the king he should have shot five or six times. As a result, Elisha tells him, Israel will only defeat Aram three times.

What is Jehoash's problem? Did he think this whole thing was childish? Did he not want to annihilate the Arameans? Did he want a buffer country between him and mighty Assyria? Maybe some of that was true. I agree with those who say the real issue, though, was a lack of zeal and enthusiasm: "He lacks zeal to be an enemy to the enemies of Israel" (Leithart, *1 and 2 Kings*, 233); "He didn't obey it [the word] enthusiastically enough" (Provan, *1 and 2 Kings*, 228); "The anger of the prophet is instigated by the king's limited faith and resolve" (Konkel, *1 and 2 Kings*, 527); "His response is half-hearted" (Olley, *Message of Kings*, 282). Jehoash is like Ahab, who previously failed to eliminate Aram at Aphek (1 Kgs 20:28). Jehoash was content with only three victories. Davis says God gave him a blank check, but he only cashed half of it (*2 Kings*, 195). The king missed his golden opportunity.

Surely we wouldn't be tempted to conduct such halfhearted religion, would we? Managing sin instead of putting it to death? Having a halfhearted prayer life? Giving sporadically, if at all, to the mission? Witnessing inconsistently? Not taking our studies seriously? Are you a three-strikes Christian? Let me encourage you to fire every arrow you have! May God forgive us for halfheartedness and give us a fresh passion today to trust His Word and act on it.

Hope in God's power over the grave (vv. 20-21). Despite the king's failure to fully embrace Elisha's word, God gave the people hope through the death of Elisha. Unlike Elijah, Elisha dies a typical death, but he performs a miracle after he dies. A group of men are burying a corpse when Moabite raiders interrupt them, forcing them to throw the body into

Elisha's grave. As soon as the dead man touches the bones of Elisha, he is revived to life. This is amazing! This incident apparently occurred a few years after Elisha's death, since the writer speaks of "Elisha's bones." I don't know of any other story like this in the Bible.

What is the point of this miracle? It certainly isn't intended to lead us to embrace a theology of relics. The church has had a history of that practice, rooted in part in this passage. If you look at a vial of Mary's milk or touch the bones of Peter, would there be healing power in these relics? If we build our church building over the site of a martyr, would that place have more power than another place? The answer of course is no. This miracle in 2 Kings is a "messianic miracle." This story displays the resurrection power of God. For those who trust in the God of Elisha, death isn't final. God is giving everyone a foretaste of the One greater than Elisha who is to come (Matt 27:52).

But there's more. This is an event that's probably also intended to give Israel hope for their future. They're about to head into exile, a death, as portended in chapters 11–16. If they stay attached to the life-giving word of the prophets, then there's hope of resurrection (Ezek 37:1-14). Elisha is dead, but God isn't, and God will continue to send prophets to speak to them, just as Elisha and Elijah have done. A body was thrown into a grave, and Israel was about to be thrown into exile (notice the same verbs in verses 21 and 23, "threw"/"banished"), but hope isn't lost. God will be faithful to His covenant, and God is the God who raises the dead. As exiled people read this story, they would have received great hope. The life-giving power of God hasn't departed. So, despite all of the sadly declining history of chapters 11–16, there's hope in the resurrection power of God and in His life-giving word.

Hope in God's compassion (vv. 22-23). There's also hope in the compassion of God. Hazael oppressed Israel, "But the LORD was gracious to them, had compassion on them." The God of Exodus 34 and Psalm 145 wouldn't utterly destroy them. The phrase "even now" is difficult. Some take it to mean He hadn't destroyed them up to that point, but now He has. But it's probably best to take it to mean "up to this point" (Davis, *2 Kings*, 202). God "still didn't cast them out of his presence" (ibid., 203). Why? We're told that this compassion was due to His covenant with Abraham, Isaac, and Jacob. This is the only mention of the patriarchs in Judges–Kings apart from 1 Kings 18:36. Provan says, "God was unwilling to destroy Israel because of Abraham, and Judah because of David. The two kingdoms are ultimately being treated the same way" (Provan, *1 and 2 Kings*, 230). God promised to bless Abraham, but the northern kingdom turned their back on God from the beginning (1 Kgs 12). Yet because of the covenant, they weren't destroyed. Hope wasn't lost.

However, this compassion shouldn't have resulted in further rebellion; it should have led them into repentance and praise. God was willing to forgive them and show compassion to them, if they would but call to Him.

Here's hope for rebels! Do you think you have sinned too badly? Do you think God cannot save you? Richard Sibbes said it well: "There is more mercy in Christ, than sin in us" (*The Bruised Reed*, 13). You're just the candidate for grace—you realize God only saves bad people. Self-righteous people don't think they need God's forgiveness.

This grace also makes me think of Jesus' teaching on forgiving others. How many times should we be willing to forgive our brothers? Seventy times seven, He tells Peter (Matt 18:21-22). In light of the patient grace of God toward rebels, let's show mercy and forgiveness to others without keeping count.

Hope in God's trustworthy word (vv. 24-25). The final note of hope comes from the fact that Elisha's word came true: three victories. How many times have we observed the fulfillment of God's word in Kings? Even though Israel is slip slidin' away, God speaks truth to them.

Kimberly and I have been watching the television series *Prison Break*. As in many television series, one of the recurring themes is that you cannot trust anyone. The characters continue to get played by different people, and sometimes they play others. But it isn't so with God's Word. It's a rock. How wonderful is it to know that God keeps His promises! Have you ever been disappointed with those who never keep their word? We don't have a God like that. We have an immutable God, that is, a God whose character never changes. He can be trusted. His Word is trustworthy, His compassions are higher than the heavens, and His power is unlimited.

The Son of David

Is there hope for the rebellious? Yes! God delays His judgment because He's offering rebels an opportunity to repent and trust in the ultimate Son of David. Will you look to the risen Christ for salvation? He is mighty and merciful to save. Micah's book concludes with an amazing vision of God's compassion on sinners:

Who is a God like You,
removing iniquity and passing over rebellion
for the remnant of His inheritance?
He does not hold on to His anger forever,
because He delights in faithful love.
He will again have compassion on us;
He will vanquish our iniquities.
You will cast all our sins into the depths of the sea.
You will show loyalty to Jacob
and faithful love to Abraham,
as You swore to our fathers
from days long ago. (Mic 7:18-20)

This God "delights" in faithful love. Will you look to Him for pardon? Will you come to Him and have your sins cast into the depths of the sea? If so, then look to Jesus, who traded places with sinners on the cross, whose blood covers the worst of sinners, who provided the ultimate display of love and mercy.

If you're a believer, will you look to Christ for strength and hope today? Paul told Timothy, in a passage on endurance, "Keep your attention on Jesus Christ as risen from the dead and descended from David" (2 Tim 2:8). Don't take your eyes off Jesus. He is the better Elisha, the risen One, who empowers us for obedience. He is the offspring of David, the One who occupies the throne. Because the tomb is empty and the throne is occupied, we can rejoice and persevere as we seek to shine as lights in a dark world.

Reflect and Discuss

1. Discuss how God's patience and anger work together in these passages.
2. God is always quick to respond to the repentance of His people. What does this teach about His character?
3. The people of Israel welcome the Lord's unnamed deliverer when they are in trouble but immediately go back to their idolatrous ways. How might Jesus' parable of the sower help explain this passage (Matt 13:1-15; Mark 4:1-12; Luke 8:4-10)?
4. Why is Elisha angry that Jehoash didn't shoot more arrows out of the window?

5. What are some ways Christians today give halfhearted efforts of repentance and obedience? Compare and contrast those to New Testament stories of Christ's obedience.

6. Describe Jehoash's response to Amaziah. Why did God allow Jehoash to defeat Judah?

7. How might God's people today be arrogant and unwilling to cooperate among themselves? Does God feel as strongly about those issues today as He did when Joash's people exhibited those characteristics?

8. Why might God's people have chosen not to completely remove the "high places"?

9. In what areas of life today might God's people be unwilling to remove sin completely?

10. In what ways do the kings of Israel and Judah fail to fulfill their divinely appointed duty as king? How does Jesus succeed in those areas?

Ruin and Restoration

2 KINGS 17:1–20:21

Main Idea: While Israel experiences the ruin of exile, Judah experiences a restoration under the leadership of Hezekiah.

I. **Ruin in Israel (17:1-41)**
   A. Do not rely on conspiracy.
   B. Worship God alone.
II. **Restoration in Judah (18:1–20:21)**
   A. Returning to true worship (18:4)
   B. Relying on God alone (18:5–20:21)
III. **Challenge 1: Crisis (18:13–19:37)**
   A. Express trust in God by requesting prayer (19:1-7).
   B. Express trust in God by praying (19:14-19).
IV. **Challenge 2: Illness (20:1-11)**
V. **Challenge 3: Pride (20:12-19)**
VI. **Remember That Ultimate Restoration Is Coming (20:20-21).**

This past week has been so refreshing. In the middle of August, the morning temperatures have been in the 60s. Football season is right around the corner, and fans are getting excited. But Penn State fans have been preparing under a dark cloud because of the horrific news about their former coach, Jerry Sandusky. This longtime coach was convicted on 45 counts of sexual abuse. Sickening. Despicable. Infuriating. I recently read where his son was changing his name because of the association with his dad. Now let me ask you: What if this coach's son grew up to be the greatest president in United States history? Would that shock you? What if he became the most influential Christian leader in the world, leading the nation in revival? Unlikely?

I definitely pray for this family and believe God can restore them and use them for His glory, just as He can use anyone who experiences His redeeming grace. The good news of the gospel is that if you had a terrible experience with your father, you don't have to end up becoming like him.

If you find this hard to believe, then consider Hezekiah. God raised up this Judean king while a dark cloud was hanging over the nation.

He led them into a time of restoration. He was the greatest king since David, yet his dad had been perhaps the most evil king in Judah's history. Here was an example of his evil father: "He even made his son pass through the fire, imitating the detestable practices of the nations" (16:3). But God, by His grace, brought restoration in a season of ruin through the leadership of this son, Hezekiah.

In these chapters we should be reminded of the grace of God, who brings refreshing fall-like seasons in our life; and like Hezekiah we should be encouraged to seek the Lord.

Ruin in Israel

2 KINGS 17:1-41

Israel's "rain delay" is over. In 2 Kings 17 the writer describes the Assyrian storm and Israel's fall into exile. Back in 1 Kings 14:15 Ahijah told Jeroboam that the Lord would "uproot" Israel and "scatter them beyond the Euphrates." But God proved to be gracious and compassionate, slow to anger and rich in faithful love, delaying judgment (2 Kgs 10:30; 13; 14:23-29). God continued to display His grace by saving Israel from various enemies through Elisha (2 Kgs 6–7), unnamed deliverers (13:5), and Jeroboam (14:27). But the previous chapters have also pointed ahead to the coming exile. The writer made us aware of the external and internal instability of the northern kingdom in chapter 15.

Do Not Rely on Conspiracy

In 2 Kings 17:1-5 we're introduced to the nine-year reigning king, Hoshea. His name sounds promising ("salvation"); unfortunately, he doesn't live up to that name. His biography in verses 1-5 sounds much like the other kings, with a few surprising exceptions. While he "did what was evil in the LORD's sight," the author adds, "but not like the kings of Israel who preceded him" (v. 2). We're left to guess about what made him stand out. However, his political power plays between Assyria and Egypt anger "Shalmaneser king of Assyria." Six times in these verses, we read of the "king of Assyria" (Davis, 2 Kings, 243). This king dominates the narrative. The angry Assyrian king first puts Hoshea in prison. Eventually, Shalmaneser captures Samaria and scatters the northern kingdom across a wide area (v. 6; 18:11). The 10 tribes of Israel are no more.

Worship God Alone

In verses 7-17 the writer provides a bit of sermon to explain why Israel went off into exile. One could give a number of reasons from a human perspective for their fall, but the writer is more concerned with the underlying problem. That problem is made clear by repetition. The verb translated as "fear" reverberates throughout this chapter—with either Yahweh or "other gods" as the object—no fewer than eight times (Yahweh in vv. 25,28,36,39; other gods in vv. 7 ["worshiped"], 35,37,38). It can also be translated "worship" or "revere." The people looked to other gods for provision, joy, satisfaction, and salvation.

We need to realize that idolatry isn't confined to shrines and pagan temples; it resides in the hearts of people who look to other things to give them what only God can give. These can be things like money, sexual pleasure, power, or success. All sin problems are essentially worship problems. The wrong god equals the wrong lifestyle.

The author warns us about the danger of rejecting the real God. We might arrange our application in four parts.

Don't reject the God who redeems (v. 7). Throughout these verses, the writer calls our attention to the exodus and the giving of the Ten Commandments. God redeemed His people "out of the land of Egypt from the power of Pharaoh," yet Israel chose to worship (fear) other gods. Instead of having lasting gratitude for Yahweh, Israel looked to other gods.

Guard your heart against ingratitude. The drift into idolatry and immorality begins there. What's often missing in corporate worship services isn't better music but a lack of "singing psalms, hymns, and spiritual songs *with gratitude in your hearts to God*" (Col 3:16; emphasis added). Marvel at the grace of God not only in corporate worship but also in daily worship. Believers must seek to cultivate the discipline to "give thanks in everything" (1 Thess 5:18).

The God of grace has delivered us out of bondage to sin and from judgment, through Jesus Christ, who has led the ultimate exodus. Thank Him for His grace! Remember this about idols: they can never give you grace; they only enslave you. When you reject the God of the Bible, you are rejecting grace. Therefore, consider what God has done for us and how foolish your other options are.

Don't reject the God who satisfies (vv. 8-12,16-17). The writer goes on to tell us of the inevitable results of idolatry. The people lived immoral lives, and they worshiped multiple false gods. Why? The psalmist explains,

"The sorrows of those who take another god for themselves will multiply" (Ps 16:4). Idols only lead to sorrow; they never bring satisfaction. Asherot, Baal, the golden calves, or Molech cannot give what the human heart longs for, namely, the God who redeems and satisfies.

If money is your idol, then you will never have enough. If you don't have any, it will crush you to the point of suicidal thoughts. If being popular is your idol, then being unpopular will crush you. If success is your idol, then you will live on a treadmill of pursuing one accomplishment after another. If sexual pleasure is your source of greatest pleasure, then no person (or image of a person) will ever thrill you enough. If a particular drug is your source of hope and strength, then you will only be enslaved, never liberated. These gods will not satisfy you. They say to you, "Serve me." But you need to preach a better sermon back to them: "In [God's] presence is abundant joy; in [His] right hand are eternal pleasures" (Ps 16:11). Deeper joy and more lasting joy are found in the presence of God.

Don't reject the God who warns (vv. 13-15). Israel knew better. After the exodus God gave Israel His law and told them how to live. He also sent prophets. But "they would not listen" (v. 14, cf. 35-40). Why? They had a heart problem. They were "obstinate like their ancestors who did not believe the Lord their God." They were like stubborn farm animals. Their stubbornness, like ours, stemmed from unbelief. Such was the history of Israel. They exasperated God with their unbelief. The psalmist recaps the history in Psalm 78 and says in verse 32, "Despite all this, they kept sinning and did not believe His wonderful works." Israel's fall into exile reminds us of the problem of "hardening our hearts" to God's word (see Ps 95:7-11).

As a result of despising God's word and resisting His warnings, "they pursued worthless idols and became worthless themselves" (v. 15). Here's another truth about idolatry: we become like whatever we worship. The psalmist says, "Those who make [idols] are just like them" (Ps 115:8). In contrast, those who behold the glory of God are "being transformed into the same image from glory to glory" (2 Cor 3:18). If you don't heed the warnings of God, then you will become like your idols: "false" (ESV) or "worthless" (HCSB). Worship really does change you! Transformation happens from the inside out.

Several years ago a four-year-old girl in North Wales had her complexion turn a yellow-orange color. The doctor discovered the reason. She had been consuming one-and-a-half liters of Sunny Delight every day. The product was largely food coloring and sugar. The manufacturers admitted that their product could turn a person orange, but only if consumed in large amounts (Davis, *2 Kings*, 250). And that's what happened. She became what she drank (temporarily). Likewise, if you're constantly drinking in a love of praise, a love of money, a love of sexual pleasure, or a love of success, it will change you spiritually. Don't reject the warnings of Scripture. Turn "from idols to serve the living and true God . . . Jesus, who rescues us from the coming wrath" (1 Thess 1:9-10).

Don't reject the God who judges (vv. 18-23). Israel's rejection of His grace and His word provoked God to anger. He removed them from His presence: "Israel has been exiled to Assyria from their homeland until today" (v. 23). In the middle of these words of judgment on Israel, the writer comments on Judah, how they also "did not keep the commands of the Lord their God but lived according to the customs Israel had introduced" (v. 19). This surely points to the coming fate of Judah. Why did God judge Israel? They had followed the ways of Jeroboam, whom they made king when the kingdom split. They persisted in sin.

Recently, despite the example of all those who had been caught and punished, several more baseball players were found to be cheating by using illegal performance-enhancing drugs. They were banished from baseball for a time. In their pride they had ignored the warnings. Most players and fans want these guys to face consequences; they want justice. God gave Israel warning after warning, but they rejected Him. Now they were banished into foreign lands. And today, don't think you are the exception to God's judgment. When God offers you grace, embrace it.

The writer continues to speak of the northern kingdom in verses 24-41. The focus in this section is still on worship. While Israel is exiled, other peoples fill the land. Assyria's king brings others from near and far to dwell there. Whom do they worship while residing in Israel's land? We read that at first they didn't worship the Lord, but "the Lord sent lions among them, which killed some of them" (v. 25). God demands exclusive worship from the nations. He isn't a tribal deity. He doesn't always send lions, but He always demands worship. The king of Assyria then actually responds better than Israel to this warning. He sends an exiled priest back to the land to instruct the people in Samaria on how to worship Yahweh.

What happened next? We read that the nations worshiped Yahweh alongside other gods. But we shouldn't read this as if God accepted such syncretism, as verses 34-39 make clear. This displeased Him, like

Israel's syncretism had displeased Him. Apparently the priest taught the corrupt worship that Israel had been practicing. Mixed worship isn't acceptable worship. Provan summarizes, "What is clear by the end of the chapter, then, is that the exile of Israel has not led to any improvement in the religion of the people who dwell in the land. . . . Nothing has changed" (*1 and 2 Kings*, 251).

The whole chapter calls us to examine our hearts. Who or what are you worshiping? Is it Yahweh plus some other god? Syncretism doesn't glorify God, and it will lead you into an unfaithful life. Enjoy creation, steward creation, and be thankful for creation, but don't worship created things. Worship the Creator and Redeemer alone. John concludes his first letter by simply and most significantly saying, "Little children, guard yourselves from idols" (1 John 5:21).

Restoration in Judah
2 KINGS 18:1–20:21

The previous chapters of 2 Kings (chs. 16–17) gave us a terrible picture not only of Israel but also of Judah. Will they head off into exile also? Not yet. What we read about in chapters 18–20 is a time of relief for the people of Judah, as a new king takes the throne during the third year of Hoshea in Israel: Hezekiah. He doesn't take after his father, Ahaz, but after his father David. His 29-year reign is briefly summarized in 18:1-8, where we see that he "did what was right in the LORD's sight just as his ancestor David had done." He isn't merely similar to David, like Asa or Jehoshaphat, but is more like a "second David." He faces his "Goliath" in Assyria's king, Sennacherib, who like Goliath boasts in himself and taunts Yahweh. He leads the people into a period of restoration. How so? He leads the people back to true worship, and he demonstrates trust in God.

Returning to True Worship (18:4)

One act that sets Hezekiah apart from previous kings is his removal of "the high places." We have grown weary of the line, "Yet the high places were not taken away" (1 Kgs 15:14; 22:43; 2 Kgs 12:3; 14:4; 15:4,35). Hezekiah, though, cut down "pillars" (symbols of male deity) and "the Asherah poles" (symbols of female deity); he also "broke into pieces the bronze snake that Moses made." This refers to the story of the serpent in the wilderness (Num 21:4-9), which was never intended for worship (Provan, *1 and 2 Kings*, 252).

Are there some idols that need to be removed from your own temple? This past week a strange thing happened. My son, James, was sleeping on the third floor, only to awaken to a bat flying around the room. He also heard something flying around in the adjacent room (the attic). He opened the door, turned on the light, and counted 12 bats! We called the "Batman" the next day, who counted 22 of these critters in our attic. He eventually removed them and solved our problem. You don't welcome bats into your house. You should not welcome idols either. However, many are more troubled by their bats than their Baals. Remove them, just as Hezekiah removed the idols from the temple. Deal with idols ruthlessly and relentlessly.

Hezekiah not only removed the idols but also led the people to cleanse the temple and celebrate the Passover. The Chronicler focuses on these events (2 Chr 29–31), while the writer of Kings focuses more on the Assyrian crisis. The two aren't opposed to each other. Hezekiah's return to true worship is linked to his stand against the enemy (v. 7). And so it is with us. Everything flows out of worship. As we focus on the Word of God, gather with the people of God, and remember the Substitute, then we begin to truly live on mission.

Relying on God Alone (18:5–20:21)

The main virtue highlighted in Hezekiah's life is his *trust*. Solomon is known for his wisdom; Josiah will be known for his reforms; Hezekiah is known for his unparalleled trust. "Hezekiah trusted in the LORD God of Israel; not one of the kings of Judah was like him, either before him or after him" (v. 5). The fruit of his trust was that he "remained faithful to Yahweh" and that he "kept the commands" (v. 6). The writer adds that the Lord was also "with him" and "wherever he went he prospered" (v. 7). So he was like David in that way: God was with him (only said of David and Hezekiah; Provan, *1 and 2 Kings*, 253).

Hezekiah also had military success. Unlike Ahaz, his father, he didn't yield to Assyria but instead "rebelled against the king of Assyria and did not serve him" (v. 7). Like David he defeated the Philistines. They were the only two kings who defeated the Philistines (Provan, *1 and 2 Kings*, 253).

In verses 9-12 the writer reminds the reader of what was going on in the northern kingdom. This context puts the bold faith of Hezekiah in perspective. In his sixth year Assyria took Samaria. What will happen to Judah? They will be threatened too. Will they trust in God?

Hezekiah's trust is challenged in various ways in the following chapters. His challenges are like our challenges. As we identify with them, let's also consider the appropriate response to them: *prayer*. Hezekiah's prayer life is worthy of emulation.

Challenge 1: Crisis
2 KINGS 18:13–19:37

The opening chapters don't begin the way we would anticipate. The new king of Assyria, Sennacherib, comes against Judah, and Hezekiah caves in. He gives Sennacherib silver, gold, and treasures from the temple and from the king's house. You might wonder, "I thought he rebelled against Assyria?" He did. But we must remember that verses 1-8 summarize his whole life. This opening story shows us a particular lapse, but that doesn't mean his whole life is measured by this one mistake. We're reminded that even the most faithful can have periods in which they cave in to pressure.

We expect to read no more of Sennacherib, but he decides the gold isn't enough. He sends his army to Jerusalem trying to persuade Hezekiah to surrender. This introduces a competing voice. Rabshakeh, Sennacherib's official spokesman, says, "Tell Hezekiah this is what the great king, the king of Assyria, says: 'What are you relying on?'" (v. 19). What does he focus on? Trust. It's mentioned in verses 19,20,21,22,24,30, and 19:30.

In his speech Rabshakeh tries to sow *seeds of doubt* in Hezekiah's heart. Like the evil one he mixes truth with error. He first questions Hezekiah's trust in Egypt. While Egypt apparently served as an ally, Isaiah said it was folly to trust in Egypt (Isa 30:1-7; 31:1-3). Sennacherib thinks it's folly to trust in Egypt because they cannot provide support. He was right about the folly of trusting Egypt, but for the wrong reason.

Rabshakeh then arrogantly asks if Hezekiah's focus of trust is "the LORD our God" (v. 22). He views Hezekiah's reforms negatively. Then he claims, "The LORD said to me, 'Attack this land and destroy it'" (v. 25). He was right in that the Lord had just used them to bring judgment on the people (17:1-23; 18:9-12). And we know that Isaiah prophesied about the Assyrians being the "rod of God's judgment against Israel and Judah" (Isa 10:5-19). But that was only part of the story (Olley, *Message of Kings*, 323).

So an ultimatum is offered in verses 26-37. The basic thrust of the ensuing dialogue is that the people shouldn't trust in Hezekiah but should choose life and not death by surrendering to Assyria. The dialogue begins with the officials requesting that Rabshakeh speak in Aramaic, the language of international diplomacy, so that the people on the wall cannot understand them. But he thinks the people should be allowed to hear his offer; otherwise they will be left to the horrific realities of a siege (eating excrement and drinking urine). He proceeds to tell the people that Hezekiah "can't deliver" them out of their hand and that they shouldn't listen to Hezekiah's words about "trusting" in the Lord. He tells the Judeans that if they will yield to Sennacherib, then they can live, and they will live in a land similar to their current land. He then insists that no god can match up against Assyria; in other words, Yahweh is no match for Sennacherib because He is as powerless as other gods. In obedience to Hezekiah's command, the people don't respond. Then the king's ambassadors report the situation to Hezekiah. How will Hezekiah respond to this rival voice? Will he cave in again?

Express Trust in God by Requesting Prayer (19:1-7)

This time Hezekiah responds appropriately. He first seeks help from Yahweh through Isaiah. He humbly puts on sackcloth and goes into the temple. His sackcloth actually represented a heart of desperation, unlike some previous examples. Then he seeks help from Isaiah. Remember, the first time he emptied the temple of wealth; now he goes into the temple for the right reason: to seek God's help. He sends his messengers to Isaiah, confessing the humiliation and powerlessness of the nation, but he holds out hope that Yahweh has heard Rabshakeh's mockery and will punish him. He tells Isaiah to "offer a prayer for the surviving remnant" (v. 5). Isaiah responds by saying,

> Don't be afraid because of the words you have heard, that the king of Assyria's attendants have blasphemed Me with. I am about to put a spirit in him, and he will hear a rumor and return to his own land where I will cause him to fall by the sword. (v. 6-7)

It's a short, powerful promise. Will it come true? Spoiler alert: yes. Check out the end of the story in 20:36-37. But let's pause and just point out how Hezekiah is asking for the prayers of the prophet. Are you seeking the prayers of God's people in your crisis?

In response Sennacherib counsels Hezekiah against trusting in God. After all, those who have tried this sort of thing before have all been destroyed. So basically nothing has changed. Jerusalem is still in a desperate position. Sennacherib is still mocking God. Isaiah's prophecy has accomplished nothing so far.

Express Trust in God by Praying (19:14-19)

Hezekiah's first response had been to seek the prayers of Isaiah. Now he prays himself. The following verses are powerful. They show us how one who trusts in Yahweh responds to fear and doubt: with faithful prayer. Consider the acrostic, TRUST:

T—take it before the Lord (v. 14). Notice the imagery as Hezekiah takes Sennacherib's threatening letter and spreads it before the Lord in the temple. He physically lays his burden before God. Biblical writers tell us to cast our burden or care on God (Ps 55:22; 1 Pet 5:7) and to let our requests be made known to God (Phil 4:6). Come to God like this: helpless and in need of grace. Why don't we do so? We must admit that at the root of prayerlessness is a feeling of self-sufficiency. If we think we can do things on our own, then why pray? Take a cue from Hezekiah and remember the words of Jesus: "You can do nothing without Me" (John 15:5).

R—recognize the greatness of God (v. 15). Hezekiah prays with an elevated view of God. He recognizes the majestic presence of God, who's "enthroned above the cherubim." He affirms the exclusive nature of God, who is God "alone." He affirms the total sovereignty of God, who is the God of "all the kingdoms of the earth." And he recognizes the unparalleled power of God, who "made the heavens and the earth." Oh, that we had a vision of God like this when we pray! Is our prayerlessness not often rooted in a low view of God? Let's "ponder anew what the Almighty can do!"

U—unload the problem to God (vv. 16-18). Hezekiah asks God to "listen closely" and "hear" and "see." He calls on God to consider the mockery of Sennacherib, who taunts "the living God." His prayer then includes a *lament*, a description of the dire situation. He states that Assyria has destroyed other nations and their gods but affirms, "They were not gods." Hezekiah isn't complaining against God; he is taking his complaint to God. He is lamenting the situation, pouring out his heart. Talk out your issue in God's presence. In our crises we get tempted to complain to other people before we pour out our hearts to God. Here's a great example for us. Unload it to the One who can carry it.

S—seek the help of God (v. 19a). His supplication is simple: "Now, LORD our God, please save us from his hand." You don't have to have

big, impressive words when you pray. Present your request to God (Phil
4:6). If you are the Father's child, tell Him what you need like a child.
Jesus said that God heard the prayer of the tax collector, who simply
said, "God, turn Your wrath from me—a sinner!" (Luke 18:13).

T—treasure the glory of God (v. 19b). The purpose of his prayer is also
simple but so important: "*so that* all the kingdoms of the earth may know
that You are the LORD God—You alone" (emphasis added). Hezekiah
isn't just praying for his own sake or for the people's sake, but for the sake
of God's glory. Davis says, "When we are concerned with God's glory we
are likely to be heard" (*2 Kings*, 289). Is this "God, glorify Yourself" not
reflected in the opening of the Lord's Prayer? "Our Father in heaven,
Your name be honored as holy" (Matt 6:9) or "make Your name great."
Oh, that we might be consumed with this desire: the glory of God being
made known among the nations!

Do you see how simple prayer is? Hezekiah faces the threat of the
Assyrians. Instead of planning, plotting, or seeking outside help, he
looks to God. Prayer doesn't eliminate the need for human solutions
(for example, Hezekiah had a great solution to get water into the city in
20:20), but our ultimate trust must always be in God alone. Corporately,
Christians sometimes look to pastors/leaders instead of to God first.
And when they bring their problems to pastors, instead of first seeking the Chief Shepherd, the pastors fail to seek God's help. They take
on a messiah complex instead of taking problems to God. Please don't
misunderstand. I think believers should always seek godly counsel. But
nothing should substitute for dependence on God. Perhaps you should
stop and pray this passage in your own words right now.

God's response. In verses 20-37 God heard Hezekiah's prayer, and He
will reverse the situation. Isaiah brings God's response to Hezekiah's
prayer in three parts.

First, we read a mocking song, or **dirge** (vv. 21-28). God speaks
through the prophet in a poetic way concerning Sennacherib. Tracing
the big picture, Sennacherib has spoken to Hezekiah about God;
Hezekiah has spoken to God about Sennacherib; and now God speaks
to Hezekiah about Sennacherib (Oswalt, *Isaiah*, 659).

In this dirge God refers to Israel as a virgin daughter who is being
oppressed. But everything will change because to mock Israel is to
insult God Himself. Then God says that Assyria's success has only come
because of His sovereign will (vv. 25-26; cf. Isa 10:5-19). This statement
is intended to humble them. In the last part of the dirge, God promises

that Assyria will go home. He says, "I will put My hook in your nose and My bit in your mouth; I will make you go back the way you came" (v. 28). House says, "The reference to the 'hook' and 'bit' reminds the original readers of the Assyrian practice of using these instruments to lead people into exile as if they were animals [cf. Amos 4:1-3]" (*1, 2 Kings*, 370). God will treat them the way they have treated other nations.

Second, the Lord will provide a **sign** for Hezekiah (vv. 29-31). The sign will occur when the Assyrians' leave. It will take two years for the land to be replenished from the Assyrian invasion, but in three years it will be back to normal. Like the crops, a remnant of surviving Israelites will grow up out of Jerusalem (House, *1, 2 Kings*, 370). How will this happen? "The zeal of the LORD of Hosts will accomplish this" (v. 31).

The third response to Hezekiah's prayer is God's specific **promise** that the Assyrians will not conquer Jerusalem (vv. 32-34). God will defend the city for His name's sake and for the sake of His servant David.

The execution of God's promises is found in the closing verse of the chapter. The angel of the Lord strikes down 185,000 soldiers. God delivers His people. "Salvation is from the LORD" (Jonah 2:9). Then we read of the fulfillment of the promise in 19:7. Sennacherib returns home and is put to death by the sword.

Are all gods the same? We hear this question a lot. The Assyrians believed that Yahweh was like the other gods—basically powerless. But God humbled the mockers and proved otherwise. David expressed what Hezekiah experienced: "There is no one like You among the gods" (Ps 86:8).

Challenge 2: Illness
2 KINGS 20:1-11

The report of Hezekiah's illness probably isn't in chronological order. House notes that "in those days" apparently refers to the general period of Hezekiah's reign. His illness must have occurred before the Sennacherib invasion (House, *1, 2 Kings*, 373n76). Regardless of when it happened, it did occur, and it serves as another case study on faith and prayer.

Hezekiah is sick and is told that he will die. Will he not live to enjoy the victory over Assyria? Once again Hezekiah takes his trouble to God in *prayer*. He appeals to his own personal character in this prayer, saying, "Please LORD, remember how I have walked before You faithfully and wholeheartedly and have done what pleases You" (v. 3). Then he "wept bitterly." Some view this petition as self-centered, but Hezekiah is really following a common Israelite pattern of the lament prayers in Psalms. He's praying a lot like David (Pss 7:3-5; 17:1-5; 18:20-26; 26:1-7; 44:17-22). Davis says, "There is no thought of sinless perfection but only of covenantal obedience" (*2 Kings*, 301).

Isaiah immediately returns to give him a revised word—that God has heard and will heal the king. God promises to give him 15 more years. Did God change His mind? Davis says, "Sometimes what sounds like a final decree is a subtle invitation" (*2 Kings*, 301). See Exodus 32:7-14 as an example.

What we should learn is that our prayers matter. Interestingly, Hezekiah will rise on "the third day" (vv. 5,8), becoming a "resurrected" king. Additionally, God says, "I will defend this city for My sake and for the sake of My servant David" (v. 6). God not only heard his prayer and promised healing but also promised that He would continue to defend the people from the Assyrians. Isaiah then calls for "a lump of pressed figs" to be applied to the infected area (v. 7). In this example we see that God may choose to work His healing through human means.

Hezekiah asked for a sign of healing (unlike his father Ahaz, who rejected Isaiah's sign in Isa 7:12). The prophet gives him a choice of signs: "This is the sign to you from the LORD that He will do what He has promised: Should the shadow go ahead 10 steps or go back 10 steps?" (v. 9). Hezekiah opts for the more difficult sign, "Let the shadow go back 10 steps" (v. 10). Thus, "His healing takes on miraculous proportions. . . . He lives under God's blessing, while Sennacherib lives under God's judgment" (House, *1, 2 Kings*, 373).

God doesn't always heal us when we pray, but sometimes He does. Regardless of the outcome, we should trust in God with our lives. Hezekiah shows us a good example of crying out to God when we're sick (Jas 5:13-14).

Challenge 3: Pride
2 KINGS 20:12-19

Once again we have an interaction between Isaiah and Hezekiah. We might call his final challenge the challenge of pride. Like other kings before him, Hezekiah became his own greatest problem. He gets puffed up with his success and his stuff, and in his pride he looks to the Babylonians instead of God for help.

It's often easier to look to God in suffering than in prosperity. When things are going well, we often lose sight of our dependency on God. As a church, it's easy to get puffed up with big numbers or "success" and start trusting in ourselves instead of God for advancing the kingdom. As a nation, prosperity often crushes dependency. How quickly we can forget the giver of gifts. As individuals, it's easy to turn into Hezekiah, failing to crush pride and cultivate humility. But we must remember that "pride comes before destruction" (Prov 16:18).

So here's what happens. Hezekiah has company over. The Babylonians pay him a visit, bringing him a present, ostensibly because the king's son "heard that he had been sick" but also to bring "letters and a gift" (v. 12; Isa 39:1ff). These letters probably had something to do with a hidden agenda (Motyer, *Isaiah*, 240). When we read that Hezekiah showed the Babylonians everything, being "pleased" to receive them (Isa 39:2), he is doing more than giving them a tour. He's showing them his resources and discussing an alliance against Assyria. Motyer captures what might have been going on in Hezekiah's heart: "Imagine them coming all that way to see me! Imagine Merodach-baladan wanting me as an ally!" (ibid.).

Isaiah knows it isn't acceptable for the king to seek such an alliance (Isa 30:1-5; 31:1-3). He takes the opportunity to tell the king about the future. He tells him that that one day Babylon will take everything in the palace, and some of the king's sons will be eunuchs in the palace of the Babylonians. We have the privilege of knowing that this won't happen for over a century, but Isaiah's word will indeed be fulfilled.

What's the problem? The Chronicler says, "God left him [Hezekiah] to test him and discover what was in his heart" (2 Chr 32:31). If this event was intended to test him, then the test had to do with *pride*, especially given his earlier problems with pride (see 2 Chr 32:24-29; House, *1, 2 Kings*, 375). Hezekiah was flattered by Babylon's interest in him and thrilled by a possible alliance, but all of it was idolatrous and arrogant. What happened to his humble trust in Yahweh to fight the enemies? We have another example like Uzziah: "But when he became strong, he grew arrogant" (2 Chr 26:16). Let us remember that "no matter our age or vocation, humility is our greatest friend and pride our greatest enemy" (Mahaney, *Humility*, 14).

Hezekiah responds strangely, "'The word of the LORD that you have spoken is good,' for he thought: Why not, if there will be peace and security during my lifetime?" (v. 19). Either this is a self-serving and unrepentant response, meaning he doesn't care about the future but just his own day, or he sees this as a "good" word because God is delaying His judgment in His grace (Davis, *2 Kings*, 306). I prefer to take the former position, given the problem of pride in the story.

Remember That Ultimate Restoration Is Coming
2 KINGS 20:20-21

The end of Hezekiah's life reminds us of the challenge of consistency. It reminds me of the 2009–10 Kentucky Wildcats basketball team. They dominated the regular season, losing only two games, but didn't reach the Final Four. Their amazing season ended with a "clang" as they shot 4 for 32 from the three-point line, including missing their first 20 three-point attempts. They go down as an impressive team that fell short of glory.

As we close the books on Hezekiah's tremendous season as king, we recognize that his reign ended with a "clang." He couldn't bring ultimate restoration. Judah's exile is coming. He accomplished a lot, but he died, and Manasseh reigned in his place. Manasseh will lead Judah into evil like Ahaz did, and soon Judah will be in captivity.

The best of kings fall short of glory. Only one King can bring true restoration: Jesus. As we finish this section, we recognize the absolute importance of worshiping and trusting in the living God. We can do this through our union with the Son of God. Jesus is the King of kings. Hezekiah was like David, but he wasn't the David that was to come. Jesus alone is the King who lived a totally sinless life, who died for idolaters, taking their judgment, and who rose on the third day to give them life in His eternal kingdom. Let's rejoice in our King!

Reflect and Discuss
1. Why are people stubborn and unwilling to obey the word of the Lord?
2. What are the consequences of Israel's and Judah's disobedience?
3. How is it possible to fear the Lord and also to serve carved images?
4. Describe some ways God's people today attempt to serve both God and idols.

5. Why is Hezekiah called the greatest of the kings of Judah who came before or after him?
6. Discuss any personal experiences with steadfastness under affliction.
7. Where can God's people today look for hope in the midst of affliction?
8. Why does God sometimes use unbelievers to expose the sin of His people?
9. Describe Hezekiah's prayer.
10. Why do you think Hezekiah responds the way he does when Isaiah prophesies that Babylon will take away everything from his house?

Humble Yourself Before the Lord

2 KINGS 21:1–23:30

Main Idea: Two kings are contrasted: Manasseh rejects the Lord; Josiah, the greatest of the kings, honors the Lord by valuing God's word.

I. **Manasseh's Idolatry (21:1-26)**
   A. The perversions he pursued (vv. 2-9)
   B. The privileges he rejected (vv. 4, 7-9)
   C. The disaster he brought (vv. 10-15)
   D. The legacy he left (vv. 16-26)
II. **Josiah's Obedience (22:1–23:30)**
   A. Value the Word (22:1-10).
   B. Humble yourself before the Word (22:11-20).
   C. Obey the Word (23:1-30).
      1. Covenant renewal (vv. 1-3)
      2. Comprehensive reform (vv. 4-20)
      3. Celebration of Passover (vv. 21-30)

Last week in our small group we were discussing the discipline of "serving." When the subject of gifts and abilities came up, I told them I don't have the gift of musical leadership. (That surprised no one.) I have tried to lead musical worship before. My first attempt was at "Baptist Men's Day." I was a relatively new Christian, eager to glorify God. While my intentions were good, my voice and guitar playing weren't. After singing three songs, playing a total of about six chords on my guitar, I sat down beside my encouraging mother, who put her arm around me and said, "You did your best, honey." That was a nice way of telling me, "Try something else." But I wouldn't be denied. About a year after my disastrous attempt at leading corporate worship, Dr. Shaddix invited me, along with my friends David and Landon, over to his house for a prayer group and encouraged me to bring my guitar. I thought, "You know, maybe small groups, not large groups, are more my thing." So I went to the group meeting prepared to lead a few choruses. I chose the short chorus "Humble Thyself" as my first selection. The only problem is I had great trouble shifting through the chords in this *very* difficult song (hint: it's not). Instead of playing, "Humble thyself in the sight of the Lord, humble thyself in the sight of the Lord. . . . And he will lift you up." I decided to just sing "Humble thyself in the sight of the Lord" over and over. The guys were locked in for the first two "humble thyselfs," but after I kept repeating it, they just burst into laughter. After receiving their mockery, I told them it was for effect. I was giving the emphasis on this phrase because they needed to hear it!

"You humbled yourself in the sight of the Lord" isn't a phrase uttered often about the kings of Judah and Israel, despite the admonition from Deuteronomy concerning the kings: "His heart will not be exalted above his countrymen" (17:20). Even the best of kings, like Uzziah and Hezekiah, fell to pride (2 Chr 26:16). The other idol-worshiping kings definitely acted in pride against Yahweh. But in these chapters we find a king who humbled himself before the Lord (2 Kgs 22:19)—Josiah. At the end of the story of Josiah, we read,

> Before him there was no king like him who turned to the LORD with all his mind and with all his heart and with all his strength according to all the law of Moses, and no one like him arose after him. (23:25)

By contrast we have a king who lived in prideful rebellion against God—Manasseh. Let's consider his idolatry that we must avoid, and then consider the obedience of Josiah that we need to pursue.

Manasseh's Idolatry
2 KINGS 21:1-26

Following the noble reign of Hezekiah, we read of this faithless reign of Manasseh. In the last chapter we noted how Hezekiah led a reformation despite having a wicked father (just as Josiah will do). Here we read how Manasseh led the nation into idolatry despite having a faithful father. He apparently reigned alongside his father a few years as well, so he had seen what a faithful leader looks like up close. Nevertheless, he's as evil as they come.

Your father doesn't have to be the determining factor in your spiritual journey (see Ezek 18). Undoubtedly fathers influence their children. But being the son of a Christian doesn't mean you will be a Christian too. On the flip side, being the son (or daughter) of an unbelieving, wicked father doesn't mean you have to be wicked. The book of

Kings shows us the importance of personally making a decision to follow the living God.

We can break down Manasseh's idolatry into four parts: the perversions he pursued, the privileges he forsook, the disaster he brought, and the legacy he left.

The Perversions He Pursued (vv. 2-9)

From verse 1 we find that this king reigned for 55 years. This makes him the longest reigning king in Israel's or Judah's history. During a period of 55 years, he utterly exhausted God's patience (23:26-27). He inflicted massive damage on the nation, so much so that even the reform of Josiah couldn't quench God's wrath; it could only delay it. Manasseh followed in the legacy of the evil kings. A good slogan for his reign would be, "Anything you can do, I can do worse."

However, instead of God sending a prophet to speak or an avenger to act, we read of little adversity in his life and then a nice burial in a "garden" (21:26). Why did God allow this king to reign 55 years? I don't know the answer. One possibility is that his reign itself was a time of judgment (Davis, 2 Kings, 310–11n5). But I wouldn't fight for this position.

We don't always know the answers to the mysteries of God's world. It appears that internally the leaders in Judah were OK with his practices. Moreover, the writer goes on to tell us that the perverted acts of Manasseh aren't his alone; he leads the *people* into more sin than the Amorites who lived there before them (vv. 9,11).

What did Manasseh do? He was the son of "Hephzibah," and he "did what was evil in the LORD's sight, imitating the detestable practices of the nations that the LORD had dispossessed before the Israelites" (v. 2). He rebuilt what Hezekiah tore down, namely, "the high places." He then reinstituted fertility worship, erecting altars for "Baal and Asherah." The author speaks of him as another "King Ahab of Israel."

Manasseh's paganism went beyond Ahab. He instituted astral worship. He "worshiped the whole heavenly host and served them" (v. 3, cf. v. 5). He built altars to the sun, moon, and stars in the temple.

Astral worship is explicitly forbidden in Deuteronomy (4:19; 17:3). Believing that the heavenly bodies influenced the events on earth was common among surrounding nations (Olley, *Message of Kings*, 340). Many today are still attracted to this practice. How opposite this is from Micaiah's vision of Yahweh being worshiped by the host of heaven, not as one among other gods (1 Kgs 22:19).

God is the Creator of moon, stars, and sun, and we aren't to worship them (Isa 40:26). Isaiah says the Babylonian astrologers who make predictions are powerless (47:13). This practice is folly, whether it's done on a popular level of a horoscope, or done for leaders seeking the heavenly hosts for determining major decisions (Olley, *Message of Kings*, 340–41). While creation is amazing, Paul warns us against worshiping creation instead of the Creator (Rom 1:25). The better a thing is, the more likely we are to make it an idol. God's creation is good and majestic, and we tend to make created people (especially those in relationship with us) or God's created nature an idol. These things cannot give you what only God can give you, namely salvation, provision, satisfaction, and meaning.

Manasseh proved to be another Ahaz. He burned his own son as an offering, violating God's word (Deut 18:10-11). He also went further than Ahaz by putting a carved Asherah pole in the temple (vv. 6-7; cf. 16:3-4). In so doing he was endorsing the worship of Asherah as the consort to Yahweh. If all of this were not enough, he also gave himself to the consultation of dark powers: he "practiced witchcraft and divination, and consulted mediums and spiritists" (v. 6). "Spiritists" involved mortals communicating with chthonic deities of the underworld (1 Sam 28:7). The author summarizes, "He did a great amount of evil in the LORD's sight, provoking Him" (v. 6). This evil was "greater evil than the nations the LORD had destroyed before the Israelites" (v. 9).

What does all this tell us? It may tell us something about Manasseh's *politics*. Did he think behaving like the surrounding nations would give Judah more favor in the eyes of the nations, including Assyria? Perhaps. Did he think his father did harm to the nation? Maybe. What we definitely learn from this story is how the *human heart* works. Humanity is incurably religious, but Nietzsche said, "There are more idols in the world than there are realities" (*Twilight*, n.p.). We are a worshiping people. We ponder the meaning of life. Animals don't do this. So the question is not *will* you worship, but *what* will you worship? Will you give yourself to myths, superstitions, the goddess of sex, or to the living God?

The Privileges He Rejected (vv. 4,7-9)

The sad reality of turning from the living God is that you are turning away from the greatest privileges you could ever enjoy. In verse 4 the writer says, "Jerusalem is where I will put My name," and then this privilege is expanded in verses 7-9.

Notice the privilege of God's **presence**. God says He will establish His name there. He will put Himself there. When you turn to idols, you are turning from the most satisfying relationship available and from a peace that cannot be found elsewhere. The presence of God now, in the new covenant, isn't found in a temple but in His people. God dwells within us, through Christ by faith (Rom 8:9).

By rejecting Yahweh, Manasseh and the people were also turning from His **favor**. God promised them security, land, and stability if they would keep His commands, but "they did not listen" (v. 9).

God has promised us a land too. Because of the work of Christ, those who are new creations in Christ are waiting for the dawning of a new creation, in which the glory of God covers the earth like the waters cover the sea (Hab 2:14). He will give us a land we didn't labor for or deserve (cf. Josh 24:13), if we will follow His Word, repenting and turning to Christ for salvation. Don't forsake the privilege offered to you.

Tragically, many trade the glory of God and His gracious privileges for their idols. In the words of Jeremiah, they have "abandoned Me, the fountain of living water, and dug cisterns for themselves, cracked cisterns that cannot hold water" (Jer 2:12-13). Idolatry is forsaking a thirst-quenching fountain for that which cannot satisfy. Think of this picture in the temple: trading the place of atonement for goddess worship; trading the bread of the Presence, a picture of God's sustaining power, for Baal; trading a prayer-hearing God, symbolized at the altar of incense, for fortune-tellers, mediums, and necromancers (Davis, *2 Kings*, 314). Manasseh says, "No thanks. I prefer the broken cisterns to the living water." And it was not because Manasseh had not been taught better or, for that matter, shown better. His dad was Hezekiah. Manasseh simply didn't care who God is. If you want to avoid the sins of Manasseh, remember that God is your greatest joy and your highest good, and you have nowhere to go outside of Him to find what your heart longs for.

The Disaster He Brought (vv. 10-15)

Judgment against Jerusalem draws near. Manasseh's sins are briefly summarized in verse 12 as the reason for the devastation. Four word pictures are used to describe the coming wrath of Yahweh. First, Yahweh says the disaster will make peoples' ears "shudder," signaling a *terrible* judgment (v. 12). Second, "the measuring [plumb] line used on Samaria" is a graphic image used by the prophets to describe God's *standard* of judgment (v. 13a; see also Amos 7:7-8). The divine architect will assess Judah as He has Samaria and Ahab. Third, He speaks of the *comprehensive* nature of His judgment with the image of "wiping" Jerusalem like a dish (v. 13b). Finally, Yahweh announces that He will "abandon the remnant of My inheritance"—the faithful followers found during Hezekiah's reform—"and hand them over to their enemies" (v. 14). This image speaks of the *helplessness* of Judah in judgment (Davis, *2 Kings*, 316).

Verse 15 reminds us of the sadness of it all. God brought this people out of bondage in Egypt, but they had a history of provoking Yahweh to anger. Manasseh put them over the top, beyond the hope of recovery (Davis, *2 Kings*, 316). Not even the reforms of Josiah could hold God's wrath back ultimately. The writer later reflects back on Manasseh, saying, "In spite of all that, the LORD did not turn from the fury of His great burning anger, which burned against Judah because of all that Manasseh had provoked Him with" (23:26).

The Legacy He Left (vv. 16-26)

The writer cannot document all of the evil of this 55-year king, but he indicates that he "shed so much innocent blood." This often refers to abusing the poor, a great offense for anyone but particularly awful for a people who themselves used to be slaves (Isa 1:15-17). Josephus records that Manasseh slaughtered the prophets daily (*Antiquities*, 10.3). Justin Martyr claims that he was the one responsible for putting Isaiah to death by sawing him in half, as possibly alluded to in Hebrews 11:37 (*Dialogue with Trypho*, § 120). At this point we aren't surprised, for when someone thinks he isn't accountable to God, his depravity has no limits.

Manasseh's son Amon takes after him, and the nation has two more years of an idol-worshiping king. Amon's reign ends when his servants assassinate him. But this death doesn't lead to the end of David's line, for the people rise up and make Josiah, his son, the king. Fascinating. For whatever reason, the people don't abandon Davidic succession. They suffered for 55 years under Manasseh and two years under Amon. Would you blame them for choosing a king from a different family? But they don't. Thus we have a delay in the judgment on Judah, and we are introduced to one of Judah's greatest kings in Judah's darkest time.

But before we move on to Josiah, there's one more note on the legacy of Manasseh. He devastated the land with wickedness. He passed it on to his son. But he also passed down *hope to sinners*. Yes, Manasseh should give sinners hope. How so? In 2 Chronicles 33:1-20 the Chronicler tells us that Manasseh repented. The Assyrians captured him with hooks, bound him with chains, and took him to Babylon. Then we read these surprising words:

> *When he was in distress, he sought the favor of Yahweh his God and earnestly humbled himself before the God of his ancestors. He prayed to Him, so He heard his petition and granted his request, and brought him back to Jerusalem, to his kingdom. So Manasseh came to know that Yahweh is God.* (2 Chr 33:12-13; see also v. 19)

Then he tried to undo the damage he had done. Remarkable! The reason Kings doesn't mention this repentance is because it didn't ultimately change the course of Judah's history. Judgment was irreversible. And apparently, his conversion didn't have much of an impact on Amon. Nevertheless, he repented personally. The Chronicler reminds us that God's grace can reach the worst of idolaters. Even Manasseh was not beyond the reach of God's transforming grace. While his previous acts had an enduring negative effect, he himself experienced God's mercy.

How do you receive such grace? Notice our theme of humility: "When he was in distress, he sought the favor of Yahweh his God and earnestly humbled himself before the God of his ancestors" (2 Chr 33:12).

Manasseh reminds us that in one sense it's never too late to turn to God in repentance. A friend this week told of a man who tried to kill himself with a shotgun after his wife left him. Somehow, despite shooting himself in the neck, he didn't die. My friend had been witnessing to this man for some time. After God spared his life, he eventually became a Christian. God's grace reaches the Manassehs. How? A person must humble himself or herself. Peter writes, "God resists the proud but gives grace to the humble. Humble yourselves, therefore, under the mighty hand of God, so that He may exalt you at the proper time" (1 Pet 5:5-6). Perhaps the testimony of Manasseh in Chronicles encouraged the exiles to remember that if they would humble themselves and repent, God would hear and restore them too.

Josiah's Obedience
2 KINGS 22:1–23:30

Judgment is coming to Judah, but it's delayed due to the stellar leadership of King Josiah. He is like a "second Moses," similar to Hezekiah, "a second David." Josiah is pictured as the ideal king as described in Deuteronomy, where we read that the king must not "turn from this command" (Deut 17:20). At the end of Josiah's reign, he indeed turned to the Lord with all his heart, obeying the Shema. The Shema is named for the first word of Deuteronomy 6:4-5—"Listen"—and it goes on, "Israel: The LORD our God, the LORD is One. Love the LORD your God with all your heart, with all your soul, and with all your strength." This confession has been echoed through the centuries by Jews, every morning and evening, and it was reinforced by Jesus, who also added that wholehearted love for God cannot be separated from love for one's neighbor. Josiah follows the Shema wholeheartedly, surpassing even Hezekiah in his devotion to the teaching of Moses. Provan summarizes Josiah's reign well: "[Josiah] is the best of all kings, but he is a king come too late" (*1 and 2 Kings*, 271).

Despite reigning after the dark spiritual days of Manasseh, Josiah leads the people into a time of reformation, much like Hezekiah led a reformation after the wicked leadership of Ahaz. Once again we see how God often uses unlikely people (the grandson of Manasseh in this case), in an unlikely time, to lead a time of reformation. God in His grace gave this generation a godly leader. How kind of Yahweh!

In the introduction of Josiah (22:1-2), we see what kind of king he is. He's a young king who took the throne at age eight. This young king is known for doing "right in the LORD's sight." The Chronicler emphasizes his passion for God at a young age: "In the eighth year of his reign, while he was still a youth, Josiah began to seek the God of his ancestor David" (2 Chr 34:3).

How early can you begin to start seeking God? Here it is: while you are "still a youth." If you are a young person reading this, begin seeking God now! Isaiah says, "Seek the Lord while He may be found" (Isa 55:6). We have a host of examples in Christian history of young people seeking the Lord—like David Livingstone who memorized Psalm 119 at age nine! Don't fail to seek God because your peers aren't doing so. You seek the Lord, taking a cue from those in the past.

The writer draws our attention to the eighteenth year of his reign in verse 3 and proceeds to tell the story of this significant year. Josiah takes the initiative in providing spiritual leadership. Consider how he "sent" or "commanded" in chapters 22–23:

- "the king sent" (22:3),
- the king "commanded" (22:12),
- "the king sent" (23:1),
- "the king commanded" (23:4),

- "The king commanded" (23:21),
- and we may add 23:24, "Josiah removed."

Josiah faithfully sets out to follow Yahweh, giving us a marvelous example of obedience to God's word. Let me point out three challenges for all of us: value the Word, humble yourself before the Word, and obey the Word.

Value the Word (22:1-10)

Josiah has much work to do, and he begins with repairing the temple, similarly to young Joash (vv. 3-7; 2 Kgs 12:1-16). As the work is being done, Hilkiah the high priest said to Shaphan, "I have found the book of the law in the LORD's temple" (v. 8). Then Shaphan returns to report to Josiah about the financial matters of the repair, and also relays, "Hilkiah the priest has given me a book" (v. 10). Shaphan and his family stand as an example of the importance of giving the word to people. Olley reports:

> [H]is son: Ahikam (12, 14) later was a protector of Jeremiah
> (Jer 26:24), and Ahikam's son Gedaliah was appointed by
> Nebuchadnezzar as governor of Judah after the destruction
> and looked after Jeremiah (2 Kgs 25:22; Jer 39:13; 41:3);
> another son, Elasha, was entrusted with Jeremiah's letter
> to the exiles in Babylon (Jer 29:3); yet another, Gemariah,
> provided the room from which Baruch read Jeremiah's scroll
> to the people, which was heard by Gemariah's son, Micaiah,
> who urged the king not to burn the scroll [Jer 36:10-17,25]
> (*Message of Kings*, 349).

Quite a legacy! Those of us who have the Word have a stewardship of getting it to people who don't have access to it.

After reading the book for himself, Shaphan proceeds to read it to Josiah. Two questions emerge: What book was found? And how long had it been missing? The answer to the first is probably Deuteronomy. Provan notes that the phrase "book of the law" is used in the Pentateuch only of Deuteronomy (Deut 28:61; 29:21; 30:10; 31:26; Josh 1:8; 8:30-35; 23:6; 24:26) (Provan, *1 and 2 Kings*, 271). As previously pointed out, Deuteronomy is the key book for the kings of Israel. What about question number two? We know that previous kings had access to it, so it must have disappeared under the long reign of Manasseh. It was apparently removed from its place beside the ark (Deut 31:26) in this period. That Manasseh wanted nothing to do with God's Word shouldn't surprise us. God's Word got lost in God's temple, and no one seemed to care until Josiah was made aware of it. How similar to our contemporary mood! My friend, have you put the Word away, or are you valuing it? Josiah is commended because he "humbled [himself] before the Lord" (22:19), and he did so by humbling himself before God's Word. He believed God Himself spoke through His Word. If we have such a high view of Scripture, then surely we would want to read it and hear it, right?

An agnostic professor at the University of North Carolina Chapel Hill, Bart Ehrman, points out the fact that many professing Christians claim to believe that God breathed out His Word (2 Tim 3:16-17), but mysteriously they don't read it. I have heard him explain the following story in a debate on the Bible:

> I'm teaching a large undergraduate class this semester on the New Testament, and of course, most of my students are from the South; most of them have been raised in good Christian families. I've found over the years that they have a far greater commitment to the Bible than knowledge about it. So this last semester, I did something I don't normally do. I started off my class of 300 students by saying the first day, "How many of you in here would agree with the proposition that the Bible is the inspired word of God?" *Voom!* The entire room raises its hand. "OK, that's great. Now how many of you have read *The Da Vinci Code?*" *Voom!* The entire room raises its hand. "How many of you have read the entire Bible?" Scattered hands. "Now, I'm not telling you that *I* think God wrote the Bible. You're telling me that *you* think God wrote the Bible. I can see why you'd want to read a book by Dan Brown. But if God wrote a book, wouldn't you want to see what he had to say?" So this is one of the mysteries of the universe. (*The Textual Reliability of the New Testament*, 13–14)

We shouldn't need an agnostic to persuade us to read the Bible. If we believe God speaks presently through His Word, will we not want to read it? Are you like these students, denying your belief by your practice? May it not be so! May God give us a heart like the psalmist: "My heart fears only Your word" (Ps 119:161). And let us value it so much that we get it into the hands of as many people as possible.

Humble Yourself Before the Word (22:11-20)

In light of hearing the Word, the focus shifts from temple repair to spiritual repair. On hearing the Word, Josiah "tore his clothes" (v. 11) as a sign of humility. This humility is affirmed later, when the prophetess tells Josiah, "Because . . . you humbled yourself before the LORD," judgment will be delayed (v. 19).

Consider three expressions of responding humbly to God's Word from Josiah's life. First, notice his **humble tenderness**. In verse 19 the writer says that his heart was "tender" (v. 11), or "responsive" (NIV), or "penitent" (ESV). The Chronicler uses the word *tender* as well (2 Chr 34:27 HCSB, ESV).

Don't respond to the word with hardness of heart but with tenderness of heart. In the New Testament James says, "Humbly receive the implanted word, which is able to save you" (1:21). Softheartedness is the good soil, which bears fruit (Mark 4:20).

Josiah exemplifies Isaiah's words: "I will look favorably on this kind of person: one who is humble, submissive in spirit, and trembles at My word" (Isa 66:2). Here's a king, trembling at the King's words.

Second, look at his **humble openness** to learn the Scriptures. Immediately he seeks to know what "the words of this book" mean for him and the nation (vv. 12-13). He doesn't simply put the book back on the shelf. He recognizes the gravity of its message and wants someone to explain it to him. Huldah explains the meaning to him in two aspects. On the one hand there is no hope. Judgment is coming to Judah. But on the other hand, judgment will be delayed because of the responsiveness of Josiah, who will go to his grave in peace and will not see the coming disaster.

Do you have a teachable spirit? Do you seek to know the meaning of God's Word? When someone teaches the warnings in it, do you get mad at them and reject it, or do you humbly repent and seek mercy? Imagine for a moment that the apostle Paul or Isaiah was coming to preach at your worship gathering next week. Do you think people would show up? Now, I know the apostle and prophet may be more gifted than your pastor, but we get to read from the prophets and the apostles every week in God's inspired Word. Do you value this privilege?

Third, notice his **humble blessedness**. God honors Josiah by granting him relief from His judgment in his lifetime. God truly looks with favor on those who honor His Word. Psalm 1 begins by saying,

> *How happy is the man*
> *who does not follow the advice of the wicked*
> *or take the path of sinners*
> *or join a group of mockers!*
> *Instead, his delight is in the LORD's instruction,*
> *and he meditates on it day and night.* (Ps 1:1-2)

Psalm 119, that amazing chapter on God's Word, opens with "How happy are those whose way is blameless, who live according to the LORD's instruction!" (Ps 119:1). Experience rich spiritual blessings by walking in God's Word.

Obey the Word (23:1-30)

What happens next illustrates the goal of receiving and understanding God's Word: obedience to it. Josiah shines at this point. His reforms are impressive, and they lead to the conclusion that he "turned to the LORD with all his mind and with all his heart and with all his strength" (23:25).

Covenant renewal (vv. 1-3). What did he do? We first read of his covenant renewal. He gathers everyone together to read the book of the Law to them. God's people have a long history of the public reading of Scripture (Exod 24; 31; Josh 8:30-35; Neh 8; Luke 4; 1 Tim 4:13; Col 4:16). God gives life to His people through His word. The reading sets up the covenant renewal, in which Josiah promises to follow the Lord wholeheartedly (see Deut 6:17; Josh 24:1-27). Then the people follow his lead.

Comprehensive reform (vv. 4-20). Next, Josiah follows the Word. It's one thing for me to tell my kids to do their chores, but it's another thing for them to do it. I don't explain their chores so they can go have small groups about it and discuss the Greek words for "mowing the lawn" and "sweeping the porch." I give them instructions, expecting them to "be doers of the word and not hearers only" (Jas 1:22). These words in James's epistle are important. James says those who are just hearing it are deceiving themselves. It's possible to deceive oneself in thinking that taking in information is sufficient. Obedience must follow.

Allow me to summarize Josiah's reforms, with thanks to Dr. Davis for providing the following "12-step 'de-Manassehfication' program":

- removing pagan vessels from the temple (v. 4),
- deposing pagan clergy (v. 5),

- pulverizing the Asherah image (v. 6),
- wrecking the male prostitutes' temple apartments (v. 7),
- defiling Judah's high places, deposing their priests (vv. 8-9),
- desecrating Tophet, the place of child sacrifice (v. 10),
- removing and destroying sun worship paraphernalia (v. 11),
- smashing royal idolatrous altars (v. 12),
- eliminating Solomon's folly (v. 13),
- destroying the props of fertility worship (v. 14),
- pulling down/defiling Jeroboam's Bethel worship center (vv. 15-16),
- and instituting a purge throughout the northern cities (vv. 19-20). (Davis, *2 Kings*, 328)

Provan calls this reform "comprehensive and thorough" (*1 and 2 Kings*, 273).

Among Josiah's acts is the fulfillment of Yahweh's word to Jeroboam I. Josiah beats the altar at Bethel to dust and defiles it by burning bones on it, which was done "according to the word of the Lord proclaimed by the man of God who proclaimed these things" (v. 16). Once again God's word is proven true. This time it's 1 Kings 13:2 coming to pass some 300 years later.

> The man of God cried out against the altar by a revelation from the Lord: "Altar, altar, this is what the Lord says, 'A son will be born to the house of David, named Josiah, and he will sacrifice on you the priests of the high places who are burning incense on you. Human bones will be burned on you.'" (1 Kgs 13:2)

Here's another reason to value the Word and humble yourself before it: *it is totally trustworthy.* Soon, Judah will see that Huldah's word will also come to pass.

Getting back to the concept of obedience, here's Josiah's example of doing the Word. Such obedience will require sacrifice, attacking idols, and reorienting our lives, and it might involve pain. But it's worth it. If you're going to remove cancer, it will involve some pain (Olley, *Message of Kings*, 353), but it will also bring healing.

Celebration of Passover (vv. 21-30). After Josiah purifies worship, he reinstitutes the Passover, following Deuteronomy 16:1-8. In celebrating the festival, he outdoes Hezekiah and even David. Judah remembers the blood of the lamb that saved them from God's wrath. The last mention of the Passover was in Joshua 5:10-12.

Then we read of more antipaganism efforts in verse 24, followed by an unparalleled commendation of his life in verses 24-25.

Despite all of these efforts, however, the wrath of God continues to burn against Judah because of the acts of Manasseh. Judgment was certain.

Consider this application. Josiah knew that his reforms could not turn away Yahweh's wrath; he could only delay it. His reformation couldn't ultimately save the nation, yet he obeyed anyway. Here's what we need to learn: "Obedience without incentives is likely genuine" (Davis, *2 Kings*, 330). He obeyed out of love for Yahweh, not for what obedience might bring practically.

The book of Job opens with a question that Josiah answered rightly, and we must seek to answer rightly. Satan asks, "Does Job fear God for nothing?" Or to put it another way, "Will Job serve God if he gets nothing out of it?" (Olley, *Message of Kings*, 351). Have you ever said, "Why should I obey now?" Perhaps you think, "I'm not going to obey God because I can't undo the past." "I won't obey, since I'm not in a position of ministry." "I'm not going to obey God, since it will never bring me out of debt." If you're considering obedience for your own self-centered reasons, then it isn't obedience. Why do we obey? Is it for what we can get in this life? No! That's prosperity theology. How many people reject prosperity theology in theory but practice it in real life? Jesus said, "If you love Me, you will keep My commands" (John 14:15). That's why we obey Jesus—we love Him. Period. We love Him because He first loved us, and those who truly love Him will obey Him. So, will you? Are you making the most of your situation right now?

Josiah eventually gets killed at Megiddo in a needless battle with the Egyptians, and his son Jehoahaz reigns in his place. The Chronicler reports that Josiah apparently tried to seek the favor of Babylon by opposing the Egyptians, but this indicated his turning from God's word, which God actually spoke through the Egyptian king Neco (2 Chr 35:22). Even the best of kings had problems. His reign ends, and now we're left to wait on the coming judgment.

Six centuries later a descendant of Josiah, Jesus, lived a life better than Josiah. His obedience was perfect. He would pray in the garden, "not as I will, but as You will" (Matt 26:39). He obeyed out of love to the Father, even though it would not ease His present suffering; He experienced agony on a wooden cross. Because of His perfect obedience in dying in our place, as the ultimate Passover Lamb, and rising from the dead, we have eternal life and the power to live out the Great Commission of teaching them to *obey* everything He has commanded (Matt 28:20).

Josiah is a wonderful example in this story. He's an example of humility and obedience; but Jesus is the ultimate hero of the story, demonstrating incomparable humility and total obedience. He's the King we need to lead us to turn away the coming wrath of God. This King can forgive the worst of sinners, those who live like Manasseh, if they will humble themselves and repent. Will you humble yourself before the King? If you will, grace is yours. If you refuse, then a judgment worse than exile is yours. You can be hidden in Christ, protected from wrath, secured forever, if you will trust in Him.

Reflect and Discuss

1. What about Manasseh makes him so evil?
2. What does it mean that Judah did more evil than the pagan nations around them?
3. Discuss ways in which severe affliction might lead God's people to question His goodness.
4. How does Christ's crucifixion illustrate God's goodness in the midst of His wrath?
5. Does God use impending judgment to warn His people anywhere else in Scripture?
6. How is Josiah's commitment to the Lord different from that of many of the kings before him? What key discovery defined his reign?
7. Josiah hears the word of the Lord, is convicted by the word of the Lord, and acts according to the word of the Lord. Discuss how each of these steps is important for the godly life.
8. How does Jesus embody the characteristics of Josiah?
9. Is it important for God's people today to value the Word of God? How might it affect their lives?
10. How does God respond to Josiah's reforms?

We Need a Better King

2 KINGS 23:31–25:30

Main Idea: Second Kings closes with a rapid downfall of four kings in Jerusalem, which magnifies the need for a better King.

I. **We Need a Better King Because We Live in a Fallen World (23:31–25:26).**
   A. Four evil kings
   B. Four applications
   C. The fallen city
II. **We Need a Better King . . . and We Have One (25:27-30; Matt 1:17,22-23)!**
   A. God fulfills His Word.
   B. A living hope

Ralph Davis likens these final chapters to the dilemma hairy men have when forced to remove a Band-Aid. Removing a Band-Aid is a big problem for men, like me, who are hairier than Chewbacca. There's no easy way to remove it, especially when it feels like it's stuck to your hairy arm with superglue. You could take it slowly, prolonging the agony, or you can just pull it off with one howl-inducing jerk. When it comes to finishing this story about God's removal of Judah, the writer seems to take the quick-rip method. There's no easy way to write this section (or preach it!). The writer could prolong the agony and give lots of detail. But he decides instead to bring the story to an end quickly, giving us the impression that he wants to hurry (and the Chronicler even more quickly, covering these events in one chapter). Our writer's message is simple: "Jerusalem is toast" (Davis, *2 Kings*, 335).

Our writer moves rapidly through the reign of four kings who reigned for a total of 22 years. Two kings reigned for three months each: Jehoahaz and Jehoiachin. Two kings reigned for 11 years each: Jehoiakim and Zedekiah. Unfortunately, everything post-Josiah goes from bad to worse. In these two chapters the writer tells us of the fall of Jerusalem. Babylon takes Judah into exile. The temple gets destroyed. The treasures are taken away. Solomon's glory departs. The book of

Kings covers about 400 years of history: from Solomon's golden age, through the divided kingdom, to the fall of Israel, and finally to this sad conclusion.

As we finish our study, I would like to consider these final chapters while also trying to reflect on the book of Kings as a whole. I have tried to magnify one dominant theme in the study: *We need a better king!* Even the best of kings proved to fall short. That theme is reemphasized here. Allow me to make two points related to this dominant theme.

We Need a Better King Because We Live in a Fallen World
2 KINGS 23:31–25:26

In the beginning of our study, I noted that 1 Kings is about *decline* and 2 Kings is about a *fall*. These books highlight the reality that we live in a fallen world and we need a Redeemer. We have to realize this fact. Consider some of the effects of the fall in these final chapters and in the wider context of Kings.

Four Evil Kings

Consider the particular kings mentioned in these final chapters. **Jehoahaz** (23:31-35) reigned for three months in 609 BC. We read little about him, other than the fact that he "did what was evil in the LORD's sight" (v. 32). Despite having a godly father, Josiah, Jehoahaz rebelled against God, doing evil.

You don't have to teach a child to rebel. "Foolishness is tangled up in the heart of a youth" (Prov 22:15). You have to teach a child the gospel. One time I got in trouble for calling kids "midget demons." I had to apologize for my statement because "midget" offended someone. I never use the term anymore. But what was curious is that no one got upset that I called their kids little *demons*! Parents know their kids are little rebels who need to change, and that change ultimately comes through the power of Christ our Redeemer.

We also see once again that just because you have a godly father, this doesn't mean you will be godly. You must respond to the gospel. Jehoahaz's dad is Josiah, yet he turns from God's ways. Be diligent in teaching the gospel in the home; perhaps your child will not depart from the way he should go.

The circumstances of Jehoahaz's imprisonment aren't described, but what is clear is that Pharaoh (Judah's overlord at the time) doesn't like him, so he replaces him with his brother, Eliakim, whose name he changes to **Jehoiakim** (23:33–24:6). The new king is a puppet king, who installs a new tax program to pay the tribute to Egypt.

Jehoiakim reigned for 11 years, from 609 to 598 BC. We read that he too "did what was evil in the LORD's sight." During Jehoiakim's reign the first deportation took place (24:1-7), which is referenced during Daniel's time (Dan 1:1-4). Judgment came on the land because of their evil. It seems that Nebuchadnezzar used foreign raiders (24:2) because his army had just encountered the Egyptians in a war, so they are an interim solution (Davis, *2 Kings*, 338). But the writer of Kings gives the real reason they went against Judah: "The LORD . . . sent them," and it happened "according to the word of the LORD."

We know more about the rebellion of Jehoiakim (aka Shallum) from Jeremiah's prophecy. Jeremiah prophesied in the days of Josiah through Zedekiah. Consider the prophet's words:

> *For this is what the LORD says concerning Shallum son of Josiah, king of Judah, who became king in place of his father Josiah: "He has left this place—he will never return here again, but he will die in the place where they deported him, never seeing this land again."*
>
> *Woe for the one who builds his palace through unrighteousness, his upper rooms through injustice, who makes his fellow man serve without pay and will not give him his wages, who says, "I will build myself a massive palace, with spacious upper rooms." He will cut windows in it, and it will be paneled with cedar and painted with vermilion. Are you a king because you excel in cedar? Didn't your father eat and drink and administer justice and righteousness? Then it went well with him. He took up the case of the poor and needy, then it went well. Is this not what it means to know Me? This is the LORD's declaration.*
>
> *But you have eyes and a heart for nothing except your own dishonest profit, shedding innocent blood and committing extortion and oppression.* (Jer 22:11-17)

We find that the king had built a sweet palace of his own while his people suffered. He also refused to compensate the builders (Jer 22:13). A true king would deliver the oppressed and do justice (Jer 22:15; cf. v. 3). Such a king doesn't sit on the throne at this time; this king doesn't know the Lord like his father did (Jer 22:15-16). Jeremiah says because of his evil reign, "They will not mourn for him" (Jer 22:18).

Further, Jehoiakim rejects God's word. We read later in Jeremiah that God in His mercy reveals His word, with an offer for repentance (Jer 36:1-3), but Jehoiakim rejects it (Jer 36:20-26). Instead of listening and turning, he burns Jeremiah's scroll (Jer 36:23).

What a picture of human depravity: oppression, indulgence, and Bible burning! If God in His kindness should give you His Word, then you should treasure it like Josiah and repent, not burn it like Jehoiakim. What are you doing with your "scrolls"?

The point is clear: repent while you can. Don't persist in unbelief. For what is coming in the end is worse than Judah's exile. The good news of the gospel is that you don't have to be abandoned (2 Kgs 21:14) because Christ became the abandoned One for us. Jesus cried out on the cross, "My God, My God, why have You forsaken Me?" (Matt 27:46). Either God's judgment will fall on you, and you will be removed from His blessing and face His wrath, or you can look to Christ as your substitute. You can be forgiven and redeemed through faith in Him. You can live every day with this promise: "I will never leave you or forsake you" (Heb 13:5).

Jehoiachin reigned for three months in 597 BC. During this time the second deportation happens (see also Ezek 1:1-3). The writer reports the awful time using the phrases "took captive," "carried off," and "deported" (2 Kgs 24:10-17). Jehoiachin basically reigns long enough to hand the kingdom over to Babylon. He's no Hezekiah. Remember how Hezekiah turned to God in desperate prayer when oppressed by the Arameans? Instead of that response, Jehoiachin "surrendered to the king of Babylon" (v. 12). As a result, thousands are carried away.

From that 597 scene, the writer takes us to 587 with **Zedekiah**. Once again a foreign king selects Judah's king, changing his name from Mattaniah to Zedekiah. He reigns for 11 years, and he's the fourth consecutive king who "did what was evil in the LORD's sight." The writer adds, "Because of the LORD's anger, it came to the point in Jerusalem and Judah that He finally banished them from His presence" (v. 20). God's patience had run out. God's wrath comes on Zedekiah and the people with full force during his reign. Before the destruction of Jerusalem, the writer reports the Babylonian siege (25:1-2). This was just the beginning of the suffering for Judah during Zedekiah's reign (read more about him in Jer 37–39).

More is said about Zedekiah elsewhere. The Chronicler adds, he "did not humble himself before Jeremiah the prophet at the LORD's command" (2 Chr 36:12). Zedekiah also "hardened his heart against returning to Yahweh" (36:13), refusing to repent. The priests were also unfaithful, as they followed "the detestable practices of the nations" (36:14). Then he says that God, in amazing compassion, continued to send messengers, but they mocked them and despised their words, bringing God's wrath (36:15-16; cf. Jer 25:4).

Four Applications

All four kings in the final chapters "did what was evil in the LORD's sight" (23:32,37; 24:9; 24:19). Kings resembling Hezekiah or Josiah don't appear again. These final kings are faithless and unreceptive to Scripture. So what can we glean from their lives in light of the rest of Kings?

Notice the need for godly leadership. Why did Judah fall? They fell because God was vindicating His holy name. God would not tolerate their rebellion (24:3-4,20; Jer 22:8-9). And poor leadership led to this rebellion and consequent judgment. We read of the shedding of blood, absence of concern for the poor, oppression, greed for gain, lack of trust in God, and rebellion against the word of God. The results are disastrous.

Nations and churches and families need good leadership. The book of Kings closes with four terrible leaders, which illustrates this basic point. Under those leaders Judah "abandoned the covenant of Yahweh their God and worshiped and served other gods" (Jer 22:9). The good news is that Jeremiah 23 follows Jeremiah 22. The messianic King, the Righteous Branch, is promised. He will "administer justice and righteousness" (Jer 23:1-8).

Realize that rebellion is boring. One of the results of a fallen world is that nothing can satisfy our hearts outside of the gospel. If you struggle through these remaining chapters of 2 Kings, then recognize that it isn't the author's fault. There isn't anything exciting about doing evil! Kings shows us that an ungodly life is a boring life.

Davis says regarding these final chapters,

> Drip . . . drip: four times we read, "He did evil in Yahweh's eyes." Nothing bracing or refreshing here, just the same stale stuff. None of the trembling of Hezekiah or enthusiastic obedience of a Josiah that gives spice and flavor and drama to kingdom life. . . . Actually, only holiness stirs and only godliness fascinates. (Davis, *2 Kings*, 336–37)

I agree. A life chasing after evil will never satisfy. Oh, it might provide some "short-lived pleasure" (Heb 11:25), but it is nothing in comparison to the riches of knowing Christ and being on mission with Him. Contrast these four kings with the prayer life of Elijah or the faith and compassion of Elisha. Which is more exciting?

Only in pursuing Christ and His kingdom will you find ultimate excitement and joy. Read the book of Acts, and you find statements about great joy experienced by those fulfilling Christ's mission (Acts 13:52). There isn't anything dull about Paul's journeys (2 Cor 6:3-10). J. Campbell White said it well:

> Most men aren't satisfied with the permanent output of their lives. Nothing can wholly satisfy the life of Christ within His followers except the adoption of Christ's purpose toward the world He came to redeem. Fame, pleasure and riches are but husks and ashes in contrast with the boundless and abiding joy of working with God for the fulfillment of His eternal plans. The men who are putting everything into Christ's undertaking are getting out of life its sweetest and most priceless rewards. ("Layman's Missionary Movement," 22)

The book of Kings shouts this: Don't waste your life. Make it count by surrendering your life to the mission of God. There you will find meaning, and there you will find joy. There's great joy in waking up every morning saying, "What do You have for me today, Lord?"

We need a better King, for apart from Jesus our hearts are restless and dissatisfied. Only in Christ can we find the "life that is real," which Paul speaks of here:

> *Instruct those who are rich in the present age not to be arrogant or to set their hope on the uncertainty of wealth, but on God, who richly provides us with all things to enjoy. Instruct them to do what is good, to be rich in good works, to be generous, willing to share, storing up for themselves a good reserve for the age to come, so that they may take hold of life that is real.* (1 Tim 6:17-19)

Even if you have wealth and toys, those things still won't bring ultimate delight. Set your hope in the glory of Christ, and you will find life.

Give attention to your heart. Notice the writer's focus on the heart throughout Kings. Even though Kings is a historical document, the writer doesn't focus on every historical detail. We noted that several kings went down in history as accomplishing great military or economic achievements, but the author of Kings reports few of these acts (e.g., Jeroboam II, Omri). Why? His purpose is to highlight something more important about a man or woman: What was the heart focused on? Did they please God? For example, he is quick to report that Abijam "was not completely devoted" (1 Kgs 15:3), but "Asa's heart was completely devoted to the LORD" (15:14). The line of David was to walk before Yahweh with "their whole mind and heart" (1 Kgs 2:4; cf. 2 Kgs 23:25). They were to trust in God and to worship God alone (Deut 17:14-20). David gave Solomon such a charge (1 Kgs 2:3-4). Josiah was commended because his "heart was tender" (2 Kgs 22:19).

Because of this focus, we read whether or not the kings did "right in the LORD's sight" up to the last king. Why? We live out of the overflow of the heart. Personal godliness is what matters. None of the kings in the northern kingdom received a positive evaluation, while the evaluation of Judah's kings is mixed. Two of them are exemplary, Hezekiah and Josiah. Six of them received qualified commendation. They did what was "right in the LORD's sight" but "the high places were not taken away."

As we read through Kings, we should be asking, Am I taking care of my heart? Am I dealing with pride? Am I dealing with anger, lust, or some other besetting sin?

With these final four kings we read about sins of greed (Jer 22:17), fear (2 Kgs 24:12), pride (2 Chr 36:12), and coldness toward the needs of others (Jer 22:3,15). All of these sins can also creep into our hearts.

If you haven't turned to Christ in repentance of faith, then begin there. You need a new heart. You need new affections. You need your heart of stone turned into a heart of flesh. If you're a believer, you need, in the words of Luther, to live a constant life of repentance. Are you dealing with fear, pride, coldness of heart, and greed?

Allow me to illustrate with one of my heroes, Tim Keller. He confesses his personal practices of dealing with his heart. In an interview he explains how he watches his heart:

> I try to do petition in the morning. I try to do repentance
> in the evening. So I try to pray in the morning and in the
> evening. In the evening I look back on what I did wrong and
> repent. But in the middle of the day I try to catch myself
> and I look for four kinds of emotions. I always pray in the
> morning, "Lord make me happy enough in the grace of
> Jesus to avoid being proud, cold, scared, and hooked." Now,

by **proud** I mean what you think, too self-congratulatory. And maybe disdainful of people who I don't think have it together. **Cold** means I'm just too absorbed in my concerns to really be compassionate and gracious and warm and joyful to the people around me. **Scared** means I'm just obviously too anxious and worried. **Hooked** means . . . when you're overworked, it means for me . . . eating. Eating things I shouldn't eat just because it's a way of keeping my energy up, and also because it's a way of rewarding myself. Or looking at women more than once. So: proud, cold, scared, hooked.

Now, in the middle of the day I get it out and say, "Have I been proud, scared, cold, or hooked in the last 3–4 hours?" And the answer usually is, "Yeah." And then I say, "How do I bring the gospel to bear on that? How does the grace of God deal with it?" And you try to catch yourself in those feelings. So basically finding problem feelings and inordinate desires, catch them when they're happening, try to deal with them with the gospel right there.

I call that "Quick Strike" on my idols around noon, if I can remember it. And repentance at night and petition in the morning. So I try to get into God's presence three times a day. (Interview by Steve McCoy, "Tim Keller on Preaching to Himself," emphasis in original)

I'm not necessarily recommending Keller's approach. I just want to show you how he realizes the importance of dealing with his own soul daily through prayer and repentance. He does what many ministers fail to do, namely, sit under their own preaching. Our hearts are prone to be proud, cold, scared, or hooked. We must cultivate a life of repentance and preach the gospel to ourselves to combat this problem.

Remember that idolatry leads to destruction. If Christ isn't at the center of our hearts, something else will be. And the result of substitute gods is destruction. You never win when you prefer idolatry.

Idolatry is a dominant theme in Kings. The idolatry of Manasseh brings the judgment of God, as mentioned in these final chapters. Jeremiah says the devastation would be so great that people from other lands would ask, Why has this happened? The only explanation would be that they had forsaken the covenant and worshiped other gods (Jer 22:8-9; cf. ch. 25).

We have read about all sorts of idols that the kings and the people have embraced, replacing the true and living God who brought them out of the land of Egypt. The writer reports the false worship of Baal and Asherah because whom you worship is the big question. The book of Kings reminds us of the critical need of answering this worship question rightly, as the people at Mount Carmel did after Elijah prayed the fire down. They said, "Yahweh, He is God! Yahweh, He is God!" (1 Kgs 18:39). Unfortunately, none of these final four kings make any effort to direct the nation to God.

An idol is anything you rely on to give you what only Christ can give you—hope, joy, security, meaning. Your idol may be drugs, peer approval, success, or sexual perversion. Sin problems are ultimately worship problems. As one young man said in our small groups, "Addiction is a worship disorder."

Within an idolatrous culture, no one thinks idolatry is a problem. The writer of Kings begs to differ. It most definitely matters. In the final evaluation of your life, your god is the most important matter. You can live like Omri, accomplishing many great things in this life, but if you aren't a worshiper of the Redeemer, then you have wasted your life and forfeited your soul.

You were made to worship the living God of the Bible. If He isn't at the center of your life, then something else is. Everything other than Christ is a cheap substitute.

The Fallen City

In chapter 25 we read the sad account of the destruction of the holy city, Jerusalem, the place where God chose to put His name (21:4). The fall of Jerusalem takes place in 587 BC. During this time Zedekiah's sons are slaughtered in front of him, and then his eyes are gouged out, making this episode the last event he sees. We also read of the third and final deportation and the execution of some Judeans.

In verses 22–26 we read of Gedaliah, grandson of Shaphan. He becomes governor of Judah under the authority of Babylon. But he doesn't survive because one among the royal family, Ishmael, kills him.

The city of Jerusalem and the temple are destroyed. We're reminded of the words of Hebrews: "For we do not have an enduring city here; instead, we seek the one to come" (13:14). The people of God await a better city. We await the new heavens and the new earth (Rev 21:1-8).

We need a better King because we aren't home yet. *Kings reveals the reality of suffering in a fallen world.* We read about all types of problems in Kings: dying children, droughts, wars, cannibalism, conspiracies, alliances, corrupt governments, injustice, violence, and oppression. This isn't how it should be. The Christian story involves a God who knows about suffering and enters into it. Jesus suffered on the cross and promised to make all things new.

The Bible is an honest book. It isn't a fairy tale. It doesn't hide the fact that we will toil and struggle all the days of our lives (Gen 3). Jesus told us, "You will have suffering in this world" (John 16:33). Don't mistake this life for heaven. We aren't home yet. Instead, look to God in trials with desperate prayer, and set your hope on the glory that will be revealed to believers when the crucified and reigning King returns (Rom 8:18).

We Need a Better King . . . and We Have One!
2 KINGS 25:27-30; MATTHEW 1:1-17,22-23

Kings doesn't have a happy ending, but it does have a hopeful ending. Yahweh hasn't forgotten His people who are in exile. The last scene takes place 26 years after the fall of Jerusalem. Jehoiachin, the last surviving successor of David (as far as we know), is now 55 years old and sits amply provided for in Babylon (Provan, *1 and 2 Kings*, 280). His story is contrasted with Zedekiah, the "mutilated man deprived of heirs" (ibid.). Here's the interesting epilogue, the final words in the book of Kings:

> *On the twenty-seventh day of the twelfth month of the thirty-seventh year of the exile of Judah's King Jehoiachin, in the year Evil-merodach became king of Babylon, he pardoned King Jehoiachin of Judah and released him from prison. He spoke kindly to him and set his throne over the thrones of the kings who were with him in Babylon. So Jehoiachin changed his prison clothes, and he dined regularly in the presence of the king of Babylon for the rest of his life. As for his allowance, a regular allowance was given to him by the king, a portion for each day, for the rest of his life.* (2 Kgs 25:27-30)

Nebuchadnezzar died, and his son, Evil-merodach, reigned in his place in Babylon. The former passed sentence on Zedekiah (25:6); the latter "spoke kindly" to Jehoiachin (25:28) (Olley, *Message of Kings*, 371). He receives a seat of honor; like Joseph he puts off his prison clothes (Gen 41:14); he dines every day at Evil-merodach's table.

God Fulfills His Word

Why is this epilogue important? It shows that the line of David is con tinuing during the exile. The writer calls Jehoiachin the king of Judah twice in verse 27 (Davis, *2 Kings*, 350). Provan notes that his reappearance is reminiscent of Joash after that earlier destruction of the royal family (*1 and 2 Kings*, 280). Jehoiachin survives miraculously in the midst of the wreckage.

The phrase "according to the word of the LORD" appears throughout the chapters. We continually say that God's Word proves true. Solomon's benediction says it all: not one promise has failed (1 Kgs 8:56). Prophets have appeared throughout Kings announcing God's word. Olley provides the following summary, demonstrating the trustworthiness of God's word, with the prediction on the left, and the fulfillment on the right (Olley, *Message of Kings*, 31):

1 Samuel 2:21-36	1 Kings 2:27
2 Samuel 7:12-13	1 Kings 8:20,24
1 Kings 11:29-39	1 Kings 12:15
1 Kings 13:1-3	2 Kings 23:16-18
1 Kings 13:20-22	1 Kings 13:26
1 Kings 14:6-16	1 Kings 14:18; 15:29
1 Kings 16:1-4	1 Kings 16:12
Joshua 6:26	1 Kings 16:34
1 Kings 17:14	1 Kings 17:16
1 Kings 21:21-24,27-29; 2 Kings 9:4-10	2 Kings 9:30-37; 10:17
1 Kings 22:17	2 Kings 22:35-38
2 Kings 1:6,16	2 Kings 1:17
2 Kings 21:10-15	2 Kings 24:2

Does this list not amaze you? You should go back and read these examples of how God sovereignly fulfills His word. He promises to raise up Solomon, to preserve David's throne forever, to split the kingdom, to raise up Josiah to crush Jeroboam's altar at Bethel, and to sweep away the houses of Jeroboam and Baasha. He promises that the widow's oil and flour will not run out. He promises with particular detail to execute Ahab, his family, and Jezebel for their evil. All of this is utterly amazing.

A few implications related to God's Word should be considered. First, **God's Word is trustworthy.** What He says, He will do. Do you believe the promises of Scripture? Build your life on His Word.

Second, **God's Word is powerful.** God was controlling the events through His word, not through human leaders. God's Word cannot be thwarted.

Third, **God's messengers will face opposition.** In the New Testament prophets are referred to as examples of persecution, with Jesus being the ultimate example of the righteous Man suffering (Matt 5:10-12; Jas 5:10). A prophet's life wasn't easy; just ask those who were hidden away during Jezebel's day, or ask Elijah and Elisha. Be prepared to suffer as you go forward in culture speaking God's Word.

Fourth, **God's Word must be obeyed, or judgment will be the result.** We have already noted how God promised to keep "a lamp in Jerusalem" (1 Kgs 11:36; 15:4; 2 Kgs 8:19; 21:7). Now we see that not even the Babylonians could stop God's purpose of bringing the ultimate King. Even a king named "Evil" could not stop it. This messianic hope isn't based on the goodness of Jehoiachin, for nothing seems to change in terms of his heart. This hope is simply rooted in the mercy and faithfulness of God (Jer 22:24–23:9).

Skipping ahead several hundred years, we find that Matthew picks up the story, demonstrating God's breathtaking mercy and faithfulness by describing the years before and after this exiled king:

> Then David fathered Solomon by Uriah's wife, Solomon fathered Rehoboam, Rehoboam fathered Abijah, Abijah fathered Asa, Asa fathered Jehoshaphat, Jehoshaphat fathered Joram, Joram fathered Uzziah, Uzziah fathered Jotham, Jotham fathered Ahaz, Ahaz fathered Hezekiah, Hezekiah fathered Manasseh, Manasseh fathered Amon, Amon fathered Josiah, and Josiah fathered Jechoniah and his brothers at the time of the exile to Babylon.
>
> Then after the exile to Babylon Jechoniah fathered Shealtiel, Shealtiel fathered Zerubbabel, Zerubbabel fathered Abiud, Abiud fathered Eliakim, Eliakim fathered Azor, Azor fathered Zadok, Zadok fathered Achim, Achim fathered Eliud, Eliud fathered Eleazar, Eleazar fathered Matthan, Matthan fathered Jacob, and Jacob fathered Joseph the husband of Mary, who gave birth to Jesus who is called the Messiah.
>
> So all the generations from Abraham to David were 14 generations; and from David until the exile to Babylon, 14

generations; and from the exile to Babylon until the Messiah, 14 generations. (Matt 1:6-17; emphasis added)

Matthew reminds us in this famous Christmas sermon that Jesus is the ultimate Son of David (Matt 1:1), descended through the line of "Jechoniah [that is, Jehoiachin] and his brothers at the time of the exile to Babylon" (Matt 1:11; see also v. 12). Matthew goes on to write that over against the statement in Kings that the Lord "banished them from His presence" (2 Kgs 17:20; 24:20), Jesus is "Immanuel: God with us" (Matt 1:23) (Olley, *Message of Kings*, 373). This ultimate King would go to the cross and be crucified under a sign reading, "King of the Jews" (Matt 27:37). And in His death Jesus was reconciling to Himself not only Jews but also all the nations who would believe.

A Living Hope

You might call 2 Kings 25:27-30 by itself a whisper of hope, but we know the rest of the story. The first readers didn't know how God's purposes would work out; only the Chronicler (who wrote later) reports Cyrus's edict to return and rebuild the temple (2 Chr 36:22-23). Further, they didn't know what would happen beyond that, when Jesus would embody the final words of the Chronicler, going up to Jerusalem Himself (2 Chr 36:23; cf. Matt 20:17-18) in order to bring salvation.

We have a "living hope" (1 Pet 1:3) because a lamp in Judah continued to burn through the years. God kept His promise to seat David's Son on the throne, and Jesus kept perfectly the covenant that none of the kings were able to keep.

How should you respond to this hope? *You should trust in this crucified, risen, and reigning King.* Jesus is the King to end all kings. Put your trust in Him. He alone can lead us out of the exile of the grave and bring us to His heavenly kingdom. We have seen a few good kings in our study, but the point is clear: we need a better king. We have what we need in Jesus! Trust in Him. Adore Him.

Second, *you should live with hope in this difficult life.* Centuries after the Babylonians, Christians faced persecution under mighty Rome (Olley, *Message of Kings*, 372). How might you encourage a church facing terrible persecution? John gives them a vision of the new Jerusalem:

> *I did not see a sanctuary in it, because the Lord God the Almighty and the Lamb are its sanctuary. The city does not need the sun or the moon*

to shine on it, because God's glory illuminates it, and its lamp is the Lamb. (Rev 21:22-23)

John's words present no faint whisper of hope. He gives a sure, unshakable word of hope. Our King has come, living the life we could not live, dying the death we should have died, rising from the dead, defeating our ultimate enemies. And our King is coming again, and we will be with Him forever. Right now we're in between the times. Let's not lose heart as we wait for the day in which King Jesus returns to establish his eternal, shalom-filled kingdom. We need a better King, and praise God, we have One! "Now to the King eternal, immortal, invisible, the only God, be honor and glory forever and ever. Amen" (1 Tim 1:17).

Reflect and Discuss

1. Why is it startling to many that God would bring such affliction on His people?
2. Describe how the people of God may have felt during this time.
3. How can Jesus' crucifixion startle people today?
4. Can sadness and mourning lead people to repentance? How?
5. What do you think the people of God longed for during this time?
6. What are some other biblical stories that sound similar to Jehoiachin's restoration?
7. How might Jehoiachin's restoration have given hope to the people of God?
8. How does Jesus' resurrection give hope to the people of God today?
9. Do you ever doubt that God will fulfill His promises?
10. In what ways have you seen God's faithfulness to His people?

WORKS CITED

Begg, Alistair. "Down in the Valley." Sermon accessed September 3, 2014. http://www.truthforlife.org/resources/sermon/down-in-the-valley.

Bimson, John J. "1 and 2 Kings." In *New Bible Commentary: 21st Century Edition*. 4th ed. Edited by D. A. Carson, R. T. France, J. A. Motyer, and G. J. Wenham. Leicester, England; Downers Grove, IL: Inter-Varsity Press, 1994.

Bock, Darrell. *Luke*. Vol 1. Baker Exegetical Commentary on the New Testament. Grand Rapids, MI: Baker, 1994.

Brown, Steve. "Spiritual Depression." Sermon accessed September 3, 2014. http://reformedsermons.org/series.asp/au/ste_brown/srs/1%20Kings.

Collins, Jim. *Good to Great: Why Some Companies Make the Leap . . . and Others Don't*. New York: Harper Collins, 2001.

Cordeiro, Wayne. *Leading on Empty*. Minneapolis: Bethany, 2009.

Davis, Dale Ralph. *1 Kings: The Wisdom and the Folly*. Focus on the Bible 11. Geanies House, Fearn: Christian Focus, 2007.

———. *2 Kings: The Power and the Fury*. Focus on the Bible 12. Geanies House, Fearn: Christian Focus, 2005.

Doriani, Daniel. "The Wise Fool." Sermon Accessed September 3, 2014. http://www.monergism.com/search?f[0]=author:35206.

Ehrman, Bart D., and Daniel B. Wallace. *The Reliability of the New Testament: Bart Ehrman and Daniel Wallace in Dialogue*. Edited by Robert B. Stewart. Minneapolis: Fortress, 2011.

Eswine, Zack. *Preaching to a Post-Everything World: Crafting Biblical Sermons That Connect with Our Culture*. Grand Rapids, MI: Baker, 2008.

Evans, Rachel Held. "Why Millennials Are Leaving the Church." *CNN Religion Blog*. July 27, 2013. Accessed April 21, 2015. http://religion.blogs.cnn.com/2013/07/27/why-millennials-are-leaving-the-church.

Ferguson, Sinclair. "2 Kings 7." Accessed September 3, 2014. http://tapesfromscotland.org/Audio7/7734.mp3 via Monergism.

————. "Experiencing Spiritual Depression." Sermon accessed September 3, 2014. http://www.sermonaudio.com/sermoninfo. asp?SID=89121017465.

Fitzpatrick, Elyse. "The Gospel Cure." *Tabletalk Magazine.* March 1, 2008. Accessed September 3, 2014. http://www.ligonier.org/learn/articles/gospel-cure.

House, Paul R. *1, 2 Kings.* The New American Commentary 8. Nashville, TN: B&H, 1995.

Hughes, Kent. *Luke: That You May Know the Truth.* Vol. 1. Preaching the Word. Wheaton: Crossway, 1998.

Hughes, R. B., and J. C. Laney. *Tyndale Concise Bible Commentary.* Wheaton, IL: Tyndale, 2001.

Jamieson, R., A. R. Fausset, and D. Brown. *Commentary Critical and Explanatory on the Whole Bible.* Oak Harbor, WA: Logos, 1997.

Johnson, Terry. "The Lord's Justice 2." Sermon accessed September 3, 2014. http://www.monergism.com/topics/sermon-manuscripts-mp3s-scripture/12-kings/audio-multimedia/chapter-1-2-kings/2-kings-09-12.

Josephus. *The Aniquities of the Jews,* 10.3.

Keller, Tim. *Counterfeit Gods.* New York: Dutton, 2009.

Konkel, August H. *1 and 2 Kings.* The NIV Application Commentary. Grand Rapids, MI: Zondervan, 2006.

Lee, R. G. "Payday Someday." Sermon accessed September 6, 2013. http://www.sbc.net/aboutus/sbvoices/rgleepayday.asp.

Leithart, Peter J. *1 and 2 Kings.* Brazos Theological Commentary on the Bible. Grand Rapids, MI: Brazos, 2006.

Lewis, C. S. *The Collected Letters of C. S. Lewis.* Edited by Walter Hooper. 3 vols. New York: HarperCollins, 2004–2007.

Lloyd-Jones, D. Martyn. *Spiritual Depression.* Grand Rapids, MI: Eerdmans, 1965.

Mahaney, C. J. *Humility: True Greatness.* Sisters, OR: Multnomah, 2005.

Marshall, Collin, and Tony Payne. *The Trellis and the Vine: The Ministry Mind-Shift That Changes Everything.* Sydney: Matthias Media, 2009.

Martyr, Justin. *Dialogue with Trypho.*

McCoy, Steve K. "Tim Keller on Preaching to Himself." *Steve K. McCoy.* February 22, 2011. Accessed September 3, 2014. http://www.stevek-mccoy.com/blog/2011/02/tim-keller-preaching-to-himself.

Meyer, F. B. *Elijah and the Secret of His Power.* Selected Works of F. B. Meyer. Accordance electronic ed. Altamonte Springs: OakTree Software, 2008.

Moo, Douglas. *The Letter of James.* Pillar New Testament Commentary. Grand Rapids, MI: Eerdmans, 2000.

Moore, Russell. "Personal and Cosmic Eschatology." Pages 858–926 in *A Theology for the Church.* Edited by Daniel L. Akin. Nashville, TN: B&H, 2007.

Motyer, J. Alec. *Isaiah: An Introduction and Commentary.* Tyndale Old Testament Commentaries. D. J. Wiseman, general editor. Downers Grove, IL: InterVarsity, 1999.

Murray, Andrew. *With Christ in the School of Prayer.* New York: Fleming H. Revell, 1885.

Murray, Iain H. *David Martyn Lloyd-Jones: The Fight of Faith, 1939–1981.* Carlisle: Banner of Truth, 1990.

Nietzsche, Friedrich. *The Twilight of the Idols and the Antichrist.* Translated by Thomas Common. DigiReads.com Books, 2009.

Olley, John W. *The Message of Kings: God Is Present.* The Bible Speaks Today. Downers Grove, IL: InterVarsity, 2011.

Patrick, Darrin. *Church Planter: The Man, the Message, the Mission.* Wheaton, IL: Crossway, 2010.

Piper, John. "Don't Avenge, but Give Place to Wrath." Sermon accessed September 3, 2014. http://www.desiringgod.org/sermons/do-not-avenge-yourselves-but-give-place-to-wrath.

———. *Don't Waste Your Life.* Wheaton, IL: Crossway, 2003.

———. "Elijah, Part 3." Poem accessed September 3, 2014. http://www.desiringgod.org/poems/elijah-part-3.

———. "There Is No Greater Satisfaction." Sermon accessed September 3, 2014. http://www.desiringgod.org/articles/there-is-no-greater-satisfaction.

Price, Ira. "The Schools of the Sons of Prophets." *The Old Testament Student* 8 (1889): 244–49.

Provan, Iain W. *1 and 2 Kings.* New International Biblical Commentary 7. Peabody, MA: Paternoster, 2000.

Quarles, Chuck. "Paul: A Model for Ministry." Sermon preached at E4 Preaching Conference, 2009.

Ryken, Phillip Graham. *1 Kings.* Reformed Expository Commentary. Phillipsburg, NJ: P & R, 2011.

Shedd, William G. T. *Dogmatic Theology.* Vol. 2. New York: Charles Scribner's Sons, 1888.

Sibbes, Richard. *The Bruised Reed.* Carlisle: Banner of Truth: 2005.

Spurgeon, Charles. "Faintness and Refreshing." Sermon accessed September 3, 2014. http://www.spurgeongems.org/vols52-54/chs3110.pdf.

———. "*God's Care of Elijah.*" Sermon accessed September 3, 2014. http://www.spurgeongems.org/vols55-57/chs3264.pdf.

———. *Lectures to My Students.* Reprint. Grand Rapids: Zondervan, 1954.

———. "Solomon's Plea." Sermon Accessed September 3, 2014. http://www.spurgeongems.org/vols19-21/chs1232.pdf.

———. "The Secret of Happiness." Sermon accessed September 3, 2014. http://www.spurgeongems.org/vols55-57/chs3227.pdf.

Thomas, Derek. "A Light in Dark Places." *Tabletalk Magazine.* March 1, 2008. Accessed September 3, 2014. http://www.ligonier.org/learn/articles/light-dark-places.

Tripp, Paul. *Dangerous Calling: Confronting the Unique Challenges of Pastoral Ministry.* Wheaton, IL: Crossway, 2012.

White, J. Campbell. "The Layman's Missionary Movement." In *Perspectives on the World Christian Movement.* Edited by Ralph D. Winter and Steven C. Hawthorne. Pasadena, CA: William Carey Library, 1981.

Wiersbe, Warren W. *Be Responsible (1 Kings).* 2nd ed. The BE Series Commentary. Colorado Springs, CO: David C. Cook, 2010.

———. *Wiersbe's Expository Outlines on the Old Testament.* Wheaton, IL: Victor, 1993.

Wiseman, D. J. *1 and 2 Kings.* Tyndale Old Testament Commentaries 9. Downers Grove, IL: IVP Academic, 2008.

Wright, Christopher, J. H. "I Never Knew Such a God Existed." *Themelios* 17, no. 2 (1992): 3.

———. *The Mission of God: Unlocking the Bible's Grand Narrative.* Downers Grove, IL: InterVarsity, 2006.

SCRIPTURE INDEX